CARIBBEAN BLOOD PACTS

A volume in the series

The United States in the World

Edited by Benjamin A. Coates, Emily Conroy-Krutz, Paul A. Kramer, and Judy Tzu-Chun Wu

Founding Series Editors: Mark Philip Bradley and Paul A. Kramer

A list of titles in this series is available at cornellpress.cornell.edu.

CARIBBEAN BLOOD PACTS

Guatemala and the Cold War
Struggle for Freedom

Aaron Coy Moulton

Cornell University Press
Ithaca and London

Copyright © 2025 by Aaron Coy Moulton

All rights reserved. Except for brief quotations in a review, this book, or parts thereof, must not be reproduced in any form without permission in writing from the publisher. For information, address Cornell University Press, Sage House, 512 East State Street, Ithaca, New York 14850. Visit our website at cornellpress.cornell.edu.

First published 2025 by Cornell University Press

Librarians: A CIP catalog record for this book is available from the Library of Congress.

ISBN 9781501784804 (hardcover)
ISBN 9781501784811 (paperback)
ISBN 9781501784828 (pdf)
ISBN 9781501784835 (epub)

GPSR EU contact: Sam Thornton, Mare Nostrum Group B.V., Mauritskade 21D, 1091 GC, Amsterdam, NL, gpsr@mare-nostrum.co.uk.

Contents

List of Abbreviations   vii

Dramatis Personae   xi

Introduction   1

1. Where the War Did Not End: The Caribbean Basin's Antifascist Struggle   9

2. The Transnational Postwar Conjuncture: The Guatemalan Revolution, 1944–1947   28

3. Counterrevolutionary Signatories: Guatemalan Reactionaries and Caribbean Basin Dictators, 1944–1947   47

4. Drawing Up Pacts: Cayo Confites and Costa Rica, 1947–1948   73

5. Building a Transnational Counterrevolution: An Anticommunist Intelligence-Sharing Network, Guatemalan Politics, and Bananas, 1948–1950   96

6. Waiting for the Colossus: British Intelligence, Guatemalan Anticommunists, and the US Congress, 1950–1952   114

7. Uncle Sam Signs On: Operation PBFORTUNE, 1952   132

8. Realizing the Counterrevolution: Operation PBSUCCESS, 1953–1954   152

   Conclusion: Dictators, Exiles, and the Caribbean Basin's Cold War   177

   Epilogue: Fictitious *Historias*   182

Acknowledgments   193

Notes   197

Note on Sources   253

Bibliography   257

Index   283

Abbreviations

AD   Acción Democrática (Democratic Action)
AEU   Asociación de Estudiantes Universitarios (Association of University Students)
ARDE   Asociación Reivindicadora Dominicana del Exilio (Dominicans in Exile Reclamation Association)
BBDO   Batten, Barton, Durstine & Osborn
CAEG   Comité de Ayuda a los Exiliados Guatemaltecos (Committee for Assistance for Guatemalan Exiles)
CCN   Comité Cívico Nacional (National Civic Committee)
CCPLH   Comité Cubano Pro Liberación de Honduras (Cuban Committee for the Liberation of Honduras)
CDP   Comité de Defensa Patria (Committee of National Defense)
CEUA   Comité de Estudiantes Universitarios Anticomunistas (Committee of Anticommunist University Students)
CEUAGE Comité de Estudiantes Universitarios Anticomunistas Guatemaltecos en Exilio (Committee of Guatemalan Anticommunist University Students in Exile)

CIA	Central Intelligence Agency
CLDH	Comité Liberal Demócrata de Honduras (Liberal Democratic Committee of Honduras)
CPG	Comité Patriótico Guatemalteco (Guatemalan Patriotic Committee)
CPLG	Comité Pro Liberación de Guatemala (Committee for the Liberation of Guatemala)
CRN	Comité Revolucionario Nicaragüense (Nicaraguan Revolutionary Committee)
CTG	Confederación de Trabajadores de Guatemala (Confederation of Guatemalan Workers)
CUEG	Comité de Unidad de la Emigración Guatemalteca (Committee for Unification of Guatemalan Immigrants)
DFS	Dirección Federal de Seguridad (Federal Security Directorate)
DGIPS	Dirección General de Investigaciones Políticas y Sociales (General Directorate of Social and Political Investigations)
FBI	Federal Bureau of Investigation
FDRH	Frente Democrático Revolucionario Hondureño (Honduran Democratic Revolutionary Front)
FEU	Federación Estudiantil Universitaria (University Student Federation)
FNDG	Frente Nacional Democrático de Guatemala (National Democratic Front of Guatemala)
FOIA	Freedom of Information Act request
FPAM	Frente Popular Anticomunista de México (Mexican Anticommunist Front)
IRCA	International Railways of Central America
IRD	Information Research Department
JLG	Juventud Liberal de Guatemala (Liberal Youth of Guatemala)
MOC	Memorandum of Conversation
MSR	Movimiento Socialista Revolucionario (Revolutionary Socialist Movement)
PAR	Partido Acción Revolucionaria (Revolutionary Action Party)
PRD	Partido Revolucionario Dominicano (Dominican Revolutionary Party)

PRN	Partido Renovación Nacional (National Renovation Party)
PUA	Partido Unificación Anticomunista (Anticommunist Unification Party)
PUC	Partido Unionista Centroamericano (Central American Unionist Party)
UDC	Unión Democrática Centroamericana (Central American Democratic Union)
UDH	Unión Democrática Hondureña (Honduran Democratic Union)
UFCO	United Fruit Company

Dramatis Personae

Dictators, Regimes, and Notable Officials/Agents
Dominican Republic
Rafael Trujillo, dictator, 1930–1961
Luis Thomen, ambassador to the United States
Joaquín Balaguer, ambassador to Mexico
Emilio Rodríguez Demorizi, ambassador to Nicaragua
Héctor Incháustegui Cabral, ambassador to Mexico
Félix W. Bernardino, consul in New York City

Honduras
Tiburcio Carías Andino, dictator, 1933–1949
Juan Manuel Gálvez, president, 1949–1954

Nicaragua
Anastasio "Tacho" Somoza, dictator, 1936–1956
Anastasio "Tachito" Somoza
Guillermo Sevilla Sacasa, ambassador

Venezuela
Marcos Pérez Jiménez, Venezuelan military junta, 1948–1950; dictator, 1948–1958

El Salvador
Maximiliano Hernández Martínez, dictator, 1931–1944
Marco Antonio Molina, chief of staff for the army

Cuba
Fulgencio Batista, Cuban dictator, 1952–1958

Colombia
Eduardo Zuleta Ángel, Colombian ambassador

Costa Rican Reactionaries-in-Exile
Rafael Ángel Calderón Guardia
Francisco "Paco" Calderón Guardia
Teodoro Picado
René Picado

Guatemalan Reactionaries and Organizations
Roderico Anzueto
Marco Antonio Archila Obregón
José Enrique Ardón Fernández
José Luis Arenas
Roberto Barrios Peña
José Calderón Salazar
Carlos Castillo Armas
Carlos Humberto Ceballos
Juan Córdova Cerna
Luis Coronado Lira
Guillermo Dávila Córdova
Domingo Goicolea Villacorta
Adán Manrique Ríos
Manuel Melgar
Carlos Padilla y Padilla
Federico Paiz Herrera
Juan Pinillos
Ovidio Pivaral
Federico Ponce
Arturo Ramírez
Carlos Salazar Jr.
Carlos Simmons

Guillermo Sosa
Miguel Ydígoras Fuentes
Comité Cívico Nacional (National Civic Committee, CCN)
Comité de Ayuda a los Exiliados Guatemaltecos (Committee for Assistance for Guatemalan Exiles, CAEG)
Comité de Defensa Patria (Committee of National Defense, CDP)
Comité de Estudiantes Universitarios Anticomunistas (Committee of Anticommunist University Students, CEUA)
Comité de Estudiantes Universitarios Anticomunistas Guatemaltecos en Exilio (Committee of Guatemalan Anticommunist University Students in Exile, CEUAGE)
Comité de Unidad de la Emigración Guatemalteca (Committee for Unification of Guatemalan Immigrants, CUEG)
Comité Guatemalteco Anticomunista (Guatemalan Anticommunist Committee)
Comité Patriótico Guatemalteco (Guatemalan Patriotic Committee, CPG)
Comité Pro Liberación de Guatemala (Committee for the Liberation of Guatemala, CPLG)
Consejo Supremo del Movimiento Revolucionario Anticomunista (Supreme Council of the Revolutionary Anticommunist Movement)
Frente Anticomunista de Guatemaltecos en Exilio (Anticommunist Front of Guatemalans in Exile)
Frente Nacional Democrático de Guatemala (National Democratic Front of Guatemala, FNDG)
Juventud Liberal de Guatemala (Liberal Youth of Guatemala, JLG)
Partido Unificación Anticomunista (Anticommunist Unification Party, PUA)
Reconciliación Democrática Nacional (National Democratic Reconciliation, Redención)

Mexican Anticommunists
Florencio Ávila
Luis Morones
Jorge Prieto Laurens
Frente Popular Anticomunista de México (Mexican Anticommunist Front, FPAM)

Antidictatorial Leaders, Allies, and Organizations
Rómulo Betancourt, Venezuelan president, 1945–1948
Acción Democrática (Democratic Action, AD)

José Figueres, Costa Rican junta leader, 1948–1949, and president, 1953–1958
Luis Muñoz Marín, governor of Puerto Rico, 1949–1965

Mexican Antidictatorial Allies
Vicente Lombardo Toledano, communist leader
Lázaro Cárdenas, president, 1934–1940

Guatemalan Democratic Leaders and Organizations
Jacobo Árbenz, president, 1951–1954
Juan José Arévalo, president, 1945–1951
Luis Cardoza y Aragón
Augusto Charnaud MacDonald
José Manuel Fortuny
Manuel Galich
Víctor Manuel Gutiérrez
Alberto Paz y Paz
Asociación de Estudiantes Universitarios (Association of University Students, AEU)
Confederación de Trabajadores de Guatemala (Confederation of Guatemalan Workers, CTG)
Partido Acción Revolucionaria (Revolutionary Action Party, PAR)
Partido Renovación Nacional (National Renovation Party, PRN)

Cuban Antidictatorial Allies and Organizations
Ramón Grau San Martín, president, 1944–1948
Carlos Prío Socarrás, president, 1948–1952
Aureliano Sánchez Arango
Eufemio Fernández
Enrique Cotubanamá "Cotu" Henríquez
Rolando Masferrer
Eduardo Chibás
Comité Cubano Pro Liberación de Honduras (Cuban Committee for the Liberation of Honduras, CCPLH)
Movimiento Socialista Revolucionario (Revolutionary Socialist Movement, MSR)
Partido del Pueblo Cubano (Ortodoxos)
Partido Revolucionario Cubano-Auténtico (Auténticos)

Dramatis Personae xv

Dominican Exiles and Organizations
Tulio Arvelo
Mauricio Báez
Diego Bordas
Juan Bosch
Juan Diaz
Esperanza Ellis
Persio Celeste Franco
Federico "Gugu" Henríquez
Juan Isidro Jiménes Grullón
Carmita Landestoy
Virgilio Mainardi Reyna
Ángel Morales
Horacio Ornes
Pericles Franco Ornes
Miguel Ángel Ramírez
Andrés Requena
Juan "Juancito" Rodríguez
Amado Soler
Asociación Reivindicadora Dominicana del Exilio (Dominicans in Exile Reclamation Association, ARDE)
Frente Democrático Dominicano (Dominican Democratic Front)
Frente Unido de Liberación Dominicana (United Front for Dominican Liberation)
Partido Revolucionario Dominicano (Dominican Revolutionary Party, PRD)

Nicaraguan Exiles and Organizations
Leonardo Argüello
Rosendo Argüello
Adolfo Báez Bone
Ernesto Cardenal
Carlos Castillo Ibarra
Emiliano Chamorro
Manuel Cordero Reyes
José Félix Córdoba Boniche
Abelardo Cuadra
Carlos Cuadra Pasos

Chester Lacayo
Pablo Leal
Juan José Meza
Alberto Ordóñez Argüello
José María Tercero
Toribio Tijerino
Edelberto Torres
Pedro José Zepeda
Comité Patriótico Nicaragüense (Patriotic Nicaraguan Committee)
Comité Revolucionario Nicaragüense (Nicaraguan Revolutionary Committee, CRN)
Partido Socialista Revolucionario (Revolutionary Socialist Party)
Unión Democrática Nicaragüense (Nicaraguan Democratic Union)
Unión Revolucionaria Nicaragüense (Revolutionary Nicaraguan Union)

Honduran Exiles and Organizations
Marcial Aguiluz
José R. Castro
Amílcar Gómez Robelo
Rafael Heliodoro Valle
Francisco Morazán
Jorge Ribas Montes
Francisco "El Indio" Sánchez
Ángel Zúñiga Huete
Comité Liberal Demócrata de Honduras (Liberal Democratic Committee of Honduras, CLDH)
Frente de Unidad Revolucionario Hondureña (Honduran Revolutionary Unity Front)
Frente Democrático Revolucionario Hondureño (Honduran Democratic Revolutionary Front, FDRH)
Unión Democrática Hondureña (Honduran Democratic Union, UDH)

Tegucigalpa and San Pedro Sula 1944 Protest Organizers
Graciela Amaya de García
Graciela Bográn
Emma de Bonilla
Argentina Díaz Lozano

Visitación Padilla
José Antonio Peraza
Angela Ochoa Velázquez
Comité Proliberación de Presos Políticos (Committee for the Release of Political Prisoners)

Central American Unionist Leaders and Organizations
Salvador Mendieta and the Partido Unionista Centroamericano (Central American Unionist Party, PUC)
Vicente Sáenz and the Unión Democrática Centroamericana (Central American Democratic Union, UDC)

United States Congresspersons
Representative, later Senator Everett Dirksen, Republican, Illinois
Senator Allen Ellender, Democrat, Louisiana
Senator Theodore Francis Green, Democrat, Rhode Island
Representative Christian A. Herter, Republican, Massachusetts
Senator Bourke B. Hickenlooper, Republican, Iowa
Senator Lister Hill, Democrat, Alabama
Senator Henry Cabot Lodge Jr., Republican, Massachusetts
Representative, later Senator Mike Mansfield, Democrat, Montana
Representative Joseph W. Martin Jr., Republican, Massachusetts
Senator Joseph McCarthy, Republican, Wisconsin
Representative John McCormack, Democrat, Massachusetts
Representative, then Senator Karl Mundt, Republican, South Dakota
Senator, later Representative Claude Pepper, Democrat, Florida
Senator Alexander Wiley, Republican, Wisconsin
Julius Cahn, counsel, Senate Foreign Relations Committee

United Fruit Company (UFCO) Officials and Allies
Edward Bernays, public relations expert
Thomas Cabot, president
Thomas Corcoran, lobbyist
Robert La Follette Jr., lobbyist
James Rowe, lobbyist
Bill Taillon, representative
Edward Tomlinson, journalist

Edmund S. Whitman, director of public relations
Samuel Zemurray, president
Batten, Barton, Durstine & Osborn (BBDO), advertising company

Franklin Delano Roosevelt Administration, 1933–1945
Henry Wallace, vice president
Eleanor Roosevelt, first lady
Sumner Welles, under secretary of state

Harry S. Truman Administration, 1945–1953
Harry Vaughan, military aide
Cornelius Mara, military aide
George Marshall, secretary of state, 1947–1949
Dean Acheson, secretary of state, 1949–1953
Spruille Braden, assistant secretary of state for American Republic Affairs
John Erwin, ambassador to Honduras
Fletcher Warren, ambassador to Nicaragua and Venezuela
Walter Thurston, ambassador to Mexico
Thomas Whelan, ambassador to Nicaragua
Rolland Welch, first secretary of the embassy in Managua
Nathaniel Davis, ambassador to Costa Rica
Edward G. Miller Jr., assistant secretary of state for Inter-American Affairs
Thomas Mann, deputy assistant secretary of state
David Bruce, under secretary of state
H. Freeman Matthews, under secretary of state
John Ohmans, Office of Middle American Affairs
Walter Bedell Smith, CIA director
Allen Dulles, CIA deputy director
J. C. King, CIA chief of the Western Hemisphere Division
Frank Wisner, CIA deputy director of plans
"Jacob R. Seekford," Castillo Armas's CIA contact

Dwight D. Eisenhower Administration, 1953–1961
John Foster Dulles, secretary of state
Henry Holland, assistant secretary of state for inter-American affairs

John Moors Cabot, assistant secretary of state for inter-American affairs
Thruston B. Morton, assistant secretary of state for congressional relations
Allen Dulles, CIA director

British Government
William H. Gallienne, British minister to Guatemala
Richard Allen, British minister to Guatemala
Emile Lecours, Information Research Department

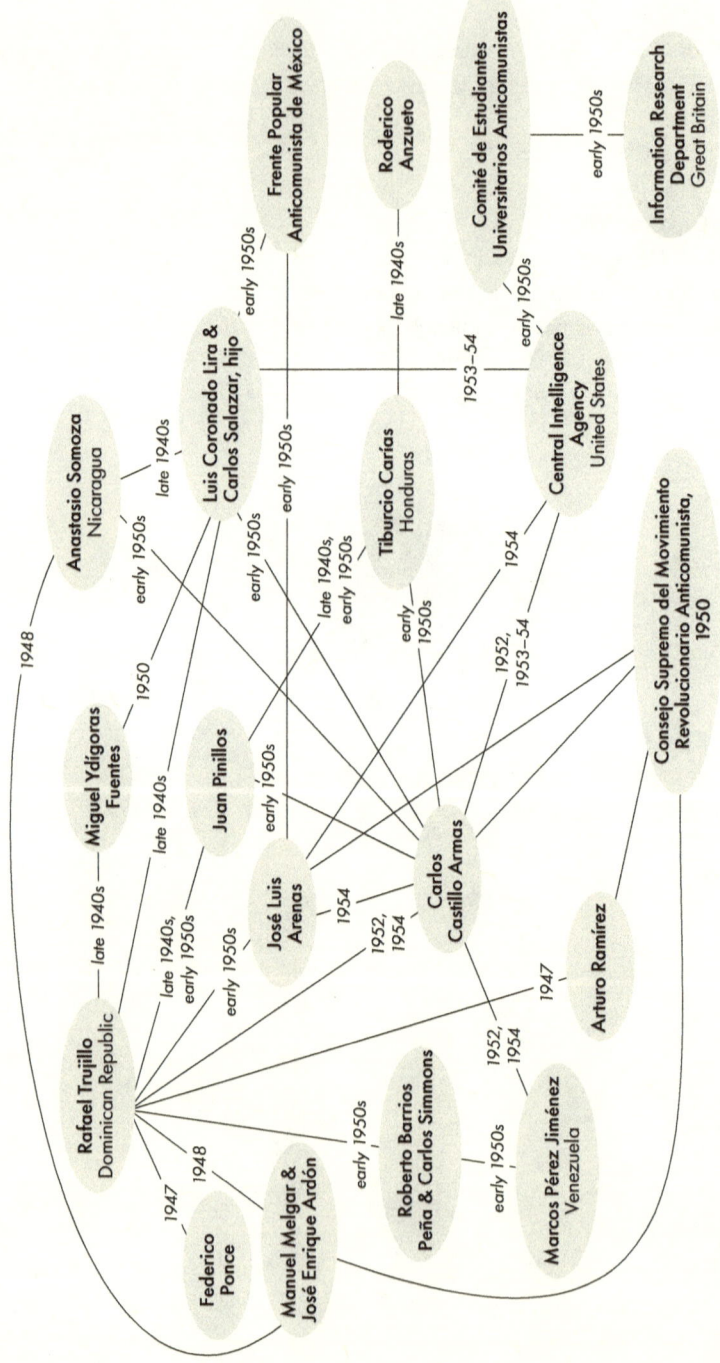

Figure 1. Connections between notable Guatemalan reactionaries, Caribbean Basin dictators, Mexican anticommunists, and British and US intelligence.

Introduction

"Thanks to God and this kindly person" who assisted his intimate subterfuge, Honduran exile Jorge Ribas Montes smuggled his testament into his wife's hands in mid-1955.[1] Imprisoned since his failed April 1954 attempt to assassinate Nicaraguan dictator Anastasio "Tacho" Somoza, Ribas Montes endured poor food, abysmal conditions, and torture at the hands of Somoza's sadistic sons. For months, mixed messages swirled across the greater Caribbean as his family and friends pondered his and his compatriots' fates. One account claimed Somoza's son "Tachito" hung Ribas Montes by the testicles; another asserted Tachito castrated Ribas Montes's colleague, Nicaraguan exile Adolfo Báez Bone, while tearing out Nicaraguan exile Pablo Leal's tongue. Even after his friends shared the official 1957 confirmation of Ribas Montes's death, details and rumors of unconfirmed brutality and horror blurred together in Central American newspapers and works by revolutionary guerrilla Luis G. Cardenal and sympathetic admirer Salman Rushdie.[2] In the end, his family and friends' best solace came from brief reminiscences, as when Nicaraguan activist Pedro Joaquín Chamorro described Ribas Montes in the dictator's prison cells "with a rosary always hanging from his neck."[3]

During that period of overwhelming uncertainty, Ribas Montes wrote his testament. He wanted to give his wife "a series of explanations of a very fundamental character about my life in order that you preserve them and, when our children are of age, teach them." Though he did not desire "to impose on my children this cause of mine," he did "want them to understand the reason why I have dedicated my adult life almost completely to the Liberation and to the Revolution of the Caribbean people."[4] In 1943, he joined reformist military officers who tried to topple Honduran dictator Tiburio Carías. Released into exile, he found sanctuary in Guatemala with like-minded antidictatorial militants and activists who had already replaced a dictator with a democratic government. Recruited as an agent for Guatemalan President Juan José Arévalo, Ribas Montes offered his military training to exiles from Honduras, Nicaragua, the Dominican Republic, and elsewhere. In 1947, he directed a unit of exiles during an abortive expedition to overthrow the Dominican dictator Rafael Trujillo. He then helped José Figueres take power during the 1948 Costa Rican Civil War. Over the next half dozen years, he served alongside a cadre of exiles and presidents devoted to eliminating dictators, culminating in the failed 1954 assassination attempt against Somoza.

Holding together this transnational struggle against multiple dictatorships was a Caribbean vision of democracy. Fighting "against the oppressors Trujillo and Somoza the same as against the despot Carías," Ribas Montes and his fellow exiles interpreted a dictator in one of their countries as part of a larger disease infecting the entire region. For ten years, these exiles gave everything against dictators who contributed to "the fundamental problem of Honduras, of Nicaragua, of the Dominican Republic, of the Caribbean, and of Latin America." Dictators enriched themselves while the people suffered "misery," "hunger," and "the lack of shelter and health."[5] Ribas Montes and his compatriots for a decade held onto this transnational determination. As he confided to his wife, his was a history of not one exile against a single dictator but an antidictatorial struggle across the greater Caribbean that went through Guatemala's Revolution.

This book is the history of this antidictatorial struggle, which, despite its international impact, has been left out of the literature on the Guatemalan Revolution, Latin America, and the Cold War. In the mid-1940s, Caribbean Basin exiles incorporated the Second World War's antifascist ideals into their local efforts against Somoza, Carías, and Trujillo. Unable to organize from their countries of origin, antidictatorial exiles turned to Guatemala, where they networked with students, workers, women's groups, and more. As a result, the nation's 1944–1954 Guatemalan Revolution became a transnational beacon of democracy, economic reform, and anticolonialism for the greater Caribbean. Those defending the region's status quo, however, did not tolerate such developments and directed their immense resources against the Revolution.

Therefore, this book is also a history of those forces' ten-year transnational counterrevolution. Guatemalan reactionaries feared any changes to their nation, dictators despised any opposition to their regimes, the United Fruit Company (UFCO) refuted any challenge to its control, and British officials distrusted any criticism of their empire. Because of the Revolution's international dimension, these entities too sought global sources of assistance. Whereas antidictatorial groups drew upon antifascism, their opponents summoned the Cold War to denounce their enemies and the Revolution as part of a communist conspiracy. When the US government ignored their pleas, reactionaries and dictators launched invasions and schemes against Arévalo's democratic government. Unrelated to the Cold War, events in 1947 and 1948 increased regional tensions as an anti-Trujillo expedition and the installation of a Costa Rican president revealed antidictatorial coalitions' potential. In response, the counterrevolution's backers escalated their efforts. Dictators organized an informal intelligence-sharing network to finance plots against Arévalo's government and help reactionaries erode Guatemalan democracy. Unable to control the executive branch of the US government, the UFCO lobbied Congress to characterize Guatemala's reforms as communist. Meanwhile, British intelligence supported Guatemalan anticommunist students.

They all failed to overthrow Arévalo or his successor, Jacobo Árbenz, but the counterrevolution's patrons continued soliciting the US government's help. In 1952, Somoza convinced the Truman administration to endorse his conspiracy to destroy Guatemala's democratically elected government, the foundation of the Central Intelligence Agency's (CIA) Operation PBFORTUNE. Despite this newfound alliance, the dictators' intelligence sharing threatened the operation's cover, so the State Department suspended the plot. However, the counterrevolution continued as reactionaries and dictators unleashed more schemes, encouraging the Eisenhower administration to authorize a coup, the CIA's 1953–1954 Operation PBSUCCESS, which sparked the Guatemalan military to depose Árbenz, destroy Guatemalan democracy, and end the Revolution. In the process, those long propelling the counterrevolution played pivotal roles, whether in reinforcing the US government's policies or rallying the US public. With reactionaries shaping the regime implanted by the US government, the antidictatorial struggle persisted over the next decades during the Cuban Revolution, the battles for Venezuelan and Dominican democracy, and the Sandinista movement in Nicaragua.

The Guatemalan Revolution and Latin America's Cold War

This book is the first account to place the Guatemalan Revolution's tragic history into that of the greater Caribbean. In a country where the government consistently limited rights, the Revolution offered Guatemalans the chance to realize political, social, and economic reforms.[6] From the mid-1940s into the mid-1950s, an ambitious but moderate coalition of nationalist democrats, socialists, communists, and more broke from decades of dictatorship and exploitation. Their transformations, including labor codes, social security, and agrarian reform, inspired citizens to build mass politics and new relationships with the state while addressing the long-standing social disparities and economic injustices defining their nation.[7] Days after a US government-induced military coup, the Revolution's opponents eviscerated this optimism with torture, mass murders, and systemic violence against reformers across the political spectrum. Subsequent regimes repeated this pattern, their atrocities becoming the norm.[8] Understandably, historians have tended to focus on why the US government chose to intervene against Guatemala's democratically elected government, emphasizing conflicts over nationalism, diverging economic policies, Cold War fears of communism, and bureaucratic divides.[9]

While adding to that discussion, this book sets the US government's policies into their hemispheric context, that is, into the transnational counterrevolution. From the mid-1940s into the early 1950s, the Revolution's opponents pursued their own agendas but wanted the US government's assistance. Unable to dictate regional matters, the UFCO lobbied influential congresspersons to shape US foreign policy.[10] This contributed to the State Department's decision to enact an interventionist policy, eventually including a covert propaganda campaign in the early 1950s. Similarly, reactionaries and dictators lobbied US officials to support a plot to invade Guatemala. Operations PBFORTUNE and PBSUCCESS relied on the transnational counterrevolution's components and actors, most clearly in the CIA and the UFCO's congressional allies rallying public support.[11] With PBSUCCESS, the US government's resources allowed the counterrevolution's creators to achieve their decade-old goal, a common occurrence during the rest of the Cold War in Latin America.[12]

While acknowledging the US government's central role, this work reveals more authors of the Revolution's end. The scholarship, at most, points out that Guatemalan reactionaries lobbied for the US government's help.[13] Coming from a tradition of right-wing forces' stifling social and economic reform since before neighboring El Salvador's 1932 Matanza, they sought the patronage of anticommunist powers outside the United States.[14] With an internationalist lens, historians have identified how landowners, Catholic activists, and admirers of Spanish fascism opposed the Revolution.[15] Instead, this book proves that reactionaries organized conspiracies, participated in the 1950 elections, and allied with Mexican anticommunists. To silence Guatemalan anticolonialism, the British government also assisted.[16] Its Information Research Department (IRD) funded anticommunist students' propaganda, an early indicator of how British officials navigated Latin America in the mid-1900s when US intervention came to overshadow British-Latin American relations, aside from matters in British Guiana/Guyana.[17]

Dictators, though, were the counterrevolution's cornerstone. The Second World War contributed to democratic openings throughout Latin America, which generally ended in the late 1940s.[18] Guatemala was a "notable exception" not just in its duration but in how its Revolution became a transnational democratic haven for antidictatorial militants due to the era's antifascist ideals.[19] Having maintained power for over a decade, dictators faced substantial challenges to their survival and could not count on the US government to defend their regimes as a hemispheric block against European fascism. Remnants of the 1920s and 1930s, they adapted to this new era by sponsoring plots against their enemies, creating an intelligence-sharing network, and helping one another. Furthermore, they interpreted regional developments through their own anticommunist lenses while trying to convince the Truman and Eisenhower administrations, often focused on European and Southeast Asian affairs, that the Caribbean Basin merited similar attention. Thanks in part to PBFORTUNE and PBSUCCESS, dictators embraced the Cold War.

The antidictatorial struggle and the transnational counterrevolution were central to the Cold War's impact in the Caribbean Basin. As in the rest of the world, Latin America's "regional proponents" of communism and anticommunism drove "overlapping conflicts" in which the Cold War "was only one among a host of other important, often revolutionary processes" shaping insurgent movements and counterrevolutionary violence.[20] Within this framework, Latin Americanist works have detailed the complexities and nuances behind local battles over democracy, dictatorship, and communism.²¹ Understandably, much of this follows events after 1959, since the Cuban Revolution and Fidel Castro's revolutionary image sparked uprisings and movements throughout the Western Hemisphere and beyond.²² Historians have noted how conservative groups, often with right-wing forces, interpreted and responded to the Cuban Revolution's seeming omnipresence in hemispheric affairs.²³

However, this post-1959 overview leaves Guatemala and much of the greater Caribbean out of the picture. Honduras's governments, economic debates, and all else are rarely acknowledged.²⁴ Trujillo's Dominican dictatorship has been a fascinating subject in US-Latin American relations while the country's numerous battles over democracy and dictatorship only spark scholarly attention with the 1965 US military occupation.²⁵ Venezuela's 1945–1948 Trienio Adeco, 1948–1958 military regime, and subsequent democratic governments, too, appear overlooked outside US-Latin American relations.²⁶ Somoza's Nicaraguan dictatorship is overshadowed by the Sandinista insurgency's efforts against his successors, as are Cuba's Auténticos and Fulgencio Batista, except as a reference to explain the rise of Castro, all of this quite confounding considering Nicaragua's and Cuba's later centrality not just in the Caribbean Basin but throughout Latin America and the world.²⁷ Meanwhile, works published outside Costa Rica are near unanimous in depicting the Central American nation as immune from much of the violence typical of the Cold War in spite of its 1948 civil war and two subsequent invasions, alongside multiple domestic conflicts between and after these events.²⁸ Most importantly, narrowing the scholarly gaze to events after the Cuban Revolution inadvertently feeds into the *teoría de los dos demonios* (theory of two demons) that sensationalizes a post-1959 radical left that committed numerous acts of violence. Though this claim is easily rebuffed when examining far-right death squads and right-wing regimes that monopolized their states' tools of violence and repression, it has manifested in a handful of works that fetishize Castro's rise and the Cuban Revolution's international reverberations.²⁹

This book resolves this dilemma by demonstrating how the Caribbean Basin's long-standing battles over democracy and dictatorship, dating back to the 1920s and 1930s, outlasted the Second World War and persisted into the 1950s. Building on years of intellectual exchanges and cultural encounters, militant democratic reformers including Nicaraguan, Honduran, and Dominican exiles invested their hopes in the Guatemalan Revolution, only for dictators to triumph with PBSUCCESS.³⁰ In those regimes' survival, many saw their democratic haven crushed due in part to the US government's

Cold War–oriented policies in the name of capitalism. They sought out new alliances or more radical solutions to restore Guatemala's decade of hope, address Honduras's economic inequality, oust a Cuban dictator, reconstruct a nation after a Venezuelan military regime's rule, build Dominican democracy, or remove a Nicaraguan dynasty. Ultimately, this book responds to scholars who encourage historians to reveal how local and regional conflicts over sovereignty, political independence, economic development, and US-based resources transcended singular dates and physical borders to create the defining battles of Latin America's Cold War.[31] With the Guatemalan Revolution and the transnational counterrevolution, the Caribbean Basin's antidictatorial struggle set the stage for a larger history of counterrevolutionary networks and violence.[32]

Book Structure

To recover the worldviews and actions of exiles, reactionaries, and others whose activities transcended the traditional boundaries of nation-states, this book turns to transnational studies.[33] Despite their disparate backgrounds, they and their allies came together based on the symbolic importance attached to democratic ideals and anticommunist ideologies.[34] Recovering this history, I follow previous works showing how similar forces drove the "Latin Americanization" and "transnationalization" of the Cold War's earliest conflicts.[35]

This book traces these conflicts' intersections and divergences. The first chapter covers how the Second World War reverberated across the greater Caribbean as exiles folded the global war against fascism into their longstanding antidictatorial struggle. They called out Somoza, Carías, and Trujillo at a time when the world seemed organized against such regimes, epitomized in the international backlash to the July 1944 Masacre Sampedrana. As the second chapter finds, an array of voices invested these ideals in the Guatemalan Revolution. Myriad democratic strands intertwined in a single Central American nation as proponents championed Guatemala's reforms and President Arévalo. In effect, the Revolution was a transnational moment uniting the Caribbean Basin's antidictatorial aspirations.

Chapter 3 reveals the transnational counterrevolution's origins. Along with the UFCO and the British, reactionaries and dictators summoned the Cold War to denounce the region's democratic surge as a communist conspiracy. Without the US government's support, they launched plots and destabilized Guatemalan politics. Events in 1947 and 1948, as chapter 4 contends, raised these conflicts' stakes. Antidictatorial coalitions behind the Cayo Confites expedition and the Costa Rican Civil War threatened the regimes. As the fifth chapter shows, dictators responded by organizing an informal intelligence-sharing network that assessed plots against Arévalo's government and supported reactionaries organizing domestic uprisings and leading the political opposition to Árbenz. Inside the United States, the UFCO unleashed a lobbying blitz that pushed Congress to denounce Guatemala's reforms as communist. The State Department's decision to intervene against Árbenz's government, chapter 6 contends, did not appease the counterrevolution's proponents. British intelligence patronized Guatemalan anticommunist students, the UFCO's congressional allies demanded a more forceful policy, dictators obtained Colombian and Cuban allies, and reactionaries teamed up with Mexican anticommunists.

The seventh chapter pinpoints these developments' collision in 1952. The Truman administration approved a conspiracy offered by Somoza that became the CIA's PBFORTUNE, but US officials failed to comprehend the counterrevolution's reach when dictators tapped into their network and jeopardized the operation's clandestine character. At the last minute, the State Department halted the scheme. Despite this controversy, reactionaries pursued their own agendas and rivalries while occupying central roles in the Eisenhower administration's PBSUCCESS. Throughout the United States, the UFCO's propaganda campaigns rallied support from the US Congress and the public, best seen in CIA-backed calls for a civilian boycott of Guatemalan coffee. For their part, British officials kept their policies in place while acquiescing to their US counterparts, who warned that any criticism of the US government's activities would place British colonialism under a microscope. Ultimately, the Guatemalan Revolution's demise resonated in the United States, Britain, and the Caribbean Basin, but the region's conflicts between democracy and dictatorship did not end.

Chapter 1

Where the War Did Not End

The Caribbean Basin's Antifascist Struggle

As exiles enlisted in the US military during World War II, many Dominicans had a complicated relationship with the United States. In a letter commending exile Juan Infante for joining the fight in Europe, Persio Franco and almost two dozen exiles prayed, "The present war is a crusade of the forces of Good," requiring "worthy men and women . . . of this prodigious Continent which seems to have been destined by God to illume the world and to establish in all parts the reign of freedom and justice."[1] From Havana, Dominican exile newspaper *Quisqueya Libre* (*Free Dominican Republic*) honored this service by raising funds for Christmas presents for soldiers' children.[2] Dominican exiles throughout the Caribbean Basin praised the sacrifices of those who died as US service members, representing the ideals of democracy on the front lines of the international war against fascism.

Still, this was the same US government that supported their home country's notorious dictator Trujillo. Wrestling with this conundrum, Franco believed those spearheading the global war against fascism had a "moral obligation to help the people of the Dominican Republic put an end to the monstrous tyranny of Trujillo."[3] "Why, if, in the name of human freedom, the police force of this great country is officially the power to help enslaved peoples to regain freedom," asked Andrés Requena, a Dominican exile who served in the US military, "why is your State Department supporting the thief and cold-blooded murderer who is morally and materially bleeding to death the Dominican Republic?"[4] Corresponding with Sumner Welles, one of the US government's Latin Americanist experts, Ángel Morales vented against the Dominican dictator and struggled to grasp the official's tolerance of Somoza.[5]

Dominican exiles' frustration regarding the US government's vocal opposition to European fascism yet steady support of Trujillo reflected their passionate embrace of the war's antifascist ideals. What US officials believed was an attempt to reaffirm hemispheric solidarity by ignoring Trujillo's rule was, to exiles, "a passive blessing of the most suppressive dictatorship" in the Western Hemisphere. Many held the United States to a higher standard, warning that "a democracy should not give moral sustenance to a dictatorship, whose principles are basically alien to a liberty-loving people."[6] This paradox of understanding that US resources bolstered Trujillo's regime but wishing for the US government's assistance against the dictatorship propelled the Asociación Reivindicadora Dominicana del Exilio's (Dominicans in Exile Reclamation Association, ARDE) plea to US President Harry Truman: "When Democracy, incarnated in the figure of the Chief Executive of the United States, gives the continental battle cry to demolish those infamous regimes [in Latin America], the oppressed countries will hurl themselves upon the arms of a Democracy that liberates them, instead of taking recourse in other beliefs which may extend to them a helping hand."[7] This warning, against the untold repercussions if the US government failed to join its ideologically aligned Caribbean allies and realize the antifascist promise inspiring the world in the mid-1940s, was quite prescient.

Caribbean Basin exiles and their allies embraced the ideals of antifascism. Into the 1940s, Trujillo, Somoza, and Honduras's Carías maintained their regimes, but students, intellectuals, and others refused to accept such authority. As with Dominicans who gave their blood and lives in the US military, exiles seized upon the global antifascist moment to legitimate and energize their years-long struggles against dictators. Although exiles held a common language and worldview built on myriad revolutionary symbols and ideals, World War II inspired new debates as the region's exiles affirmed the seemingly global agreement to oppose dictators. Ultimately, antifascism expanded and facilitated connections among a growing, transnational array of militant antidictatorial exiles.

Caribbean Basin Dictators and Antidictatorial Exiles

Of course, Dominican exiles were not alone in keeping a close eye on the United States and its government. Already, the United States and its people intimately tied itself to much of the Caribbean Basin, its encounters during the 1800s ranging from ideological exchanges and a toothless Monroe Doctrine against European interventions in the Western Hemisphere to taking half of Mexico's territory in the late 1840s and filibustering expeditions in Cuba and Nicaragua. At the turn of the twentieth century, the 1898 Spanish-American-Cuban-Filipino War opened a profound wave of US interventions throughout the region, including military occupations in Cuba, the Dominican Republic, Haiti, and Nicaragua. It took a few dozen years, but US officials finally seemed capable of enforcing the Monroe Doctrine and reshaping the region's affairs to serve their nation's interests.[8]

The Caribbean Basin, though, was far from an empty laboratory for these imperialist experiments. Whenever possible, its peoples still made use of the US empire's ideals and resources in the hopes of improving their respective communities. Despite the immense violence unleashed by their respective occupations, Cubans, Puerto Ricans, Nicaraguans, and Haitians believed US institutions and democratic ideals might offer the means to strengthen their respective communities, even trying to reshape US imperialist mandates to serve their own ends. In fact, those ideals helped bring together like-minded allies from across the Americas, facilitating transnational anti-imperialist networks including insurgent guerrillas, civil rights organizations, and more stretching from Central America into the United States.[9] Between such resistance and the Great Depression, Herbert Hoover's and Franklin Delano Roosevelt's administrations implemented the Good Neighbor Policy to turn away from the past decades' occupations and respect the Latin American principle of nonintervention in one another's internal affairs. As US forces withdrew and left behind a conflicting portrait of their nation's democratic ideals and imperialist government, those especially adept at incorporating US resources for their own ends were a coterie of Caribbean Basin dictators who held power from the 1930s into the Second World War.[10]

Nicaragua endured this tension as Somoza took control of the newly created Guardia Nacional (National Guard) to assassinate anti-imperialist Augusto Sandino in 1934 and seize the presidency in 1936. Over the next years, Somoza played political parties against one another and cultivated alliances with workers, peasants, and other groups thanks to affordable housing, social welfare, and government projects.[11] To those fearful of another foreign invasion, Somoza was the favored leader preventing instability, with local journalists warning US officials, "Everybody . . . took [Somoza] as a sort of an American agent performing some kind of an errand in Central America [who] spoke as President Roosevelt's mouthpiece."[12] Those accepting his rule received his patronage, but critics faced repression and expulsion. Repeatedly, Somoza freed political prisoners, welcomed back exiles, and accepted unenforceable governing pacts. As Somoza intended, his opponents detested any who compromised their positions in pursuit of security or sacrificed their ideals in the hopes of making a measure of progress at home. Such divisions hindered a unified opposition and cemented Somoza's rule. The result, this "false democracy" as his enemies termed it, was nothing more than a "lie."[13]

Events in the 1940s exposed this "lie." Anti-Somoza activism proliferated, emanating from students who in August 1944 demanded the restoration of democratic liberties and Somoza's removal from power.[14] In response, he suspended the very constitutional guarantees presented as evidence of his "democracy." Even critics such as Manuel Cordero Reyes and Carlos Cuadra Pasos, who admitted Somoza's reign initially offered stability, marveled that he no longer hid his policies of censorship and torture.[15] To bolster his "democracy," he tried tapping into the global antifascist struggle by establishing relations with the Soviet Union and inviting Mexican communist Vicente Lombardo Toledano to visit Nicaragua.[16] Using his regular bag of tricks, Somoza in 1947 welcomed back exiles and granted amnesty to opponents for a managed election of Leonardo Argüello, whom he expected to act as his puppet. Instead, Argüello tried weakening the influence of Somoza and his Guardia, who ousted the newly elected president and unleashed violent reprisals.[17] This postelection repression dramatically increased the number of exiles abroad, frustrating neighboring countries' security institutions, from Mexico's Dirección General de Investigaciones Políticas y Sociales (General Directorate of Social and Political Investigations, DGIPS) to Costa Rica's Seguridad Pública (Public Security).[18] Upon leaving Nicaragua, the poet Alberto Ordóñez Argüello described the regime as "living in an atmosphere akin to that of servitude."[19] Despite Somoza's hold over the Guardia Nacional, some officers, including Lieutenant Adolfo Báez Bone, joined Argüello abroad.[20]

In Honduras, Carías's policies mirrored Somoza's. Presenting himself as a bulwark against the Great Depression's instability, Carías received significant support from business interests, industrialists, and landowners.[21] When in 1936 he dissolved the legislature and extended his power, these sectors endorsed his regime. "Pragmatically" manipulating local politics, he allowed followers to engage in graft and corruption while promoting select enemies to divide the opposition. Any who challenged the dictator faced his secret police.[22] Similar to descriptions of Somoza's regime, the US Federal Bureau of Investigation (FBI) admitted that Honduras's government was "theoretically" a "democratic form of government," but "in practice" Carías "thoroughly dominated" the nation.[23] Despite their common enemy, Honduran exiles were divided over politics and personal animosities. Furthermore, theirs was another Central American nation whose dictator profited off his seemingly close relationship with the US government.[24] Carías not only made US Independence Day a Honduran national holiday but had his congress confer honorary citizenship upon Roosevelt.[25] Throughout the mid-1940s, his government published favorable articles claiming "that a change of Government in Honduras would have a prejudicial effect on the Allied war effort."[26] His supporters blamed any criticism on "the famous bogey" of "quintacolumnismo" (Fifth Columnism) and "Comunismo" (communism), even though international observers found "no evidence of Nazi machinations or of the bogy of comunism [sic]."[27]

Honduran exiles too turned to the Second World War. Noting that the dictator's newspapers published admiringly of international fascism, Honduran democratic activist Ángel Zúñiga Huete claimed Carías followed in the footsteps of his fascist "teachers" to become "a grand tropical reflection of [Benito] Mussolini and [Adolf] Hitler."[28] In stark contrast to their past years' disagreements, over a dozen exiles united and begged Carías to recognize the ideals of Honduran democracy and the Atlantic Charter.[29] For the first time in years, the dictator seemed vulnerable, with the writer Rafael Heliodoro Valle believing "Carías's situation could not be more precarious, and it is a fact that the time approaches for the 'invasion' [for] the downfall of the satrap."[30] Journalist José R. Castro suggested that Carías's only option was to release political prisoners and provide amnesty for hundreds of exiles scattered across the Americas.[31]

In the Dominican Republic, Trujillo embodied the dictator's most outlandish qualities. Through the Dominican police-turned-military, he profited off domestic frustrations and offered a stable state he claimed would deter foreign intervention.[32] When Trujillo authorized a corrupt 1947 reelection, some championed him as a barrier against domestic disturbances and anarchy.[33] His manipulation of US politics ranged from the bombastic, as when constructing a George Washington monument replica, to the subtle, as when recruiting US diplomats' sons as military advisers.[34] Trujillo fostered a white racial identity that culminated in the 1937 Haitian massacre when, for almost a week in early October, his soldiers joined Dominicans in slaughtering hundreds of Haitians working in local agricultural enterprises. Waving off international repercussions, Trujillo deployed well-connected diplomats and public relations firms. To contrast his image against Nazi persecutions, he opened a small agricultural settlement for a handful of Jewish refugees, this Sosúa settlement being proof of his supposed democracy.[35] These managed generosities played upon US leaders' personal sympathies, such as funneling donations to the National Fund for the Prevention of Infantile Paralysis during Roosevelt's administration.[36]

With these tools, Trujillo constructed a personalist dictatorship. US officials admitted he ran "the most efficient government" the Dominican Republic ever witnessed that "operat[ed] primarily for the personal enrichment of himself, his relatives, and his satellites" with his "greed result[ing] in the impoverishment of the Dominican people, economically and morally."[37] One British official summarized, "Trujillo feels that he is the State and the interests of the country are his interests."[38] Between his childhood obsession with titles and his early career in putting fake medals on his uniforms, he lived up to his nickname "Chapita" (Bottlecaps) by gathering the titles of "Generalísmo of the Armed Forces," "Founder and Supreme Head of the Partido Dominicano" (Dominican Party, PD), "Benefactor of the Nation," "Benefactor of Humanity," "Restorer of Financial Independence," and "First Journalist of the Republic" simply for owning the newspaper *La Nación*.[39] Mexican officials highlighted how the entire nation revolved around Trujillo, with every decree, law, statue, and monument labeled as products of the "Era de Trujillo."[40] There were no outlets for political activism beyond the PD, with the party's motto, "Rectitud, Libertad, Trabajo, Moral" (Rectitude, Freedom, Work, Morals), honoring the initials of Rafael Leonidas Trujillo Molina.[41]

Those watching Trujillo's firm grasp inside his nation's borders acknowledged that his most influential opponents challenged his regime from abroad.[42] In *Quisqueya Libre*, Juan Bosch and others wrote about the "tyrant's" corruption and brutality.[43] Political activist Ángel Morales helped US journalist Albert Hicks publish in 1946 *Blood in the Streets*, one of the first widely read accounts of Trujillo's regime.[44] Carmita Landestoy followed with a text detailing his monopolization of domestic industries and control over the PD.[45] One of the Partido Revolucionario Dominicano's (Dominican Revolutionary Party, PRD) most circulated publications was *La historia del hombre que se proclamó igual a Dios* (*The History of the Man Who Proclaimed Himself*

Equal to God). Though resembling others in tracing Trujillo's rise to power, what set this publication apart was its mockery of the dictator's unsurpassed ego, whether in his renaming the capital city and oldest settlement from European colonization Santo Domingo with his own name, Ciudad Trujillo; making his preteen son a general and his son's birthday a national holiday; or demanding the national motto be "Dios y Trujillo" (God and Trujillo).[46] Nevertheless, the dictator's control seemed impenetrable, with Trujillo in 1947 immediately voiding agreements for communist- and student-led political organizations intended to placate his critics.[47]

Between Sandino and Uncle Sam

Before the war's end, antidictatorial figures were already blending the global conflict's antifascist ideals with their local aspirations. For example, Sandino's image long embodied transnational antidictatorial solidarity, whether in Honduran exiles' support or numerous works on the "assassin" Somoza.[48] Some had stood with him in the 1920s, his memory needing no reminder during subsequent decades. The Unión Democrática Centroamericana's (Central American Democratic Union, UDC) Cuadra Pasos and Pedro José Zepeda served Sandino in Mexico, and journalist Carleton Beals offered support for exiles and allies akin to that given when interviewing Sandino and criticizing the US government's Nicaraguan occupation in *The Nation*.[49]

Thus, few were surprised at repeated references to the Nicaraguan revolutionary in the 1940s. In early 1945, Central American exiles paid homage to Sandino at Mexico City's Monumento a la Independencia (Monument to Independence) simultaneously with the Chapultepec Conferencia Interamericana sobre Problemas de la Guerra y de la Paz (Inter-American Conference on Problems of War and Peace).[50] On the streets, in the Biblioteca Nacional (National Library), and at the Cámara de Diputados (House of Deputies), DGIPS agents found exiles distributing prints of *Por la unidad americana* (*For American Unity*) and *El abrazo de la muerte* (*The Embrace of Death*), all denouncing dictators.[51] Poets and intellectuals regularly convened on the anniversary of Sandino's assassination, and the resulting compilations interpreted the antidictatorial struggle as honoring the anti-imperialist's legacy.[52]

In contrast, exiles' admiration of the United States vacillated. This was not the first time US-endorsed declarations for democracy and self-determination resonated globally, but in the greater Caribbean the US government's contradictory tolerance of dictators stood out.[53] As early as 1940,

Zúñiga Huete asked US Vice President Henry Wallace if Roosevelt's administration would support those toppling "their tyrants" or defer to "the devilish dictators infesting Spanish America."[54] Based on "the cooperation that the people—the people!—favorably give to [the United States] in this great combative disaster promoted by the powers of the Rome-Berlin-Tokyo axis," the UDC begged Sumner Welles that "Washington stop providing weapons and money" to "the antidemocratic governments of Central America," which would "only be of use after beating the authentic enemies of totalitarian regimes."[55] In a letter to Roosevelt, the UDC's Vicente Sáenz warned that the president's "promise and fight for democracy and human dignity" could be realized only if the US government rejected dictatorships.[56] Only two years after the war's end, the Partido Unionista Centroamericano (Central American Unionist Party, PUC) warned that the "second part of the conflict" would not end unless all realized "the promise of organizing the world democratically and in perfect harmony" as Roosevelt envisioned.[57]

Their country held up as the stereotypical banana republic, Hondurans passionately argued over the US government's role. Critics scorned unqualified support for the UFCO and exploitive regimes, yet Amílcar Gómez Robelo believed US-based entities could help guide Latin America, now that the Colossus of the North "ha[d] its eyes open to the lighthouse that, in the darkness of this night that we live, is illuminating the path of free men, and hopefully will continue illuminating thanks to the influence of the new ideas . . . that will have to be reality after this war in spite of all the reactionaries and in spite of all the skeptics." He and others remembered the US government of the past decades that accepted dictators as reliable and friendly to US-based economic interests yet believed the US government during the Second World War "undoubtedly is interested in our countries' heading toward authentic and tolerable democracy."[58] For almost a dozen years, Zúñiga Huete detested how dictators manipulated the US government's Good Neighbor Policy to depict any opponent as violating the nonintervention principle.[59] During the war, though, he encouraged the policy's "reform" and invested his faith in the deluge of expressions for self-determination and democracy.[60]

Many grappled with this paradoxical role ascribed to the United States, a beacon of democratic hope while complicit in the rise and entrenchment of dictatorial regimes. Although some Nicaraguans associated the US government's policies with Somoza, Cordero Reyes and Cuadra Pasos interpreted the Good Neighbor Policy as one that allowed intervention against dictatorial regimes, comparing the situation to that of one who could not stand by while witnessing abuses next door.⁶¹ This argument endured into the early 1950s, when they contrasted the Good Neighbor against "the Bad Neighbor, the tyrant that enslaves and exploits his people and does not respect human life," and hoped the US government might help remove Somoza.⁶² Doubts persisted, leaving Honduran feminist Graciela Bográn wondering if the US government's oft-repeated call for "continental solidarity" in the fight against fascism would ever target Carías.⁶³

Dominican exiles were especially conflicted due to Trujillo's cultivated relationships with US officials. Summoning antifascist ideals, female exiles were "openly fighting against tyranny."⁶⁴ One was Esperanza Ellis, the daughter of Gerardo Ellis Cambiaso, expelled soon after Trujillo assumed power, and the brother of Gerardo Ellis Guerra, whose death was popularly attributed as retribution for their father's anti-Trujillo activities.⁶⁵ When a writer for the *Washington Times-Herald* praised Trujillo in March 1944, Esperanza wrote back that the dictator's role in the Haitian massacre and her brother's murder were proof that "Trujillo is the Hitler of the New World." Not only did Esperanza claim that she and other Dominican exiles lived "with the hope for the day when all representatives of decency and freedom in the United Nations will have crushed those criminals" suppressing democracy, but she sent a copy of her letter to Eleanor Roosevelt.⁶⁶ While lamenting "that there are people like [the newspaper's writer] in America," the Dominican exile told the first lady, "I admire and respect you so much, Mrs. Roosevelt; it is people like you that have made me love your country."⁶⁷ In exile, women and men felt frustrated at the disparity between the US government's antifascist rhetoric and pro-dictatorial policies.

Antifascist Linkages

As the Second World War ended, the struggle against fascism remained alive in the greater Caribbean. The US government's Office of the Coordinator of Inter-American Affairs used antifascist texts such as the Four Freedoms, Roosevelt's January 1941 justification for defending Britain against German aggression, and the Atlantic Charter, Roosevelt and British Prime Minister Winston Churchill's August 1941 call for people throughout the world to receive self-government, to reinforce hemispheric solidarity against the Axis Powers. To US officials, the war's naval battles, industrial sabotage, and proclaimed lists against Nazi sympathizers in the Caribbean Basin ended in 1945.⁶⁸ To exiles, the war's antifascist promise was not fulfilled until all dictatorial regimes fell.[69] Honduran exiles highlighted how, during the Great Depression, Carías's newspaper *La Época* applauded the nationalism and economic policies of the "Nazi-Fascist regimes of Europe."[70] Publishing texts from Venezuela and Cuba, the PRD temporarily renamed itself the Unión Democrática Antinazista Dominicana (Democratic Anti-Nazi Dominican Union, UDAD), and *Quisqueya Libre* stated that Trujillo's and Hitler's regimes shared similar goals and policies.[71] *En Marcha*, the newspaper of the Comité Liberal Demócrata de Honduras (Liberal Democratic Committee of Honduras, CLDH) in Mexico, compared Carías's supposed years of "peace" to those under Hitler and Mussolini, all invoking order at democracy's expense.[72]

Quickly, such figures and organizations invoked the war's antifascist symbols. Sáenz and the UDC portrayed the various movements against dictatorships as "the start of the application in Central America of the Atlantic Charter," held up as a global antidictatorial text.[73] Cuadra Pasos and Nicaraguan exiles quoted Roosevelt's words from the Atlantic Charter's second anniversary: "We recognize the fact that our enemies are not only Germany, Italy, and Japan: they are all the forces of oppression, intolerance, insecurity, and injustice which have impeded the forward march of civilization."[74] Repeating these same words, the Unión Democrática Nicaragüense (Nicaraguan Democratic Union) urged "sincere antifascists" to denounce Somoza's "bad use" of armaments provided by the US government.[75] Others followed suit with the Four Freedoms, which the PUC summoned to champion Argüello's 1947 candidacy against Somoza's corrupt influence.[76] Similarly, the Frente Democrático Revolucionario Hondureño (Honduran Democratic Revolutionary Front, FDRH) endorsed the United Nations (UN) as part of its own "ideological, spiritual, and economic revolution."[77]

Many exiles feared that, if they did not seize upon the war's antifascist ideals, there would never be another chance to eliminate their region's dictatorships. In the early 1940s, dictators tried manipulating the exigencies of war to defend their regimes. "I greatly fear," Heliodoro Valle outlined, "the dictators and those that support them with force will stress the necessity that they remain as contributors to the work of reconstruction."[78] In the mid-1940s, antidictatorial forces pushed back. Those with the Unión Democrática Hondureña (Honduran Democratic Union, UDH) in San Pedro Sula hoped the UN would shield anti-Carías organizations against their dictator's political and physical assaults.[79] In a message for the Honduran people, the CLDH in Mexico summoned the Atlantic Charter as a "symbol . . . of freedom for the world of the future" and a "new international order" that could not wait any longer.⁸⁰ Likewise, one exile in *Quisqueya Libre* insisted that, as the war in Europe came to an end, their own war to realize democracy in the Caribbean Basin, to bring the ideals of the Atlantic Charter to their home countries, must continue.⁸¹

For these reasons, they paid close attention to Spanish dictator Francisco Franco. Democratic organizations sent letters to Roosevelt, Churchill, and Joseph Stalin offering to help European refugees repatriate to fight "the German invader and its fascist agents" and assisting Spanish exiles against Franco as "a valiant contribution to the Cause of the United Nations."⁸² Similarly, Cuban antifascists offered immense support, with labor organizations under the Confederación de Trabajadores de Cuba (Confederation of Workers of Cuba, CTC) denouncing Franco's "fascist regime."⁸³ To all of them, the survival of Franco's regime was a warning that fascism was not dead in Europe or Latin America. In Costa Rica, citizens put together the Comité de Ayuda al Pueblo Español (Committee for Help for the Spanish People) to lobby for the end of diplomatic relations with Spain.⁸⁴ The nation's Casa Presidencial (Presidential House) received numerous petitions to break relations with Franco's Spain, with adherents identifying Franco's regime as "the focus of fascist infection in the postwar world" and insisting, "If our country was one of the first to support the fight against Hitler, we should be one of the first to break relations with this regime, [an] enemy of world democracy."⁸⁵

For those targeting dictatorships, Franco was proof that the international conflict against fascism had not yet concluded, a message Sáenz professed during a 1946 UN radiobroadcast across Latin America. Breaking relations with Franco's "Nazi-Falangist regime" was not a violation of the nonintervention principle but representative of "the America of Bolívar, Hidalgo, San Martín, O'Higgins, Juárez, and José Martí."⁸⁶ Sáenz and Gómez Robelo justified their democratic crusades by pointing out how Latin America's dictatorial regimes admired Franco's Falange.⁸⁷ Likewise, Nicaraguan exile Juan José Meza highlighted Somoza's role as Franco's "great friend," reiterating that Germany, Italy, and Japan's surrenders should not denote the end of antifascism.⁸⁸ Stressing that Trujillo remained one of Franco's staunchest defenders while most members of the UN had broken relations, Requena and ARDE questioned why the world's leaders and governments criticized Franco when "there exist[ed in the Dominican Republic] another dictatorship bloodier even that [sic] the one which is oppressing Spain today and relatively more gloomy and implacable than the infamous one of Hitler's in Europe."⁸⁹ Just as they demanded that the Atlantic Charter and other symbols of antifascism should outlive the Second World War's official conclusion, antidictatorial groups summoned Franco's regime as evidence that the war for democracy was far from over.

By merging local goals and global ideals, antidictatorial exiles injected new energy into their transnational networks. In late 1945, the Unión Revolucionaria Nicaragüense (Revolutionary Nicaraguan Union) notified Mexican officials that Central American students would attend the Universidad Nacional Autónoma de México as "brothers in arms" opposed to all the region's dictators.[90] The students and poets making up the Comité Cubano Pro Liberación de Honduras (Cuban Committee for the Liberation of Honduras, CCPLH) denounced Carías as complicit in Hitler's and the UFCO's activities by allowing Nazi officials to operate in Honduras and welcoming entities who profited off Honduran resources.[91] From New York, Latin American and Spanish exiles coauthored letters to the UN's founding delegates in San Francisco denouncing Franco, Somoza, Carías, and Trujillo, whose regimes defiled the international institution's democratic ideals.[92]

Dominican exiles expertly networked throughout the greater Caribbean. In Cuba, *Quisqueya Libre* repeatedly described independence heroes Martí and Máximo Gómez as historical links between Cubans and Dominicans.[93] Some in the 1930s, including Dominican-born and Cuban-raised Enrique Cotubanamá "Cotu" Henríquez, helped found the PRD and joined the Auténtico political party against Cuba's dictatorships.[94] Celebrating one hundred years of Dominican independence, exiles stood with Cuban labor unions, backed by the Allied nations' flags and portraits of Roosevelt, Churchill, Stalin, and Martí.[95] Due to their efforts, the struggle against Trujillo's regime was a collective war against Caribbean Basin dictatorships. Poet Nicolás Guillén and Cuba's Federación Estudiantil Universitaria (University Student Federation, FEU), Lombardo Toledano and the Confederación de Trabajadores de América Latina (Confederation of Workers of Latin America, CTAL), Venezuelan poet Andrés Eloy Blanco, and Beals joined the UDAD's compilation *América contra Trujillo* (*America Against Trujillo*).[96] While petitioning for their government to grant persecuted Dominican students asylum, Mexico's FEU and the Asociación de Estudiantes Hispanoamericanos (Association of Hispanic American Students, AEH) proclaimed that "the Second World War has produced dramatic conditions that divided Humanity into two irreconcilable groups" of democracy and fascism where "the imminence of a democratic victory should not be just military but fundamentally political," and the Dominican Republic "could not be an exception."[97]

The Masacre Sampedrana in Honduras

The greater Caribbean's antifascist struggle was best embodied in the Masacre Sampedrana (San Pedro Sula Massacre), the July 1944 massacre of Honduran protesters in San Pedro Sula by Carías's forces.[98] Over the previous months, Carías's rule sparked significant domestic opposition. The prior November, Ribas Montes of Carías's presidential guard and reformist military officers tried to arrest the dictator and form a new government before being found out.[99] After the conspirators sat in prison for a month, the UDC joined Honduran exiles to solicit Churchill's intervention. In any other circumstance, the organization's anticolonial orientation would have placed its members against the vocally proud British imperialist. Here, though, the UDC petitioned Churchill on the basis of the antifascist ideals he represented. Ribas Montes's plot was an outgrowth of the "inextinguishable desire in the Honduran people's soul to solidly set their institutions on a democratic base." This "truly heartbreaking . . . internal struggle for [democracy] in various American countries" and "sacrifice of many patriots' lives," the UDC proclaimed, was embodied in the "elevated proposals consigned in the Atlantic Charter." Now, they beseeched Churchill to "interject his valiant influence" on behalf of "the United Nations that nobly discussed establishing an empire of democracy" and free the conspirators.[100]

As the conspirators and numerous political prisoners remained in Carías's jails, Honduran women planned public protests. The following May, a group of prominent women spearheaded a march in Tegucigalpa to rally public support for clemency.[101] Their informal organization boasted among its number the poet Angela Ochoa Velázquez, labor activist Graciela Amaya de García, feminist Visitación Padilla, writer Argentina Díaz Lozano, daughters of multiple generals, and Emma de Bonilla, wife of former Honduran dictator-president Policarpo Bonilla. On May 29, the women set out from the Catedral de San Miguel (Saint Michael Cathedral), and hundreds of like-minded civilians enlarged their ranks. At the Casa Presidencial, Fernando Zepeda Durón, editor of Carías's *La Época*, allowed only three to enter for a heated but fruitless exchange with the dictator's allies. Afterward, the march headed toward the US Embassy where workers, students, and more cheered for Roosevelt and the Atlantic Charter. A few days later, the women regrouped, baptized themselves the Comité Proliberación de Presos Políticos (Committee for the Liberation of Political Prisoners), and prepared a second march for July 4. As the women drew up their plans, Carías's police detained and interrogated the protests' leaders for organizing a "center of rebellion."[102]

Despite these suppressive actions, the march commenced as planned. Blending their protest against Carías into the victories against Hitler and Mussolini, participants held flags representing the newly formed UN's members; canvases of Roosevelt and US Independence Day; and banners proclaiming the Atlantic Charter, the Four Freedoms, and the phrase "Liberty or Death." With between two thousand and three thousand participants, the march wound its way toward and overwhelmed the Plaza Morazán, honoring Honduran president and Central American hero Francisco Morazán. Speeches, songs, poems, and Honduras's national hymn celebrated Morazán, Roosevelt, Central American freedom, and the "country of [George] Washington," echoing onward as the march arrived at Comayagüela's Parque La Libertad (Freedom Park). In its midst, students demanded a "¡Huelga!" (strike) unless Carías stepped down. Despite brief appearances from some of the dictator's supporters, the marchers concluded around nine o'clock that night after returning to the Parque Morazán.[103] The July 4 march was a tranquil protest.

That peace made events on July 5 all the more devastating. Before eight o'clock in the morning, police dispersed through Tegucigalpa's streets, threatening any businesses that joined the students' strike. The rest of the day was replete with participants arrested and taken to the jails, while speakers and students, men and women, endured police beatings. From morning until night, participants flooded the Mexican and Salvadoran embassies to request asylum.[104] Officials attacked and injured women, who often bore a gender-specific protection from such reprisals, and stories circulated of how agents broke the arm of Ribas Montes's sister.[105] This special attention may have enabled some women to be released from jail and given house arrest, but it was a small luxury.[106]

These events rippled outward from Honduras. Noting similarities to their own struggle against Trujillo, Dominican exiles in Cuba applauded the women while mocking Carías for instituting martial law against those pleading their case on behalf of political prisoners and free elections.[107] In letters to fellow exiles, Heliodoro Valle took note of this escalating energy throughout the greater Caribbean and encouraged colleagues to lobby their nations' governments against Carías. "We believe that it is the most psychological moment, all because of the latest news related to the manifestation that the women had made in Tegucigalpa."[108] Because Honduran women had picked July 4 for their march, the "day of liberty for the great nation of the North" and the "anniversary of the Independence of the United States," their antidictatorial fervor intersected with the global antifascist spirit.[109]

Events at San Pedro Sula, though, overshadowed all else that transpired and brought international attention on the dictator. As in Tegucigalpa, organizers with Graciela Bográn purposefully chose July 4. However, the regime's suppressive measures forced the committee to request prior authorization from Carías's minister of war, Juan Manuel Gálvez. Two hundred kilometers northwest of the capital city, Gálvez and San Pedro Sula's Cariísta (pro Carías) officials on July 5 granted permission for the march to take place the next day, provided the protest was silent and followed a prescribed route. Though surprised to have even received such authorization in light of the repression taking place in Tegucigalpa, the committee accepted. On the morning of July 6, women, workers, and students commenced their protest. While remaining on the approved path, the movement incorporated more and more sampedranos (San Pedro Sula residents) holding the flags of the United States and other Allied nations while distributing flyers requesting the dictator's resignation. Some exiles later alleged participants shouted denunciations of the dictator, but most exiles and British reports confirm it was a silent protest from beginning to end, even as numbers increased to as many as seven hundred. Along the way, Gálvez's soldiers followed their every step, but protesters arrived without incident at the final destination, the Droguería Nacional (National Drugstore), believing their uninvited and armed stalkers merely aimed to intimidate.[110] As exiles later alleged, this was far more than intimidation; it was the perfect staging ground for a massacre.

The specific spark behind the Masacre Sampedrana remains unclear.[111] Concluding the march, organizer José Antonio Peraza came forward to thank everyone for their support and good behavior. As he walked to a store building to speak to the crowd, the escort of soldiers and police began surrounding the protesters, Bográn claimed.[112] When Peraza reached the store's second floor, Cariísta official Mayor Ángel Funes confronted him. Funes insisted that there could be no speech, and Peraza swore he only intended to give a few words to disperse attendees. A British vice consul, who visited San Pedro Sula days later, was told Funes pulled out a gun, which he waved in the air to stop Peraza. Some claimed protester Alejandro Irías reached out to prevent Funes from shooting, only to be shot; others suggested Irías, pushed by protesters behind him, accidentally knocked Funes to the ground, who took out a tear gas bomb, which failed to go off but "made a lot of noise."[113] From the crowd, Bográn thought Funes had taken out a hand grenade to throw into the marchers.[114] In the midst of the confusion, either Funes or one of the armed Cariístas shot

Irías. With that bullet, the masacre ensued. The vice consul heard that the soldiers and police "lost their heads and started firing on the crowd indiscriminately."[115] Bullets tore into the fleeing civilians, gunning down men, women, and children. Blaming "stupidity and mismanagement" on the part of Cariísta officials, the British ambassador reported, "The police who were armed with automatic rifles in many cases shot the people from pure joy of killing—I am told that one of the official gunmen was seen pumping bullets into the body of a 14 year old boy lying in the gutter."[116] There was never an official count of the total number of protesters; estimates range from a few hundred to just over a thousand. Week to week over the next years, the number reported butchered by Cariístas in San Pedro Sula varied, with conservative guesses in the dozens and other approximations going as high as two hundred. Because the soldiers carried machine guns and followed the march along Gálvez's prescribed path that ended at a closed-off area in front of the droguería with another number of soldiers and police armed with automatic weapons, survivors understandably felt Cariísta officials under Gálvez orchestrated the massacre.

This massacre reverberated throughout the Americas as proof of the cruelty behind Carías's regime. Delivering this news were newly exiled survivors and sympathizers seeking asylum.[117] From El Salvador and Guatemala to Cuba and Mexico, they tapped into antifascist ideals and denounced the "Nazi-Cariísta assault troops" unleashed upon "citizens that made use of their human rights."[118] Having helped organizers, Gómez Robelo insisted the protests were evidence that the Second World War bolstered anti-Carías opposition.[119] In 1945, a group of Hondurans, while being expelled, took a moment at Toncontín Airport to compose a brief recrimination of Carías, the "Nazi-fascist" dictator, whose self-proclaimed "peace" ignored the "desire of the United Nations," whose regime "betray[ed] the Atlantic Charter," and who was an "enemy of humanity." In writing their names, they claimed that their signatures would stand alongside the 179 murdered, 194 wounded, and 185 arrested during the massacre.[120] Four years after the atrocity, when Carías allowed managed elections that ensured his chosen successor Gálvez would take over, exiles in Mexico warned that the incoming president was the "Massacrer of the People of San Pedro Sula."[121]

Antidictatorial figures and groups throughout the Caribbean Basin joined Honduran exiles in remembering the Masacre Sampedrana. In Guatemala in 1945, intellectuals helped Hondurans put together a one-year commemoration, publicized by *Mediodía* with massive articles written by Hondurans, Guatemalans, and more.[122] The CCPLH honored the "fight for the dignity and democracy of the people of America" alongside "the nations struggling against Totalitarianism."[123] In a similar vein, students and the antifascist Asociación Mexicana Pro Francia (Pro-France Mexican Association) joined exiles in Mexico to swear that the "blood of the martyrs [of San Pedro Sula] was not spilled in vain."[124] The CLDH in Mexico paired the transnational array of hymns and poems with participants' testimonies and letters in the compilation *Homenaje a las Víctimas de San Pedro Sula* (*Homage to the Victims of San Pedro Sula*), in which one writer designated Carías the "Hitler" of Honduras and a "canned Mussolini."[125] Crystalized with the Masacre Sampedrana, the Caribbean Basin's antidictatorial sentiments and the Second World War's antifascist ideals melded into regional opposition targeting the Honduran dictator.

Watching El Salvador but Heading to Guatemala

Within this environment, exiles, intellectuals, and students turned their attention to the April 1944 uprising against Salvadoran dictator Maximiliano Hernández Martínez. As Martínez's ouster commenced, *Quisqueya Libre* noted different egos, since no one compared to Trujillo's demand for statues and titles, but recognized that both dictators "perverted the popular conscience, making half the country spy on the other half."[126] Across the greater Caribbean, marches, speeches, and writings honored the forty-four executed during the uprising and compared Martínez to other "oppressors of liberty," calling his successor, Honduras's Carías, Nicaragua's Somoza, and Guatemala's Jorge Ubico "the four horsemen of the apocalypse in Central America." On radio stations, Ordóñez Argüello, journalist Castro, and others criticized the Atlantic Charter's seeming "ineffectiveness," since the "great democracies" had not taken any measures against Central America's "hitleresque governments."[127]

Unexpectedly, it was not El Salvador that became their haven for democratic activism but Guatemala, a country whose June 1944 revolution against Ubico served as the beacon for their continuing struggles. There, students put together a solidarity group, Juventud Liberal Hondureña (Honduran Liberal Youth).[128] Castro received a job with one of Guatemala's newspapers, as did others fleeing Carías's violence in Tegucigalpa, Comayagüela, and San Pedro Sula.[129] Alongside the resulting outpouring of antidictatorial articles, the country's radio stations amplified exiles' voices.[130] Buoyed by a civic spirit including "masons, rotaries, lions, students, universities, workers, farmers," and more, Gómez Robelo disseminated the Atlantic Charter's ideals as part of a "campaign [of] the continental press in a decisive fight against Carías, Somoza, and Trujillo."[131] For those unable to partake of the international antifascist moment from their respective nations of origin, Guatemala became the locus for the region's transnational antidictatorial networking.

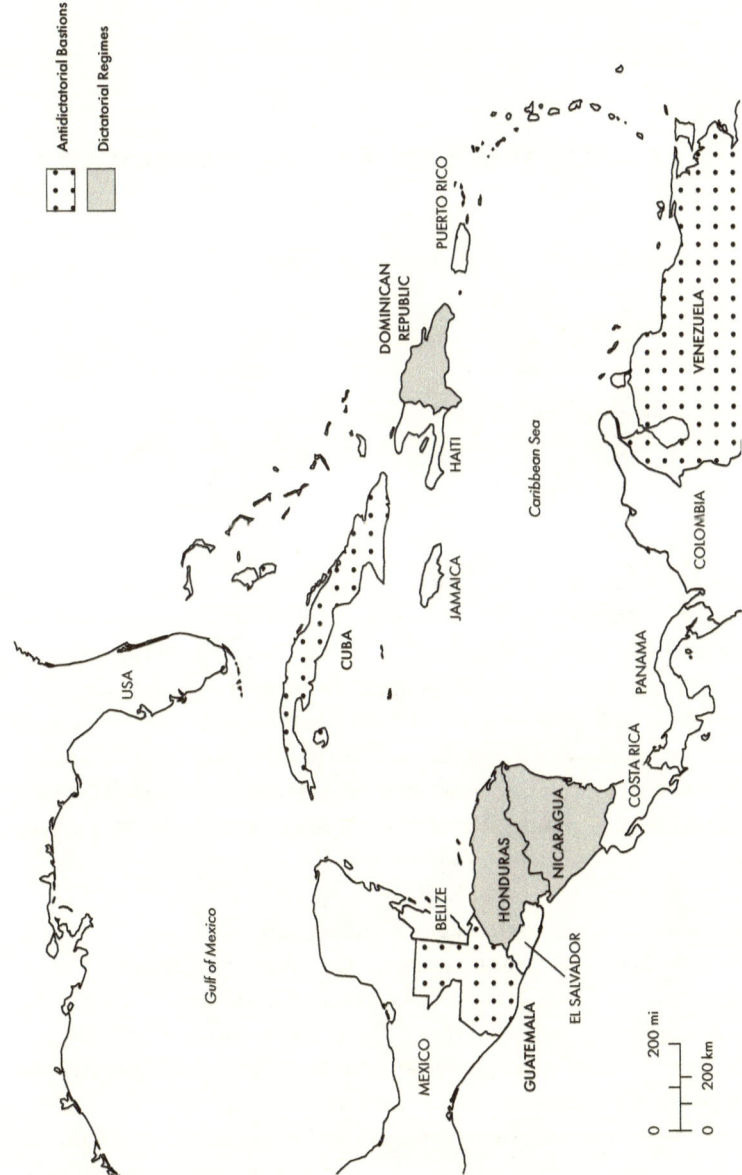

Figure 2. Map of Caribbean Basin, 1944

Chapter 2

The Transnational Postwar Conjuncture

The Guatemalan Revolution, 1944-1947

In much of the world, various nations spent mid-August 1945 celebrating. For their peoples, August 15 and the surrender of Japan's empire was the Second World War's official end. Guatemala's newly elected president had a different message the following day. "The war has ended. The Allies have paid a terrible price in blood, life, and resources to defend liberty in all the countries of the world," proclaimed Juan José Arévalo before addressing those across the greater Caribbean who needed no direct acknowledgment. He swore, "Now begins the second phase of this great war with the purpose of assuring that those sacrifices will not have been in vain and to implant the democratic ideal in all nations. Particularly our America should not consent to the existence of totalitarian regimes under a democratic disguise. Guatemala has the first democratic government in its history. We hope to soon see the same privilege reach other American lands that wish for it."[1] Honduran, Nicaraguan, Dominican, and other exiles were repeatedly demanding the realization of the Atlantic Charter and the Four Freedoms. Now, Arévalo invoked their claims.

The 1944 Guatemalan Revolution immediately transformed into the greater Caribbean's bastion of antidictatorial sentiments and antifascist ideals. Due to exiles' activism and Arévalo's democratic image, Guatemala emerged as the region's epicenter for those standing against dictatorships. There, exiles and like-minded compatriots networked while sketching out hopeful solutions to the dilemma of dictators. By the time Arévalo joined a fellow democratic leader in diplomatically isolating Trujillo, Guatemala's transnationalized Revolution embodied the hopes of many in the Caribbean Basin.

Bringing Antifascism into the Guatemalan Revolution

With the greater Caribbean's full attention on the Second World War and the uprising in El Salvador, the onset of the 1944–1954 Guatemalan Revolution took many by surprise even though Jorge Ubico's regime shared many characteristics with its regional counterparts. Ubico took power during the Great Depression's uncertainty and promised local elites and business interests economic stability and the suppression of communism.[2] He never withheld his admiration of European fascism, declaring in interviews, "I admire Hitler." Meanwhile, his officials enforced his policies with an array of secret police and domestic spies under General Roderico Anuzeto, this "despotic hand" forcing many into exile.[3] In Mexico, nationalists and labor activists, including Lombardo Toledano, welcomed Guatemalans and their efforts "against the Dictators of the World."[4] There, Guatemalan intellectual Luis Cardoza y Aragón joined the UDC's Sáenz, Meza, and Heliodoro Valle in summoning the war's antifascist ideals.[5] Journalist Clemente Marroquín Rojas compared Ubico to Hitler and Mussolini, calling the Central American dictator "the first friend of Franco."[6] During the 1942 Río de Janeiro Conference to discuss World War II, Marroquín Rojas joined others to point out an apparent contradiction. Latin American governments were supposed to "battle for united action and the hope of the Continent against the totalitarian dictators which menaces [sic] the peace of the world." However, they counted among their members Ubico, who was "not a democratic ruler" but a dictator forcing the "popular masses of many Central American and Insular nations" under the "slavery imposed by the tolerance of the nations which now speak as standard bearers of democracy." Exiles also questioned the US government's hand in these matters. On one hand, the US government bore much of the responsibility for their current situation due to "Washington [having been] the author of all these little rulers of America." On the other hand, they conceded that "it is the spirit of the immense American

Ruler [Roosevelt] which has started all" the current criticisms of fascism and totalitarianism bolstering their aspirations.[7]

In mid-June 1944, teachers and students in the capital city went on strike against Ubico's repressive measures.[8] Middle-class professionals joined the protests, and Guatemalans denounced their dictator's policies as those of "Nazi-fascists" and the "enemies of democracy."[9] Upon Ubico's unexpected resignation, a military junta under General Federico Ponce, one of the departing dictator's confidantes rumored to have been selected by Anzueto and fellow Ubiquistas to ensure the regime's spiritual continuation, sought to suppress this democratic activism.[10] Ponce's officials forced vocal figures like journalist David Vela into exile while antidictatorial and antifascist messages swirled.[11] As Anzueto's agents tracked them, Marroquín Rojas, Vela, and others in Mexico and El Salvador saw little difference between Ubico and Ponce.[12] Ponce's request that Carías send military supplies, planes, and explosives to attack Guatemala City only solidified his image as a venomous remnant of Ubiquismo.[13] Following Ponce's expulsion, an unprecedented wave of political participation enveloped the nation, with the Guatemalan Revolution memorialized by Cardoza y Aragón as a decade of "spring in the land of eternal tyranny."[14] With the military and a governing triumvirate assuming control before forthcoming elections, myriad debates emerged over how to institutionalize the social ambitions, economic reforms, and political goals proffered over the past weeks.[15]

Among the Revolution's admirers were Caribbean Basin exiles who found a common antifascist cause in the elimination of the region's dictators. At the Universidad de San Carlos, unions welcomed Nicaraguan exile Edelberto Torres and Guatemalan intellectual Manuel Galich while members held flags of the UN's members as a "democratic and antifascist act" and envisioned the Revolution as "an omen, a hope, a promise for the liberation of Central America."[16] Addressing the triumvirate of Captain Jacobo Árbenz, Major Francisco Javier Arana, and civilian Jorge Toriello, Honduran exiles praised the Revolution as a "triumph . . . that opens for Central America a new era of authentic Democracy" they sought in their home country.[17] Zúñiga Huete concluded, "Guatemala's democratic movement has initiated a new era of institutional life in Central America."[18]

Consequently, Guatemala's Revolution was a transnational epicenter of antidictatorial networking. The Asociación de Estudiantes Universitarios (Association of University Students, AEU) endorsed student protests "to put into practice in their country the principles of democracy and liberty that served as the standard for the United Nations in their recent fight against totalitarianism."¹⁹ In *Mediodía*, Honduran exile and Árbenz's future secretary Francisco Morazán was one of many who used the Revolution's surge of newspapers, pamphlets, and other political outlets to denounce the unjust "peace" of Latin American and fascist dictatorships.²⁰ Likewise, *El Imparcial* disseminated materials from the UDC and CTAL encouraging the "Isolation of Central American Dictatorships."²¹ This activism captured regional observers' attention. Before the end of 1944, the Dominican ambassador in Guatemala City remarked on the nation's "incessant revolutionary propaganda."²² He later reiterated that Guatemala was "the central point for the enemies of the three Central American dictatorships" of Carías, Somoza, and Martínez's successor in El Salvador.²³

Arévalo as an Antidictatorial Figurehead

An immeasurable amount of attention and activism gravitated toward Arévalo, the teacher who became a focal point nationally as the Revolution's first president and transnationally as an antidictatorial patron. The first Guatemalans to offer their names and their organizations' support to Arévalo encompassed many who had endured exile, including Cardoza y Aragón, the AEU, and local political parties.²⁴ Traveling, Cardoza y Aragón found Arévalo's name reverberating among numerous people and groups.²⁵ Through such positive descriptions of the previously unknown teacher, exiles came to admire Arévalo. From Mexico City, Heliodoro Valle described an intense admiration coming from his friends, Cardoza y Aragón and Vela.²⁶ The CLDH in Mexico's members were amazed at the enthusiasm for Arévalo's candidacy among their compatriots, including Guatemalan intellectual Alberto Paz y Paz.²⁷

Arévalo was a stark contrast to the region's dictatorships. Influenced by German philosopher Karl Christian Friedrich Krause, Arévalo termed his ideology spiritual socialism, which sought to balance individual liberty and private property with labor rights and democratic organization. This worldview shaped his support for the Revolution's plethora of reforms, including an eight-hour labor code, social security, and more, which aimed to gradually reduce Guatemala's economic inequities.²⁸ These ideals did resonate with some exiles, such as the FDRH, which supported his spiritual socialism as a "democratic socialism" that recognized "humanitarian tendencies" and "the divine essence of the man's soul" that should not be sacrificed by any "capitalist or socialist orthodoxy."²⁹

Arévalo's ideology further transnationalized the Revolution's appeal among democratic groups throughout the greater Caribbean. A group of Salvadorans sent an album of their signatures simply to express "their fervor for the cause of liberty," and another endorsed Arévalo's warning that Central America "can only have five democracies or five dictatorships."[30] The Unión Femenina ProDefensa de la Libertad de Guatemala (Women's Union in Defense of Guatemalan Liberty) in Mexico City cheered Arévalo's "democratic ideals" and supported his candidacy.[31] To a Nicaraguan exile, the "strength and sincerity of the Central American youth" ensured their "faith in" the new president.[32] During 1946's May Day celebrations, Arévalo gave a passionate speech on behalf of workers and American democracy. Over in San Pedro Sula, where the Masacre Sampedrana transpired, the Sociedad de Obreros "La Fraternidad" ("The Brotherhood" Society of Workers) read Arévalo's speech, which the local newspaper, *El Norte*, republished. Lamenting they could only read his words without getting to hear his voice, the society composed a tribute it admitted might be "hyperbolic." Arévalo was "an ideological promise," "a revolutionary symbol," "the standard for the vindications of Central America," and "the expression of the isthmus's popular soul" for the workers of Honduras and Central America.[33]

Just as appealing were his open criticisms of dictatorial regimes. In May 1945, José Castro sent copies of Arévalo's speeches to fellow Honduran exiles.[34] Alongside his Guatemalan friends Cardoza y Aragón and Vela, Heliodoro Valle offered to write editorials lauding Arévalo.[35] In the early 1950s, Ordóñez Argüello compiled hundreds of statements, writings, interviews, and publications from those who admired the teacher. Throughout *Arévalo visto por América* (*Arévalo as Seen by America*), Arévalo's democratic ideals and militant antifascism echoed. Among multiple student organizations, in newspapers across the Western Hemisphere, from Caribbean Basin to Peruvian Aprista exiles, and among anti-Franco organizations between Argentina and Cuba, all included in the massive compendium recounted his sympathy for and encouragement of their antidictatorial causes.[36]

This sympathy manifested in Arévalo and his government's moral, economic, and military support for antidictatorial groups. In early 1946, Mexican agents confirmed Guatemalan military officials were selling and transporting munitions to Nicaraguan exiles.[37] In addition to chapters in Mexico and El Salvador, the FDRH opened one in Guatemala.[38] Among the group's associates was Guatemalan legislator José García Bauer, whose support merited an honorary credential.[39] In December 1944, Honduran exiles claimed Árbenz promised "material support to the Honduran exiles in order to overthrow [their] dictatorial and despotic regime." Deliberations over such assistance split some exiles. There were numerous historic examples of inter-American solidarity going back to when Nicaragua's government supported Francisco Morazán in the early 1800s to restore Honduras's government, but hanging over such offers were questions about how Hondurans would react to "the specter of Guatemalan intervention."[40] In light of their factional schisms, Heliodoro Valle hoped they would unite to follow Arévalo against Carías.[41] Receiving these offers of support, he and the FDRH presented the Revolution as proof they could overcome the constant "partisan, personalist" divisions Carías exploited. "Today more than ever," Heliodoro Valle wrote, "one has to have faith that the dictatorship has its days counted," thanks to the hope they invested in the Revolution, the "repudiation of Franco" at San Francisco, and "the political environment there is in this hemisphere."[42]

Unionism, Franco, and Doctrines Against Dictatorships

Due to the Revolution's transnational ideals, activists blended and intertwined various antidictatorial doctrines. Among them was a powerful strain of Central American unionism.[43] Since the first years of independence, unionists advocated for an intraregional mechanism to facilitate closer relations. More importantly, an umbrella organization of democratic allies would hopefully prevent the domestic coups, civil wars, and foreign interventions that spawned dictators among the region's smaller nation-states.[44] In fact, the two most prominent organizations, Sáenz's UDC and Salvador Mendienta's PUC, often hosted local forums where attendees denounced those regimes.[45] From Guatemala, the Unión Patriótica Centroamericana (Central American Patriotic Union, UPC) claimed a union would break down the national barriers hindering the region's antidictatorial activism.[46] No longer would "tyrants" and "old despotisms" undermine the "cultural, intellectual, and economic development of [the Central American] people" by exploiting nation-states' borders and playing the people against one another.[47]

Arévalo's personal support for the unionist ideal, in turn, solidified adherents' passionate embrace of the Revolution.[48] His government's proposals for regional identification cards were tentative and stillborn, but small measures garnered the attention of unionists, including a Costa Rican section of the UDC.[49] Salvador Mendieta directly urged Arévalo that removing any dictatorship would be a "triumph for the unionist cause" and bring about "the fundamental social, economic, political, and international revolution of Central

America, the indispensable base for Iberoamerican confraternity, the cornerstone of continental solidarity."⁵⁰ As the Guatemalan president gave his blessing to unionist meetings, Castillo Ibarra and Nicaragua's Partido Socialista Revolucionario (Revolutionary Socialist Party) hoped he would protect unionists and exiles seeking refuge in Guatemala.⁵¹

Those exiles admired unionists' antiauthoritarian spirit. Ordóñez Argüello believed a union or even a greater Caribbean confederation could topple Somoza and Carías.⁵² During the transnationalized Revolution, unionist organizations and meetings brought together a broad range of antidictatorial figures, including socialists, communists, and more.⁵³ Under the PUC, the Club Femenino ProUnión (Women's Pro Union Club) and the Comité Femenino ProUnión Centroamericana (Women's Pro Central American Union Committee) in Quetzaltenango welcomed all classes and races to learn the unionist ideal.⁵⁴ In November 1944, the UPC convened a program including Central American exiles, speakers from the Universidad Nacional de Guatemala, student activists with the AEU, and the UPC's Sección Femenina.⁵⁵

Similarly, Arévalo joined the Revolution's adherents in denouncing Franco's fascist regime.⁵⁶ Upon Ubico's and Ponce's expulsions, Guatemalan civilians demanded that action be taken against the Spanish fascist, and the governing triumvirate broke diplomatic relations with Franco's government, preceding the UN decisions to keep his regime out of its international organizations.⁵⁷ "The people of Guatemala, that have achieved their liberty by means of overthrowing dictatorships of totalitarian regimes, possess genuinely democratic aspirations," the revolutionary junta declared, and Franco's regime "was of the type clearly totalitarian" with "an ideology and origins repugnant to the principles of the [Guatemalan] revolution." Thus, Decree 17 ceremoniously suspended the country's diplomatic relations with Franco.⁵⁸ After his election, Arévalo endorsed the act as links between the anti-Franco cause, antidictatorial sentiments, and the Revolution escalated. Throughout, the Confederación de Trabajadores de Guatemala (Confederation of Guatemalan Workers, CTG) and other labor organizations lobbied the UN to keep out Franco's regime.⁵⁹ An adviser to the UN's Guatemalan delegation, Sáenz assured Spanish exiles that he would continue fighting on their behalf.⁶⁰ Into the early 1950s, Spanish exiles networked with Guatemalan intellectuals and Caribbean Basin exiles in support of their common antidictatorial cause.⁶¹

Opposition to Franco was not the lone international inspiration from which the Revolution's admirers borrowed. In the mid-1940s, positions put forward by US Assistant Secretary of State Spruille Braden and Uruguayan diplomat Eduardo Rodríguez Larreta dovetailed with similar doctrines. An experienced US government hand regarding inter-American affairs, Braden gained attention for his efforts to undermine Juan Perón's populist government based on the Argentine's tolerance of Nazis and hesitance to follow the US government's leadership, but this criticism also targeted Franco's and Trujillo's dictatorial policies. For his part, Larreta suggested that American governments could take up limited forms of multilateral intervention against regimes relying on force or violating human rights.[62] Coming from North and South America, these two doctrines, Braden's antidictatorial thesis and the Larreta proposal, overlapped neatly with antifascist ideals circulating across the Caribbean Basin. ARDE claimed Arévalo's crusade against dictatorial regimes was a continuation of the Second World War with a "new inter-American politics" and "a new version of the 'Good Neighbor' thesis."[63] In Guatemala's *El Imparcial*, one former exile pleaded for Braden to apply his antidictatorial doctrine to not just Franco in Spain and Perón in Argentina but also "the Hitlers and Mussolinis of Honduras and Nicaragua."[64] *Quisqueya Libre* put Braden's words about freedom on its June issue next to an excerpt of the Dominican national hymn.[65]

Although the Larreta Doctrine greatly appealed to those who interpreted such a measure as necessary in a region mocked for its stereotypical dictators, some dreaded how the policy could be manipulated or abused. Furthermore, the doctrine acknowledged that undemocratic figures abused the nonintervention principle. Nevertheless, Braden's popular image dominated the discussion. Coming from an assistant secretary of state, his words suggested that the US government's embrace of antifascist policies was not limited to matters outside the Western Hemisphere. As Gómez Robelo summed up, Braden represented a US government "interested in setting countries on the path of a progressive democracy."[66] Most nations outside of Arévalo's Guatemala would not approve the Uruguayan's proposal, but Gómez Robelo considered the very suggestion an opportunity; observing the debates and gauging everyone's position regarding the Larreta Doctrine would "clarify and ascertain the ambiguous continental attitude against tyrants." At the very least, "Washington" was no longer "the head of the [forces of] reaction in America."[67] A sole representative of the US government provided the energy and even legitimacy to grasp what antidictatorial ideals and multilateral proposals like the Larreta Doctrine envisioned.

The Imperialism of European Colonialism and Foreign Investment

Woven into these discussions were impassioned debates over colonialism and foreign investment. More than a century since most Central American nations gained independence and half a century since the Spanish lost their last Caribbean territories, many did not forget the remaining British, French, and Dutch territories in Trinidad, French Guiana, or Curaçao.[68] Additionally, these European governments were the same ones that requested global support on behalf of democracy during the Second World War while failing to produce tangible plans for their colonial subjects' independence. Further impacting the Revolution was the issue of Belize/British Honduras, a Central American colony to which Guatemalans staked claim.[69]

Running the gamut from complaints that Britain failed to recognize Latin Americans' sovereignty over regional matters to the war's larger ideals, anticolonialist sentiments could not be removed from the Revolution's energies. Some have downplayed the sincerity or likelihood of these Guatemalans' demands regarding Belize, highlighting the issue as political theater behind demands for territorial gains.[70] However, anticolonialism was a significant aspect of the Revolution's democratic goals.[71] Arévalo's diplomats reported on figures and organizations throughout Latin America endorsing Guatemala's rights over Belize based on the UN's charter.[72] Referencing the international atmosphere against colonialism, Guatemalan newspapers cheered the US government's 1945 offer to arbitrate the entire matter.[73] Later that year at the Universidad de San Carlos, students during their traditional Huelga de Dolores (strike) included posters of the Atlantic Charter, parodies of Hitler, and placards on Belize.[74]

Lending their voices to the Revolution, antidictatorial exiles interpreted colonialism as another insult to local sovereignty. Looking over Europe's lingering hold in the greater Caribbean, Juan Bosch complained, "For the American conscience these colonies in their continental land are an embarrassment and, above all, nuisance." He lambasted French Guiana as a "penal colony," lamented how the Netherlands extracted resources from Surinam, mocked Britain for justifying its colonial policies in Guyana/British Guiana as part of the war's efforts, and feared for Belize's future, whether under Britain or a local strongman who would "continue exploiting without end the Guatemalan people."[75] From Mexico, Bográn and the FDRH endorsed Arévalo's position on Belize as reflective of their "struggle to liberate their country from the yoke of tyranny" and the "accession of a democracy like the one that the people of Guatemala truly enjoy."[76] Unionists enthusiastically cheered the Revolution's anticolonial stance. In 1945, Mendieta hoped that the US government, even with reservations, offered its "sympathy" on behalf of the "termination of European colonialism in America."[77] Borrowing from the Atlantic Charter and the Good Neighbor Policy, Sáenz lobbied Venezuelan President Rómulo Betancourt to join Arévalo at international venues and rally support for anticolonial proposals.[78] This was not a far stretch. From his pre-presidential writings to his presidential speeches, Arévalo envisioned a union of Central American states that would ward off aspiring dictators as well as colonizers.[79]

In these debates were questions related to foreign investment's role and multinational corporations' power. For the past decades, companies such as the UFCO and International Railways of Central America (IRCA) profited off the region's resources thanks to carefully cultivated relationships with local officials.[80] Under these arrangements, they expected gratitude but no meddling in their dealings, the result being domestic resentment at host nations' limited financial gains. For example, IRCA officials in 1944 feared the public would learn that the company paid five hundred thousand dollars in taxes in the United States but downplayed its profits to reduce Guatemalan taxes.[81] This resentment often manifested in Honduras, the country mocked as a banana republic. Gómez Robelo denounced how Carías allowed international corporations to operate at costs lower than what others endured, as when the UFCO acquired railroad construction rights valued at five million dollars for only two hundred thousand dollars. This was a betrayal of the country's potential, and the UFCO's political support for Carías was an additional insult.[82] Somehow worse was the daily reminder that Hondurans who worked for Carías's regime and newspapers occupied important positions in the UFCO.[83] As British officials concluded, the UFCO had "a rather deciding voice in the affairs of Honduras" and was described "as the Sixth Power [among the five nations] in Central America."[84]

For a century, critics lambasted the obvious links between extractive industries and local regimes that promised stability and security at the expense of workers' rights and traditional ways of life; World War II merely added to their arguments. Following Ubico's ouster, workers in Tiquisate struck against the UFCO, crying, "Down with the Gringos."[85] At a local meeting commemorating the anniversary of Martínez's ouster, attendees turned their attention to the UFCO and IRCA, issuing passionate denunciations of the companies.[86] Such complaints intertwined with those of locals, including groups like the Alianza Femenina Guatemalteca, who sought to uplift impoverished laborers and the Central American nation's economic plight.[87] Heliodoro Valle and Honduran exiles joined Guatemalans, unionists, and veterans of the Mexican Revolution to endorse Arévalo's criticisms of foreign monopolies.[88]

Links between the US government and multinational corporations remained a frequent point of contention, but Guatemalans and Caribbean Basin exiles into the late 1940s maintained a genuinely favorable view of the United States. When Arévalo's government passed a new labor code in 1947, Guatemalan officials noted that Braden and his colleagues did worry the legislation specifically targeted US-based enterprises.[89] After officials attempted to allay such concerns, Braden spoke favorably of Arévalo's government and the Revolution, casting aside what he saw as overblown anticommunist fears and bolstering his national appeal.[90] Likewise, Gómez Robelo and other exiles held Braden in a positive light. The exile interpreted Braden's antidictatorial position, the Good Neighbor Policy, and the Atlantic Charter, with its call that "the people of the world without exception could have access to the rights that had been denied them," as conducive for criticisms of the UFCO and any such entity that held immeasurable influence.[91] In March 1945, students organized a "strike," a serious though celebratory tradition wherein participants used face painting and enormous banners to unleash their frustrations with local concerns as well as global issues. During their first march in years, students tapped into the Second World War's international energies. Their signs demanded Belizean independence and portrayed the UFCO as a monopoly exploiting the Good Neighbor Policy to Central America's detriment.[92] This repeated during May Day activities in 1949 when protesters' signs called out, "The great Roosevelt would never let Guatemala down over Belize," "Kick out the English pirates," "America for the Americans," and "Out with the Falangist dogs!" Others questioned, "Why no Monroe Doctrine for Belize?" and "Why has Guatemala been thrown open to Franco's myrmidons?" Denouncing their nation's status as a "semicolonial regime" under the UFCO, Standard Oil, and other extensions of an "imperialist power" jeopardizing local sovereignty, labor leaders tied together the Revolution's anticolonialist energy with their deeply held frustrations with multinational corporations.[93]

Diagnosing Dictatorship

Antidictatorial figures did not limit their plans to the simple expulsion of dictatorial regimes; eliminating an illiberal ruler was only part of the larger discussion. In the Revolution's atmosphere, exiles and sympathizers recognized that dictatorships were a symptom of the larger diseases plaguing the Caribbean Basin. Despite the militant spirit sweeping the region, some feared the consequences of armed struggle and interference in host nations' internal affairs.[94] Heliodoro Valle was one who hoped diplomatic solutions could avoid violence, feeling "more optimistic than ever" that the UN's opposition to Franco indicated that "little by little [the world was] tightening the noose that will choke the dictatorships."[95] Other Hondurans aimed to tackle the dictatorial dilemma "without resorting to arms."[96] Similarly, the Comité Revolucionario Nicaragüense (Nicaraguan Revolutionary Committee, CRN) in Mexico endorsed Arévalo and other governments' using diplomatic means to isolate "totalitarian regimes" in America in the hope it "would avoid much blood."[97] Tragically, regimes appeared ready to outlast the democratic moment. After Somoza's 1947 coup against Argüello, Nicaraguan exiles appreciated various governments' gestures of ending diplomatic relations but worried such measures would fail to remove the dictator.[98]

In this vein, many exiles felt diplomacy, propaganda, and protests fell short of the requisite actions to realize Caribbean Basin democracy. For years, exiles somehow survived as the world ignored American regimes relying on force. Now, the world wielded every available resource including violence to remove fascist dictatorships. Watching World War II, many accepted bloodshed to remove long-standing dictatorships. Dominican exiles with Juan Diaz insisted they needed to go beyond moral opposition and actually "fight" dictators.[99] Although unionists usually endorsed pacifist measures for a democratic Central America, Sáenz presented the uprisings against the region's dictators as evidence that tyranny was on its way out thanks to the global conflict.[100] For exiles who endured years of repression and persecution throughout the Western Hemisphere, the Second World War's example sharply contrasted against the nonintervention principle dictators long manipulated.

The dictators' efforts to remain in power through force spurred many revolutionaries to turn to violence. Castro articulated this concept, alleging that it was Carías's "illegal regime" and its reliance on "embezzlement and violence" that sparked the "frequent attacks, plots, and insurrections against the dictator's life."[101] Gómez Robelo too believed "dictatorships" must be removed through the use of "force," since pacific measures had been "counterproductive and dangerous."[102] Another factor was exiles' increased networking thanks to the transnationalized Revolution. Through their interactions, they learned about one another's failed efforts and wondered if violence remained the only option.

Tulio Arvelo was one Dominican exile who spent years focused on peaceful means to remove Trujillo. In the mid-1940s, regional developments and new relationships with militant exiles, he admitted, "positively influenced my convictions regarding the true nature of the ruling regime in our country," leading him to embrace violence.[103] The symbolic figurehead channeling various antidictatorial ideals, Arévalo also faced this conundrum. Half measures and diplomatic gestures improved his image but did little beyond offering moral comfort to those still waiting for democracy to arrive in their countries of origin. During his first year in office, Arévalo confessed his growing fear that the "democratic nations of the continent" would fail to achieve "an effective system for asphyxiating the . . . totalitarian governments that still remain in America."[104]

Although all agreed on their shared crusade against dictatorial regimes, there remained the question about what the resulting democratic governments would be. Some exiles interpreted democracy as merely the antithesis of dictatorship. In his correspondence with fellow Dominican exiles, Miguel Ángel Ramírez sought "to see our countries free and under completely democratic regimes."[105] Others, such as the FDRH, were a bit more specific. Building on their conception of a spiritual or democratic socialism that protected the individual, the organization opposed "unpopular and inhuman" regimes that were nothing more than "totalitarian systems of the left or the right."[106] Influencing their definition of "dictatorship" and "totalitarian" were historical experiences with dictators who conflated their selves with the state and nationalism. Therefore, the path to democracy would begin with structures that identified collective needs alongside individual rights, as Nicaragua's Partido Liberal Nacional outlined. They warned that dictatorships, either "personal or collective," suppressed national sovereignty, free expression, the law, cultural vibrancy, and workers' rights; only a "republican, democratic, and representative system of government" would be the "ideal formula" to enshrine the citizens' rights.[107]

Antidictatorial exiles were also aware that dictators did not seize power in a vacuum. Political schisms, impoverished economies, competing national interests, and foreign interventions produced myriad regimes. Gómez Robelo described their common pursuit "for the best and most prompt solution of our great problem in Honduras." Their country was "enslaved" and in "pain and disgrace," but it was not simply their dictator's fault. Tragically, Honduras's political parties allowed their "personal attitudes or interests" to splinter their nation.[108] Zúñiga Huete agreed. He described the "understandably combative attitude" shaping those enduring "twelve years of exile . . . against the dictatorial regime" of Carías. In the face of a personalist dictatorship, he opposed any attempt to build a political ideology around one figure.[109] From the FDRH to the CLDH, fears that Carías's removal would bring to power a new dictator weighed on exiles' aspirations. Honduran exiles in Guatemala, though, saw these divisions and debates as a sign of progress, representative of the "obligatory discussions [and] expressions of new political tendencies" dictatorships denied.[110] In a similar vein, Dominican exiles believed that their disagreements would be secondary to their primary aim of removing Trujillo.[111]

To establish a common ground, antidictatorial exiles summoned the legacies of Latin American revolutionaries. Tapping into historically prominent and popular figures allowed diverse exiles to sketch a shared foundation of what a postdictatorship democracy should resemble. Those standing against Caribbean Basin dictatorships sought to follow the example of Cuba's Martí, Venezuela's Simón Bolívar, and others who fought for independence. Opposing dictators throughout the region, they were responding to Bolívar and Morazán's calls for inter-American solidarity. As had Martí, Sandino demonstrated that democracy was free of foreign intervention and imperialism. Building upon these common values, exiles charged Somoza, Carías, and Trujillo for betraying their people and their history. As Ramírez elaborated, foreign interests exploited the Caribbean Basin thanks to the armed forces directed by dictators and military regimes arrayed against their own people. Thus, the "representative forces of international imperialism" operated through "dictatorships and tyrants" to serve personal interests, foreign governments, and multinational corporations. Under a "Movement for the Liberation of the Caribbean," Ramírez hoped to promote "the democratization" and "the political liberation and emancipation of all the countries and colonies of the Caribbean." Reinforced by a "Bolivarian league of the Caribbean" or other supranational organization, the people would "adopt a democratic and revolutionary doctrine, based on the high principles of Bolivarian and Martian ideals" with individual nations governed by a "democratic republican system."[112]

The FDRH looked beyond Carías's removal and aimed to help "a great movement of the popular masses" that would "bring to Honduras an integral revolution, as political and economic as social, artistic, and cultural."[113]

In a 1955 letter to his wife, Honduran revolutionary Jorge Ribas Montes had to explain his reasons for fighting not just against the dictator in his country of origin but those throughout the greater Caribbean, so he utilized the examples of multiple champions, past and present, of Latin American independence. He quoted Martí's "Tres Heroés" (Three Heroes) to legitimate his own stance "against those that rob the people of their liberty." Morazán "thought in terms of Central America" and Bolívar of Greater Colombia, just as Ribas Montes needed to remember all those struggling under Carías, Somoza, and Trujillo. He drew inspiration from the words of his friend, Dominican exile turned Cuban politician Cotu Henríquez, who complained that Latin America had only "five cents of democracy" to its name. Dictators profited off the region's resources and spirit while preventing what should be the region's material progress and its people's liberty. This Honduran exile had to give his life "to liberate the Caribbean, implant in it just regimes, to form a block of nations" from which to tackle economic, agricultural, and industrial problems and return the region's "richness" and "dignity" to its peoples. This, Ribas Montes wrote, was the same idea of Martí, Bolívar, Morazán, Máximo Gómez, and Sandino, as well as his contemporary allies Cotu and Ramírez.[114]

Horacio Ornes was another Dominican exile seeing in the postwar environment an inter-American democratic spirit. Those who participated in armed movements against dictatorships aimed "to fulfill a duty and to defend a principle that is common to all people of America." "They are not Costa Ricans, Nicaraguans, North Americans, or Dominicans," he proclaimed. "They are our brothers, defending the highest and richest ideals of the people and belonging to the Great Country that Bolivar dreamt and Martí predicted."[115]

Latin America's democratic symbols and the Second World War's antifascist hopes guided militant exiles through the mid-1940s. One Honduran exile summarized how, facing the dictatorships' "oppression," they "hoped that the [Chapultepec Conference was] the basic point for their freedoms and for the development of the beautiful principles backed by the Atlantic Charter." Such ideals, whether freedom of the press or speech, were just one step closer to "the Democratic mold" of governments in the United States or Mexico that could provide "morality and the respect for these institutions," foundational elements of a civil society moving away from "despotic and dictatorial governments." Together, they could combat and rehabilitate those caught under the "Nazi-Fascist structure" undergirding dictatorships.¹¹⁶ Peraza reminded fellow Hondurans of the Revolution's inspiration, where Arévalo and the Guatemalan people's moral support continued without end. Although there had not been any grand effort to marshal all the region's people, Arévalo "could not be better and his intents could not be more favorable."¹¹⁷ The events of 1947, though, weighed upon the exile. In that year's first months, Trujillo staged a managed election, Somoza deposed Argüello, and Carías held onto power. The vexing year challenged the exile's optimism, but he remained steadfast. After all, Arévalo and the Revolution were still "ardently fighting to shake off the yoke of the tyranny that still oppressed" him and others.¹¹⁸

Denouncing the Dominican Dictator

For those wanting proof that the Revolution's ideals endured, Arévalo delivered. Since Ubico's removal, Guatemala became a hotbed of anti-Trujillo activities and publications.¹¹⁹ In the midst of the antidictatorial ideals circulating throughout the greater Caribbean, Trujillo ordered his officials abroad to monitor Dominican exiles, spread favorable propaganda, and prevent any publicity damaging to his reputation.¹²⁰ During the mid-1940s, the Dominican ambassador in Guatemala City admitted he could not fulfill these directives. All he could do was suggest that Arévalo's government "would not be able to end relations with ours without doing so at the same time with those of Carías and Somoza" due to the resulting demands of "the student mass and the refugees of those two countries."¹²¹ Paradoxically, the Revolution's democratic aspirations were good news for Trujillo's officials, as it seemed antidictatorial groups would not accept half-hearted diplomatic measures against a sole dictator.

Further frustrating Dominican officials were new ties between the Revolution and Venezuelan democracy. In October 1945, reformist military officers helped the democratic party Acción Democrática (Democratic Action, AD) and its leader Rómulo Betancourt take power. Already a nation whose people loathed the dictator on the other side of the Caribbean, this distaste grew in part because of Betancourt, who never hid his hatred of Trujillo.¹²² In office, Betancourt commemorated the Four Freedoms and spoke admiringly of the Guatemalan Revolution.¹²³ Immediately, Arévalo's government granted full recognition to Betancourt's government and sent a special delegation to attend all related ceremonies.¹²⁴ With trepidation, Dominican officials watched when Betancourt in late July 1946 visited Guatemala. He brought a statue of Bolívar to give the nation; Arévalo awarded the Venezuelan leader the nation's highest honor, the Orden del Quetzal. Later, Betancourt gave a speech encouraging more "diplomatic boycotts" against dictators, further incensing Dominican officials worried about the two presidents' amicable relationship.¹²⁵

This was about far more than nation-state alliances or personal rivalries because Trujillo despised the near omnipresence of Dominican exiles in all these affairs. The Revolution already served as a beacon for anti-Trujillo activities and publications, as when Pericles Franco Ornes sent Arévalo a copy of his *La tragedia dominicana* (*The Dominican Tragedy*), but Venezuelan democracy compounded all of this.¹²⁶ Dominican exiles had worked closely with Betancourt and other Venezuelans during their years in exile, and Bosch served as Betancourt's secretary and became an intermediary to Arévalo.¹²⁷ By early 1946, the two leaders privately wrote each other of their "giving all our moral support to the democratic opposition" and "just cause" of anti-Trujillo groups and discussed how to build a "block" against other regimes. Betancourt admired Bosch as their "mutual friend" who was a "paladin of one of the most just causes in our America today: that for the liberation of the Dominican people from the primitive and grotesque dictatorship that oppresses them," an "identical sentiment" he found in Arévalo.¹²⁸

Backed by an array of antidictatorial supporters, Arévalo in July 1947 broke diplomatic relations with Trujillo's Dominican Republic. This single gesture seemed to bring together, as had the transnationalized Revolution, all the democratic inspirations and antifascist ideals unleashed in the mid-1940s. Predictably, Dominican exiles were among the first to celebrate. ARDE cheered Arévalo's decision and expressed its members' "hopes [for the] restoration [of] democracy [in all] oppressed countries."¹²⁹ Cotu wrote Arévalo personally while Juan Isidro Jiménes Grullón sent a book as a token of gratitude.¹³⁰ Rather than a gift, Bosch sent an "emotional hug."¹³¹ The Frente Unido de Liberación Dominicana (United Front for Dominican Liberation) in New York, the Frente Democrático Dominicano (Dominican Democratic Front) in Caracas, and exiles in Puerto Rico embraced Arévalo's measure.¹³²

It was not just Dominican exiles who applauded the Guatemalan president; this reprimand of Trujillo's regime resonated for all continuing their own struggles against dictatorships. Augusto Charnaud MacDonald and

José Manuel Fortuny with Partido Acción Revolucionaria's (Revolutionary Action Party, PAR) Executive National Committee lifted up Arévalo's action as "putting in practice a new legal conception of international relations" that challenged "electoral farces" and "armed coups."[133] In Chimaltenango, PAR members described their pride in Arévalo as an "authentic and exemplary democrat," and members in Antigua agreed.[134] Partido Renovación Nacional's (National Renovation Party, PRN) Executive Committee too cheered the action.[135] Another Guatemalan described his pleasure in the "revolution."[136]

Guatemalans were not alone in sharing their pride in ending their government's relations with Trujillo's regime, for Arévalo's action became a transnational democratic symbol. Cuba's Movimiento Socialista Revolucionario (Revolutionary Socialist Movement, MSR) compared Arévalo to the Cuban revolutionary Antonio Guiteras.[137] Including the FEU, Cuban student organizations joined Dominican exiles to cheer Arévalo's action.[138] Ordóñez Argüello and Castillo Ibarra described Arévalo's action as part of a "continental attitude" in service of the "salvation [of] America," and the Comité Patriótico Nicaragüense (Nicaraguan Patriotic Committee) argued that Arévalo's action uplifted those in the Dominican Republic, Nicaragua, and Spain who lived under regimes that refused to enact the Four Freedoms or the UN's idea of human rights.[139] On behalf of "young Honduran revolutionaries," Morazán described Arévalo's opposition to Trujillo's "continuist pretentions" as "confirming once again [the] indisputably democratic nature" of the Revolution, and multiple members of the FDRH offered their solidarity.[140] Holding a similar respect for the Guatemalan president, Lombardo Toledano sent a CTAL representative to present plans for a convention to discuss the "remnants of fascism and the activities of falangism and sinarquismo and their links with the dictatorships" of the region as well as "the fight for democracy."[141]

Preparing for War

A decade after the Guatemalan Revolution's auspicious beginning, Horacio Ornes remained one of Arévalo's friends and admirers. The democratic energies and antifascist ideals of the era inspired his turning against Trujillo's regime, and Ornes joined the public celebrations on behalf of the Revolution and Arévalo's suspension of diplomatic relations. Half a dozen years later, the exile wrote Arévalo in 1954: "You had the best comprehension of the problems facing not just Guatemalans but all America."¹⁴² Ornes was just one of many in the greater Caribbean who saw in Arévalo and the transnationalized Revolution the hopes promised by the Second World War.

In Guatemala, Ornes joined others who sought to topple their respective dictators and spread democracy across the region. As Heliodoro Valle summarized, "If Somoza leaves, the neighbor will have to pack up his bags."¹⁴³ Gómez Robelo argued that, "in Central America, organic peace will not come while there exist people subdued to brutal dictatorships like those in Honduras and Nicaragua."¹⁴⁴ Any dictator would bolster a fellow authoritarian regime; therefore, the contrapositive for Gómez Robelo was that removing Somoza from Nicaragua would resonate outward and undermine Carías in Honduras.¹⁴⁵ Each dictatorship was a barrier to any legitimate and sustainable solution to every country's underlying problems. Gómez Robelo articulated, "The salvation of Honduras is in the hands of Hondurans, more today than ever, and perhaps, or perhaps not, in this salvation of our country is the salvation of Central America."¹⁴⁶

Out of Mexico City, CRN applauded Arévalo and hoped he would offer "the same treatment to the tyrant Somoza." The letter's adherents were a cross stitch of antidictatorial activists, from unionist Meza to anti-Somoza leaders Cuadra Pasos and Chester Lacayo to a young exile named Ernesto Cardenal.¹⁴⁷ Sáenz and the UDC succinctly put such aspirations into words when praying that "it will not be possible to halt the democratization impulses in Central America" and that the promises of the transnationalized Revolution ripple into Nicaragua and Honduras.¹⁴⁸ Unfortunately, those opposed to such ideals also understood this, for Caribbean Basin dictators refused to stand by and tolerate any popular threat to their respective regimes.

Chapter 3

Counterrevolutionary Signatories

Guatemalan Reactionaries and Caribbean Basin Dictators, 1944–1947

Although he never divulged much to his family, Carlos Padilla y Padilla was one of the more notable Guatemalan reactionaries trying to overthrow Arévalo's government. In March 1945, the physician played a central role in a failed coup. The plot was straightforward; Padilla, Colonel Arturo Ramírez, and their allies tried bribing members of the Guatemalan Army, offering as much as two thousand dollars a month to the governing triumvirate's Colonel Francisco Arana, to prevent Arévalo from taking office.[1] Into April, Guatemalan officials suspended constitutional rights while rounding up and exiling suspected participants. Abroad, reactionaries resumed their conspiratorial activities. Thanks to the censorship system designed to monitor Nazi sympathizers in Latin America, US officials intercepted cryptic letters and phone calls among Padilla, Ramírez, General Roderico Anzueto, and others.[2] Censors struggled to grasp the finer points of these conversations since Padilla and his collaborators purposefully used "double talk and Guatemalan slang" to mask their plans, but it was clear the discussants were organizing some kind of movement.[3] By mid-1945, US officials asserted that "plans were definitely afoot for a political coup in Guatemala."[4] The FBI concurred, believing Padilla was searching for money once again to bribe officers in the Guatemalan Army.[5]

Scattered information on Padilla's activities trickled in, thanks to the FBI's contacts and US officials' conversations with their Central American counterparts. Desperate for funds, Padilla sought dictators' patronage. Barely two months after his first plot, he headed to Nicaragua. In Managua, he met with members of Somoza's Guardia Nacional, the editor of Somoza's newspaper *Novedades*, and the dictator.[6] Next, Padilla flew to Honduras, meeting in Tegucigalpa with Carías's minister of foreign affairs, the editor of Carías's newspaper *La Época*, and the dictator.[7] To gather intelligence, US officials accepted visits from reactionaries desperate to gain favor and undermine others' reputations.[8] As would repeatedly happen over the next years, another reactionary divulged Padilla's activities to US officials: the doctor was assuring everyone "that he had been promised aid in the form of money and arms" from Somoza and Carías in order to launch an invasion with air support coming from five of Carías's planes.[9]

Now, US officials had to investigate the two dictators' involvement. In Nicaragua, US Ambassador Fletcher Warren approached Somoza. Asked about Padilla's activities, the dictator admitted "that he had seen [Padilla] for a few minutes" but "did not comment further." This surprised Warren, for it was "the first time" Somoza had "shown any apparent reluctance in discussing any matter."[10] Carías and his foreign minister denied promising any support to Padilla.[11] In their final determination, these US officials doubted the dictators' involvement. For his part, Warren believed Somoza would not use his resources to intervene in regional matters.[12] The US ambassador in Tegucigalpa, John Erwin, issued a similar statement about Carías's possible role, assuring his superiors in Washington, DC, "it is scarcely conceivable that such aid would be forthcoming from Carías, whose policy during the twelve years he has held office has been to refrain from interfering in the internal affairs of his neighbors and to refuse to tolerate their interference in Honduran affairs."[13] The FBI agreed that Somoza and Carías would not want to intervene in regional affairs.[14] Still, there was one unnamed US official who, reading Erwin's claim that Carías's involvement would be "too fantastic for credence," sarcastically commented, "O yeah?"[15]

In July 1946, Padilla backed a handful of Guatemalan military officers conspiring to kill Arévalo and others.[16] That December, the reactionary endorsed another abortive plot.[17] The following March, Arévalo's foreign minister reached out to US officials to share information provided by Salvadoran officials "to the effect that Guatemalan exiles under the leadership of Padilla in Honduras intended to fly over Guatemala City . . . and drop bombs."[18] Additionally, Padilla's colleague Luis Coronado Lira had a plane in Honduras prepped for this plot. The Guatemalan military went on high alert, since the conspiracy coincided with local antigovernment protests and shared the same details reported over the past years. Once again, US officials remained skeptical of the dictators' alleged involvement and the actual plots, with one US official casting aside a recent conspiracy as nothing more than "improbable."[19] They, however, failed to grasp the local stakes. As Padilla later told his son, Somoza had suggested using explosive and incendiary devices to air-bomb Guatemala City and induce a military coup against Arévalo's government. Although he assured his family that he quit the scheme in opposition to the plan's destruction and civilian casualties, the truth is that domestic events and other plots derailed the affair.[20] Unknown to and even hidden from US officials, Central American dictators were funding Guatemalan reactionaries' conspiracies to destabilize Guatemala's government.

For some, the Guatemalan Revolution brought together the Second World War's antifascist ideals and the greater Caribbean's democratic aspirations. For others, regional disturbances were proof of a grand communist plot. During the Revolution's first days, reactionaries and dictators blamed Guatemala's rapid changes on foreign actors and communist machinations. UFCO representatives alleged that a new labor code targeted the multinational corporation in order to destroy symbols of capitalism. Opposing any criticism of their country's global dominion, British observers feared a network of communist-inspired states would manipulate the UN and weaken their empire. All summoned anticommunism in order to justify their positions, but reactionaries and dictators were the first to come together and describe themselves as part of a global crusade. Seeing around them a communist conspiracy, they unleashed myriad plots that sparked constitutional suspensions and radicalized domestic politics in Guatemala.

Reactionaries and Dictators Against the Guatemalan Revolution

In the Revolution's first days, opponents fled the country or faced exile due to their allegiance to or activities under Ubico's regime. Many were prominent military or political officials such as Anzueto, who directed Ubico's secret police. Ramírez had occupied multiple positions, fleeing after his involvement in a protester's death and Padilla's March 1945 plot. Usually escaping the public eye, Juan Pinillos appeared throughout Central America as a member of Ubico's Secret Service and Foreign Service. Some reactionaries came from the upper class, disputing the Revolution's reforms and searching for political opportunities or influence. Coronado Lira and Carlos Salazar Jr. were lawyers for wealthy coffee elites, and Salazar was the son of Ubico's minister of foreign relations and worked for the IRCA.[21] Arévalo's government initially employed Juan Córdova Cerna, a UFCO lawyer, as the nation's ambassador to Mexico, but he soon renounced the position.[22]

In the mid-1940s, Mexico became a base for reactionaries. Some sought means of help or work to provide for themselves.[23] Others were conspiratorial actors, smuggling armaments or engaging in seditious activities. Following the nonintervention principle, the Mexican government tasked agents from its DGIPS and Dirección Federal de Seguridad (Federal Security Directorate, DFS, formed in 1947) to monitor reactionaries' activities, usually with little success.[24] Due to medical issues, familial relations, or plans to return to their country of origin, many resided on the Guatemala-Mexico border, with Tapachula and Huixtla in Chiapas as busy hubs of activity.[25] Further complicating everything were reactionaries' conflicts with one another. In early 1946, Mexican agents confirmed that Manuel Melgar was working with the Comité de Unidad de la Emigración Guatemalteca (Committee for Unification of Guatemalan Immigrants, CUEG). When interviewed, he not only denied being in the CUEG but insisted the claims came from "enemies" among fellow reactionaries.[26] When DGIPS agents interviewed Ponce and Marco Antonio Archila Obregón, the two alleged that the Guatemalan Embassy paid another reactionary to publish "libel[ous]" articles and assassinate Ponce.[27]

Guatemalan and Mexican officials' best efforts to monitor reactionaries' activities resulted only in warnings. In Tegucigalpa, Guatemalan officials identified Padilla, Pinillos, and others networking, but nothing was proven.[28] In October 1945, *Mediodía* put out a pamphlet, *Radiografía del Complot* (*X-Ray of the Plot*), summarizing the first years' conspiracies, but it lacked concrete details.[29] Furthermore, some had at their disposal money from their grafts or the confiscation of properties under Ubico's regime.[30] Officials suspected Adán Manrique Ríos was smuggling weapons but had no financial evidence.[31] In January 1947, the Guatemalan Embassy shared intercepted correspondence between reactionary Ovidio Pivaral and an arms merchant, "Tobías José," involving a deal for ten thousand units of an unspecified item and a C-38. The only reason this correspondence came to light, though, was that a gunrunner approached Arévalo's government.[32]

Right away, DGIPS agents interviewed Pivaral and employees at the local hotel in Tapachula where reactionaries convened but obtained no actionable intelligence.[33]

What was apparent was that reactionaries charged Arévalo and the Revolution as beholden to foreign, totalitarian ideologies. Throughout the Caribbean Basin, elites conflated challenges to the status quo with subversive ideologies and presented themselves as legitimate defenders against alien threats to the region's traditions, Catholic religion, and social order. In this worldview, communism dominated labor activism, reformist nationalism, and anti-imperialism whether in the 1910 Mexican Revolution or Sandino's movement. Conservatives alleged that Mexican officials, aligned with Lombardo Toledano and former president Lázaro Cárdenas, leveraged the popularity of their nation's economic reforms and socialist ideals to spread communism. Though this lacked evidence, the imagined specter of a Mexican-Soviet communist alliance bolstered regional opposition to leftist movements.[34] Whatever connections did manifest between the Communist International and Latin America were rife with ideological disagreements.[35] Nevertheless, regimes suppressed not just communist organizations but also most leftist challenges based on this anticommunist trepidation.[36]

As the Guatemalan Revolution took hold, reactionaries immediately blamed Mexico, the Soviet Union, and fascism. In 1945's *La Confabulación Nazifascista y Comunistoide Revolucionaria en América* (*The Revolutionary Nazi-Fascist and Communist Confabulation in America*), a self-proclaimed "liberal exile" argued that a fascist-communist alliance of Argentina's Perón and the Soviet Union sparked the Revolution.[37] In his writings to Mexican, British, and US officials, including Truman, Ponce warned that Arévalo and "Nazi-fascist claws [were] taking advantage" of the Second World War's turmoil.[38] In Mexico, reactionaries published a newsletter, *Boletín: Emigración Democrática de Guatemala* (*Bulletin: Democratic Emigration from Guatemala*), whose September 1945 issue repeated Archila Obregón's claims that Arévalo fell under a "Nazi-communist" ideology while in Argentina.[39] Though contradictory, this trope reassured reactionaries that recent events, in Guatemala or elsewhere, tied back to an international conspiracy to destroy their nations rather than local discontent with the prevailing social order or economic conditions. This belief shaped *Xequijel*, the bulletin of the Juventud Liberal de Guatemala (Liberal Youth of Guatemala, JLG). Supposedly, the Revolution's author was Konstantin Umansky, the Soviet official serving in Mexico and Central America during World War II before his 1945 death.[40]

Therefore, opposition to the Revolution was a noble effort that would, as Padilla wrote to Anzueto, help their nation "shake off the Nazi-communist and anti-American yoke."[41]

As the antifascist component of their exaggerations dissipated, reactionaries relied on their anticommunist claims. Railing against what he insisted was a communist attempt to destroy Guatemalan nationalism and Catholicism, Coronado Lira alleged that Arévalo was creating "a totalitarian state equal to that of Russia."[42] Despite personal disputes, reactionaries spread one another's writings, as when the Comité de Defensa Patria (Committee of National Defense, CDP) included Coronado Lira's publications in *La Tribuna de la libertad: Voz de los Guatemaltecos en el destierro* (*The Gallery of Freedom: Voice of the Guatemalans in Exile*), where he begged his brethren to "not allow the washing away of the colors [of the sky blue and white Guatemalan flag] to become red or the symbolic Quetzal of our freedoms to change into the sickle and hammer of communist totalitarianism."[43] His words appeared next to those of Archila Obregón because both alleged that Lombardo Toledano planted "the exotic seed of communism" in the "soil of America" and transformed their nation into an "instrument of Russia."[44] This was how reactionaries understood the Revolution's economic and social transformations. One reactionary warned that "strong cells" of "international communism" took over radio stations and railroad properties to direct all labor agitation.[45] Pinillos wrote US officials that the "Mexican Embassy in Guatemala [had] organized all the movements" behind the Revolution, and Arévalo was "determined to move forward with this plan [from] Lombardo Toledano" and "establish a small dependency of the Soviet Union."[46]

Casting the Revolution as a joint Mexican-Soviet conspiracy cemented reactionaries' shared identity. After their expulsions, they created organizations in Mexico, Nicaragua, El Salvador, and Honduras charging Arévalo's government as a communist regime implanted under foreign design. The Frente Nacional Democrático de Guatemala (National Democratic Front of Guatemala, FNDG) and the Unión Democrática Nacional de Guatemala (National Democratic Union of Guatemala) protested before the Guatemalan Embassy in Mexico City on behalf of Guatemalans exiled under suspicion of participating in the March 1945 plot.[47] Ramírez was in the Unión Popular Revolucionaria Guatemalteca (Guatemalan Revolutionary Popular Front).[48] Padilla and Coronado Lira's CDP purportedly represented "the voice of thousands of Guatemalans in exile" and spread radio transmissions and articles in Nicaragua, Honduras, and El Salvador.[49]

In *Guatemala bajo el signo rojo* (*Guatemala Under the Red Flag*), the Comité Patriótico Guatemalteco (Guatemalan Patriotic Committee, CPG) and José Calderón Salazar contrasted the "chaos of a Revolution promoted by the Soviet Union" against Guatemala's "national and Christian tradition."[50] One of the broader organizations was the Comité de Ayuda a los Exiliados Guatemaltecos (Committee for Assistance for Guatemalan Exiles, CAEG). Petitioning the UN, the group claimed to represent 103 Guatemalans in Mexico, 82 in El Salvador, 20 in the United States, 12 in Costa Rica, 11 in Honduras, and 9 in Nicaragua, including Ponce, Anzueto, Ramírez, Padilla, and Coronado Lira. All these Guatemalans were supposedly guilty of nothing more than disagreeing with Arévalo's government, a "sovietizante regime" that forbid "freedom," "the free operation of political parties," and "the freedom of free ideas."[51]

The Revolution's open support for antidictatorial, antifascist ideals threatened the region's dictators and their definition of the nonintervention principle. Before Ubico's fall, dictators welcomed exiles into one another's countries, only to suppress political activities and allow their allies' agents of surveillance and repression to operate in one another's countries.[52] The Revolution tore apart this unwritten agreement as Somoza's and Carías's newspapers lambasted exiles' "odious campaign[s] of defamation."[53] Throughout the mid-1940s, the two dictators complained that Arévalo's government allowed "Central American exiles [to] have a free hand" and "shamelessly encourage[d]" antidictatorial activities, including border incursions and armed movements.[54] They too viewed these developments as part of an international communist conspiracy, which legitimated their regimes as anticommunist. Somoza insisted that Arévalo was a communist puppet "acting at the instigation of Mexico and, ultimately, the Soviet Union."[55] Carías's officials agreed that Arévalo's "communistic" government "was taking orders from outside the country," that is, "from Soviet Russia."[56]

To the dismay of reactionaries and dictators, US officials in the postwar years treated these exaggerated anticommunist claims as meritless. In mid-1946, the US Embassy in Guatemala City opened its report "Communism in Guatemala" by saying, "There is no evidence to prove that there exists in Guatemala at the present time a Communist party or other type of Communist organization." Though reformers sympathized with or even picked up communist ideas, "Communist charges are the most popular of all charges used by the opposition against the Government, and they are used with great frequency."[57] Investigations proved that Arévalo was not some Nazi-fascist-communist but "desired a moderately liberal and constitutional stable form of government" with "no close relations with extremists [or] sympathy for either Communists or Fascists."[58] When meeting with the Revolution's opponents, US officials refuted any solicitation to endorse anticommunist intrigues, with one warning to a reactionary—"I cannot mix up in your internal political affairs," which "would be against my country's wishes and certainly against my own desires"—becoming something of a mantra.[59] Indeed, the repetitive claims inadvertently nudged US officials to oftentimes ignore reports on reactionaries and dictators' relationships.[60]

Proclaiming Their Part in the Global Anticommunist Crusade

Although desirous of the US government's resources and support, reactionaries and dictators needed no approval to launch their machinations. Their anticommunist lexicon allowed them to find common cause against Arévalo's government and the Revolution. They did not depict their shared opposition as simple efforts to take back their previous standings in their home country or remove bastions of antidictatorial exiles. Rather, they looked at their local and regional conflicts through a Cold War lens and saw themselves as soldiers in a hemispheric struggle against communism. Although anticommunism had often served as an ideological shield, what changed in the mid-1940s was how the Revolution's opponents used the Cold War to attach additional urgency to their local and regional conflicts. Claiming that the Soviet Union aimed to strip the United States of its allies in Latin America, they depicted themselves as the Caribbean Basin's best defense in this global anticommunist crusade.

They reinforced their diatribes by alleging that their countries were the first target in a hemispheric communist conspiracy. According to Ponce, Arévalo sought to disrupt the "security of the United States and Central America" in order to "attack the powerful" symbol of capitalism, the United States.[61] The JLG attributed regional disturbances to the Soviet Union's plans to seize territory from the Panama Canal through Belize to Alaska.[62] In one memorandum, Padilla outlined how "Mexican expansionism" implanted in Arévalo's government "a totalitarian tyranny with communist tendencies" to "sow confusion" across the Americas "in the event of a future war between the United States and Russia."[63] "With the necessary resources that had been provided by the Soviet government through Lombardo Toledano," according to Pinillos, Arévalo converted Guatemala into communism's forward base.⁶⁴ Reactionaries even compared their situation to anticommunist refugees from Eastern Europe. If the UN and other international organizations were to stand against the Soviet Union, they needed to pay attention to Central Americans struggling against a regime similar to those in Poland and Romania.⁶⁵ Dictators agreed; Arévalo's government was a "communist" regime "planning aggression against the other Central American governments" and "a danger to the peace of the isthmus."⁶⁶

Positioning themselves as defenders of hemispheric security in the emerging Cold War, Somoza and Carías patronized reactionaries during the mid-1940s. Pinillos, Padilla, Anzueto, Coronado Lira, and Ramírez all received the dictators' largesse. Pinillos met regularly with Honduran officials, who arranged some of the reactionary's travels and meetings in Tegucigalpa.⁶⁷ Pinillos emerged as a key node between reactionaries and dictators.⁶⁸ Unknown to the US government, Carías funded an early plot led by Padilla and Anzueto.⁶⁹ What US officials did notice was how often Padilla boasted of his relationships with Nicaraguan and Honduran officials. When approached about such claims, Honduran officials blamed one another while promising to clear up the matter.⁷⁰ By 1947, Somoza was directing the reactionary's flights while organizing plots and acquiring armaments.⁷¹ Like Padilla, Coronado Lira bragged about the dictators' financial support to potential allies, making him a mainstay among typically rivalrous reactionaries.⁷²

This loose network spearheaded numerous projects against Arévalo's government. Guatemalan newspapers and Arévalo's government lacked substantial evidence on these contacts, but US, British, Dominican, and Guatemalan reports combined offer insights into some links. Some Guatemalan officials interpreted rumors that Somoza and Carías were using their own economic enterprises to transport armaments as "gossip."⁷³ In contrast, Dominican officials in October 1945 concluded that "Carías and Somoza contributed money sent through their legations in Guatemala for [a recent] plot to overthrow doctor Arévalo."⁷⁴ Salvadoran officials often notified their Guatemalan colleagues about weapon shipments and reactionaries' movements on their border.⁷⁵ In Mexico City, Guatemalan officials tried to verify these relationships but only concluded that Somoza and Carías trusted some reactionaries more than others.⁷⁶ In July 1947, US officials notified Guatemalan officials of a plot under Ramírez financed by Somoza.⁷⁷

Discouraging the few plots that came to its attention, the US government failed to grasp these conflicts' extent. Throughout the Caribbean Basin, all swore that their governments adhered to the nonintervention principle.⁷⁸

At best, some US officials speculated that rumors of collaboration did not relate to the dictators but to lower-level officials.[79] Thus, they did not comprehend the depth of the region's ideological animosities. For Arévalo and the exiles, their efforts to rid their region of dictators were the fulfillment of Latin American democratic aspirations and World War II's antifascist promise. Dictators also justified their opposition by blending hemispheric and international goals, depicting themselves as defending the nonintervention principle through their patronage of reactionaries and striking against a government whose very toleration of antidictatorial activism threatened their regimes. Overthrowing Arévalo's government and installing a regime less willing to undermine neighboring dictators would restore the prewar status quo and their interpretation of nonintervention. Furthermore, reactionaries and dictators blended the Cold War and their local grievances to reaffirm their anticommunist ideology.

Bringing in the Dominican Dictator

Whereas the limited source material offers a general overview of how reactionaries petitioned and networked with Central American dictators, Dominican files provide a revelatory case study. In 1947, Dominican officials used anticommunism to explain away Arévalo's decision to suspend diplomatic relations with Trujillo's regime. In order to lobby the Dominican dictator, Ramírez, Pinillos, and General Miguel Ydígoras Fuentes seized upon this regional conflict to depict anti-Trujillo activism as communist. Utilizing the same ideas and tropes in their public writings and communications with US officials, reactionaries' letters to and conversations with Dominican officials championed Trujillo as a fellow anticommunist soldier defending the greater Caribbean from Mexican and Soviet influence.

When Arévalo suspended diplomatic relations, Dominican officials blamed a grandiose communist plot disrupting regional peace and hemispheric security. Privately, they asserted that the entire affair was "designed to try to prove that we represent an inconvenience for the harmony and unity that define the fraternal coexistence of the peoples and governments of this Continent."[80] Their public remarks followed this script, asserting that the suspension was not "surpris[ing]" in light of Arévalo's "demagogic tendencies and of his efforts to guide the policies of his Government by the communistic ideology which he personally professes." By highlighting a communist conspiracy "interrupting the rhythim [sic] of collective harmony and in breaking the unity which consolidates the peoples and the Governments of the Americas, united in their democratic ideals," Trujillo's officials repudiated Arévalo and exiles' antidictatorial activism and characterized their regime as an anticommunist bulwark.[81] Arévalo was the "Central American Delegate to implant communism" throughout the Western Hemisphere.[82]

Guatemalan reactionaries also seized upon Arévalo's decision as evidence that communism dominated their former country. In Mexico City, a reactionary organization offered articles to the local press defending Trujillo's regime against Arévalo's "communist and pernicious ruling."[83] One of the CPG's pamphlets reproduced an article from a Catholic, anticommunist journalist in the Mexican newspaper *El Universal* that charged Arévalo with threatening "continental unity" and following the "irritated attitude assumed by Russia" on the eve of the Río de Janeiro Conference.[84] Their defenses of Trujillo hit their mark, for the CPG's Calderón Salazar caught Dominican officials' attention when he denounced the suspension.[85] As in their defenses of Somoza's and Carías's regimes, reactionaries imprinted on this regional conflict over democracy and dictatorship a Cold War struggle in which the Soviet Union conspired with local communists to destroy hemispheric security.

And, as with Central American dictators, reactionaries sought an advantageous alliance with Trujillo thanks to their shared anticommunist worldview that championed their mutual opposition to Arévalo's government as a virtuous stance against international communism. The first reactionary to secure Dominican officials' hospitality appears to have been Ramírez. Already inundating US officials with writings charging Arévalo as a servant of Mexican and Soviet communism, Ramírez recognized the suspension of diplomatic relations as the perfect opportunity to lobby for an anticommunist patron. As he told US officials, Arévalo's action against Trujillo had "been only for the goal of disrupting continental harmony."[86] On July 8, 1947, Ramírez repeated these claims in his first letter to the Dominican dictator. He hit hard on the common refrain that minimized the region's antidictatorial efforts into a communist plot: "The communist outbreak in Central America was born from the continued efforts of Vicente Lombardo Toledano and the Soviets to the South of Mexico . . . to insert spearheads into the Continent." He implored Trujillo, "I write to you, respectfully, in order to inform you that there is a means of exercising the first step toward the establishment of a sanitary measure that will clean the American Continent of this Siberian leprosy." Here, Ramírez combined his and Trujillo's opposition to Arévalo's government by invoking their shared roles in defending the Americas from international communism. He beseeched the dictator to support an emerging plot against Arévalo's government and fight the Cold War, pleading, "The entire world is expecting this sanitary measure . . . to constitute a real dam against the advance of communism in the economic sense." He lauded Trujillo, saying, "Global Democracy will have in you a paladin."[87]

This shared anticommunist identity against their mutual enemy resonated with Trujillo, for the dictator ordered his officials to receive Ramírez.[88] Accompanied by Pinillos, Ramírez met with Dominican officials in Tegucigalpa and shared his latest memorandum, "Exposición sobre los asuntos relacionados con Guatemala" (Exhibition regarding the affairs related to Guatemala). The text contained the common allegation that Arévalo's Guatemala was the "most disciplined and abject disciple of Soviet Russia in Central America."[89] What stood out, though, was Ramírez's explanation of his plan to overthrow Arévalo's government. Reactionaries in Nicaragua, likely with Somoza's support, would pass through Honduras, with Carías's blessing, to invade Guatemala.[90] Ramírez promised assistance from the dictators but did not intend for the invasion to topple Arévalo's government. Rather, the resulting chaos would induce various governments' mediations. At this juncture, Central American, Dominican, and US officials would request that Arévalo's government provide amnesty and political representation to Ramírez and others, who would then oust Arévalo.[91]

Although other events halted Ramírez's plot, Dominican officials now had a working relationship with reactionaries. For example, Pinillos remained a reliable source of intelligence, frequenting Trujillo's legations and embassies in Central America almost as often as he did those for Somoza and Carías. In late August 1947, Dominican officials relayed to their superiors information Pinillos provided on reactionaries' armaments and supplies.[92] The next month, he reported on changes in Guatemala's military.[93] Throughout, all parties utilized their anticommunist ideology to interpret regional events. When discussing anti-Trujillo plots, Pinillos said, "The Russian Embassy in Mexico has had jurisdiction in Guatemala and has been sending delegates (unofficially) to remain in clandestine communication with Arévalo." All "money" for anti-Trujillo ventures was "provided from Russia to Guatemala through unofficial Agents and Vicente Lombardo Toledano."[94] Anticommunism was not a superficial camouflage; Dominican officials repeated and reiterated these claims all the way up Trujillo's personalist bureaucracy.[95]

These meetings gave Trujillo the opportunity to fund schemes against Arévalo's government, one of the earliest coming from Ydígoras Fuentes. In contrast to his contemporaries, Ydígoras Fuentes was the Guatemalan ambassador in London, likely to keep him from fomenting conspiracies at home.[96] This was for naught, as he networked with Trujillo's officials in Europe. One of the prominent generals whose name was floated as a potential successor to Ubico, Ydígoras Fuentes disagreed with the Revolution's reforms. However, he did not immediately reach out to Trujillo for material support to oust Arévalo. As did others, he contacted Dominican officials following Arévalo's suspension of diplomatic relations. In a conversation with the Dominican ambassador in London, Ydígoras Fuentes guaranteed that his strong reputation in the Guatemalan Army would convince leading military officers to back an uprising against Arévalo's government, but he required "an assistance of fifty thousand dollars."[97] As with Ramírez's plot, local events deterred these plans, but the relationship endured.

Dominican officials made use of Ydígoras Fuentes due to their shared worldviews. He provided officials with various writings decrying Arévalo's government and charging "the Mexican Embassy" and "Soviet money" with sparking the Revolution.[98] He forwarded letters from conservative Guatemalans who attributed local and regional disturbances to a consortium of Mexican and Soviet communists.[99] Most representative of their collaborative relationship was how Dominican officials in Ciudad Trujillo ordered their staff in Mexico City to try to republish Ydígoras Fuentes's documents in the national press.[100] By reducing the Revolution and anti-Trujillo activism into a communist conspiracy, Dominican officials gained an influential reactionary, and Ydígoras Fuentes received a patron who provided him with at least thirty-five thousand dollars over the next years.[101]

Eroding the Constitution and Weakening Public Support

Thanks to dictators' assistance, reactionaries organized multiple plots against Arévalo's government. Most were halted or fell apart due to infighting, lack of funding, or Guatemalan officials acquiring just enough intelligence to intervene, sometimes with the help of regional allies. Though the majority were stillborn, these projects' potential and failed launches rippled throughout Guatemalan politics. Upon hearing of these schemes, Arévalo's government suspended the constitution while rounding up possible suspects but provided the public little conclusive evidence due to the reactionaries' and dictators' efforts in masking their activities. Consequently, civilians felt overwhelmed by a deluge of constitutional suspensions and mass arrests. This directly contributed to a growing sense of fear, repeated in Guatemalan newspapers and international observers' reports, that Arévalo's government was building a totalitarian regime and repressing opponents. Thus, reactionaries and dictators fueled the radicalization of Guatemalan society during the Revolution's formative years.

This pattern originated with Padilla and his allies' March 1945 conspiracy. Through April, Guatemalan officials suspended constitutional guarantees while arresting multiple individuals.[102] To explain the contradiction in a government boasting respect for democratic rights yet appearing to ignore them, officials shared what little information they knew. They broadcast over the radio, trying to reach a population with a high illiteracy rate, to describe this scheme.[103] Some Guatemalans, though, doubted the claim's veracity while criticizing the government's reaction. An outlet for followers of Guatemalan liberalism and Ubico's regime, *El Demócrata* splashed its front page with the title, "Various honorable people were detained today." The newspaper emphasized how its director, *El Mercurio*'s director, and others were arrested.[104] Strengthening this reaction was how many detainees were leaders of political parties or had been presidential candidates during the 1944 election that Arévalo won: Manuel María Herrera of the Partido Nacional de Trabajadores, José Gregorio Díaz of the Partido Acción Nacional, Teodoro Díaz Medrano of the Partido Constitucional Democrático. Although the government arrested Padilla, Ramírez, and others whom US censors linked to the plot, Guatemalan officials could not proffer much evidence. Meanwhile, antigovernment critics opposed the arrests as violations of the country's constitution.[105]

In effect, the prevalence of antigovernment plots and government arrests fed political doubts about the stability and democratic legitimacy of Arévalo's government. In Guatemala, there were a handful of protests against the constitutional suspension.[106] From Mexico, the FNDG argued in statements to *La Prensa* and *Novedades* that officials were attempting a "purge" of legitimate opposition.[107] This forced the Guatemalan Embassy in Mexico City to defend its government's actions in another newspaper, *El Nacional*, but this defense provided no new information.[108] After all,

Guatemalan officials and perhaps even the FNDG itself did not recognize how many of the very reactionaries held up as victims were traveling the greater Caribbean in search of material and financial support for their antigovernment projects.

What information was disseminated to the public lacked details. When the government rounded up suspects linked to Padilla in September 1945, Guatemalan newspapers reported on the arrests.[109] *El Imparcial*'s October 8 issue opened with a massive headline—"El complot a luz" (Details of the plot)—and highlighted the number of suspected participants who came from prominent positions in Ubico's regime.[110] However, the article had little insight into the plot, for the government knew only that conspirators were bribing military officers and did not have solid evidence about Padilla's role in the affair or his networking with dictators. Arévalo's government gave to the nation's newspapers and radio stations what was already becoming the typical, broad explanation as authorities arrested almost one hundred suspects.[111]

The most damning aspect of these intrigues was how Arévalo's government could not prove links between reactionaries and their foreign patrons. With multiple conspiracies happening simultaneously, details and evidence blended together or completely diverged. Another issue was the danger that publicizing what little knowledge Guatemalan officials did have could jeopardize their few successful agents, as seen during an October 1947 conspiracy. One Guatemalan agent, "Ramón Delgado," infiltrated a group in San Salvador. That October, "Delgado" was with Coronado Lira when a Honduran military plane arrived with Padilla on board. Padilla told Coronado Lira and "Delgado" that their "cargo" would be brought to the Honduran Legation. Soon after, Coronado Lira showed the agent their "cargo": guns "to liquidate Dr. Arévalo, Colonel Arana, and Major Árbenz" because "you have to remove them in order to overthrow the Guatemalan government."[112] Had Guatemalan officials shared this intelligence with others, reactionaries may have identified the source. In addition, another plot unrelated to Carías and Coronado Lira almost transpired, derailing officials' attention. Just days later, Coronado Lira and his allies were assuring US officials of their noninvolvement.[113]

This October 1947 conspiracy was also an example of how reactionaries profited from the chaos they denied generating. First, they defended any extralegal efforts against Arévalo's government as necessary due to what they alleged was the very need to eliminate an unconstitutional regime, an outgrowth of their anticommunist worldview. In their conversation with

US officials, Coronado Lira and his colleagues complained that Arévalo had "repeatedly violated the Constitution, by such acts as the repeated suspension of constitutional guarantees, and has thus constitutionally disqualified himself for the Presidency, which makes attempts to oust him entirely consistent with the spirit of constitutionality and democracy."[114] Second, they sidestepped their own involvement in the projects, provoking constitutional suspensions and debates over Arévalo's government. In effect, reactionaries and their allies propelled a cycle: counterrevolutionaries launched conspiracies that sparked constitutional suspensions; these suspensions fomented domestic and international criticism that the government suppressed legitimate antigovernment opposition; and reactionaries and those expelled from Guatemala took this as evidence to justify their pursuing conspiratorial plots with foreign assistance. This cycle spun into the early 1950s while undermining Guatemalan political stability.

Almost Blowing Up Guatemala City

The 1947 Ponce-Trujillo air-bombing conspiracy encapsulates how a failed plot radicalized Guatemalan politics.[115] Akin to others, Ponce did not attempt to network with Dominican officials right after his expulsion from Guatemala. Rather, his summer 1947 scheme coincided with Arévalo and Trujillo's political dispute. That June, Ponce met with US officials in Mexico City where he repeated his typical tirade charging Arévalo "as a Communist." Of course, he was not trying to acquire official assistance from the US government. Referencing the importance of a united Western Hemisphere during the Cold War, he felt "the United States as the leader of democratic nations should . . . be kept informed of possible developments . . . if something should happen in the near future in Guatemala." For their part, US officials treated Ponce as another reactionary hoping "to interest the United States Government in their cause."[116] A couple of weeks later, Arévalo suspended diplomatic relations with Trujillo's regime. Immediately, Ponce reached out to Dominican officials in Mexico City, his messages warmly received and opening a channel of communication with Trujillo.[117]

Over the next month, Ponce built a project to air-bomb Guatemala City. He hoped that an unexpected torrent of explosives on Guatemala's capital city would shock civilians and military officers to overthrow Arévalo's government. He felt confident enough in his plan to again approach the

US Embassy in Mexico City on August 21. Actually, he had not intended to mention the air-bombing scheme. As did most reactionaries, he simply wished to champion "his ideals of fighting Communism and establishing a gov[ernment] that will cooperate with the" United States and reiterate how "Somoza and Carías had been [the US government's] best friends among the Central American Republics." Still, he wanted to keep the State Department abreast of possible developments as he prepared to launch his "revolution," so he shared a manifesto and a phonograph he would distribute throughout Guatemala after taking power.[118]

The manifesto, though, gave away Ponce's plans. Reading it, US Ambassador Walter Thurston was taken aback at a reference to the "serial bombardment which had just taken place over some points of the capital." He remarked "that it would be a matter of great regret if [Ponce] should bomb Guatemala City killing civilians," but Ponce "replied that he would only bombard certain strategic points." Right after Ponce left, Thurston messaged his superiors in Washington, DC.[119] Receiving a reliable report that a reactionary was planning to air-bomb Guatemala City, the State Department ordered its embassies to notify respective nations' authorities.[120] By August 25, Mexican officials had interviewed Ponce about his scheme, and Ponce had denied the entire affair, attributing all accusations to his "enemies" among other reactionaries. Unable to prove anything definitive, the Mexican authorities ended the investigation with their typical warnings for Ponce to keep out of any political activities.[121]

He ignored their counsel. Two days later, Ponce visited the Dominican Embassy in Mexico City to solicit "economic aid to initiate operations."[122] The next day, Trujillo approved.[123] Dominican officials over the next weeks helped Ponce work with a Mexican gunrunner to acquire armaments, large amounts of explosive material, and at least three airplanes. With this arsenal, Ponce planned to air-bomb Guatemala City while reactionaries invaded from Mexico and Honduras.[124] However, the scheme's cost increased, and Ponce in mid-September asked for additional funds to pay the gunrunner.[125] Trujillo, though, decided that the reactionary needed to increase his own contribution to the affair and refused to provide more money until the invasion took place.[126] With Ponce and Trujillo arguing over the payments, the gunrunner feared being defrauded, so he approached the Guatemalan Embassy and offered to sell the conspiracy's armaments and details if officials covered the outstanding balance.[127]

Between the US government's warning and the gunrunner's proposal, Arévalo's government had a nearly complete picture of the larger framework behind Ponce's conspiracy, but the Guatemalan public received only pieces of information over the course of a rather long process. First, on September 16 Arévalo's government suspended the constitution for thirty days.[128] Initially, Guatemalan officials did not share any details with the public, as they only knew what Ponce told Thurston, which Mexican officials could not confirm. Following the gunrunner's offer that revealed Trujillo's involvement, Arévalo on September 27 spoke on the radio regarding the past years' plethora of conspiracies and the dictator's regime but still did not divulge additional information.[129] Finally, on October 3, the Guardia Civil went on the radio and laid out the entire affair, including Trujillo's involvement and the gunrunner's role.[130] The following day, *El Imparcial* and other newspapers published the resulting report.[131] A few days later, Arévalo's government again suspended most constitutional guarantees, using the same justification as with the previous suspension while alleging an ongoing antigovernment plot that coincided with the Revolution's October 20 anniversary.[132]

Although Guatemalan officials obtained a significant amount of intelligence on the Ponce-Trujillo air-bombing plot, the slow dissemination of details and rumors of other conspiracies sowed confusion. When officials asked the US government to halt Ponce's planes in the United States, there was no clear indication whether the planes were in Florida or Texas, leading US officials to wonder if this was an overreaction to their month-old warnings.[133] In November, Ponce told US officials that other reactionaries purchased planes in Florida for a different scheme, leaving them wondering which group was behind which plot.[134] Some Guatemalans, such as those with the PRN, endorsed the constitutional suspensions as necessary to protect the country.[135] At the beginning of the next year, PAR's executive committee defended how Arévalo's government stood against "the Trujillos, the Somozas, etc., who patronize and finance these machinations."[136] Others opposed the suspensions or did not believe the government's claims. *El Imparcial* and *La Hora* printed crucial information about the Ponce-Trujillo air-bombing plot but questioned the repeated constitutional suspensions, since officials used the same arguments with no new details.[137] US and British officials too wondered if the constitutional suspensions were cover to persecute conservative figures.[138]

Reactionaries and dictators manipulated this confusion to their advantage. Petitioning the UN, reactionaries cited the constitutional suspensions as evidence that Arévalo's government was totalitarian.[139] One organization asked the Río de Janeiro Conference to intervene in Guatemala to protect "liberal and conservative opponents."[140] The CAEG, whose list of exiles included Ponce, compared the constitutional suspensions to the Soviet Union's political persecutions.[141] From the Dominican Republic to Central America, dictators had their officials and newspapers reduce the complexity of Guatemalan affairs and these constitutional suspensions to "communist" intrigues.[142] In the meantime, Ponce never faced any consequences because officials could not produce sufficient evidence to extradite him.[143]

The uncertainty shaped by reactionaries' and dictators' projects hovered over Guatemalan politics for years. In mid-1951, Arévalo claimed that thirty out of thirty-two known plots received some form of foreign assistance, but he never provided sufficient evidence or details of such machinations.[144] During a late October 1948 uprising near Puerto Barrios, Arévalo's government suspended the constitution. This continued off and on and ended up delaying results from the late 1948 local elections and voting for the early 1949 municipal elections. Antigovernment critics seized upon this turmoil, while political parties and Guatemalan newspapers wondered if Arévalo's supporters were derailing the political process.[145] Although Arana's failed 1949 coup was a domestic matter, officials' contradictory reports sometimes blamed foreign intervention, and Trujillo's regime exacerbated local fears by sending out radio broadcasts that claimed to be warnings for Arana. Rumors of international influence in the affair endured, encouraged by Somoza's newspapers, which interviewed Arana's chauffeur.[146] This also emboldened some of the government's supporters who brushed off any and all local opposition as representative of a foreign conspiracy. When an anticommunist figure beat the Guatemalan government's favored candidate during Guatemala City's December 1951 mayoral election, the candidate did not accept the results at first. Instead, he "issued a truculent statement about the result of the elections, in which he followed the usual line of blaming clerical reactionaries and foreign imperialistic companies."[147]

Two More Voices of Concern: The United Fruit Company and the British Goverment

For their part, UFCO and British officials also tapped into anticommunist ideologies to justify their respective institutions' anxieties about the Revolution. The postwar years' militant aspirations unleashed a barrage of criticism against the powerful institution and British colonialism. As had reactionaries and dictators, the transnational corporation's and the European power's representatives summoned the Cold War to defend their opposition to the Arévalo government's support for economic reforms and decolonization. Although there is little clear evidence that UFCO or British officials played a great hand in antigovernment plots before the late 1940s, both vilified the Guatemalan Revolution as a communist tool.

Central to the UFCO's corporate worldview was its self-proclaimed mission in spreading material and social progress by expanding capitalism throughout Latin America. UFCO officials boasted of their "creating habitable farmlands out of the [region's] jungles and lagoons," as well as "housing, roads, railroads, ports, communications, power plants, hospitals, schools, and churches ... when local governments could not build them."[148] Victor Cutter incessantly proclaimed that his corporation provided the "forms of industrial and commercial development which must precede the intellectual and cultural development of the great masses of the peoples" in the Western Hemisphere.[149] The UFCO's public image revolved around its facilitating the work of scientists, archaeologists, anthropologists, and others who eradicated tropical diseases, examined historical sites, and spread recent innovations in sanitation and health care.[150] Not only were most of these practices equally beneficial to the company's finances and reputation, but the UFCO also wielded these accomplishments against any criticisms, resulting in a paternalistic logic demanding gratitude from workers and governments. Throughout Latin America, corporate officials stressed that their wages were higher than smaller businesses in the local vicinity, which labor activists conceded.[151] This reinforced the company's contention that it was, according to one chairman, "second to none in its faith in Latin America's future and its commitment to the economic and social development of that area."[152]

The corporation, though, revoked these gifts when deemed necessary. Internal reports documented how supervisors and managers reduced wages at their workers' expense, even forcibly recruiting women and children, to compensate for lost hours.[153] In contrast to their public proclamations, officials privately admitted that, during any "drastic economy program," such as one seen in Almirante, Panama, their "laborers' earnings ... no longer allowed them any except the most limited kind of existence."[154] If labor organizations or government regulations sought to moderate these policies, the company refused to negotiate, even silencing proposals for minimum wages.[155] One second, the company held up labor codes as proof of its beneficial relationships with Latin American nations.[156] The next, officials manipulated those codes to halt international unions' inroads or dispute any strike's legitimacy.[157]

The company defended its practices while blaming communism for any challenge to its influence. Before the Second World War, some company officials like W. Cameron Forbes championed fascism, Mussolini, and Franco for standing against "Russian influence" and the "Red menace" in defense of "the Christian religion."[158] UFCO vice president and general counsel Victor Folsom insisted that agrarian reform proposals were cover for "fostering violent revolution" and the "communist mechanism for collectivization."[159] In Victor Cutter and others' worldview, communists took advantage of "the morbid fancies and the sullen inner feeling of inferiority enjoyed by most Mexicans" to exploit Latin American nationalism.[160] Into the early 1950s, representatives suggested that critics borrowed their "totalitarian and antidemocratic thesis" from communism, Nazism, and fascism.[161]

This ideology collided with the Revolution and Arévalo's government. Labor activism shaped a handful of new codes and proposals, culminating with the 1947 Labor Code. The legislation was a hodgepodge of advances and limitations for workers, recognizing unions but limiting agricultural unions' strength or standardizing eight-hour workdays but exempting agricultural enterprises with less than fifty employees.[162] Nevertheless, the UFCO interpreted the Labor Code's very existence as communist. One internal memorandum alleged Arévalo was "either a Communist or a fellow traveler" who associated with communists, due to his endorsement of labor unions and the Labor Code.[163] IRCA President J. P. Armstrong was convinced that Lombardo Toledano and Mexican-based communists provoked all labor agitation against US-based businesses.[164] Talking with US and British officials, UFCO representative Bill Taillon suspected Guatemalan and Mexican communists were doing the bidding of Soviet superiors.[165]

Officials added import to their conflict by tapping into the Cold War and depicting the corporation as a symbol of capitalism under assault by international communism. As part of the global war, the Soviet Union "selected" the UFCO "as a 'whipping boy,'" a "symbol of such Communist semantics as 'imperialists,' 'reactionaries,' or 'Wall Street capitalist.'"[166] Guatemala, the UFCO believed, was "chosen by the Kremlin as a focal point in the ideological war against the United States and free democracies in the Western Hemisphere." The Soviet Union aimed to weaken the Western Hemisphere by taking over the IRCA's railroads near the Panama

Canal and converting Guatemala into "the beachhead of international communism in the Western Hemisphere." Arévalo's "undying hatred for the United States and its business concerns," "international communists," Guatemala's "communist element . . . passing the Labor Code," and "an association with Communist Russia and its agents" together conspired against the corporation and capitalism.[167] Officials were doing more than simply defending their business interests in Guatemala; they were pushing back against the Soviet Union's master plan "in Latin America . . . to turn the Western World . . . into an anti–United States camp in an effort to isolate and weaken . . . the world struggle for freedom."[168]

Further frustrating UFCO officials was their dread that the US government was failing to defend the company's interests against this assault. For decades, the UFCO expected the State Department to uphold a "sound and consistent policy" defending US citizens and businesses in Latin America.[169] With generally amicable relations between the US and Guatemalan governments in the mid-1940s, the corporation saw itself as a lone seer warning of the communist scheme taking hold.[170] The truth is that the State Department did act on the UFCO's behalf multiple times and discouraged their Guatemalan counterparts from discriminating against US-based businesses.[171] This did not appease the company because any challenge to its interests was an unforgivable slight. During a late-1948 workers' slowdown at a UFCO loading station in Puerto Barrios, Taillon did not understand why Arévalo refused to intervene against the labor unions, even after the US ambassador lectured Guatemalan officials about the disruption's impact on further US investments.[172] When the matter settled, Taillon privately declared victory because the resulting contract included concessions the company was willing to make alongside a better rate for loading bananas.[173] Nevertheless, Taillon and his associates continued blaming communism for all disputes.[174]

This also shaped how British officials interpreted their colonial issues with Guatemala.[175] Into the Second World War, they appreciated how Ubico moderated nationalist claims to Belize and privately assured the British government that he would not pursue any action.[176] His removal, though, unleashed debates over the Belize question, which US officials offered to arbitrate. The British Foreign Office believed that Arévalo's government "unscrupulously" manipulated anticolonialism and mantras such as "Belize is ours" to "divert attention from the Government's shortcomings."[177] Misunderstanding rumors about a plot against Carías's regime, they deployed warships to deter any potential invasions of Belize, the matter allayed by US officials' interjections. Afterward, the War Office suggested deploying troops in case Arévalo's "irresponsible Guatemalan government" stoked a border incursion.[178] Into the late 1940s, the War Office sent ships, monitored pro-Belize organizations, and misinterpreted local conflicts as anticolonial conspiracies.

Behind this concern over Guatemalan nationalism and decolonization was anticommunism. British officials believed international communists sought to exploit anti-imperialist sentiments and weaken Britain's influence and position at the global level, a fear exacerbated by the Cold War. The Foreign Office asserted, under British imperialism, "Everything is being done for the advancement of [colonial] inhabitants [and] self Government" thanks to positive, tangible benefits for their subjects. Meanwhile, the Soviet Union conspired to exploit lower-class frustrations and historical grievances by turning the colonized against their stewards. Anticolonial proposals at international venues were deceptive efforts to build "a powerful bloc in the United Nations" where communists would "distract attention from the economic condition" of what was lost by deserting the colonizers.[179] Nationalist propaganda "creates an atmosphere of hatred on which the propaganda of Communism thrives," one Foreign Office official remarked. "Every weakening of G[reat] Britain and the US represents a corresponding gain of strength for the Soviet Union."[180] Since "communist and nationalist methods are in many cases identical," another official concurred that the Soviet Union profited from the "dangers" of all anti-imperialist propaganda.[181]

The British government, especially its Foreign Office, believed communists spearheaded almost every anticolonial demonstration or project to strengthen the Soviet Union. During May Day festivities in 1947, Guatemalans carried signs criticizing Franco and the Truman Doctrine, but British officials focused on anticolonial slogans. "America for the Americas, Belize for the Guatemalans"; "Belize is Guatemalan Territory"; and "We require an outlet to the sea through Belize, otherwise our Petén will die" supposedly drew from communist inspiration.[182] Actually aimed against British imperialism, the phrase "Pan Americanism—'America for the Americans'" was somehow "clearly Soviet-inspired" and "anti–United States slogans."[183] Ultimately, British officials reduced the Revolution to a communist scheme. Cabinet changes, welcoming Spanish exiles, suspending relations with Trujillo's regime, and more were proof that Arévalo had aligned himself with international communism.[184] Arévalo's government established relations with the Soviet Union not due to the war's antifascist moment but his being "considerably under the influence of Mexico."[185] This messaging was controlled by Lombardo Toledano, whom British officials claimed was constructing one of the Soviet Union's communist blocs within Latin America thanks to his exploitation of revolutionary nationalism.[186] Through labor organizations, he somehow spread communism throughout the Western Hemisphere.[187]

Within this international conflict, some British officials looked favorably on the numerous difficulties facing Arévalo's government. Guatemala's democratic opening, with the constant movements of antidictatorial exiles and political refugees, perturbed the Foreign Office, who suspected "it provides an admirable opportunity for the infiltration of Communist agents, briefed to cause as much trouble as possible to the British in the British Honduras dispute."[188] Arévalo networked with regional allies including Betancourt while spreading "Guatemalan propaganda" and "actively exploiting" anticolonial sentiments.[189] As one official determined, "The 'democratic bloc' is a thorn in our flesh as far as anticolonial agitation is concerned."[190] Consequently, the Foreign Office cast antigovernment uprisings as temporary relief from anticolonialism. Following constitutional suspensions in October 1945, one official jotted down, "I hope the Guat[emalan] Gov[ernment] are going to have lots of internal trouble, but I think we sh[ould] not be wise to believe that either they or any eventual successors will give up the Belize agitation easily."[191] Another noted that the flurry of suspensions "suggests that the Guatemalan Gov[ernment] may be too busy with internal affairs to pay much attention to Belize for the present."[192]

The Forgery

Illustrative of the anticommunist scorn thrown against Arévalo's government, a document began circulating throughout the Caribbean Basin in the mid-1940s. According to gossip among diplomatic officials, some unnamed opponent got his hands on a letter that merited immediate republication in Central American and Caribbean newspapers and pamphlets. Allegedly, this letter was written by Arévalo to the Soviet chargé d'affaires in Mexico City Vasili Yakubovsky and dated March 18, 1945. The letter assured the Soviet official that "all is progressing well," with Arévalo's government having achieved "the unification of the working and agricultural masses in this little nation." Soon, Arévalo would nominate Cardoza y Aragón as the country's representative in Moscow. The letter concluded by thanking Yakubovsky for his "spiritual and economic help." At the bottom was Arévalo's signature.

The letter was a forgery. It was not simply that the "tone" and "contents" of the letter did not conform to Arévalo's writing or ideas.[193] The US Office of Central America and Panama Affairs identified seven signs of forgery, from how the letter misspelled "Vasili Yakubovsky" as "Basili Pyakubovsky" to a simple comparison of the letter's forged signature and Arévalo's actual signature.[194] Mexican authorities agreed that, "from the crude signature to the language in the forgery," the "falsification [was] clumsy and crude."[195] Cardoza y Aragón had spoken with Soviet representatives in Mexico City in late 1945 and when he traveled to Sweden, but any results were insignificant beyond exchanging polite diplomatic pleasantries based on a postwar respect.[196]

Those with a good relationship with Arévalo's government did not fall for the forgery. Meanwhile, frustrated with reactionaries' rants, US officials observed Ponce, Ramírez, Coronado Lira, and others distributing and publicizing the forgery.[197] Reactionaries were "so embittered and prejudiced" that they tried sharing what was obviously "unreliable and inaccurate information."[198] Mexican authorities excoriated the republication and distribution of the forgery as coming right up to the line of engaging in political activities.[199] In contrast to Guatemalan officials' inability to provide actionable intelligence on antigovernment conspiracies, the forgery gave credence to the charge that reactionaries failed to abide by the laws surrounding asylum in Mexico.[200]

For the Revolution's many opponents, the forgery was perfect evidence that Arévalo was pushing a communist plot to convert Guatemala into a Soviet puppet state. The newspaper *Diario Latino* in San Salvador seems to have first republished the forgery. From there, it appeared throughout the greater Caribbean. In Mexico City, Archila Obregón provided copies to his allies.[201] They published the forgery alongside other writings charging Arévalo with welcoming communism with no regard for the Western Hemisphere's spirit of "Pan-Americanism" and "Continental Defense," a gross violation of the "tranquility and sovereignty of our beloved Guatemalan country and with her that of all the sister nations of Central America."[202] Like-minded organizations incorporated the forgery into their writings and compilations, with headlines like "Traitor to the Christian Faith" in the CDP's *La Tribuna de la Libertad* and the CPG's *Guatemala bajo el signo rojo*.[203]

The forgery would never go away. When Carías's newspaper *La Época* reproduced it, the dictator's son handed a copy to US officials at the UN.[204] In 1946, members of Arévalo's government, who thought they knew Coronado Lira's character before his exile, swore he could not be the one to author or disseminate such propaganda.[205] US officials confirmed Coronado Lira and Salazar were mass producing republications, and the two brought up the forgery during their October 1947 antigovernment plot as evidence Arévalo was a communist.[206] Two years later, in the midst of rumors of international intrigues in Guatemala during Arana's death, it reappeared.[207] Following a failed 1949 invasion by antidictatorial exiles to oust Trujillo, Somoza's newspaper *Novedades* printed it.[208] The forgery, and the multiple plots sparking constitutional suspensions, haunted the Guatemalan Revolution.

Chapter 4

Drawing Up Pacts

Cayo Confites and Costa Rica, 1947–1948

In June 1948, Dominican exile Bosch assessed the past years' developments. In a confidential report for newly elected Cuban President Carlos Prío Socarrás, Bosch claimed, "Truly Central America is a political and social volcano, with eruptions that started in June 1944," right before the Guatemalan Revolution took hold. Soon after, Arévalo enacted a foreign policy to weaken dictators. Ideally, overthrowing any dictator would not only prevent a "secret alliance" among them but convert their country into a springboard for additional projects. Although a 1947 expedition against Trujillo failed, Arévalo supported a 1948 antidictatorial coalition that installed an ally in Costa Rica. Hopeful for the next years, Bosch believed these events favored those standing against "cowardly dictators like Somoza, Carías, and Trujillo."[1] What he did not know, though, was that those dictators had reached the same conclusion: they feared that Arévalo, Bosch, Prío, and their allies might convert the democratic promise of the mid-1940s into a reality. To push back, the region's dictators were building the "secret alliance" Bosch dreaded.

This chapter explores how tumultuous events within the Caribbean Basin in 1947 and 1948 reshaped the conflicts unleashed at the Second World War's end. In the summer of 1947, Arévalo and his allies supported an antidictatorial effort to overthrow Trujillo's regime. Although international pressure halted what became known as the Cayo Confites expedition, dictators started sharing intelligence with one another as a common anticommunist defense. Failing to air-bomb Caracas in early 1948 and eliminate Arévalo's democratic allies in Venezuela, dictators discussed the necessary means to destroy Guatemala's government. This collaboration escalated during subsequent events in Costa Rica, where Arévalo helped install a friendly government. As 1948 came to an end, dictators coalesced into an informal network of self-proclaimed anticommunist regimes seeking to turn back the recent years' wave of antidictatorial energy by cooperating against their mutual enemies.

An Abortive Antidictatorial Shot: Cayo Confites, 1947

What became the Cayo Confites expedition united, for one brief moment, much of the Caribbean Basin's antidictatorial energy.[2] A truly bombastic plot emerged in mid-1947 to overthrow Trujillo through a combination of naval invasions, aerial bombardments, and internal uprisings. Spearheaded by Dominican exiles, the plan brought together various exiles, Cuban students and politicians, and multiple democratic presidents to topple Trujillo. Quickly derailed due to its publicity and the US government's calls to limit regional conflict, the abortive expedition sent a clear message regarding the region's antidictatorial passions.

Into 1947, Dominican exiles continued their networking. Bosch, Jiménes Grullón, and others in the PRD long sought to unite their compatriots scattered across Cuba, Puerto Rico, and New York. Despite years of partisan disputes and ideological divisions, they capitalized on events in the mid-1940s and drew together fellow exiles. Additional momentum came from wealthy and newly exiled Juan "Juancito" Rodríguez. Having spent months sneaking part of his fortune out of the Dominican Republic, Rodríguez in 1946 agreed to assist anti-Trujillo plots. Joining him was Miguel Ángel Ramírez, who over the next years would serve as a military adviser and influential link to Rodríguez, Dominican exiles, and their transnational allies. By 1947, Rodríguez had purchased a small arsenal. Between Rodríguez's financial contribution and the PRD leadership, a core movement solidified. Now, the exiles reached out to ideological colleagues in Cuba, Guatemala, Venezuela, and Haiti.

Cuba became the plot's hub. Its president, Ramón Grau San Martín, sympathized with Dominican exiles. He and his political party, the Partido

Revolucionario Cubano-Auténtico (Auténticos), had a long history of anti-dictatorial activism and close relations with exiles. Among its leaders were Cotu and Eufemio Fernández, a Spanish Civil War veteran and vocal anti-Trujillo militant, and Bosch was an intermediary between Auténticos and exiles while serving as one of Prío's advisers. In fact, anti-Trujillo activism was one of the few issues capable of uniting, temporarily, Cuba's fractious political organizations and personalities. Having recently broken from the Auténticos, Eduardo Chibás and the newly formed Partido del Pueblo Cubano (Ortodoxos) endorsed the plot, as did Rolando Masferrer and the militant MSR. Most plentiful, though, were Cuban students. An array of student organizations, such as the FEU, and leaders, including Fidel Castro, sent volunteers. Thanks to this popular support and the Auténticos' governmental resources, Cuba was the plan's launching pad.

Guatemala's Arévalo and Venezuela's Betancourt contributed. Betancourt allowed some members of the Venezuelan military to provide resources and guidance.[3] Arévalo agreed to assist by facilitating the participants' movement and purchasing additional weapons through Argentine President Juan Perón. Many Haitians were aware of Trujillo's repeated interventions in their nation's affairs and sympathized with anti-Trujillo movements, so Guatemalan, Cuban, and Venezuelan representatives tried lobbying Haitian President Dumarsais Estimé.[4] Likely due to the Haitian government's knowledge of the strength of Trujillo's regime, Estimé offered little material support for the plot.[5]

Nevertheless, Rodríguez's resources, the presidents' support, and Cubans' enthusiasm were enough for Dominican exiles to draw up their plan. From Cuba, exiles and their allies would launch joint air and naval strikes. Simultaneously, other exiles would cross from Haiti into the Dominican Republic while anti-Trujillo activists within the country rose up. Together, the multifront assault and its shock-and-awe tactics would erode Trujillo's military forces and destroy the illusion of the dictator's popular support. On paper, the plan was many times larger than anything ever envisioned. Exiles amassed at least two hundred submachine guns, fifty machine guns, one thousand automatic pistols, over a dozen bazookas and three hundred rockets, hundreds of bombs and explosives, three mortars, three antitank guns, and two thousand hand grenades, along with a small navy of seven ships, including two torpedo boats, an assault ship, and two landing craft vessels, and an air force with sixteen planes, including six P-38 fighters, a B-24 bomber, a B-25 Mitchell bomber, and troop carriers.

The transnational links behind the already unwieldy plot expanded. Though there would never be an exact number, observers and participants estimated that hundreds of Cubans, possibly just over a thousand, attempted to participate. In 1945, Meza and the UDC had reached out to Arévalo to introduce Nicaraguan Rosendo Argüello.[6] Cheering on the plot, Argüello depicted the expedition as part of the recent years' "glorious campaign," promising "a victory . . . not only for you but for America and humanity, since the dictator whom you will fight is outside the laws of humanity and divinity."[7] By July 1946, Arévalo had sent Meza to network with the "Cuban-Dominican-Venezuelan group in Havana" and assess the available resources.[8] The next year, Argüello helped arrange introductions between Arévalo and Ribas Montes, recently released amid the international backlash from the Masacre Sampedrana. Argüello championed Ribas Montes as "one of the most hardworking and valiant soldiers of the liberating army of Central America."[9] In the span of just a few weeks, Ribas Montes joined Ramírez as two of Rodríguez's trusted confidantes. Additionally, Argüello and his new friend, Costa Rican José Figueres, paid for a handful of technicians to assist the expedition.[10]

Into July 1947, the plot kept growing. Volunteers came through the Hotel San Luis, owned by Spanish exile Cruz Alonso, who handled much of the plot's transportation and food through his import/export business. A onetime soldier against Sandino in the 1920s before his rupture with and exile from Somoza's regime, Abelardo Cuadra joined.[11] Dominican exiles Arvelo, Amado Soler, Federico "Gugu" Henríquez, and Virgilio Mainardi Reyna enlisted, as did Dominican labor activist Mauricio Báez. Before the month's end, Cotu assured Arévalo that over three hundred men were organized while another three hundred waited for training. Still leading were the Dominicans who would "have the great honor in going to the line of fire against the tyranny of Trujillo." At their side were "other Latin Americans and a great number of Cubans," including veterans of past battles against Cuba's dictatorships, the Spanish Civil War, and World War II.[12] Reflecting this transnational support behind the affair, participants divided into battalions under Cubans Fernández and Masferrer, Honduran Ribas Montes, and Dominican Diego Bordas, with companies reflecting a similar dispersion of nationalities. Battalions' names honored Nicaraguan anti-imperialist Sandino and Cuban independence hero Máximo Gómez. By mid-July 1947, they felt confident to invade the Dominican Republic the following August.[13]

The escalating size and popularity of the plot brought immense chaos. As US and Dominican officials heard rumors and confirmed minor aspects of the scheme, Grau had participants move from their original base in Holguín to the beaches of Cayo Confites on Cuba's northeastern coast. This unexpected change upended much of the planning, as did poor weather and a lack of supplies and sanitation. Rivalries broke out as Dominican exiles felt frustrated that, following the relocation, Cubans occupied most leadership roles. As the initially unifying effervescence of a bold anti-Trujillo strike faded away, violent threats and even physical attacks broke out among rival Cuban leaders. Thanks in part to journalists from the Associated Press's Latin American staff who were on Trujillo's payroll, newspapers reported the expedition's activities with articles specifically citing the Cuban, Guatemalan, and Venezuelan governments' involvement.[14] US officials pressed their Cuban counterparts for clarification, and by September the expedition had imploded due to international pressure and the disastrous situation on the beaches. Grau ordered Cuban authorities to arrest participants while seizing Rodríguez's arsenal. A small comedy of errors erupted as ships attempted to escape and Fidel Castro dived into the sea to swim for land, but Cuba's navy detained most of Rodríguez's vessels.

As the expedition fell apart, it remained a beacon of antidictatorial optimism. Some, like Honduran José Castro, felt dejected that removing Trujillo would come at a later date; he lamented, "The failure of the Dominican revolution of Juan Bosch and company has been a failure of Honduras and Nicaragua, for Santo Domingo was only the first chapter for the Army of American Liberation, the most noble of recent times and one of the most audacious and unselfish that I can remember."[15] Fortunately, Auténticos prevented any lasting reprisals against participants. While holding more than one hundred Cubans for joining the abortive expedition, Grau's government provided dozens of passes and tickets to help them return to their home provinces.[16] Alonso once again used his import/export business to arrange travel for the participants, including Nicaraguan José María Tercero, Ribas Montes, and Dominicans Horacio Ornes and Ramírez.[17] By mid-January 1948, Auténticos had transported most of Rodríguez's arsenal to Guatemala where Arévalo's government acquired additional resources.[18] Now, Castro prayed, Cayo Confites's unrealized promise would have a better chance thanks to Arévalo's and Guatemala's democratic sympathies.[19]

The new question was not whether to organize another expedition but which dictator to target. Nicaraguans Toribio Tijerino and Cuadra Pasos suggested redirecting their resources against Somoza, whose forces were far smaller than those of Trujillo.[20] To evaluate this possibility, Arévalo sent a representative to interview Nicaraguan exiles. Immediately, the messenger recognized the factional infighting, much directed against Emiliano Chamorro and the Conservatives.[21] To curtail this dissension, Arévalo summoned representative exiles to Guatemala City in November 1947. Having financed the recent affair, Rodríguez spoke on behalf of Dominican exiles. To allay the Nicaraguan exiles' divisions, Arévalo brought together Tijerino for the Partido Conservador (Conservatives), Rosendo Argüello for the Partido Liberal Independiente (Independent Liberals), and recently ousted president Leonardo Argüello. Focusing on their shared goals against all dictators, representatives signed the Pacto del Caribe (Caribbean Pact). The overarching idea was the same seen at Cayo Confites: fighting Trujillo and Somoza was "one common cause," but the underlying question was how to make their dream of deposing dictators a "more and efficient" reality; how would they create "in these two sister countries political regimes of social justice and of true respect for human dignity?" Simply put, they agreed to coordinate their resources. Rodríguez swore to provide sufficient materiel and lobby Auténticos on the Nicaraguan exiles' behalf. For their part, Tijerino and Argüello would help fight Trujillo's regime, offer Nicaraguan bases for future expeditions, and repay Rodríguez's generosity, should they succeed in overthrowing Somoza.[22] Embodying their shared visions for the Caribbean Basin, they now had a pact to outline their next steps.

Dictators Helping Dictators: A Counterrevolutionary Pact

Simultaneously, dictators drew up their own pact. Despite its failure to touch Dominican soil, the Cayo Confites affair was tangible proof of the greater Caribbean's democratic aspirations against not solely Trujillo but all dictators. Now, they feared that an attack against one dictator was not some happenstance but a regional security threat. Beginning in late 1947, Trujillo, Somoza, and Carías took their first steps to share intelligence on what they deemed a communist danger. There had long been rumors of collaborations among the region's dictatorships, but the Cayo Confites expedition's transnational makeup aroused the beginnings of the dictators' informal anticommunist pact.[23]

In December 1947, Somoza ordered his ambassador in Washington, Guillermo Sevilla Sacasa, to contact his Dominican counterpart, Luis Thomen.[24] Nicaraguan officials had succeeded in embedding among Cayo Confites's participants at least one informant, who alleged that the expedition was part of a "revolution with a totally communist veneer" that would not stop at Trujillo's removal. With their armaments funneled to Guatemala, the conspirators were building new "bases of operation" under Arévalo's protection. Their regimes targeted, Somoza, through Sevilla Sacasa, "offered to provide" Trujillo with "whatever additional information" his officials would unearth.[25] Carías, too, sent at least one official to participate in these early intelligence exchanges.[26] Presenting any antidictatorial entity as a communist intrigue, these dictators interpreted recent events as a common security threat that required mutual cooperation. Almost immediately, they deployed this newfound collaboration in hopes of eliminating Arévalo's ally in Venezuela, Betancourt.

In early 1948, the dictators' cooperation deepened with a plot to air-bomb Caracas and destabilize Betancourt's government. Trujillo's rivalry with the Venezuelan democrat went back years but hit new levels when Betancourt assisted antidictatorial exiles.[27] From 1945 into 1947, Trujillo quietly financed antigovernment propagandists and conspiratorial Venezuelan reactionaries. In fact, the FBI was actively investigating a recent attempt by Dominican officials in Miami to acquire explosive materials.[28] To circumvent US officials, Trujillo and Venezuelan reactionaries were searching for a new staging ground, which is when the dictators' nascent alliance came into play. First, Trujillo provided reactionaries with one hundred thousand dollars. Then, Somoza offered the use of one of Nicaragua's easternmost ports, Puerto Cabezas. Backed by two dictators, reactionaries set into motion their plot: flying planes over Caracas and air-bombing Venezuela's capital to spark a domestic uprising. From late 1947 into early 1948, Trujillo's air force helped transport planes and explosives into Nicaragua. Reactionaries also hired US mercenaries to purchase equipment, all the while falsifying their paperwork to hide their activities from US officials.[29]

Serendipitously, Arévalo uncovered this plot. Facing the conspiracies targeting his government, he had authorized intelligence operations in Nicaragua, with agents having to cross into the country through Mexico to cloak their origins.[30] These efforts increased when, after Ponce's air-bombing plot, Arévalo began ordering officials "to be on the lookout for the anticipated arrival of military equipment from the Dominican Republic" while suspecting Trujillo was reinforcing "Somoza['s] eventual aggression against Guatemala."[31] Complementing warnings from elsewhere, informants confirmed the arrival of Dominican planes offloading their cargos in Puerto Cabezas, the heart of the Caracas conspiracy.[32] Arévalo shared this information with Betancourt, who notified the US government.[33] In February 1948, US officials and Betancourt asked Somoza's government about the planes' arrival and the reactionaries' ongoing activities.[34] Just as Dominican officials had called for the US government's assistance to halt the Cayo Confites expedition the previous summer, Venezuelan officials solicited US officials' intervention.

And just as Auténticos helped antidictatorial exiles by detaining and then hiding the armaments, Somoza aided his own allies in a similar fashion. First, Nicaraguan officials claimed to have seized the participants' planes to prevent any hostilities against another government.[35] Next, Somoza covered up his fellow dictator's involvement. As he explained in a private message to Trujillo, US officials had derailed the plan, so he pretended to cooperate while quietly sabotaging any investigation. Seizing only two of the planes and a few pilots, Somoza provided cover for most participants by hiding four other planes.[36] As became clear over the next weeks, this cooperation hit its mark. US officials failed to complete a thorough investigation of the plot, merely warning Somoza, Betancourt, and Arévalo against intervening in other nations' affairs.[37] Although Arévalo's agents had provided the necessary intelligence that allowed Venezuelan officials to prevent the conspiracy from taking off, both governments lacked any concrete information on the growing links between Somoza and Trujillo.[38]

After the Caracas plot, the dictators expanded their intelligence sharing to include conspiracies against Guatemala's government when Ponce again solicited Trujillo for help. This time, though, Trujillo asked for advice. He ordered a special ambassador to meet in Washington with Sevilla Sacasa. Together, they evaluated Ponce's plot, when Sevilla Sacasa worried that "the requested economic assistance seemed very substantial." Complicating matters was that they knew little about Ponce's influence within the Guatemalan army. Although Ponce boasted of having many "friends among the military lot in Guatemala," Sevilla Sacasa doubted this influence due to Ponce's years in exile. Any uprising against Arévalo depended on the Guatemalan Army, but its organization had changed, with most showing "great loyalty" to current head Colonel Francisco Arana. They recognized that Central America's most powerful military played a crucial role during the 1944 removal of Ubico and remained a pivotal institution, so a successful uprising needed to penetrate the army's ranks, or at least have its leaders' consent. Consequently, Sevilla Sacasa suggested that Ponce write a list of contacts to better measure whether the reactionary could garner the required popular and military support.[39]

There are multiple reasons Ponce's 1948 solicitation sparked the first dialogue on a reactionary's conspiracy. His request came right after Dominican and Nicaraguan officials held their first meetings concerning the Cayo Confites expedition. Having already financed one of Ponce's failed plots, Trujillo sought additional advice from his colleagues who had more experience working with the factious Guatemalans. In less than one year, Trujillo had sponsored two air-bombing conspiracies that fizzled out. Now, the regimes were networking against Arévalo's government. What had been a series of scattered plots over the past few years was becoming a coordinated, though informal, system to evaluate reactionaries' strengths and weaknesses. In the span of a few weeks, two regimes built a loose alliance where officials shared intelligence, evaluated conspiracies, and assisted one another against their enemies. This networking quickly came into play as a new crisis in Costa Rica grabbed everyone's attention.

The Costa Rican Civil War of 1948

The Costa Rican Civil War took many in the Caribbean Basin by surprise, because the country appeared relatively immune from the regional tensions. In fact, most discussions of Central American politics highlighted Costa Rica as ideal, held up as proof that stable governments and economic systems were possible. However, the nation's political situation was on edge in early 1948 as its politics hit a point of crisis. Beginning in the early 1940s, a unique alliance enacted various reforms such as a labor code and social security.[40] Reflecting the dynamism seen elsewhere, this coalition included Catholics, labor activists, and communists who supported President Rafael Ángel Calderón Guardia and his 1944 successor, Teodoro Picado. These alliances and social reforms frustrated Costa Rican conservatives and anticommunist reformers, among them planter José Figueres, who was exiled to Mexico in 1942.[41] There, Figueres built a relationship with Nicaraguan exile Rosendo Argüello. In 1947, the two traveled to Cuba to make contact with the Cayo Confites participants.[42] While Argüello represented Nicaraguan exiles at the various meetings, Figueres financially contributed.[43] The support of unionists Meza and Mendieta further bolstered Argüello's antidictatorial credentials and positioned him as a signatory to the Pacto del Caribe.[44] Meanwhile, Figueres's reputation grew. By the end of 1947, another Nicaraguan exile, Ordóñez Argüello, opened the doors at Guatemala's Palacio Nacional to introduce Arévalo to Figueres.[45]

Figueres's decision to solicit Arévalo's intervention in Costa Rican affairs remains a contentious issue. With Calderón Guardia entering the 1948 presidential election with a coalition that included communists, Figueres joined fellow conservatives and reformist anticommunists to back Otilio Ulate. Violence, intimidation, protests, fraud, and strikes dominated late 1947 and early 1948 with a heavily contested February vote.[46] Confronted with complaints from both candidates' supporters, the recently created Tribunal Nacional Electoral (National Electoral Tribunal) at the end of the month declared Ulate the victor, yet Calderón Guardia's allies in the legislature threw out the popular vote, handing Calderón Guardia the presidency and unleashing popular violence. On March 12, Figueres declared war. Whereas Figueres had been preparing for war since 1947, antidictatorial exiles faced a dilemma about whether to take a side in a conflict appearing unrelated to the regional skirmishes over democracy and dictatorship.[47] Calderón Guardia was a popular figure thanks to alliances and policies in line with those envisioned by reformers throughout the Western Hemisphere, so this left many wondering whether to support Figueres.[48]

The final decision, though, would be based on not reforms within Costa Rica but Calderón Guardia's alleged alliance with Somoza. Nicaraguan exiles complained that Calderón Guardia and his Calderonistas always halted plots against the dictator next door. Ordóñez Argüello denounced "the anticonstitutional excess of Caldero-communism" that "betrayed Nicaragua's desire for liberation through the entente with Somoza," and Bosch claimed these Calderón Guardia–Somoza dealings continued under his successor Picado.[49] Arévalo's officials repeated these charges, going so far as to suggest Somoza interfered in Costa Rican politics on Calderón Guardia's behalf.[50] In a 1945 confidential report, Guatemalan officials insisted that the two Costa Rican presidents had financial arrangements with Somoza that compelled them to prevent any border skirmishes and hinder the activities of anti-Somoza exiles.[51]

This was how Figueres, Arévalo, and antidictatorial exiles judged Costa Rican matters. By December 1947, Figueres endorsed the Pacto del Caribe and warned that Calderonistas, "supporters of Somoza," would try to steal the election.[52] Arévalo, financial patron Rodríguez, and their allies needed to help Ulate secure the presidency and gain "the advantages of having a reliable friendly country." If not, Costa Rica would be "definitively what is the Southern front for Somoza," thereby losing "the common fight for us all."[53] Figueres offered to repay any assistance by converting the country into a launchpad for movements against other dictators.⁵⁴ This idea, incorporating Costa Rica as part of the larger antidictatorial vision, resonated with Rodríguez. He saw Figueres as an ally who would "honor the noble crusade of liberating our people oppressed by assassins and vulgar murderers." Agreeing to assist Figueres and Ulate now, Rodríguez looked forward to Costa Rica's "firm participation in order to solve later the situation of all countries of the Caribbean area that find themselves subjugated by despotic regimes."⁵⁵ Arévalo likewise presented this idea to Betancourt. Removing Costa Rica's pro-Somoza government, antidictatorial exiles could target Somoza's Nicaraguan regime. In the span of a week, forces would move against Carías in Honduras. Perhaps two weeks later, Trujillo would fall. With Costa Rica as part of an antidictatorial alliance, their governments would serve as a bulwark against dictatorial schemes and cooperate at international venues to expel colonialism, whether Europe from Belize and the Guianas or the United States from Puerto Rico.⁵⁶ As the civil war commenced, Figueres expressed his gratitude in a language that his antidictatorial allies appreciated: "This fight will not end until we free the American world of Trujillos."⁵⁷

Thus, the forty-day Costa Rican Civil War of 1948 became a lodestar for the region as Figueres and his allies took on Calderón Guardia. Initially, Calderonistas had the advantage, with the Picado government's forces joined by communist militias. However, Figueres's forces seized San Isidro Airport to establish a route between Costa Rica and Guatemala that allowed Arévalo to send Rodríguez's armaments.⁵⁸ Soon, antidictatorial exiles joined Figueres in Costa Rica.⁵⁹ Among them were Dominicans Ornes, Ramírez, Soler, and Mainardi; Nicaraguans Rosendo Argüello, Báez Bone, and Tercero; and Hondurans Ribas Montes, Morazán, and Francisco "El Indio" Sánchez.⁶⁰ With such resources and allies, Figueres took advantageous positions along the Atlantic coast, allowing an uninterrupted channel of resources and information between Costa Rica and Guatemala.⁶¹ Bolstered by these early wins, Rodríguez held up the civil war as "not only victory in Costa Rica but, also, the victory of the entire movement of liberation in the Caribbean."⁶²

Just as Arévalo and antidictatorial exiles supported Figueres in hopes of acquiring a base for their activities, Somoza and Carías were invested in the outcome, sharing what a Salvadoran official described as a "secret pact" that was "ostensibly an anticommunist pact but which, in effect, is anti-Arévalo."⁶³ Against this backdrop, rumors swirled that Somoza's officials were assisting Calderón Guardia's forces in the civil war's first days. Notifying Arévalo of the first days' successes, Figueres included reports that the Guardia Nacional intervened, and Guatemalan officials estimated that six hundred Guardia Nacional troops were participating.[64] Admitting that they had requested Somoza's planes, Calderón Guardia and Picado's general denied receiving any outside assistance.[65] There were also rumors that Calderón Guardia asked for Carías's help.[66] Monitoring these transnational alliances, the US and Mexican ambassadors described this civil war as an international conflagration.[67] Subsequent days brought increased fears as more communists joined Calderón Guardia's forces, reflecting the Calderonistas' desperation.[68] Antidictatorial exiles helped capture their opponents' munitions and Puerto Limón on April 10.[69] By then, Picado believed his government would collapse without sufficient support, so he reached out for Somoza's direct assistance.

On April 16, Picado enlisted Calderón Guardia's brother, Francisco "Paco" Calderón Guardia, as a "confidential agent."[70] Joined by one of Picado's officials, Paco headed for Managua to "solicit [Somoza's] cooperation." The messengers depicted Costa Rica's violence as an outgrowth of the regional conflict. Those seeking to overthrow Picado's government were "Guatemalans and members of the opposition of Honduras, El Salvador, the Dominican Republic, and other mercenaries" with the "financial and material assistance of certain foreign governments." They were "convert[ing Costa Rica into] a Central American war" that would target Somoza's regime. To push back, Picado through his two representatives "authorized the Nicaraguan Government to occupy those locations deemed convenient in Costa Rican territory, for the purpose of protecting [Nicaragua's] border and avoiding any penetration into Nicaraguan territory."[71] Picado's representatives purposefully presented a change of government in Costa Rica as a direct threat to the dictator's security but unknowingly offered Somoza the perfect way to secure another regime's involvement.

Hours after receiving Picado's request, Somoza reached out to Trujillo. Throughout early April, Somoza had kept Dominican officials informed about Central American matters and especially the civil war. However, Picado's solicitation offered Somoza the means to incorporate Trujillo into the civil war and leverage their formative alliance. On April 17, Somoza sent a messenger to the Dominican Republic with a plea for assistance. Based on Picado's request, Somoza could "demonstrate how the revolutionary movement in Costa Rica threatens to spread to Nicaragua, Honduras, El Salvador, and the Dominican Republic." Arévalo and Betancourt were providing the "financial and material assistance" to Figueres for a change of government. Included in these resources was the Cayo Confites arsenal. In response to Picado's petition, Somoza planned to order his Guardia into "strategic locations on Costa Rican soil." He could count on his soldiers but lacked the appropriate "war materiel" to ensure victory, so, on behalf of Trujillo's "demonstrations of friendship" and "well recognized anticommunist attitude," Somoza asked for the necessary resources to fight against "the common goals that our gratuitous enemies Arévalo and Betancourt pursue."[72]

Whether this solicitation worked remains unknown, for international pressure ended the civil war. As early as mid-March, US and Latin American officials issued notes protesting any government's interference in Costa Rican affairs, with Calderón Guardia and Figueres asking US officials to help their respective sides.[73] In mid-April, US and Mexican representatives caught wind of Calderón Guardia's requests for Somoza's assistance. This added to the rumors of Somoza's "launch[ing] an all-out invasion of Costa Rica," either pushing Costa Rican communists to switch sides from Calderón Guardia to Figueres to fight any Nicaraguan invasion or precipitating an official international conflagration if Arévalo's government declared war on Somoza's regime.[74] Hoping to limit the spread of the civil war, participants agreed with mediators to reach a final pact as soon as possible.[75] Of course, this did not immediately halt all violence within the nation. At the end of April, Nicaraguan forces crossed the border and attacked a handful of Costa Rican locations, and the nation's people would endure local violence in the civil war's aftermath.[76] From international observers' perspective, however, the Costa Rican Civil War had concluded.

Their loss in the civil war solidified the dictators' alliance. Over the next days, Picado insisted he never requested or permitted Somoza's Guardia to enter Costa Rican soil and blamed his representatives and Somoza for overstepping their authority.[77] This allegation perturbed Somoza, who shared copies of Picado's and the messengers' petitions with US officials and portrayed his actions as a legitimate response to those who sought "a conflagration in all Central America and the Caribbean."[78] He even defended his deployment of troops into Costa Rica as an appropriate measure to ensure Nicaraguan sovereignty.[79] Most importantly, Somoza kept intact his alliance with Trujillo. In early May, Somoza ordered Sevilla Sacasa to travel to Ciudad Trujillo. There, Sevilla Sacasa provided photocopies of relevant documents and assured Trujillo that his ally had not acted blindly.[80] Consequently, Dominican officials backed Somoza's charges against Figueres's transnational coalition for disrupting "the interest of peace and inter-American solidarity." Dominican officials depicted Figueres's allies as communist and beholden to "antidemocratic foreign doctrines," in spite of Calderón Guardia's alliance with Costa Rican communists.[81]

The "Legión" Emerges

The civil war further energized the Caribbean Basin's dynamics. Once held up as semi-immune to the area's tumult, the nation took a central role in the region's conflicts. In fact, their success in Costa Rica inspired Rodríguez, Ornes, and others to term their loose coalition the Legión Caribe (Caribbean Legion), often reported as the Legión del Caribe. In the shadow of their false start on Cuban beaches, this name added fame and suggested a united front. Rodríguez and Ornes tried bringing together all exiles into an official structure, best evidenced in an accounting book where Ornes tabulated its finances.[82] Most agreed on their overarching goal to remove Caribbean Basin dictators, but political divisions persisted. As a result, this so-called Legión would never be a cohesive front and only officially existed for a few months. Nevertheless, these Legionarios (Legionnaires) would remain committed to their pursuit of democracy, their moniker's mythical prestige stoking the dictators' fears.

Figueres's victory had relied on the assistance of Arévalo, Betancourt, and those making up this Legión under the Pacto del Caribe. Right away, Figueres began fulfilling his part of the bargain, allowing Costa Rica to provide antidictatorial sanctuaries. However, the civil war cast international attention upon Figueres's foreign alliances, with US officials especially active in discouraging disruptions and changes of government. Facing this pressure, Figueres issued an official break with the Legión to placate US officials, as historians have correctly highlighted.[83] His private actions, though, betrayed his public position. Whether in leading Costa Rica's post–civil war junta, as the nation's elected president, or outside public office, Figueres remained a key antidictatorial ally, offering his estates and resources. In fact, he repeatedly wielded his image as a vocal anticommunist, pro-US leader to aid his compatriots, as when providing haven to those fleeing dictatorships and persecution. Figueres had turned to Dominican exile Ramírez, who recognized the US government's pressure to avoid additional regional conflicts, for advice and guidance while issuing his public rupture with the Legión.[84] Although Rodríguez and some critics resented this rupture, most Legionarios and Arévalo acknowledged Figueres as a quiet friend.[85]

The triumph in Costa Rica uplifted antidictatorial exiles' hopes. Ramírez credited this victory to their alliances and their spirit of "freedom."[86] He and Honduran exile Morazán tied this optimism for the Caribbean Basin's future to the continued support of Figueres's Costa Rica, Arévalo's Guatemala, Betancourt's Venezuela, and the Auténticos' Cuba.[87] The latter was quite significant, thanks to the 1948 election and peaceful transfer of power from Grau to Prío. Soon, Dominican and Nicaraguan exiles alongside Arévalo and Figueres updated the Pacto del Caribe. They divided their activities into zones targeting Somoza's Nicaragua and Carías's Honduras, planning to remove Somoza first.[88] When writing a personnel chart detailing the Legión's leadership and membership, they included a brief paragraph outlining their vision. Any "success" could only come if they remained in agreement and put aside their "personal preferences" to focus on their larger goal.[89]

Political and personal tensions weakened these grand visions. Weeks after the civil war's end, multiple Nicaraguan exiles agreed to form a provisional government in the event of Somoza's ouster.[90] Some joined Cuadra Pasos, Meza, Tijerino, Tercero, Báez Bone, and Castillo Ibarra to endorse a "Promesa de Adhesión y Lealtad a la Causa Revolucionaria de Nicaragua" (Promise of Adhesion and Loyalty to the Revolutionary Cause in Nicaragua).[91] Others with Chamorro boasted of their own "revolutionary plan."[92] However, these projects were stillborn as exiles jockeyed for leadership. Argüello's personality and actions frustrated many, and his onetime friend and colleague Figueres soon cut ties.[93] Some exiles detested Chamorro and the Conservatives while holding up Torres and the Liberals as better beneficiaries of Arévalo and Figueres's support.[94] Competing bands vied for influence and resources, resulting in scattered border incursions and squandered plots. Guatemalan officials and Dominican exiles grew disillusioned with the Nicaraguan exiles' infighting and disunity that came with numerous petitions requiring Arévalo's personal mediation.[95] Though all swore to serve in the "fight against the tyranny of Somoza" and other dictators, few successful ventures materialized.[96]

Honduran exiles lobbied for assistance just as passionately while facing similar strife. Their declarations and pleas stressed unity as a consistent theme. For example, the Frente de Unidad Revolucionario Hondureña (Honduran Revolutionary Unity Front) in San José specifically leveraged their "unit[y]" in favor of the "armed struggle against the despotic regime implemented by Tiburcio Carías" in order to secure the Legión's, Arévalo's, and Figueres's support.[97] Ribas Montes, Sánchez, and Marcial Aguiluz received military assistance, as did another group. All agreed to fight for "the liberation of . . . the Caribbean and the Central American isthmus," but disunity plagued them.[98] Before the civil war, Carías once again promised free elections and allowed opponents more leeway to criticize him, allowing many exiles to return to their country of origin and their families.[99] Most notably, Heliodoro Valle accepted an offer to return and work for Carías's approved successor, Gálvez, who had been in San Pedro Sula during the Masacre Sampedrana. Exiles who refused to give up their fight castigated Heliodoro Valle, and the UDC expelled him "for his betrayal to democracy and union with the Honduran dictatorship."[100] Facing these divisions, the Legión's reputation would always be more powerful than its actual, brief existence.

Costa Rica Again: The December 1948 Invasion

That reputation propelled dictators to turn closer to one another. US officials hoped the region's turbulence had died down; instead, Somoza, Carías, and Trujillo complained that Figueres contributed to the communist conspiracy gripping the greater Caribbean. This frustrated international observers in light of Figueres's anticommunist credentials and the alliance between Somoza and Calderón Guardia, who had worked with Costa Rican communists. Dictators, though, merely conflated all developments under the same communist plot they blamed for the past years' disturbances. Nicaraguan officials swore it was the Arévalo–Lombardo Toledano cabal using communist "funds" to disrupt hemispheric security.[101] Carías's defenders admitted that Calderón Guardia had some communists on his side but insisted that the "activities of the communist triangle" of Guatemala, Cuba, and Venezuela allied with Costa Rica aimed to attack Nicaragua and Honduras.[102]

Calderón Guardia fought hardest to put the "communist" label on Figueres. Likely due to his new alliances, Calderón Guardia distanced himself from his past years' work with his nation's communists and claimed that Figueres was "more of a communist than" the leader of Costa Rica's communists.[103] Less than two months into his exile, Calderón Guardia met with the State Department. For the better part of an hour, he described himself as "friendly to the US" and "anticommunistic."[104] The State Department's Latin American experts were astonished that Calderón Guardia attempted to brush aside his relationships with Costa Rican communists. Furthermore, Calderón Guardia claimed that US Ambassador Nathaniel Davis, deciding not to intervene in Costa Rica's election, caused the civil war. These US officials were not impressed that the exiled Costa Rican was claiming it was "all Davis' fault for not having given the nod to Calderón" and insulting their government's attempt to stay out of another nation's affairs.[105] With US officials writing him off, Calderón Guardia relied on someone else to shape US opinion in his favor, Latin American affairs expert Sumner Welles.

Calderón Guardia and Welles had crossed paths when the former was Costa Rica's president and the latter an influential voice in the State Department. However, Welles was pushed out of office, thereby limiting his influence on US policy.[106] Seemingly unaware of what transpired, Calderón Guardia saw Welles as an ally who could spur the US government to reconsider its support of Figueres. In response, the State Department, ignoring Calderón Guardia's petitions, passed the exile's papers to Welles.[107] Frustrated that the US media and international attention focused on the Cold War in Europe while overlooking the greater Caribbean, Welles asked Calderón Guardia to share "any evidence" of external intervention in Costa Rican affairs.[108] His concern with communist activities in the region led him to also ask Sevilla Sacasa for useful evidence.[109] Before receiving any such material, though, Welles was already publishing editorials in *The Washington Post* denouncing Figueres for secret alliances with communists.[110] To prove Welles's charges, Calderón Guardia and Sevilla Sacasa sent articles from Trujillo's propagandists and Somoza's outlets.[111] Central to this lobbying was playing up anticommunism, which required changes to the historical record and claiming Calderón Guardia's administration had not worked with communists. No, he lied, the communists supported his policies on their own accord. Cognizant of the UFCO's importance among US political circles, he also presented Figueres's demands for new contracts with the Boston-based firm as a violation of international law.[112] It appeared that this lobbying worked, as Welles assured Calderón Guardia that the State Department would examine Central American matters.[113] He would even ask his friend, *The Washington Post*'s editor, to investigate everything.[114]

Bolstered by this good news, Calderón Guardia portrayed events in Costa Rica as an outgrowth of an international communist conspiracy aiming to weaken the United States in the Cold War's first years. He proclaimed that Figueres, Arévalo, and Betancourt were "being Soviet," with Figueres's "orientation [as] collectivist" while Arévalo and Betancourt led "Russophile governments." Together, the "cardinal orientation of the movement initiated in Costa Rica by Arévalo of Guatemala and Betancourt of Venezuela [was] substantively Russophile and adverse to the United States."[115] Backed by the Soviet Union, Arévalo and Lombardo Toledano spread their influence to arrest "the imperialism of the United States."[116] Thanks to this lobbying, Welles disseminated these anticommunist claims in editorials in *The Washington Post* and the *New York Herald Tribune*, some read by the State Department. However, this did not change US policy toward Costa Rica and left Calderón Guardia reliant on the dictators.

This odd coalition of anti-Figueres forces had started its plans to retake Costa Rica right after the civil war, its activities unknown to international observers. From May into August 1948, dictators shared information on their mutual opponents, paying close attention to Costa Rican matters. Antidictatorial exiles seemed to strengthen their networks of support, and all dictators distrusted Figueres's public claims about no longer working with exiles.[117] Having stayed out of the civil war, Carías joined Somoza and Trujillo in monitoring Arévalo, Figueres, and anyone associated with the Legión who planned to "overthrow the Constitutional Governments of Honduras, the Dominican Republic, and Nicaragua."[118] Carías shared his agents' intelligence on what they believed was the Legión's "plan to attack the *dictatorships of the Americas*, that is, Honduras, Nicaragua, and the Dominican Republic."[119] Believing themselves besieged by communist forces, dictators warned that the Legión's Costa Rican bases could penetrate their Central American lands while targeting Trujillo.[120] It was their responsibility, Somoza rallied, to ensure inter-American security.[121] As such, the dictators unified behind Calderón Guardia.

In September 1948, Calderón Guardia began sharing his plans with Dominican officials. Typical of those who sought Trujillo's support, Calderón Guardia stressed his anticommunist orientation and explained that a few Mexican officials were allowing his allies to purchase armaments, including two planes on the way to Puerto Cabezas, the port used for the Caracas plot.[122] Although the Nicaraguan dictator had no difficulties helping anyone opposed to Figueres and Arévalo, Somoza and Calderón Guardia hoped for Trujillo's assistance to fulfill their "military plan" to invade Guanacaste, a Costa Rican province with many citizens sympathetic to the Calderonistas. To accomplish this, Somoza wanted Calderón Guardia "to personally meet with Trujillo over some matters of importance." Circumventing commercial routes, Somoza made available a military plane at Puerto Cabezas.[123] Although arrangements were set in motion, Dominican officials in Ciudad

Trujillo had to pause them while Trujillo was away.[124] This did not mean the Dominican dictator disapproved of such plans.

Instead, Trujillo's assistance came into play inside Mexico, where Calderón Guardia's allies were purchasing the invasion's materiel. While Calderón Guardia waited in Managua, Somoza ordered his officials in Mexico City to meet with their Dominican counterparts and ask Trujillo for permission to "cooperate" with Calderón Guardia's brother, Francisco "Paco."[125] Soon after, Trujillo ordered his officials in Mexico City to work with Paco and purchase armaments.[126] Immediately, the Dominican attaché called Paco on the telephone to arrange a meeting the very next day, September 26. That morning, the attaché "made the offer of the cooperation" to Paco. They also agreed that Paco should produce a "memorandum" detailing "of what this cooperation w[ould] consist." The next day, he complied.[127] Although quite brief, his memorandum outlined the typical anticommunist point that Figueres, Arévalo, Betancourt, and Prío were creating "the Socialist Republics of the Caribbean." To this end, Figueres and Arévalo had "international agreements" to "wage war throughout Central America and the Dominican Republic." Calderón Guardia had the support of other governments, influential Mexican officials, and Welles in the United States to lead a movement into Costa Rica; the Calderonistas were "practically ready," thanks to their recent purchases of armaments, but lacked the money, "thirty thousand dollars," for a plane and transportation. This would be well worth the "investment," Paco promised, because the armaments themselves were worth three times this cost. As a further incentive, he promised that Calderonistas would pay back this expense upon retaking their nation and accessing their financial assets.[128]

Trujillo's "cooperation" proceeded. In early October, Dominican officials asked Paco to travel to Ciudad Trujillo, which had been Calderón Guardia's suggestion in early September.[129] Because he could not leave Mexico while purchasing weapons and networking with his allies, Paco suggested sending an envoy.[130] Over the next days, he met with Dominican officials in Mexico City.[131] In mid-October, he put forward the name of a suitable compatriot to network between Calderonistas and Dominican officials.[132] When Somoza asked to arrange the requisite trip from Mexico City to Ciudad Trujillo, Dominican officials shut down the proposal because Trujillo "had decided not to pay favorable attention to this proposition."[133] It appears that Dominican officials chose, in light of Paco's work in Mexico City and the regional disturbances, to avoid having notable Costa Rican exiles travel to the Dominican Republic, for any publicity or diplomatic scandal could jeopardize their arms purchases. Furthermore, the Cuban ambassador in San José, who also traveled to Tegucigalpa to investigate matters, reported Calderón Guardia's "obtaining support" and receiving "large sums of money" for their activities.[134] Guatemalan agents deployed to Nicaragua to surveil Somoza's activities in Puerto Cabezas spent "three months" following "evidence that materiel had been sent by boat" from the Dominican Republic.[135] Unlike earlier shipments, any Dominican materiel sent to Puerto Cabezas was not intended for Venezuela, since the country had suffered a change of government following a military coup weeks before. Between Somoza's making available Puerto Cabezas for Calderonistas, Dominican assistance in Mexico, and Dominican shipments to Puerto Cabezas, Trujillo joined Somoza in sponsoring Calderón Guardia's efforts and becoming a patron of the December 1948 invasion of Costa Rica.

This brief December 1948 invasion failed. On December 10, Calderonistas crossed from Nicaragua into Guanacaste, as Calderón Guardia and Somoza planned. Upon learning of the invasion, Figueres requested the intervention of the newly formed Organization of American States (OAS) and the United States.[136] Two days after the invasion started, the US ambassador in Managua discouraged Somoza from supporting the conflict.[137] The invading forces retreated, and the OAS convened a council of Latin American officials to visit San José and investigate what it saw as a Costa Rica–Nicaragua dispute.[138] As with the attempt at air-bombing Caracas, Somoza took the blame for the entire affair while Trujillo avoided any attention. Despite the many rumors about the Dominican dictator's involvement, US officials never obtained any actionable intelligence.

Preparing for More War

As 1948 came to an end, US officials were overwhelmed at the intense rivalries and tensions dominating the greater Caribbean. After the civil war, Somoza boasted to US officials that he entered into an anticommunist alliance with Carías, which US officials interpreted as just another of the dictator's neverending complaints about regional intrigues against him.[139] Carías's officials bombarded the US government with similar warnings.[140] As the year progressed, the seemingly endless series of conflicts weighed heavily on US officials. The State Department's heads came to agree with the dictators that the Legión was "of course a danger to the peace of this part of the world."[141] Arévalo's central role in intervening in Costa Rica and backing the Legión added further frustration. In early 1948, the US ambassador in Guatemala City commented to his British counterpart on his "becoming uneasy at recent recrudescences of 'antigringoism.'"[142] Months later, Arévalo's antidictatorial adventurism had become a "serious concern."[143]

US officials' desire for regional stability stood in stark contrast to antidictatorial leaders' plans. Cardoza y Aragón characterized the tumult of 1948 as a cataclysmic shift for the greater Caribbean.[144] For Jiménes Grullón, the year's developments were positive and offered the best chance to spread democracy throughout the Caribbean Basin. He believed Carías's successor, Gálvez, would at least steer the country away from the dictator's policies and maybe even work alongside Arévalo and Figueres, leaving Somoza "completely isolated" and weakening Trujillo.[145] Some may have shared this optimism, but Ornes believed that the year was concluding in a "war of nerves," with Arévalo, Betancourt, Figueres, and Cuba's Auténticos standing off against Trujillo, Somoza, Gálvez, and Carías, who would never completely relinquish his control.[146] Arévalo's government was at the center of this "war." At the end of 1947, Cotu had warned Arévalo of what they were facing. "Trujillo will make all possible effort," he warned the Guatemalan president, "to interfere, to help the other dictators." Well versed in the dictator's foreign policies, Cotu outlined, "[Trujillo] has a wide vision of the problem, an accurate vision; he knows that in defending the other dictators, fighting the revolutionary governments, he is defending his own regime. Therefore, the entire revolutionary undertaking that bears such a name in Central America is, and *has to be* from its launch, a war against Trujillo."[147]

Arévalo understood this "war" with the dictators but believed 1948 ended in his favor. In October, he boasted of such matters to Spanish Republican representative Luis Nicolau d'Olwer. He was "hopeful in the antidictatorial position" of Prío, "satisfied with Costa Rica" under Figueres, and prepared if "one of the Central American dictatorships" were to launch an attack against his allies. In light of the US government's intervention in the civil war, d'Olwer interjected, "surely the United States w[ould] not permit it." Arévalo responded that, "obviously, if the conflict were lengthy, [the US government] would make the movement end, but if it were to triumph in 3 days, [the US government] would accept it as fait accompli." "In the jocular tone in which the President sometimes speaks of matters very serious," d'Olwer recounted how Arévalo remarked, "'There is no war in Central America because we have no arms, but even if it is with machetes the conflict will explode.'" Now, Arévalo "hope[d] that between Guatemala, Cuba, and Venezuela he will be able to form a democratic front that will succeed in eliminating the dictatorships of the Caribbean and Central America."[148]

Arévalo agreed with Cotu's prediction that this "war" or "conflict" would envelop the region, but he failed to grasp how true Cotu's warning was. The Cayo Confites expedition, the Caracas plot, and the Costa Rican Civil War had set the foundation for the dictators to organize a network aimed at winning this war and destroying the antidictatorial threat. What Arévalo and his allies did not foresee was that subsequent events would undermine his democratic alliance while the dictators would not be alone in waging a war against Arévalo's government and the Guatemalan Revolution.

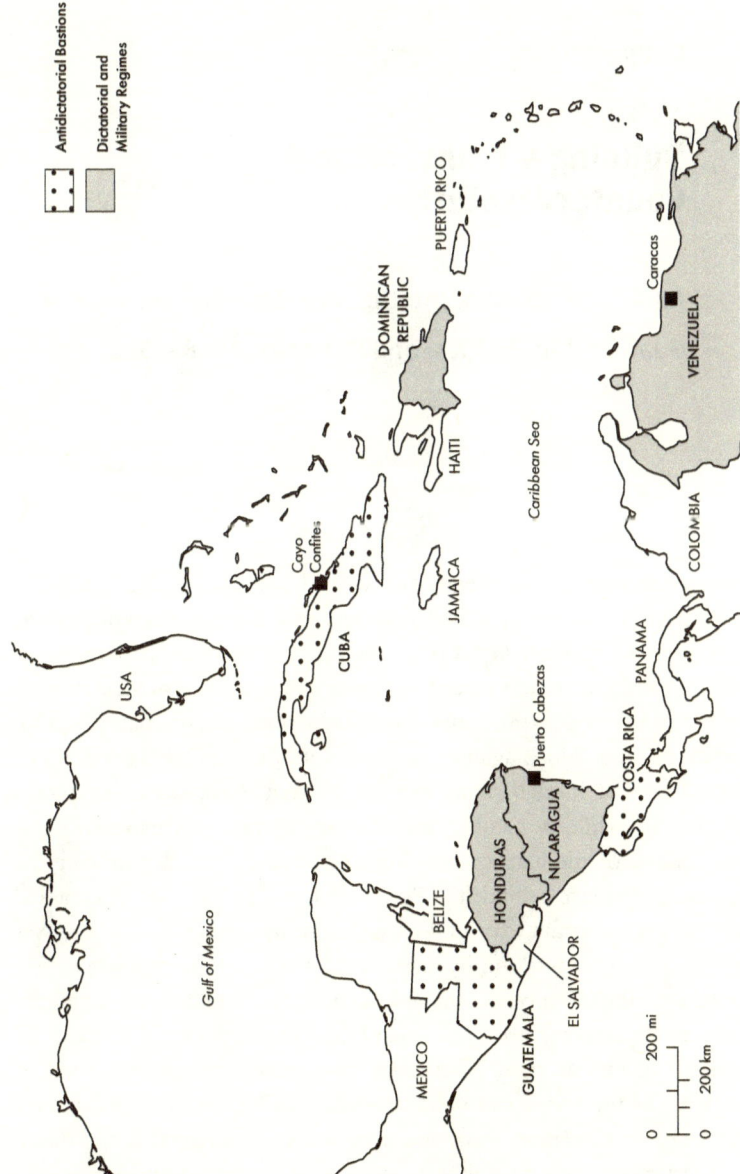

Figure 3. Map of Caribbean Basin, 1948

Chapter 5

Building a Transnational Counterrevolution

An Anticommunist Intelligence-Sharing Network, Guatemalan Politics, and Bananas, 1948–1950

In early November 1950, Betancourt wrote his friend Luis Muñoz Marín, the governor of Puerto Rico. Two years earlier, a military coup ousted the AD government and installed a junta that curtailed democratic freedoms, imprisoned dissidents, and forced opponents into exile. Now, Betancourt vented that US and Latin American governments at international venues operated as a "block against Russia and its satellites" and condemned "the violations of human rights that the Eastern European governments perpetrate[d]" while remaining silent about Venezuelan matters. These "states, leaders of the hemispheric front," had no qualms denouncing the atrocities taking place behind "the European Iron Curtain," yet when asked about "the Iron Curtain existing in the [Western] hemisphere," there was only "the most cautious and hypocritical of silences." He was most disillusioned with the US government and its "politics of indifference, from the country that claims for itself the leading role in the universal crusade for the validity of human rights" but turns away from "the daily violation of these rights by the hemisphere's dictatorships." With the US government's ambivalence on this issue, "various democratic governments" found themselves succumbing to this Caribbean Iron Curtain, a "mano dura" (iron fist) of regimes that wielded their "ostentatious and spectacular anticommunist affiliation" while destroying the very "political forces" that were "authentically democratic."¹

In the aftermath of Cayo Confites and events in Costa Rica, dictators expanded their regional alliance. Profiting from Venezuela's military coup, their informal intelligence sharing allowed officials to cooperate when analyzing and financing reactionaries' plots against Arévalo's government. Into the early 1950s, reactionaries cultivated international support and sabotaged Guatemalan politics. Simultaneously, these efforts received indirect support. Unable to control the US State Department or the White House, the UFCO unleashed a lobbying blitz that galvanized Congress's criticism of Guatemalan affairs. For its part, the British government cautiously initiated an arms embargo while one of its intelligence officers became familiar with antigovernment organizations.

Against the Guatemala-Costa Rica-Cuba Axis: A Network of Dictators and Reactionaries

Sparked by events in 1947 and 1948, the Caribbean regimes escalated their networking. A key development was the November 1948 Venezuelan military coup when military officers ousted the AD government and installed a junta that gradually consolidated under Lieutenant Colonel Marcos Pérez Jiménez's repressive leadership. Asked about their decision to end the nation's nascent democracy, the junta's leaders cited dissatisfaction with domestic and foreign issues, including Betancourt's support for antidictatorial exiles.² Unsurprisingly, dictators embraced the new regime as an anticommunist ally, for they shared common enemies as Betancourt and AD-in-exile joined Dominican, Nicaraguan, and Honduran exiles.³ Evident in what little correspondence remains from these tumultuous years, Betancourt, Bosch, and others networked thanks to the material support of like-minded colleagues.⁴ Though contentious political and personal issues remained, exiles were committed to their shared vision of a democratic Caribbean Basin free of dictatorial and military regimes.⁵

This transnational nature galvanized the regimes' fears and collaboration.⁶ Despite the Legión's disbandment, officials summoned its name as a descriptor for a motley group of exiles targeting any regime at any point, proof of a boundless threat. Venezuelan officials could not track only AD-in-exile who met with various Caribbean Basin exiles.⁷ Doing due diligence, Nicaraguan and Dominican officials with intelligence on a Legión plan against the Venezuelan junta sent it along.⁸ Venezuelan officials likewise had to share reports regarding a possible attack by Betancourt and the Legión because it was unclear whether the intended target was their regime or Trujillo's due to exiles' transnational relationships. Of course, Dominican officials then forwarded this material to Nicaraguan officials for the exact same reason.⁹ When provided these reports, US officials failed to confirm their veracity or identify Caribbean Basin regimes' cooperation.¹⁰ In contrast, the regimes subsumed all opponents into the sinister Legión that they claimed sought to replace them with Soviet-inspired communism.¹¹

As a result, regimes deployed their intelligence sharing to evaluate and propel multiple plots against Arévalo's government, one of the exiles' bases of support.¹² Myriad reactionaries requested assistance, but officials networked to determine the plots most likely to succeed, beginning with one from veteran conspirators Coronado Lira and Salazar. In March 1948, Somoza summoned the former and offered him "men, money, and arms" to "get busy and start a revolution in Guatemala as soon as possible."¹³ Coronado Lira then traveled to the Dominican Republic and received Trujillo's support before joining Salazar in San Salvador.¹⁴ While the two organized, Carías's officials ordered another reactionary, Colonel Carlos Humberto Ceballos, to assist, his military credentials a resource to appeal to Guatemalan military leaders who determined a coup's success. However, infighting splintered the project after Ceballos criticized his fellow reactionaries and repeated rumors that Carías was not invested in a shared anticommunist defense, a Dominican attaché scolding him that "the threat from Guatemala [was] a mutual issue for the three" dictators.¹⁵

Unlike Ceballos, the next reactionary, Melgar of the CUEG, was quite cognizant of the regimes' alliances. In September 1948, he went to the Dominican Embassy in Mexico City to deliver a memorandum, claiming, "the Republics of Central America and the Caribbean have a duty to fight at all cost in order that in Guatemala, Cuba, and Venezuela there exist governments that prepare the people" to take up an anticommunist role in the Cold War. Due to this common goal, Melgar petitioned Trujillo to lobby Carías for an invasion of Esquipulas during the upcoming January 1949 religious pilgrimage. Backed by Colonel José Enrique Ardón Fernández's military contacts and José Calderón Salazar's Catholic prestige, Melgar needed only Carías's permission for the "necessary storage of the armaments" and "the hospitality and guarantees to the military leaders that must move from Honduras to Guatemala at the appointed time."¹⁶ Tapping into their transnational alliance, Trujillo shared Melgar's proposal with Somoza, who agreed to lobby Carías.¹⁷

Though Melgar's invasion never took off, possibly due to regional issues in late 1948, the regimes' networking continued. In September 1949 in Puebla, Mexico, General Roderico Anzueto asked for Trujillo's assistance in a plot, and the dictator again asked for his allies' input. Trujillo ordered Dominican Ambassador Joaquín Balaguer, who was already coordinating Dominican intelligence work in Mexico City, to obtain the Nicaraguan ambassador's opinion.[18] Together, the two examined Anzueto's proposal of ten thousand dollars to "produce" a popular uprising and overthrow Arévalo's government. Based on this presentation, both ambassadors sent positive reports to their respective dictators.[19] Nevertheless, Anzueto disappointed his cheerleaders by refusing to help the Nicaraguan ambassador who took point on making arrangements. Frustrated, Balaguer asked for the Honduran ambassador's advice, who warned that Anzueto had already "wasted" Carías's funds. Casting aside Anzueto, the ambassadors turned to another reactionary, Colonel Arturo Ramírez, who required one hundred thousand dollars.[20] Over the next weeks, Balaguer met with his fellow ambassadors as well as the chief of staff for the Salvadoran Army, Colonel Marco Antonio Molina, who championed Ramírez as the "true representative of the military class of Guatemala."[21] As Salvadoran officials joined the regimes' intelligence-sharing network to identify the reactionary best able to launch a coup with the Guatemalan military's support, their attention turned to the country's 1950 presidential election.

Foreign Influence in Guatemalan Politics: The 1950 Election and Base Militar Uprising

As they had over the previous years, the regimes and reactionaries' efforts outside Guatemala corroded politics inside the country. On the eve of the 1950 presidential election, their network remained active as ever while receiving reactionaries' petitions. Among the petitioners was an unknown Guatemalan military officer, Colonel Carlos Castillo Armas, preparing his own military uprising that would catapult him into regional fame. As conservatives organized political parties at the state and national level, they remained unaware that some of their leaders happened to be those requesting and receiving the regimes' financial support for the abortive, failed conspiracies behind the constitutional suspensions and political tensions driving local grievances. Unknown to many inside Guatemala, these outside forces propelled the central issues at the heart of the nation's 1950 election and Base Militar uprising.

One of the high-ranking soldiers loyal to Colonel Francisco Arana, Castillo Armas did not participate in Arana's failed 1949 coup or his followers' subsequent uprising, though he was arrested and released after some weeks.²² In mid-January 1950, Castillo Armas confided to a CIA source his belief "that the only way to change the present government in Guatemala was by means of an armed coup." Despite what he described as "his reputation for sincerity and honesty" among Guatemala's military commanders and alliances with "men on the outside of the army," he lacked the "arms" to realize this ambition and "was, therefore, thinking of contacting Somoza or Trujillo." Incorrectly believing that other reactionaries "had met with no success," he claimed that those who petitioned the dictators "had no standing or power in Guatemala and that this must have been known to Somoza and Trujillo" when rejecting such proposals. Though failing to grasp the extent of the regimes' network, Castillo Armas did know that there existed a potent source of foreign support, and he believed that he fit the criteria with "a good chance of success in getting arms from Somoza or Trujillo."²³

He was wrong. Days after divulging his aspirations, Castillo Armas secured a meeting with the network's officials in San Salvador. Initially, he expected his intended audience to be Somoza, for whom he prepared a list detailing the materials required for his plot, but the dictator believed that the "international situation" was an inopportune time for a meeting. This left the responsibility for evaluating Castillo Armas's petition to Somoza's ambassador, the Dominican chargé d'affaires, and Salvadoran Chief of Staff Molina. As with Ramírez's plot a few months prior, they together critically examined Castillo Armas's petition and rejected its "excessive" cost of almost a million dollars. They also disputed his claims of national influence since he could not call upon any powerful "civilians" or "military support."²⁴ Over the next months, he continued organizing his scheme, likely with Somoza's blessing.²⁵ At this point in time, though, most members of the regimes' intelligence-sharing network did not look favorably upon Castillo Armas.

While Castillo Armas schemed, observers watched the preparations surrounding Guatemala's November 1950 presidential election. Arévalo and the nation's revolutionary parties, including the PAR and PRN, backed Jacobo Árbenz.²⁶ Plenty of local groups opposed Árbenz, especially due to the increasingly public presence of Guatemalan communists José Manuel Fortuny and Víctor Manuel Gutiérrez. Putting up candidates in various districts, opposition parties' leaflets claimed Árbenz would follow Fortuny and Gutiérrez to "hand Guatemala over to Russia."²⁷ Conservatives denounced Arévalo for, on the "orders emanating from the Red Zone of Moscow," allowing a foreign ideology, "international communism," to "infiltrat[e]" the nation.[28] Though their stance against external influences was genuine, foreign sources were actually boosting their local activism.

The leading opposition candidate was Ydígoras Fuentes, who had approached Dominican officials about a coup in 1947 and received from Trujillo at least thirty-five thousand dollars. In July 1949, Ydígoras Fuentes again solicited the dictator's help to reshape Guatemalan politics, not through an uprising but through the 1950 election. If elected, Ydígoras Fuentes would, first, reestablish diplomatic relations with the Dominican Republic and, second, "pay back every last centavo of the loans received" from Trujillo, "plus interest." More important than reimbursing the dictator, he would maintain "international order" and, built upon their "anticommunist bonds," prove his "gratitude" to his Dominican patron.[29] It is unclear if any of his political allies inside Guatemala knew of such agreements. Backing Ydígoras Fuentes's candidacy were multiple political parties, including the Partido de Unión Democrática (Democratic Union Party), Juventud Nacionalista (Nationalist Youth), the Partido Unificación Anticomunista (Anticommunist Unification Party, PUA), and Reconciliación Democrática Nacional (National Democratic Reconciliation, Redención).[30] Across the country, these parties had committees holding their candidate up as a "paladin of public liberties" while unaware of his international assistance.[31]

Neither did they know that, in the midst of the election, Ydígoras Fuentes sent his representatives to request more support from the region's regimes. In April 1950, reactionaries including Pinillos were in Tegucigalpa visiting various legations and embassies.[32] Acting as Ydígoras Fuentes's messengers, they asked dictators to "support, if possible, [Ydígoras Fuentes's] presidential aspirations." Additionally, they hoped for "facilities to prepare and launch from Honduran territory a revolutionary movement against the ruling regime in Guatemala" if Ydígoras Fuentes were to win the election but be denied office. Though empathetic, Honduran officials conditioned their assistance "on the attitude that the Yankee Government and the United Fruit Co[mpany] assume on the subject."[33] Serendipitously, Pinillos began sharing with Caribbean Basin officials a memorandum asserting that the US government did back Ydígoras Fuentes against Arévalo and the "international communists" following "the orders of Russia."[34]

Conservatives were left in the dark not only about their candidate's arrangements with Caribbean Basin regimes but also that their grievances originated in great part with those leading their political parties. As the government was never able to provide sufficient evidence that reactionaries obtained international support for their schemes, disenchanted Guatemalans turned to Juventud Nacionalista, the PUA, or Redención to denounce constitutional suspensions and protest what they believed were authorities' "continuist ambitions" to suffocate legitimate political opposition. In mass petitions, Juventud Nacionalista demanded a government free of the "dangerous demagogic practices" and "constant restriction on the use of [their] constitutional guarantees."[35] Tragically, their frustrations led them to those responsible, for those behind some of those abortive uprisings and coups led the opposition parties. At the head of Redención were Luis Coronado Lira, the party's first vice president, and Carlos Salazar Jr., the party's president and secretary general. Thus, conservatives were doing more than distributing handouts that compared exiled Guatemalans to unfairly persecuted political prisoners.[36] Their campaigns inadvertently capitalized off Coronado Lira's and Salazar's actions and resources, including money received from the region's dictators to produce handouts, leaflets, and pamphlets.[37]

Nowhere was reactionaries' success in blurring together legitimate and illegitimate activities more apparent than when Arévalo's government repressed the opposition parties' campaigns. Following a skirmish between the Guardia Civil and members of the opposition, Guatemalan officials blamed "a political minority" for "subversive expression and actions" going back to the Revolution's onset and instituted a suspension of constitutional liberties in the middle of July.[38] Conservatives' ire was further incensed when days later the Junta Nacional Electoral (National Electoral Board) declared Redención's and the PUA's electoral registrations invalid. Throughout the election, Salazar pushed back on public claims that the opposition party was "terrorist."[39] All along, he warned his party's members that authorities were conspiring to sabotage the citizens' "sacred constitutional rights."[40] Upon being declared illegal, Salazar and Coronado Lira could now issue a manifesto excoriating what they termed a "Muscovite barbarity" to ensure the Arévalo government's "continuismo." Rather than restraining the PAR and those "perfectly identified with the international communist party," the board had targeted the "political rights" and "constitutional rights" of the nation's "independent parties fighting communism."[41] As usual, Guatemalan officials failed to produce sufficient proof of Ydígoras Fuentes's, Salazar's, or Coronado Lira's relationships with Caribbean Basin regimes. Remaining silent about their complicity, these reactionaries portrayed themselves as political martyrs and gave voice to those who feared Arévalo's government was silencing legitimate political opposition. Reactionaries tapped into the frustrations their regional networking unleashed, while regimes' officials and newspapers republished anti-Arévalo and anti-Árbenz manifestos.[42]

As it had over the past half dozen years, this cycle sent into exile new reactionaries, most notably the PUA's José Luis Arenas. In contrast to Redención's leaders, who had networked with regimes since the mid-1940s, Arenas only appears to have done so during the 1950 election. Despite condemning Arévalo's government as beholden to the foreign ideology of communism, Arenas traveled the greater Caribbean for his own international support, justifying his transnational anticommunist alliances as a necessary weapon to retake his nation of origin.[43] By September, Arenas joined Mexican anticommunists, including Luis Morones and Jorge Prieto Laurens of the Frente Popular Anticomunista de México (Mexican Anticommunist Front, FPAM).[44] Agreeing that Lombardo Toledano and Soviet agents were "converting [Guatemala] into a . . . Russian beach on the American continent," Arenas and the FPAM agreed to organize an international congress "with the goal of uniting the anticommunist patriots for [their shared] ideals, that is, America's traditional freedom, continental solidarity, and the crystallization of the Western Hemisphere's defense."[45] Afterward, Arenas requested a meeting with Trujillo to "have an exchange of ideas regarding a continental anticommunist campaign." While waiting, he traveled to the United States.[46] By early November, Arenas returned to Central America, where he impressed Carías and received permission to travel to the Dominican Republic.[47]

Against this backdrop, Castillo Armas launched his Base Militar attack on November 5, 1950, in order to spur a military uprising. As Gleijeses has confirmed, Castillo Armas had approached Ydígoras Fuentes to collaborate, but the latter maintained the same position shared with Honduran and Dominican officials: he would support such action only after the election.[48] However, Castillo Armas's uprising did receive other reactionaries' support, including Arenas and Arturo Ramírez. Joined by Guillermo Dávila Córdova and Ardón, Castillo Armas, Arenas, and Ramírez announced the Consejo Supremo del Movimiento Revolucionario Anticomunista (Supreme Council of the Revolutionary Anticommunist Movement).[49] Castillo Armas and Arenas may have been the most recent reactionaries to build relationships with Caribbean Basin regimes, but Ramírez was an experienced veteran while Ardón supported Melgar's abortive 1948 invasion. Of course, the council ignored such matters, issuing manifestos calling for Guatemala's civilians and military to "take up arms to save the country from the hands of COMMUNISM that ha[d] taken root in Guatemala under the domination of arevalismo."[50]

Representative of reactionaries' networking, the council was equally representative of its members' failure to achieve their goals. The Base Militar attack failed, the Guatemalan military refused to turn on its government, and Ydígoras Fuentes handily lost to Árbenz. Castillo Armas went into exile after bribing his way out of prison, joining Ydígoras Fuentes, Ramírez, and others abroad. These schemes during 1950 may not have achieved the desired goals, but they contributed to the tense political situation in Guatemala. By February 1951, Arenas was arranging meetings in Honduras, securing agreements with Somoza, and coordinating with other reactionaries in El Salvador.[51] As Árbenz entered the presidency, the regimes' network continued patronizing reactionaries' plots to bring the Revolution's end.

Convincing the Legislature: The United Fruit Company's Congressional Lobbying

Another force was in motion during these events. In early 1949, a Dominican official reported that the UFCO was spending a million dollars to oust Arévalo, including a plot involving the Nicaraguan ambassador in Tegucigalpa.[52] This coincided with claims that Ramírez received the corporation's support. During the election, observers noted that the UFCO feared Árbenz would further his predecessor's work against the company, possibly forcing its exit.[53] Such rumors held at least a grain of truth, as the UFCO vociferously opposed labor strikes as well as the Guatemalan Congress's decision to reconsider the company's decade-old contracts.[54] The election was important enough that the UFCO sent a lobbyist to Guatemala, who lamented to a colleague, "We lost to the Commies."[55] With only scattered reports regarding the links between the corporation, regimes, and reactionaries, it is difficult to determine precisely how such efforts overlapped. Despite not having materials to definitively show the corporation's involvement to shape Guatemalan politics in financing plots or influencing the presidential election, sufficient evidence demonstrates that the UFCO sought to achieve its goal by influencing politics in another country, the United States.

In the United States, the UFCO was plenty experienced in public relations. After the Second World War, its staff worked with Edward Bernays, the founder of modern public relations, to publish pamphlets and influence "group leaders and opinion molders."[56] Advertiser Jean Wade Rindlaub crafted the Chiquita Banana cartoon mascot that public relations firm Batten, Barton, Durstine & Osborn (BBDO) popularized through dolls, banana-based recipes, and cannon towel giveaways.⁵⁷ Through popular literature and recipe books, the UFCO put front and center bananas' dietary benefits and the corporation's role in making the food accessible to the US consumer.⁵⁸ While these campaigns cemented the UFCO's image in US culture, events in Guatemala following the 1947 Labor Code took the corporation aback, and executives sought to do more than merely republish glowing articles about their wartime contributions, archaeological ventures, or public health campaigns.⁵⁹

At first, the UFCO employed this public relations apparatus to make Guatemala a topic in US politics, trying to tap into the growing anticommunist fears sweeping the United States during the Cold War's early years. BBDO assisted multiple US-based conservative causes, so its partner Bruce Barton reached out to David Lawrence, the conservative journalist and *U.S. News & World Report* publisher.⁶⁰ He suggested that Lawrence discuss US policies in Latin America such as the Point IV program, a US assistance program for Latin America to develop the hemisphere's economies and technical capabilities while deterring communism's inroads, but Lawrence was hesitant to take up a story without a suitable audience.⁶¹ Pivoting, Barton tried to sell the issue to conservative journalist George Sokolsky.⁶² He wanted to present the UFCO to the US public as a crucial Cold War ally, outlining in a memorandum, "Nearly every natural product for which we are presently dependent on the Orient is growing or can be grown at our own front door, in the countries of Central America." The UFCO was essential in developing abaca and hemp for the US Navy, and Barton described the corporation's production of rubber, quinine, and coconut oil as "a 'living' stockpile [which] does not deteriorate, but rather appreciates in value."⁶³ However, nothing came from these efforts. Outside of a handful of stories, the US public overlooked Guatemala and most Latin American affairs while focused on Europe and China.

Instead, it was the UFCO's congressional lobbying campaign that successfully raised the Guatemala issue. Because the corporation refused to divulge its activities at the time, historians have believed UFCO lobbyists were marginal actors waiting for the United States to interpret Guatemalan nationalism as communism in the early 1950s.⁶⁴ However, the UFCO did not bide its time. Instead, the company employed its agents, notably Thomas "the Cork" Corcoran, to lobby Congress in order to turn the US government against the Revolution. Having served the Roosevelt administration, Corcoran was close to prominent US officials. He was also involved in US-based conservative causes, such as the Free China movement.⁶⁵ These qualities made him an adept lobbyist to help the UFCO put its anticommunist message before Congress. In early 1947, he joined UFCO President Samuel Zemurray, newly hired lobbyist and former senator Robert La Follette Jr., and UFCO officials traveling Central America.⁶⁶ Hired in 1948, Corcoran immediately returned to the region to learn about the Labor Code.⁶⁷ Thanks to his Free China work, he kept the UFCO aware of the schedules of periodicals such as *Reader's Digest* and journalists with Hearst Press.⁶⁸ While amplifying his colleagues' efforts, Corcoran excelled at networking with US congresspersons.

At first glance, Corcoran's work appeared daunting, for no congressperson brought up Guatemala before 1949. Many were familiar with the UFCO due to its large presence in Latin America. When preparing to travel through Central America, Senator Bourke Hickenlooper (R-IA) relied on the corporation, with La Follette offering to help with arrangements while Hickenlooper socialized with UFCO and IRCA officials, including Taillon.⁶⁹ Still, Hickenlooper only received positive reports on US-Guatemalan relations.⁷⁰

To change this, Corcoran and his fellow lobbyists started a campaign directed at prominent senators and representatives. This built on the UFCO's established connections, as when Corcoran sent materials to Claude Pepper, the Democratic senator of Florida, a state whose ports the company used.⁷¹ Likewise, Senator Lister Hill (D-AL) made clear that those "in Alabama like the United Fruit Company" and "any help to the Company" would be "gratifying."⁷² He networked with Representative John McCormack (D-MA), a reliable ally of the Boston-based company.⁷³ Their shared Catholic faith, work with New York Cardinal Francis Spellman and anticommunist Catholic leaders, and opposition to Chinese communism facilitated their collaboration.⁷⁴ With these congressional allies, Corcoran hoped to reshape US policy. "Unless the State Department gets firm about it," he complained to McCormack in 1949, "Guatemala will Communize the whole of Central America."⁷⁵

Representative Mike Mansfield (D-MO) epitomized what initially seemed to be UFCO lobbyists' uphill battle. In 1948, Mansfield joined Representative Donald L. Jackson (R-CA) in Colombia for the Ninth International Conference of American States when US Secretary of State George Marshall asked the two congresspersons to travel through Central America for an assessment after the Costa Rican Civil War.⁷⁶ By mid-April, Mansfield reported productive meetings with Figueres, who criticized some of the UFCO's "evils," acknowledged the corporation's "good," and sought a balance between private investments and national sovereignty. This positive impression continued in Guatemala. There, Mansfield pushed back against some US citizens' insistence that Arévalo was "too socialist." He respected Arévalo's "right ideas" and deemed critics of the Guatemalan president "wrong."[77] This view shaped Mansfield and Jackson's resulting report for the House Committee on Foreign Affairs. They warned that Latin Americans needed "to balance their watchfulness against Communist penetration" against the repetitive "use of the Communist tag to label one's enemies" and disputed anticommunist charges against Figueres without mentioning any conflicts with Arévalo.[78] Lobbying Congress, the UFCO's agents cultivated a relationship with Mansfield. Upon receiving a copy of Jackson and Mansfield's report, UFCO President Thomas Cabot reached out. Cabot took "one slight exception" to the report, a single paragraph where the congresspersons noted how "plantation workers" had to endure "the critically low standard of living found in all too many of the Latin American republics." This observation collided directly with the UFCO's claims that their workers enjoyed higher pay than other farmers or workers, so Cabot invited Mansfield to visit UFCO's Costa Rican plantations and "fully appreciate the true difference in favor of the banana worker." Within weeks, Mansfield took up Cabot's offer.[79]

Journalist Edward Tomlinson's efforts complemented Cabot's. In articles in *Reader's Digest* and prominent US newspapers, Tomlinson minimized any disruption of hemispheric solidarity and US leadership as a byproduct of international communism. "Stalin," the journalist alleged, wanted "to dominate Latin America" in order to bring down his real "target," the United States. The Costa Rican Civil War and labor activism were "the beginning of the Communist drive for America."[80] He wrote glowingly on the UFCO and networked with company officials, seeing the corporation's work in Latin America as emblematic of US investments, which the Soviet Union and communism sought to "destroy."[81] Tomlinson agreed with company officials that international communism manipulated extreme nationalism by blaming US-based companies for poor working conditions and political upheavals, so the company subsidized his ventures.[82]

This provided the opening for UFCO agents to change Mansfield's mind about Guatemala. When no congressperson was questioning US-Guatemalan relations, Tomlinson sent his articles from *The Washington Star* to Mansfield.[83] Simultaneously, Corcoran sent Mansfield a memorandum on Point IV, complaining that Latin American countries refused to ensure the "fair and equal treatment of foreign investment." Alongside Argentina and

Colombia, Corcoran argued, Guatemala with its Labor Code was "one of the most flagrant cases of unfair and discriminatory treatments of American interests." "Under influence which is directly traceable to Communist action," the Code, "ostensibly written for the benefit of the laboring class, ha[d] been so worded and administered as to discriminate only against the largest American enterprise in the country."[84] Characterizing his reports as "nothing more" than "background information," Corcoran had "given identical memorandums to several people who might be interested in the Central American situation."[85]

This lobbying drove the first congressional speeches on US-Guatemalan affairs in 1949. On February 14, Senator Henry Cabot Lodge Jr. (R-MA) spoke first, his entire speech lifting liberally from Corcoran's UFCO memorandum on Point IV. He alleged that the "new code, supposedly written for the benefit of everyday citizens, has been devised and is interpreted so as actually to discriminate solely against the most extensively invested American enterprise in that country." He even stated all matters were due to "actions, which, I am informed, can be directly traced to Communist influences."[86] Three days later in the Senate, Pepper denounced the Labor Code, saying, "For instance, President Arévalo himself advised the United States Ambassador, so I am informed, that a certain law was obviously intentionally discriminatory against this American company, and that he, the President, thought it was a machine gun aimed at the head of this American company, and that he, the President, agreed that the discrimination should be removed, and that he would do everything possible to effect its removal."[87] As Pepper finished, Hill jumped in to reinforce Pepper's points, repeating Barton's memorandum to Sokolsky about the UFCO's developing abaca, hemp, rubber, and more for "a living, growing stockpile, so as to free us from our dependence upon the Far East for these strategic products."[88]

On February 21 in the House, McCormack spoke on the Labor Code, no one noticing that he used the exact same words as Pepper had four days earlier in the Senate: "President Arévalo, I understand, *himself advised the United States ambassador* that the *law was obviously intentionally discriminatory*; that *he, the President, thought it was a machine gun aimed at the head* of the United Fruit Co., and that *he, the President, agreed that the discrimination should be removed*, and that *he would do everything possible to effect its removal*."[89] Three days later, Representative Christian A. Herter (R-MA) elaborated on these complaints to blame Guatemalan labor unions for delaying banana shipments and Arévalo's government for "discriminatory influence . . . against responsible American capital."[90] Right after, Mansfield added to

McCormack's observations. As had Lodge in the Senate, Mansfield used the UFCO's Point IV memorandum, saying the Labor Code, "ostensibly written for the benefit of the laboring class, ha[d] been so worded and administered as to discriminate against the largest American enterprise in the country." Though he left out Corcoran's claims about "Communist action," Mansfield repeated verbatim the corporation's description of the Labor Code as "not only unfair but discriminatory."[91] All six speeches in Congress in 1949 about Guatemala occurred in the same month, with at least five delivered by congresspersons lobbied by UFCO agents and deriving directly from the company's materials.

Into the early 1950s, the UFCO's congressional allies continued receiving and repeating lobbyists' materials. Corcoran and La Follette expanded their reach, networking with additional congresspersons, including Senator Everett Dirksen (R-IL).[92] Mansfield, McCormack, and others remained in contact with UFCO officials and agents.[93] Tragically for the historical record, many of their discussions were off the books, leaving behind convoluted and unclear messages. In March 1949, Corcoran sent Mansfield materials, writing, "The enclosure is the answer to a letter which you will receive tomorrow morning which has been written to you for the record which the writer has shown to us and to which he does not expect you to respond." Indeed, Corcoran admitted, this was quite an unwieldy, unhelpful description of the situation, so he would soon call Mansfield.[94] Joined by Senator Alexander Wiley (R-WI), McCormack remained the most vocal collaborator. In early 1950, he sent a speech draft to Corcoran, which after editing was delivered in Congress on April 3.[95] Although its work with allies in the greater Caribbean remains unclear and did little to silence Guatemalan nationalism or labor activism, the UFCO did secure the assistance of one of the branches of the US government.

The British Choose Caution

Meanwhile, British officials' views of Arévalo and the Guatemalan Revolution continued conflating anticolonialism and communism. In mid-1948, the British minister in Guatemala City, William Gallienne, admitted that Arévalo was not "a real communist" but "would probably not mind if his country came under Soviet domination as long as he could achieve his ambitions of gaining British Honduras and leading a Central American union."[96] Hoping to prove this predetermined theory that an anticolonialist would sacrifice his country's sovereignty, British officials requested any "evidence that the Guatemalan Government is acting, directly or indirectly, as the agent of the Cominform" by whipping up "the anticolonial agitation."[97] The only "evidence" produced was the 1945 Arévalo-Yakubovsky letter, which US officials warned was a forgery.[98] Still, British officials looked favorably on the myriad tensions facing Arévalo's government while avoiding direct intervention.[99] During the 1950 election, Gallienne preferred Ydígoras Fuentes, arguing that, "since left wing here means communism and chauvinism, a benevolent dictatorship might be better for the people and for our relations."[100] Nevertheless, British officials avoided anything that could be considered political involvement.[101]

Under this caution, the Foreign Office did initiate an arms embargo on Guatemala. By late 1949, British officials pressured corporations to refuse business with Arévalo's government based on regional conflicts and the dispute over Belize. When denying the Western Arms Corporation licenses to sell rifles, British officials succinctly summarized, "the Foreign Office have strong political objections to the supply of any equipment whatsoever of this nature to Guatemala, not only because of the potential threat to British Honduras, but also because there is considerable danger that it might be used to equip the Caribbean Legion and ultimately in some attempted invasion of, say, Nicaragua or the Dominican Republic."[102] Trying to expand the embargo, the Foreign Office sounded out Canadian and US officials to limit weapons purchases.[103] In mid-1948, officials considered lobbying the State Department using the same reasons given to arms manufacturers but hesitated in light of US officials' attempts to standardize armaments and increase the US market in the Western Hemisphere.[104] This "unofficial arms embargo" or "secret embargo" endured, "very cautiously," into the early 1950s.[105]

Caution also defined the Foreign Office's efforts under the Information Research Department (IRD). At the end of 1947, US officials learned that the British government was increasing its pro-British, anticommunist propaganda campaign in Latin America.[106] Along these lines, the Foreign Office established the IRD in 1948 to rebut anticolonialism and communism across the globe, much of their work taking place in Cold War hot spots such as Southeast Asia and the Middle East.[107] For the greater Caribbean, the IRD's work came out of the British Embassy in Caracas under intelligence official Emile Lecours.[108] From the late 1940s into the early 1950s, Lecours guided his staff's work, which usually consisted of disseminating translations of anticommunist materials to IRD posts throughout the Western Hemisphere.[109] Building off the Foreign Office's earlier work in the region, IRD materials appeared in local newspapers and anticommunist outlets, such as the short-lived *El Ciudadano*, desperate to fill pages for readers.[110] Into 1951, US officials in Caracas worked with Lecours and the IRD on some anticommunist propaganda but were never fully briefed on the Foreign Office's policies.[111]

To keep his already overworked, short-staffed office's mission going, Lecours took some liberties in his duties while helping other departments, often to his supervisors' chagrin. In early 1950, he took a tour of Latin America in which he overstepped his orders and stopped in Guatemala. He then traveled to the Dominican Republic, again outside his official duties.[112] There, Lecours attended an informal reception where he met with Dominican and Venezuelan officials. Overlapping with the regimes' interviews with Castillo Armas and other reactionaries, Lecours shared some intelligence on Venezuelan purchases of British planes and his own concerns that the Legión was organizing in Cuba.[113] Upon returning to Caracas, Lecours telegrammed information on Guatemalan affairs to British officials in Ciudad Trujillo.[114] Soon after, an individual described as Lecours's "right party friend" asked for more information on these matters.[115] This flurry of atypical exchanges, all over telegram rather than in diplomatic pouch, caught the attention of Lecours's superiors.[116] Right away, the Foreign Office reprimanded the IRD official for participating in "anticommunist work which is not suitable for an Information Officer without special training." Though some inquired as to whether Lecours was assisting another department, the Foreign Office believed that he had made his trips to Guatemala and the Dominican Republic at his own behest.[117] Into 1951, the Foreign Office adhered to its cautious policy toward Guatemala, but their head anticommunist propagandist in the Caribbean Basin was behaving a bit zealously when networking with the Guatemalan Revolution's opponents.

Nudging the State Department

At the end of 1950, US officials refused to violate the ideal of nonintervention in hemispheric affairs, opposing any action by the UFCO during Guatemala's presidential election. In May 1950, Corcoran approached Deputy Assistant Secretary of State for Inter-American Affairs Thomas Mann and asked if the US government planned to involve itself in the election. Mann rebuked the lobbyist, writing that "any attempt by the Government to intervene would not only be counterproductive, but would meet with opposition in Guatemala, in the other American republics, and in the United States itself." When Corcoran pressed forward to suggest covert intervention by the UFCO and other parties, Mann again rebuffed the idea, warning that such action would likely be uncovered and destroy "hemispher[ic] solidarity and the Inter-American system."[118] Trying to circumvent Mann, Corcoran approached CIA Deputy Director Allen Dulles, who refused to act without the State Department's permission.[119] As Árbenz took office, the UFCO's agents had yet to convince the State Department to intervene but remained hopeful. After all, Mann had remarked to Corcoran, "I would not like to try to guess what the policy in the future might be if it were definitely determined that the Guatemalan Government and people had fallen under the totalitarian control of Communist elements."[120] International events favored the UFCO and those waiting for that "future" as the Cold War encouraged a rightward shift in US policymaking.

By 1950, US officials' fears of communist inroads into Guatemala escalated.[121] Exacerbated by the McCarthyist anticommunist paranoia gripping US domestic politics, the State Department's Latin Americanist experts were placing greater weight upon the supposed threat of international communism to the Western Hemisphere and the vaunted inter-American system.[122] Weeks before the Korean War began, it was Assistant Secretary of State for Inter-American Affairs Edward G. Miller Jr. who summarized this growing concern. In April 1950, Miller declared, "Communist political aggression . . . bears directly on the purpose of the Monroe Doctrine, which is as much our national policy today as it ever was." This was not the first time a high-ranking State Department official highlighted the dangers posed by communist expansionism, but this warning was coupled with his lecture "that the doctrine of nonintervention never did proscribe the assumption by the organized community of a legitimate concern with any circumstances that threatened the common welfare. Such a collective undertaking, far from representing intervention, is the alternative to intervention. It is the corollary of nonintervention."[123] Lacking much detail, observers could only speculate at when Miller's State Department would deem such an intervention, supposedly in the spirit of nonintervention, a necessity. A few months into Árbenz's presidency, that moment would come.

Table 1. Congresspersons chart

Congressperson	Party	State	UFCO Relationship
Rep. John McCormack	D	MA	- Worked with lobbyist Thomas Corcoran - Lobbied by lobbyist Robert La Follette Jr. - Gave "machine gun" speech - Approved interventionist policy
Rep., later Sen. Mike Mansfield	D	MO	- Worked with lobbyist Thomas Corcoran - Received materials from journalist Edward Tomlinson - Repeated UFCO Point IV memorandum
Sen. Henry Cabot Lodge Jr.	R	MA	- Repeated UFCO Point IV memorandum
Sen., later Rep. Claude Pepper	D	FL	- Gave "machine gun" speech
Sen. Lister Hill	D	AL	- Lobbied by UFCO official Joseph W. Montgomery - Repeated BBDO memorandum
Sen. Allen Ellender	D	LA	- Lobbied by UFCO official Joseph W. Montgomery - Supported interventionist policy
Sen. Alexander Wiley	R	WI	- Led Senate Foreign Relations Committee as Counsel Julius Cahn worked with UFCO public relations expert Edward Bernays
Rep., later Sen. Everett Dirksen	R	IL	- Lobbied by lobbyist Thomas Corcoran - Lobbied by lobbyist Robert La Follette Jr.
Sen. Bourke Hickenlooper	R	IA	- Lobbied by lobbyist Robert La Follette Jr. - Lobbied by UFCO public relations expert Edward Bernays - Worked with Senate Foreign Relations Committee Counsel Julius Cahn and CIA on coffee boycott

Chapter 6

Waiting for the Colossus

British Intelligence, Guatemalan Anticommunists, and the US Congress, 1950–1952

Many wondered if Árbenz's election would take the Guatemalan Revolution in a different direction. US officials hoped the new president would be a reliable ally, the UFCO dreamed of restoring its unchallenged dominion, and dictators thought he might renounce his predecessor's foreign policy. Instead, Árbenz charted his own course, backing reformist policies and remaining an ally of antidictatorial exiles such as Ribas Montes.[1] Unlike Arévalo, Árbenz drew the wrath of not only those long opposed to the Revolution but also the US government. After implementing an interventionist policy to destabilize Árbenz's government, one official forewarned, "A good deal more blood would have to flow in Guatemala before a sufficiently strong reaction against the regime would be possible."[2]

By 1951, Miller and Mann's State Department judged Guatemala a communist base and approved an interventionist policy to weaken Árbenz's government. Deeming this policy insufficient, the British Foreign Office unleashed its IRD, which expanded its propaganda campaign and financed anticommunist organizations. Going into 1952, those behind the counterrevolution felt emboldened: the UFCO's congressional lobbying campaign appeared triumphant, regimes gained an ally in Cuba, and reactionaries solidified their anticommunist alliances in Mexico. Despite such progress, all still wanted the US government to take a more influential role in undermining Guatemala's democratic moment.

The US Government Departs from Nonintervention

Into the late 1940s, the Revolution's opponents dealt with a State Department that vacillated in its assessments of whether Arévalo's government was "communist, crypto-communist, under communist influence, or not communist at all," as one US official admitted to historian Piero Gleijeses.[3] Focused on events outside the Western Hemisphere, Secretary of State Dean Acheson delegated US–Latin American relations to his experts Miller and Mann.[4] Despite their knowledge of the region, the two constantly mistook Guatemalan nationalism for radicalism and anti-US sentiments.[5] Fortunately, Guatemalan officials made clear their commitment to the United States during the Korean War and with their legislature's signing the Inter-American Treaty of Reciprocal Assistance, or the Rio Treaty.[6] Looking forward, Miller and Mann cast Arévalo as a moderating influence and believed Árbenz's 1950 election would empower centrists.[7] In the hemispheric context, the State Department's lukewarm treatment of Arévalo's government, or even receptivity to a coup, paled next to the abortive conspiracies and sensational propaganda unleashed by the Revolution's foes.[8]

Quickly, Árbenz disappointed Miller and Mann. When the State Department warned the new president about persons influenced by communist ideas, Árbenz allowed them to publish pro-Soviet materials and operate in the open.[9] This spurred the State Department's growing fears that international communism profited from the nation's intense nationalism and undermined the military's role.[10] These assessments dovetailed with military attachés' characterization of former Legionarios' antidictatorial, anti-imperialist stance as cover for "a general opposition to the United States ... follow[ing] the Communist line."[11] Árbenz's presidency allowed communists to increase their numbers and occupy important positions, which Miller and Mann believed weakened inter-American security.[12]

Months into Árbenz's presidency, the State Department chose to undermine Guatemala's democratically elected government. In June 1951, Mann outlined a new policy that he admitted was "the first of its kind since the establishment of the Good Neighbor Policy," that is, "a violation of the Nonintervention Agreement." Now, the US government would cut trade and reduce funds for various projects so that, under "certain economic pressures," anticommunist forces would rise against their government. With a faltering economy, "the center and right elements in Guatemala will see that it is necessary to get together and clean their own house."[13] Right away, they discussed how to subtly weaken Árbenz's government by withholding technical and financial assistance, limiting sales of weapons, and preventing loans. Most important, they needed to cautiously implement this policy so that Guatemala's government would not have "any tangible grounds" showing the US government "attempting to intervene in her internal affairs."[14] It was time, Miller determined, "to put the squeeze on the commies in Guatemala."[15]

Whatever doubts Miller and Mann had, the UFCO's congressional allies reassured them. The biggest risk was that this policy "would strengthen the hands of the nationalists and communists" if discovered, a danger Deputy Under Secretary of State H. Freeman Matthews and US officials with less experience on Latin American matters recognized. Fortunately, Mann "talked to people on [Capitol] Hill," where McCormack, the House's majority leader and the UFCO's vocal ally, "state[d] that he would back us on our policy toward Guatemala."[16] Likewise, Senator Allen J. Ellender (D-LA) a year later investigated the Árbenz government's requests for road-building equipment. Explaining the rejection of the requisite export licenses, a State Department official "declared, in confidence, that it is not the department's public stand, but that relations between this government and Guatemala have become 'strained' due to Communist infiltration of the government and the 'resulting action against US interests.'"[17] Ellender, having spent the past weeks receiving the UFCO's materials and "accumulating data" regarding "Communist infiltration into Guatemala," did not push the matter further, thereby endorsing the interventionist policy.[18]

As had Ellender, the UFCO's allies moved to support this new policy. In late June 1951, La Follette sent McCormack Tomlinson's latest article for his "file" of Guatemalan materials.[19] The next month, McCormack delivered a lengthy speech about the "small but highly active and vocal group" of communists controlling Árbenz's government. These communists manipulated anti-US sentiments, all under "the spell of Soviet propaganda," in order to "cause Guatemalan policy to be subservient to the Kremlin's design of world conquest."[20] Initially, *Diario de Centro América* and other newspapers assumed McCormack "was briefed by" the UFCO and ignored the speech.[21] After a few days, though, newspapers using British propaganda seized upon the UFCO-backed screed. Marroquín Rojas's *La Hora* and his son's *La Hora Dominical* republished McCormack's speech, while an editorial in Vela's *El*

Imparcial connected these issues to larger national problems.[22] Mirroring its actions in the United States, UFCO lobbying disseminated anticommunist materials throughout the Guatemalan press. The Revolution's opponents celebrated. With the media spending days on McCormack's speech, Guatemalan officials responded with interviews and ads throughout the Western Hemisphere, exactly what UFCO agents desired. "This is blood finally drawn," Corcoran cheered. "I can't think of any better position for you to be in than to have these fellows trying to explain with paid ads in the American newspapers that they ain't Communists. This is making them play the game just where you would like to have it played—on your own home ball lot."[23] "The speech hit home," Mann agreed in a note to McCormack about how "the opposition press ha[d] given favorable editorial treatment" to the speech and forced "the Government-controlled press . . . to rebut it."[24] A UFCO-inspired speech in Congress, amplified by Guatemalan allies of British intelligence, fit perfectly into the State Department's interventionist policy to encourage internal resistance against Árbenz's government.

Nevertheless, some doubted whether the new policy was sufficient since it would take time for Miller's "squeeze" to produce tangible results. Mann confided to British officials "that there were signs of growing Congressional concern about Guatemala" and "thought that there was a strong liklihood [sic] that if the present relatively mild measures did not produce any effect, stronger measures would have to be adopted."[25] Having helped facilitate this policy, the UFCO's agents were, of course, waiting for such "measures," as were British officials.

British Intelligence and Guatemalan Anticommunists

Also pursuing a more forceful policy was the British government. After years of seeming indifference, US officials "were very anxious to collaborate" and updated the Foreign Office about the interventionist policy.[26] Initially, the Foreign Office celebrated this camaraderie, deeming the policy "satisfactory" for a strengthened arms embargo and agreeing to "cooperate to the fullest extent."[27] As one official remarked, "it would be a pity not to profit from the State Department's present interest in Guatemala and their unprecedented readiness to cooperate with us in anticommunist activities."[28] This congeniality was short-lived. The US government's economic sanctions seemed insignificant with Guatemala's coffee exports unaffected. To maintain an image of noninterventionism, US officials used technical excuses to explain away cuts to road-building equipment and cotton shipments, but this paradoxically prevented Guatemalan officials from learning that the US government was demanding a change in their government, the policy's entire purpose.[29]

What especially upset British officials was the US government's refusal to defend colonialism. Indeed, the Foreign Office worried that their US counterparts exaggerated and misunderstood communism. Árbenz's government seemed less preoccupied with Belize and more communist, that is, "pro-British and pro-communist," yet the Foreign Office thought US officials misunderstood this nuance and "exaggerate[d communism's] progress."[30] Even in 1952, British officials mocked how US evaluations arrived "to the hasty conclusion often . . . that everything moving under a bush is a 'commie.'"[31] Though they had waited years for the State Department to act, British officials believed these concerns overshadowed the anticolonialist issues. In spite of the interventionist policy, the State Department was still not "giv[ing] equal seriousness to anti-Americanism in general and Moscow['s] incitement against G[reat] Britain's colonial position in the Western Hemisphere."[32] Since US officials refused to agree that anticolonialism was a communist ploy, the Foreign Office did not embrace the interventionist policy, with one official warning, "We are concerned about the possibility that we may take practical steps to cooperate in the policy which the State Department outlined, only to find that they have reestablished friendly relations with a Guatemalan Government of slightly different political complexion."[33] Over the next year, some British officials lectured their US counterparts, saying, "We must try to make sure that the US remembers that the enemy is communism and that their position would not be 'bettered' if Guatemala were to switch back to the old scapegoat," the British government.[34] The Foreign Office was also taken aback by US officials' seeming ambivalence on weapons trafficking, such as that by Hubert "the Black Eagle" Julian, which circumvented the governments' arms embargo and could be used in Belize.[35]

This sentiment influenced the IRD's evaluation of Guatemalan affairs. With the interventionist policy, the Foreign Office suggested collaborating on intelligence projects.[36] To assess this possibility, IRD agent Lecours visited Guatemala in August 1951.[37] There, he grew disillusioned. Multiple publishers of British propaganda, such as *El Impacto*'s Marroquín Rojas, identified him as "a high-powered British intelligence officer who had come to this country to study Communist infiltration."[38] *La Hora*'s Baltazar Morales cheered that Lecours's "presence" and "interest . . . was for them a sign that the great powers were at least taking into account the seriousness of the

Communist Movement in Guatemala and the repercussions it could have in the rest of Central America." Despite such optimism, only one of those "great powers" appeared willing to help. "Prominent anticommunists," Lecours reported, "have expressed to me in conversation the hope that the United States will impose ... economic sanctions on Guatemala."[39] Actually, the State Department had just implemented its interventionist policy, but no one felt its impact, just as Mann foresaw. Lecours's disappointment grew when the US cultural attaché admitted "his own hands were tied" and he "was under instructions from the State Department to avoid giving rise to any accusation that the United States were interfering in the internal affairs of Guatemala."[40] Anticommunists, the very people the interventionist policy meant to rally, were in the dark.

Believing themselves abandoned by one power, anticommunists solicited another's patronage. In Guatemala, Lecours made "contact with various groups of persons who are actively fighting Communism," "distributing anticommunist propaganda in the towns and villages," and "organizing anticommunist committees." They "offered to distribute material" the IRD provided but lacked "sufficient funds" and "the experience necessary to carry out their underground work." Therefore, he suggested a permanent IRD office in Guatemala where officers could carry out these projects. Reflecting his typical zeal, he argued that "there is no reason why anticommunist work should not be openly undertaken," since Árbenz's government tolerated communist publications. The British government needed to provide the "monetary assistance" and "leadership" to sustain these organizations. If they were to wait for the State Department's interventionist policy to work, the nation would "transition from a republic to a soviet ... in a relatively short space of time unless prevented by strong pressure from outside."[41] Hoping to collaborate with US officials, the Foreign Office shared Lecours's suggestions, only for the State Department to confess that it was "at present very far from thinking of a campaign to bring down the Guatemalan Government."[42] This was further evidence of what Lecours and Guatemalan anticommunists already believed: the US government's interventionist policy seemed impotent.

This weighed on the Foreign Office when witnessing an outpouring of anticommunist activism. During the summer of 1951, market women and Catholics protested Árbenz's government for removing nuns from the nation's largest orphanage.[43] Anticommunist organizations such as Arenas's PUA pounced on what it claimed was a communist plot to destroy the nation's sovereignty and Catholic faith.[44] The protests and resulting suspension of constitutional liberties inspired the formation of the Comité de Estudiantes Universitarios Anticomunistas (Committee of Anticommunist University Students, CEUA). Days after its September 1951 creation, CEUA issued manifestos defending Catholicism and denouncing all the "traitors to the Country, those bad Guatemalans," who gave their nation over to communism, a "harmful international doctrine."[45] Organizing committees across the country, members gave away flyers and handouts warning against "fifth columns" under "the orders of the Kremlin" and demanding "no more 'vivas [hurrahs]' to Russia or Stalin."[46]

On November 25 and 26, 1951, CEUA joined the Comité Cívico Nacional (National Civic Committee, CCN) in hosting the Convención Nacional Anticomunista (National Anticommunist Convention), hailed in the invitations as the nation's first anticommunist rally.[47] As outlined by CCN Secretary General Colonel Roberto Barrios Peña and CEUA Secretary General Guillermo Sosa, the convención included representatives from all of Guatemala's anticommunist organizations.[48] As expected, the convención tapped into opposition to the Arévalo and Árbenz governments' frequent constitutional suspensions, recommending attendees avoid "discusiones callejeras" (open discussions) and "tumultos" (riots/marches), which would be deemed illegal.[49] Under the convención, the CCN put forward ten "ponencias" (reports/conclusions) and CEUA put forward six. Most of these were typical anticommunist demands: denounce Guatemalan officials who attended communist meetings, organize an anticommunist newspaper, champion the constitution's Artículo (Article) 32, which prohibited foreign political parties and which anticommunists argued applied to any communist organization. Reflecting local grievances with constitutional suspensions and conspiracies that Mexican communists controlled Guatemalan affairs, the longest sections defended the right to vote and denounced international communism and Lombardo Toledano.[50]

Here, at the intersection of this escalating antigovernment activism and their own frustrations with the interventionist policy, the Foreign Office took up Lecours's calls to support Guatemalan anticommunists. An official from the British Legation in Guatemala City attended the convención and reported "great enthusiasm" from attendees, the "overwhelming majority of those present [being] students and workers" as "young people predominated."[51] Afterward, Lecours returned to Guatemala, where he made contact with CEUA's leadership.[52] In a memorandum, CEUA proclaimed itself an umbrella organization with anticommunist "cells" and "regional conventions" across the country. They gave the IRD a list of over one hundred "collaborators" and described their alliances with the PUA, the CCN, and anticommunist groups of Catholics and market women.[53] To prove their capabilities, they provided photographs of recent protests, with marchers holding signs for the Liga Anticomunista Escuintleca (Escuintla Anticommunist League) and Universitarios Anticomunistas (Anticommunist University Students) as well as slogans denouncing "The Soviet Paradise" and demanding "Down with the communists."[54] They also gave copies of their myriad leaflets, pamphlets, and posters: "The Hydra of Communism," "Attention Anticommunists: See what is the Communist Ten Commandments," and "We are anticommunists."[55] Most suggestive of the IRD and CEUA's tentative networking was a multicolored stencil used for producing posters, "Out with Communism! Guatemala for Guatemalans!"[56] As had reactionaries for the past years, CEUA held up its activities as necessary to liberate the nation from international communism.[57]

CEUA, similar to newspaper publishers using IRD propaganda, recognized the British government as a potential source of assistance. Hoping to "obtain the support of some industrialists and business men," CEUA stressed its reliance on "voluntary contributions from a few farmers and persons who belong for the most part to the lower and middle classes." As 1951 came to an end, the organization spent its three thousand quetzales on transportation, the convención, and almost five million leaflets. Unsurprisingly, UFCO subsidiary IRCA provided "free transport," but this was not sufficient. Pleading for financial assistance, it required at least one thousand quetzales for rent, staff, materials, travel, and something labeled "secret services." Additionally, CEUA wished for a cinematograph, photography and audio equipment, and everything necessary to produce radio broadcasts or purchase radio spots.[58] Immediately, Lecours championed CEUA as an authentic and successful wellspring of local anticommunism. Repeating his conclusion from mid-1951, he told his superiors, "I feel that they should be helped because, as far as I am aware, this is the first time that, at any rate in Latin America, groups of men and women have banded together to fight against Communism."[59] A week later, he reiterated his position that the IRD should support CEUA.[60]

By early 1952, the British Foreign Office, not the US State Department, became these Guatemalan anticommunists' patron. First, the IRD and CEUA collaborated in publishing anticommunist materials throughout Guatemala. Some of these anticommunists were "precisely those who did us good service and ran considerable risks as our contacts for the distribution of anticommunist IRD material," the British Minister admitted in August 1954. An "outstanding example . . . was one of the leaders of [the] anticommunist student body during the Árbenz Government," CEUA's Domingo Goicolea Villacorta.[61] Second, CEUA received the funds necessary to host a radio broadcast, an operation for which they requested financial assistance in late 1951.[62]

This international support bolstered CEUA's activities and Guatemalan anticommunism into mid-1952. Following the convención, CEUA joined the CCN, the PUA, the Comité Anticomunista de Estudiantes de Ciencias Comerciales (Anticommunist Committee of Commercial Sciences Students), and the Comité Central Anticomunista Femenino (Feminine Anticommunist Central Committee) in organizing the March 23, 1952, anticommunist march.[63] They aimed to unite thousands of Guatemalans for what participants dubbed the Gran Manifestación (great demonstration) to repudiate foreign ideologies, specifically international communism.[64] The PUA summoned Artículo 32 to denounce Soviet influences, and the CCN's flyers held up the Guatemalan flag and national hymn as nationalist symbols.[65] Invitations urged Guatemalans to "eradicate from the homeland the harmful communist doctrine, the cancer that corrodes the hearts of the country."[66] Paralleling reactionaries' transnational alliances, CEUA boasted that US, Mexican, and Salvadoran anticommunists participated.[67] Likewise, CEUA warned that Árbenz's government, like Arévalo's, implanted provocateurs to spark violence, deploy force, and suspend the constitution.[68]

Such conspiratorial assertions gained impetus when, during the Gran Manifestación's preparations, officials arrested one of CEUA's officers, Federico Paiz Herrera, who happened to be Castillo Armas's brother-in-law. At first, officials claimed to be unaware of the arrest, before charging Paiz Herrera without conclusive evidence for participating in bombings and armed uprisings, only to then release the anticommunist showing physical signs of abuse and torture.[69] For the rest of the year, CEUA published flyers showing Guatemalan officials beating Paiz Herrera under the "system of torture used in the modern 'revolutionary' prisons in the Soviet style."[70] Some referenced previous dictatorships while others depicted his torture as a violation of Guatemalan law, the norms of a civilized nation, and the UN's Universal Declaration of Human Rights.[71] According to CEUA propaganda, the persistent constitutional suspensions, whether under Arévalo's or Árbenz's government, contradicted and undid the Revolution's lofty ideals.[72]

Though content with this antigovernment activism, the British government's covert financial assistance was not limitless support. While preparing, CEUA proclaimed that, even if their manifestation accomplished nothing material, they would "declare a COLD WAR against all communists or semicommunists." To "defend our homeland, our religion, and our lives as free men and not controlled under the Soviet Yoke," they announced, anticommunist Guatemalans would not greet, speak to, sell to, or buy from communists.[73] Such threats were not necessary, for an estimated thirty thousand Guatemalans attended the Gran Manifestación to demand banning communism in accordance with Artículo 32, expelling foreign communists, removing communists from Árbenz's government, and restructuring the government's internal policies and foreign relations. To pacify these anticommunists, Árbenz invited a delegation for a meeting. In the spirit of Lecours's call for the Foreign Office to provide "leadership," CEUA and its fellow organizations sent CCN's Carlos Simmons to the British Embassy for advice.[74] There, Simmons asked for names of suspected communists who needed to be expelled from the country, but British officials offered no names. Instead, Simmons went to the US Embassy, whose staff suggested that he call out Guatemalan officials for already knowing the communists' names. The anticommunists' representatives did just this, and the meeting went as expected. When Árbenz's government responded that communist organizations in Guatemala were not totalitarian, the anticommunists highlighted the official suppression of CEUA's radio broadcasts.[75]

In spite of the links between CEUA and the IRD, both were seeking the US government's largesse. In fact, CEUA had petitioned the US government while meeting with the IRD, providing similar materials to both international powers.[76] Alongside Lecours's memorandum on CEUA was a memorandum in which unnamed Guatemalan anticommunists, probably Castillo Armas's allies, solicited armaments. They pleaded "that the situation, owing to the activities of the students, . . . is most favorable for an armed movement, which could be timed to coincide with a general stoppage of commerce, industry, and all the vital forces of the country."[77] British officials refused to provide this form of assistance, instead redirecting the petitioners to their US counterparts. Since any armed movement could set off a governmental suppression and wipe out all anticommunist forces, the Foreign Office "agreed that the Americans have both the main responsibility and the chief means of combating Communism in Guatemala" and forwarded Lecours's reports to the State Department.[78] This was not the Foreign Office's only attempt to encourage the US government's aid. During the demonstration, the US air attaché in Guatemala City divulged to British officials "that, if the demonstration of 23rd March proves to have been ineffective, the anticommunists will have to resort to other means and will need large sums of money."[79] British Minister Gallienne concurred. In the ninth paragraph of his report on the Gran Manifestación, Gallienne wrote, "I think it is clear that the demonstration of March 23rd has failed to impress the Government and that the anticommunists have, for the time being, shot their bolt. They will now have to consider their next steps, and unless they are to abandon the struggle, they must make a greater show of strength."[80] His superiors agreed and concluded, "I think it is in our interest to stimulate the State Department's concern about the present regime."[81] They recommended sharing Gallienne's report with US officials but left out that ninth paragraph's last sentence, "This will need money, and it may be that the Americans will help to provide it."[82]

Congress Champions the Cause

At the same time, Guatemala was receiving greater attention in the US press and Congress, much of this due to UFCO lobbyists' work. Agents certainly did not author all articles. Some journalists tapped into long-standing false claims, as when *The Washington Post*'s Duncan Aikman alleged Lombardo Toledano and Soviet provocateurs took over Guatemala in the Revolution's first days.[83] The activities of certain Guatemalan communists, notably Gutiérrez's December 1951 Moscow trip, merited some lines.[84] Overall, US press coverage was from those not well versed on Latin America. In February 1952, *The Washington Daily News*'s Ludwell Denny published a series of articles: "Marriage of Convenience: Communist Clique Runs Guatemala," "Economic Suicide in Guatemala: Reds Out to Wreck United Fruit Co.," and "Central America Rich Field for Reds."[85] Denny's reporting was atypical since his notable articles from the mid-1940s into the early 1950s covered Spain, Yugoslavia, and Britain for the Scripps-Howard Newspaper Alliance.[86] Lacking any knowledge of Latin America, Denny depicted Guatemala as a land where communists manipulated the "inferiority complex of the mixed-blood minority" who were too busy "worshiping the pagan gods of their Mayan ancestors" to recognize the Soviet-directed plot taking place in Guatemala City, an "alien capital of mixed breeds and whites."[87] One reason for Denny's remarks was that a source for his and other journalists' reporting was the British minister, whose superiors celebrated that his "session with these writers has reaped a rich reward" now "that the heat has been turned onto the US."[88]

Meanwhile, UFCO agents found additional means to lobby Congress, relying heavily on their Massachusetts-based allies. After Denny's articles appeared, La Follette sent McCormack all of the journalist's writings.[89] A few days later, McCormack inserted Denny's articles, Aikman's *Washington Post* item, and one from *Time* magazine into the *Congressional Record* and launched into a speech. "Now," he warned, "new confirmation comes from irreproachable independent sources that this Guatemalan penetration by the Soviets has reached the point that Guatemala is now truly a Soviet Guatemala. We of the United States have to recognize that we have a full-fledged Soviet beachhead on our flank—and that the Latin American nations which are friendly to the United States have a full fledged Soviet beachhead on their flank too."[90] Representative Joseph W. Martin Jr. (R-MA) joined to repeat that "reliable American newspaper observers" had confirmed "the fact that international communism . . . is successfully establishing a beachhead in Guatemala." Encapsulating the UFCO's propaganda, Martin declared, "International communism is using the Guatemalan situation to destroy the inter-American system which has been painstakingly created over the course of many years, and to disrupt and dislocate the solidarity which, up until now, has existed among all of the American Republics."[91] La Follette and other UFCO officials thanked McCormack for his speech, but their work was not finished.[92]

Next, agents used the congresspersons' words for their propaganda. After McCormack's and Martin's performances, Corcoran's associate James Rowe sent Mansfield the articles and McCormack's and Martin's *Congressional Record* statements.[93] In early March, Mansfield complained on the House floor, "The Communist minority in [Guatemala] has increased its power through placing selected party members in key government posts. Political parties have been manipulated and combined, Communist Party members have gone to Moscow for instructions, and American corporations have been forced to bow to exorbitant demands." He then inserted into the *Record* an item from *Newsweek*, the outlet with which Corcoran worked.[94] The day after, Rowe followed up with Mansfield to share a new article from Denny.[95] In "Latin American Reds," Denny referred to the Árbenz government's treatment of the UFCO and IRCA based on the "unusual House debate" in which McCormack and Martin "joined to warn that Guatemala has become a Stalinist 'beachhead' in this defense area."[96] Pretending to be unaware of any collaboration between the UFCO, McCormack, and Martin, Rowe asked Mansfield if there would be "perhaps some cooperation" between the two Massachusetts congresspersons and "wonder[ed] what [the State Department was] doing about all of this, if anything."[97] The unfounded complaints by

McCormack and Martin that Árbenz's government was a Soviet puppet, initiated by the UFCO's agents, had become the lobbyists' and even some journalists' evidence.

This propaganda was then fed into the UFCO's various ventures. Diplomatic officials throughout the Western Hemisphere noted press coverage of McCormack's and Martin's speeches. Some, including a British official, marveled at the two, "who [were] bitter enemies, for once agreeing on something."[98] One reason for this coverage was that Corcoran used the UFCO-backed controversy for material that appeared in outlets with whom he networked, including *Newsweek* and *The New York Times*.[99] Out of Corcoran's efforts, McCormack's and Martin's speeches appeared in the Spanish-language edition of *Newsweek* in early March 1952.[100] Agents subsequently fed this back to their public relations expert Bernays for "books on Communist propaganda" and a "white paper."[101]

Most notably, the UFCO's congressional lobbying directly influenced the State Department. The same day he sent Denny's articles to McCormack, La Follette wrote Senators Hickenlooper and Dirksen.[102] Dirksen knew that La Follette worked for the UFCO yet claimed the corporation's treatment was a dangerous sign for other US-based enterprises. Writing to Hickenlooper, he repeated the typical refrains that "the Reds are making Guatemala a beachhead" and that "this country has been designated as headquarters for the Red network on this Hemisphere."[103] On February 26, Hickenlooper assured them both that the Senate was about to act. Spurred by their letters, he met right away with Senator Theodore Francis Green (D-RI), chair of the Senate's Subcommittee on Latin American Affairs. The two agreed that the subcommittee would convene that afternoon to discuss Guatemala with Miller or someone representing him.[104] Hickenlooper's assurances to Dirksen and La Follette made their way to Corcoran, who included this among his lobbying's myriad victories: "We have both parties on a bipartisan basis calling in the House for the 'elimination' of the Guatemalan cancer and putting it up to the other Latin American nations that it is to their own interest that the elimination be effected." On the same day Hickenlooper updated Dirksen and La Follette, Corcoran updated Zemurray, saying, "There has also been a formal meeting of the Latin American Sub-Committee of the Senate Foreign Relations Committee (Green, Sparkman, and Hickenlooper) with Eddie Miller to discuss the necessity of doing something about the situation" in Guatemala.[105] In spite of the State Department's interventionist policy, Congress and the UFCO demanded more.

Gaining Allies in 1952: Fulgencio Batista's Coup and Eduardo Zuleta Ángel's Mission

Coincidentally, events outside the United States bolstered regimes' strength, starting with the 1952 military coup in Cuba. Into the early 1950s, Dominican officials complained that Auténticos granted anti-Trujillo exiles asylum, and AD-in-exile found there the "most ready support."[106] Therefore, the regimes' informal intelligence sharing repeatedly monitored these dealings.[107] Fortunately for them, Fulgencio Batista's March 1952 coup reshaped the region's dynamics. To hold off a forthcoming election he was likely to lose, Batista and his military allies seized power, forcing political opponents into exile.[108] As in 1948, regimes celebrated. Somoza's *Novedades* immediately cheered this strike against the "Figueres-Betancourt-Arévalo axis."[109] Costa Rican officials noted the only defining aspect of Batista's vague foreign policy was his goal to obtain a "great understanding" with neighboring governments.[110] Actually, this was Batista's plan. In August, the Cuban ambassador in Washington sent three of Batista's speeches to the Dominican ambassador, who appreciated the new dictator's description of Prío's government as "a regime . . . breaking the principle of nonintervention."[111]

As with Venezuela in 1948, regimes rapidly incorporated the Cuban dictatorship into their intelligence sharing. Weeks after taking power, Batista's officials reported that Auténticos, in Cuba and abroad, were rallying opponents.[112] Cuban military intelligence identified Prío, Aureliano Sánchez Arango, and Auténticos-in-exile as key leaders with the training and resources to undermine the newly installed dictator.[113] As part of their mutual defense, Batista's officials shared their intelligence with the region's regimes. Trujillo's journalist in Cuba, José Arroyo Maldonado, networked among Cuban, Dominican, and Venezuelan officials to deliver reports on arms purchases by "communists" under anti-Trujillo exile Ramírez. Cuban officials then sent this information to Batista's Servicio de Inteligencia Militar (Military Intelligence Service).[114] In early May, the Cuban naval attaché detailed that his staff improved their intelligence services to monitor Auténticos-in-exile thanks to their receiving their counterparts' reports on weapon sales to Sánchez Arango and Betancourt.[115]

The 1952 coup cast a larger spotlight on Guatemala's continuing haven for antidictatorial activism. "The political aspect had changed favorably," regimes' officials recognized, but they needed to keep an eye out for "future machinations."[116] The coup put a friendly regime inside Cuba but pushed militant Auténticos-in-exile into Árbenz's Guatemala.[117] Throughout the year, Cubans traveled there to join anti-Batista organizations and plots.[118] The network kept its other eye on Figueres's activities, sharing reports of his purchasing and storing armaments in Costa Rica for "his attempts to disturb peace in Central America and the Caribbean."[119] This materiel was supposedly transported and distributed among Auténticos-in-exile, AD-in-exile, Dominican and Nicaraguan exiles, and Arévalo.[120] Their claims that these figures were Soviet agents at the head of "a communist offensive in our America with the goal of overthrowing the governments of Colombia and Venezuela" opened the door for meetings in 1952 with Colombian Ambassador Eduardo Zuleta Ángel.[121]

Akin to Batista's regime, Colombian officials joined this intelligence-sharing network due to a common transnational threat. Colombia's Conservative government opposed the overlap between Colombian Liberals, AD-in-exile, and Figueres. Colombian and Venezuelan national security intertwined thanks to Figueres's friendship with Betancourt, whose presence in Costa Rica added to "the difficult situation" facing the network's allies in "Central America, Colombia, and Venezuela."[122] Hence, Colombian officials worked with their Venezuelan counterparts in the hope of tracking Figueres's purchases of armaments.[123] From these exchanges, Venezuelan and Colombian intelligence officials discussed "the possibility of making a sort of bloc in which Venezuela, the Dominican Republic, Cuba, Colombia, and Nicaragua would participate against the activities developing in Costa Rica, Mexico, and Guatemala."[124] To accomplish this task, Colombian Ambassador Zuleta Ángel became his government's primary agent for sharing information with the network's members. In mid-1952, his government officially sent him on an economic tour of Latin America. Unofficially, he held numerous meetings to share intelligence on the Caribbean Basin's anti-dictatorial forces and cement a "bloc of mutual defense" against Figueres's regional influence.[125] Of course, there was little secrecy around his activities, with newspapers in multiple countries noting the true reason for Zuleta Ángel's mission.[126] However, no report surmised that he was contributing to a new plot from Castillo Armas to overthrow Árbenz's government.

Moving in Mexico, Hoping for the United States

Into mid-1952, reactionaries kept networking with like-minded compatriots. In Mexico, some had sworn off political activities, but a handful remained quite involved, among their number Ponce, Salazar, and Archila Obregón.[127]

One reason was that those still conspiring had received the regimes' largesse over the past years. This was most evident when Trujillo's infamous official Félix W. Bernardino visited Mexico in late May 1952. Bernardino formally served as the Dominican consul in New York City but informally carried out the dictator's repressive policies throughout the Western Hemisphere.[128] His appearances in Havana or New York City dovetailed with the assassinations and murders of anti-Trujillo exiles including Báez in Cuba or Requena in New York.[129]

This time, Mexican security agents noticed that Bernardino's trip coincided with a surge of reactionaries' activities. First, Bernardino met up with a few prominent reactionaries. Second, a new association, the Comité Pro Liberación de Guatemala (Committee for the Liberation of Guatemala, CPLG), inserted anticommunist handouts into the capital city's newspaper *La Prensa*. To investigate this political activity, the DGIPS sent agents to the CPLG's address. Upon arriving, agents did not find the CPLG's signs; there were only signs for the FPAM, the same Mexican anticommunist organization with whom, two years earlier, Arenas signed a pact to collaborate in fighting Guatemalan communism. The DGIPS was unaware of Arenas's networking between the FPAM and Dominican officials but assumed they were assisting this CPLG.[130]

During the DGIPS's investigation, propaganda against Árbenz's government continued appearing in Mexico City. The CPLG in September announced that Arbencistas were "traitors to the country" who "turned [Guatemala] over to the concealed Soviet yoke." Árbenz's policies were an extension of Arévalo's "'diplomacy' that had disrupted the peaceful Central American life."[131] In October, *El Universal* published an editorial from FPAM leader Prieto Laurens. Echoing the unproven allegations found throughout the region, Prieto Laurens claimed "the Red Conclave of Guatemala" was home to "Soviet submarines" and the "headquarters" for "Soviet agents in Guatemala." Their goal was "to attack and to take power in all countries of the American Continent," establishing a "base to collaborate effectively with the USSR in its fight against Yankee imperialism." Fortunately, the FPAM and other anticommunist Mexicans were aware of this plan, having witnessed in their own country how the Russian Embassy and the Czech and Polish legations were working hand in hand with CTAL, the Partido Comunista Mexicano (Mexican Communist Party), the Amigos de la URSS (Friends of the USSR), and the Intercambio Cultural Mexicano-Ruso (Mexican-Russian Cultural Exchange).[132] The FPAM then disseminated a handout alleging that Árbenz's government was under the thumb of the "Red Czar of Moscow" and "selling its country to Communist Russia." "The Reds," it warned, "threaten Mexico from the South with the support of the 'Fifth Column' of traitors as well as the thousands of Communist Refugees in our country." The supposed "evidence" of the international communist conspiracy emanating from Guatemala to destroy Mexico's sovereignty was the forged 1945 Arévalo-Yakubovsky letter.[133]

If this flurry of activity were not enough to convince the DGIPS of the FPAM and the CPLG's authentic collaboration, Prieto Laurens offered a memorandum detailing their shared ideology. The FPAM may have operated as the umbrella organization for the CPLG and Guatemalan reactionaries, but their worldview was real. Prieto Laurens and his colleagues sought to inform the Mexican public about the "sovietizante labor" of Árbenz's government. This drew them to the plight of these Guatemalans, who were only guilty of their "antitotalitarian ideology" and "victims of the persecutions of the pro-Soviet government" of first Arévalo and then Árbenz.[134] Under the FPAM, the CPLG's leadership included Salazar, one of the reactionaries most experienced in cultivating transnational alliances, and Ardón, who joined Arenas on the Consejo Supremo that backed Castillo Armas's Base Militar attack.[135] Thus, the CPLG's bulletins and propaganda were not just produced by lone Guatemalans, Prieto Laurens declared, "It is the work of us, Mexicans, in defense of the freedom of that unfortunate brother country."[136]

As with the CPLG and the FPAM's collaboration in Mexico, reactionaries built up their transnational alliances. At the end of 1951, Castillo Armas traveled through Panama toward Nicaragua "to be closer and in contact with his friends."[137] Fearful of being monitored by the DGIPS or Guatemalan officials, Arenas used a passport with a fake name, though this rudimentary subterfuge remained amateurish and inadvertently prevented his entering the Dominican Republic in March.[138] This did not slow him down, however, for he was in Nicaragua the next month. During April 1952 meetings, he updated the Venezuelan military attaché on his and Castillo Armas's tentative plans to launch a coup against Árbenz's government, information that was immediately shared with Dominican officials.[139] Possibly, Castillo Armas's activities were something of a known secret, as Padilla even referenced them in conversations with US officials.[140] What they did not share, though, was that Castillo Armas and his patron Somoza were preparing to ask the US government to join their counterrevolutionary alliance.

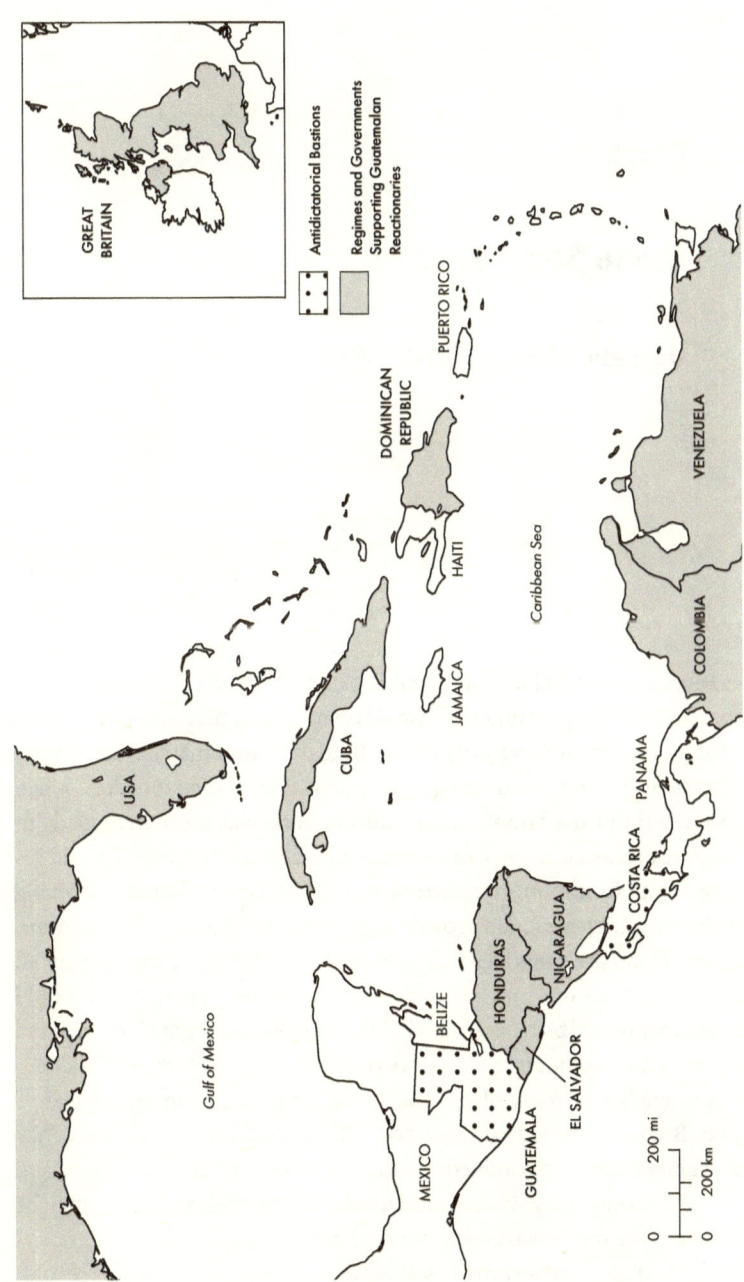

Figure 4. Map of Caribbean Basin, 1952

Chapter 7

Uncle Sam Signs On

Operation PBFORTUNE, 1952

In February 1951, Miller and Mann debated whom to send to Guatemala to represent the US government during Árbenz's inauguration. At the top of their list was Assistant Secretary of State Braden, whom many in the greater Caribbean celebrated for his mid-1940s opposition to dictatorships. When approached about the honor, Braden admitted he was more than glad "to express our gratification over Árbenz's assurances that he wished to rid his country of the Communists and to play with the United States." Believing at the time that Árbenz could provide stability for US-Guatemalan relations, Miller and Mann liked this idea, only for Braden to dictate, "I would then tell [Árbenz] that there was only one way—repeat *one way*—in which he could do so and that would be to seize and kill the top seven or eight Commies and that I meant *kill* and not imprison or deport." In early 1951, they considered Braden's suggestion "too violent" and chose not to send him. At the end of the year, Braden boasted that those two officials had reversed course. They "now acknowledge," he confided to a friend, "that my advice was good and that it was the only thing which could have done the trick and that it may be too late even for such measures to succeed at this time."[1]

In 1952, the US government joined the transnational counterrevolution. That year, dictators and reactionaries approached two global powers, the United States and Britain, to patronize schemes to overthrow Árbenz's government. In the process, Somoza and Castillo Armas lobbied Truman's military aides and sparked a bureaucratic conflict. Serendipitously, this inspired the State Department to participate. With the US and not the British government backing the plot, the CIA's Operation PBFORTUNE built on the transnational counterrevolution. It imploded, however, when US officials failed to comprehend the reach of those who had spent over half a dozen years trying to realize what had only just become the US government's goal.

Lobbying Uncle Sam

Years of reactionaries and regimes networking and conspiring, with some assistance from the UFCO, collided as they lobbied for the US government's support. Before the 1950s, the CIA paid little attention to Latin America in comparison to other regions distinctly subsumed by the Cold War, though Guatemala's "pronounced anti-US attitudes" stood out.[2] As had the State Department, the CIA by mid-1951 saw Árbenz in an unfavorable light, an opening for the UFCO's agents to offer their resources.[3] Soon, Corcoran met CIA officials to solicit "assistance" for Castillo Armas and his ally Juan Córdova Cerna.[4] Castillo Armas's relationship with the UFCO remains unclear, for he may have established a relationship on his own, through a regime, or through Córdova Cerna who had been one of the corporation's lawyers.[5]

In early 1952, the CIA sought to understand the forces opposed to Árbenz's government. In January, the agency identified three prominent reactionaries: Castillo Armas with the UFCO, Ramírez, and Ydígoras Fuentes.[6] With limited knowledge of the region's intrigues, agents noted links between Castillo Armas, Somoza, Carías, CEUA, and the CCN, and a March report elaborated on Somoza and Carías's patronage of Castillo Armas.[7] Still, the CIA did not know that for half a dozen years dictators, sometimes individually and sometimes jointly, financed multiple reactionaries. For a thorough evaluation, chief of the Western Hemisphere Division Colonel J. C. King ordered agents to make direct contact with Castillo Armas and assess the reactionary's alliances.[8] Revealing that the US government was moving against Árbenz, these contacts may have begun influencing reactionaries' alliances, for Castillo Armas and Ydígoras Fuentes the same month signed a "Pacto de Caballeros" (Gentlemen's Agreement) to unite their forces.⁹ For years, reactionaries depended on regimes for financial assistance while lobbying US officials, but this was the first time the US government expressed interest. To obtain such largesse, Castillo Armas's allies assured the agency that he was "willing to delay his movement until he is given the green light."[10]

The State Department's concerns escalated with the Árbenz government's Decree 900, the Agrarian Reform. Backed by governmental credit, loans, expanded infrastructure, and labor committees, peasants received titles to uncultivated lands from large estates whose owners would be compensated on the basis of their tax returns. In a country where illiteracy and poverty defined daily life for the majority, Decree 900 offered an alternative path for economic development and social reform. Though envisioned and implemented by communists, Decree 900 resembled moderate, reformist ideas implemented by US officials elsewhere during the Cold War. Nevertheless, US officials judged the program too radical.[11]

The State Department's reaction to the Agrarian Reform reinforced its interventionist policy. In April 1952, Miller and Mann's staff implemented a covert propaganda campaign in which US embassies and legations were to reproduce negative materials on Guatemala and communism in local newspapers and other outlets.[12] Complaining "that there is little appreciation throughout Latin America and in Guatemala of the inroads which Communism has made in that country and the threat that it presents to the unity and security of the hemisphere," the State Department would use this propaganda to rally "public opinion in Guatemala" and the Western Hemisphere.[13] By that point, the IRD had been the primary producer of anti-communist materials, its staff disseminating in May 1952 alone more than thirty articles through Guatemalan newspapers.[14] Under pseudonyms such as "Raúl Pichardo," IRD-authored pieces titled "What Is a Communist?" and "Communist Infiltration in Costa Rica" appeared in Marroquín Rojas's *La Hora* and *El Impacto*, Vela's *Imparcial*, and elsewhere.[15] The next month, US officials were distributing numerous articles critical of Árbenz's government, including those from "Raúl Pichardo."[16]

Castillo Armas's primary patron, Somoza, was also taking action. At the beginning of 1952, the dictator used a medical operation in Boston to request an official state visit. Ambassador Thomas Whelan, as well as some military officers and congresspersons, believed Somoza at least deserved a military decoration, but Miller rejected the request.[17] The White House's recent renovations had delayed state visits, making any spontaneous event potentially "embarrassing." "Extremely fond" of the dictator, Miller only approved alternative arrangements and military decorations.[18] Maneuvering around such inconveniences, "Somoza invited himself" for an early May visit, forcing Miller to recommend the "minimum courtesies due a Chief of State."[19] Here, Somoza's lobbying gained support from Truman's military aides, General Harry Vaughan and Colonel Cornelius Mara.

Vaughan was a passionate anticommunist susceptible to lobbying and flattery. In the late 1940s, Republicans investigated Vaughan for accepting gifts related to shipments of freezers.[20] Though nothing improper was officially uncovered, the scandal became fodder for journalist Drew Pearson's reporting on corruption and earned Vaughan's ire. Years later, Mara defended his colleague: "I was so angry at Drew Pearson. He was my special hate."[21] To push back on these allegations, Vaughan characterized his critics as part of a "smear campaign."[22] These efforts provided the opportunity for infamous antisemite Gerald L. K. Smith to start a correspondence with Truman's aide.[23] Smith, too, hated Pearson, not for reporting on corruption but for allegedly being a "strategic part of the antichristian, antichurch, procommunist underground movement in the world."[24]

Defending Vaughan as a "patriot" standing against "left wingers, spies, Communists, and stool pigeons," Smith contacted the aide, sending an anti-Pearson pamphlet as a "tribute to a great patriot who has the moral courage to stand up against the most vicious conspiracy of ridicule and character assassination in the history of our Nation."[25] This flattery worked, and Vaughan asked for a dozen "interesting pamphlets" of which he "hope[d] to be able to make good use."[26] During their brief friendship, Vaughan hosted Smith for dinner and introduced the antisemite to Mara.[27] Although the two aides soon stopped answering Smith's correspondence, Vaughan's character allowed such a figure to get close to Truman's staff.

Along the same lines, reactionaries and dictators networked with the aides. Into the early 1950s, Vaughan learned about the region's political tensions so as to avoid offending regimes hostile to those friendly to the US government.[28] US-Guatemalan tensions, though, did not dull his personal tastes or desire for military decorations. During a Central American trip coinciding with Árbenz's inauguration, the State Department denied the inclusion of Truman's military aides, which could seem "improper," create "trouble" if awarded military honors, or escalate tension at a time when US officials hoped Árbenz would be a "moderate."[29] Rather than recognizing these issues, Vaughan tried to remain, forcing the under secretary of state to defend his staff's decision.[30] Furthermore, Vaughan and Mara's interpreter was veteran reactionary Padilla, who had somehow gained enough influence to position himself near Truman's aides.[31] It required the protests of Honduran Ambassador Heliodoro Valle and multiple State Department officials to remove Padilla.[32] Meanwhile, no one complained of the aides' cordial relationships with dictators. In Nicaragua, Somoza regularly treated the two to luncheons at Managua's Hotel Majestic and receptions at the Club Terraza.[33] Later that year, Trujillo awarded Vaughan the Orden al Mérito Juan Pablo Duarte (Juan Pablo Duarte Order of Merit).[34]

Familiar with regional tensions and enjoying the dictators' graces, Vaughan in early 1952 tried upgrading Somoza's visit. Circumventing the State Department, he declared himself "an authority on Central America" and pled for Truman to give Somoza "some recognition plus a dinner and a 'kidney medal.'"[35] Truman replied halfheartedly, telling his aide to handle the matter with the State and Defense Departments and noting, "It is going to be rather difficult to take care of him, but we will manage it some way."[36] Vaughan leveraged this to upgrade the visit to include a meeting with Truman and a small luncheon.[37] He then pushed for more, claiming to have "spoken to [Truman] concerning the proposed visit" and, despite "some embarrassing aspects," the US government "had to give Somoza the honors due his office," including "the customary medal of Commander of the Legion of Merit." Trying to verify Vaughan's assertions, Miller only dissuaded the aide when warning that any oddities would bring "the wrath of the American press on us and on Somoza." Possibly due to his encounters with Pearson, Vaughan relented.[38] Though it would not be an official visit, Vaughan succeeded in improving Somoza's trip to include time with the US president.

Somoza used this upgraded visit to lobby the Truman administration to overthrow Árbenz's government. Thanks to the dictator's jovial personality, much of this was cloaked in good humor and informalities. When touring with Vaughan, the two joked about how Somoza could use nuclear bombs to carve a canal in Nicaragua.[39] He used this frivolity to hint at his conspiratorial goals. At the luncheon with Truman and other US officials, attendees broached the subject of Árbenz's government, and Somoza remarked, "Just give me the arms, and I'll clean up Guatemala for you in no time." Supposedly, those present "laughed" and "took it as a good joke."[40] Later, Truman gave Somoza a tour of the White House.[41] In the renovated kitchen, the two "alone" discussed classified matters.[42]

This lobbying continued during official meetings with Truman, Acheson, Miller, and Vaughan. To all, Somoza admitted he "was prepared to take the initiative in overthrowing the present regime in Guatemala."[43] Somoza and others, whom US officials did not realize made up a network, would provide material support to Castillo Armas and his allies for an invasion. Any complaints at regional or international venues, whether the OAS or the UN, would be set aside thanks to the regimes' representatives.[44] With this "behind-the-scenes approval," all the US government needed to make public was its "noncritical attitude."[45] Somoza believed, "If the United States would even turn its back for a short time, the Central Americas could clean up the situation."[46]

The lobbying appeared to succeed only because of Vaughan. Acheson admitted that the US government opposed Árbenz's government but offered nothing substantive. As Somoza would tell everyone, Miller consistently rejected these proposals.[47] The State Department's position drowned out Truman's seeming interest, at which point Vaughan seized the initiative to assure Somoza that the US government would provide the necessary "assistance."[48] Leaving the United States, Somoza did all possible to nurture his relationships with Truman's aides, his best links to the US government's support. Circumventing the State Department and supposedly acting on Truman's orders, Vaughan offered Somoza an airplane to return to Nicaragua.[49] Showing his gratitude, the dictator offered the aides more medals, while Mara accompanied Somoza to Managua for various ceremonies.[50]

Somoza's lobbying through the aides hit its mark. In Managua, Mara openly endorsed the dictator's plans. During a party at Whelan's house, Somoza and Mara "talked rather openly of the attempt on Guatemala to be made with Nicaraguan and US backing."[51] Mara's boldness surprised Whelan, who asked John Ohmans from the Office of Middle American Affairs about the matter. When pressed, Somoza "referred to the Guatemalan situation and expressed his views that the communists were in control there and were creating a cancerous growth in the Americas." To remedy this, the dictator planned to "get arms into the hands of the Guatemalan oppositionists to help contribute to the downfall of the present rulers there." As promised in Washington, Somoza "said he could facilitate this arms movement to the proper people in Guatemala without any involvement for the United States." Mara then interjected to criticize the State Department. Following Somoza's brief description of the conspiracy, Mara "expressed his own view that [the State Department's] Guatemalan policy was too weak and vacillating and that [the State Department] should take strong action." As if this were not enough, he blamed Miller and Mann specifically for "not acting strongly enough with Guatemala."[52] In front of the State Department's own officials during a semiformal event, Truman's military aide lambasted the interventionist policy and openly endorsed Somoza's plot.

Returning to the United States, Mara encouraged Truman to endorse Somoza's conspiracy. On July 11, he wrote the president a memorandum, saying, "A gentleman in whom you have confidence advises that the situation in Guatemala has reached such a stage that some positive action is necessary." Repeating reactionaries and regimes' allegations, Mara warned that people throughout the Western Hemisphere felt the US government was "condon[ing]" or "fully approv[ing]" Árbenz's government. It was time the State Department should "decide on some stringent action and implement it in a sudden move."[53] The aide then handwrote a message to Truman: "Somoza . . . could clean up the Guatemala regime with 10,000 rifles and one million rounds without ever involving [the] US."[54] On July 17, Ohmans and Whelan interviewed Mara, who did not hide his lobbying and admitted writing the materials. Despite petitioning Truman, though, Mara could not give a clear answer about the response.[55] Meanwhile, Somoza informed his allies of the aide's assurances.[56] Possibly due to his own personalist regime where aides to a head of state could wield immense influence over bureaucratic officials, Somoza failed to grasp the divisions between Vaughan and Mara's grandiose promises and a reticent State Department.

As reactionaries continued to learn, the State Department seemed inflexible. At the end of May, the CCN's Barrios Peña met with State Department officials to ask what the US government would do to help Guatemalan anticommunists, only to be lectured on the US government's "traditional policy of noninterference and nonintervention." Gaining no material assistance, the reactionary remarked, "The United States, as the power of preponderant influence in the Western Hemisphere, could not escape taking notice of the situation on moral and humanitarian grounds if on no other."[57] In mid-July 1952, with only Truman's military aides endorsing Somoza and Castillo Armas's plot and a State Department making known its commitment to nonintervention, any "green light" seemed unlikely.

Finding Scapegoats

The lobbying by Truman's aides and Somoza inadvertently became a factor to obtain the State Department's approval. Following their May orders, CIA contacts confirmed Honduran president/dictator Gálvez's backing of

Castillo Armas.⁵⁸ Into June, sources investigated the reactionaries.⁵⁹ Some contacts presented Castillo Armas and Córdova Cerna's connections as best, but others preferred the underground opposition inside Guatemala under the CCN's Simmons and Barrios Peña.⁶⁰ As always, reactionaries' divisions persisted, leading some to consider timing Simmons's uprising with Castillo Armas's invasion.⁶¹ Weighing upon the CIA's decision-making was the fear of an unsuccessful anticommunist uprising. Waiting for additional support, Castillo Armas, Simmons, and others stressed that they had suspended their tentative plans the past months but could not hold back much longer. An antigovernment uprising, done poorly, would fail without proper backing, giving the government sufficient cause to destroy "all effective anticommunist opposition in Guatemala." Although Castillo Armas appeared best positioned, the CIA concluded that it was imperative to support all reactionaries with "token assistance" to maintain their "continued confidence" and prevent a premature movement.⁶²

On July 10, State Department and CIA officials met to assess the situation. Dreading an abortive anticommunist uprising, Deputy Director Allen Dulles and his staff put forward three central questions:

1. Does [Miller and Mann's State Department] want the change in government envisaged in the Summary?
2. Would [the State Department] like it to be assisted covertly?
3. Would [the State Department] oppose it?⁶³

Miller appeared open to the CIA's intervention, provided it remained hidden, a point Mann vociferously reiterated.⁶⁴ Based on the State Department's response, and its own confidence in keeping its role hidden, the CIA believed it had permission to proceed. When informed that Miller and Mann had "not answered clearly but by implication positively," Director Walter Bedell Smith scheduled a meeting with Under Secretary of State David Bruce.⁶⁵ On the basis of the resulting conversation, Bedell Smith approved the CIA's assistance.⁶⁶

The agency commenced supporting Somoza and Castillo Armas's plan. Though lacking a nuanced understanding of such relationships, the CIA identified the regimes' and UFCO's important roles. First, the agency intended to inform Somoza and Gálvez "that any assistance they give to Castillo [Armas] will not reflect to their discredit."⁶⁷ Second, officials met with the UFCO's representatives. Although Bedell Smith approved material support, the agency would remain at arm's length, only facilitating shipments.⁶⁸

As the UFCO learned, the CIA stressed that the corporation and its allies, whose "interests were materially involved," would be the ones to "pay the bill."[69] The UFCO's representatives were quite amenable to this arrangement, Corcoran celebrating how "the people interested in Guatemala [had] decided that, as soon as they get their ducks in a row," they would make the necessary arrangements. He even believed they "need not worry about State's feelings being hurt—they have recently asked for just help as [the UFCO] is offering."[70] To the lobbyist, the US government was realizing the corporation's long-standing goal.

With the State Department's seeming approval and the CIA's facilitating assistance, participants agreed to blame any difficulties on Truman's military aides and Somoza. On July 21, some of the same officials convened in response to complications regarding the CIA's covert assistance.[71] Right away, participants addressed Miller and Mann's fears about the US government's involvement, the same fears that permeated the interventionist policy. To allay such concerns, Dulles noted Bruce's approval and showed a cable to demonstrate the agency's commitment to their covert role.[72] He emphasized that, thanks to the UFCO and regimes' financial resources, the CIA did not have to provide direct assistance; the reactionaries' patrons had ample funds. At most, according to Dulles, the CIA's agents and contacts would lead Castillo Armas's organization to the necessary armaments or perhaps help in their delivery. No matter, "all activities, with respect to the hardware, would be restricted as far as [they] were concerned to this country, and handled through cutouts." Most importantly, Dulles warned that any current inaction would prevent any future action. If Castillo Armas's invasion commenced without the requisite support, anticommunist forces would be obliterated, with the US government receiving the "blame" despite its nonparticipation.[73] Here, Mann mentioned the controversy stemming from Mara's lobbying Truman, information confirmed by the State Department four days earlier. This is precisely where the military aides and Somoza's actions worked to the CIA and State Department's advantage. Building off his warning that the US government would be criticized even if it was not to participate, Dulles "suggested that this again was evidence that if anything happened, there would be plenty of other persons to blame for it."[74] If the plot were uncovered, the aides' and Somoza's lobbying would be the scapegoat, allowing the CIA and the State Department to redirect blame toward those who had made no secret of their support for Castillo Armas. These figures not only put forward this plot but also provided a possible cover up.

With a pact to blame the aides and Somoza, both departments got to work. The next day, Dulles ordered agents to locate suitable ports and prepare the armaments' shipping manifests, possibly through New York City to Puerto Cabezas, Somoza's favored easternmost port.[75] Meanwhile, Miller began compartmentalizing his office's role in the affair, officially distancing his staff from the plot yet unofficially allowing it to move forward, in order to ensure the State Department's plausible deniability.[76] Although his staff learned of Mara's lobbying on July 17, they documented this encounter on July 21, the same day as Miller's meeting with the CIA.[77] Next, Miller wrote his superior, Freeman Matthews, to warn that "Mara's activities in regard to Nicaragua and Guatemala [were] potentially dangerous."[78] Freeman Matthews relayed this note on "Mara's extravagant ideas" to Acheson just "in case."[79] Simultaneously, Miller called on Whelan. To ensure a clear separation between the State Department and Truman's aides, Miller instructed Whelan "to inform Somoza that the State Department was not interested in sponsoring a 'covert' aggression on any American State." However, "Miller indicated to Whelan that he thought some support for Somoza might be coming from the Army."[80] In essence, Miller shielded the State Department from any allegations that his staff violated the nonintervention principle while allowing the CIA to move forward and hanging any potential backlash upon Truman's aides.

This compartmentalization came into play immediately when US officials in Managua made these points clear to their Nicaraguan counterparts. In early August, Ambassador Sevilla Sacasa lunched with Mara. When Mara mentioned Vaughan's efforts to get weapons, Sevilla Sacasa repeated what he had been told: this matter needed to go through the Department of Defense before receiving the State Department's approval.[81] Apparently, the military aides and Sevilla Sacasa devised a solution to solicit armaments while keeping the State Department at a safe distance: the Mutual Defense Assistance Program (MDAP), a relatively new aspect of US foreign policy that allowed the US government to provide military assistance to allies threatened by communist aggression.[82] Mara and Vaughan encouraged the Department of Defense to incorporate Nicaragua under the MDAP, which then only required the State Department's approval. In Washington, Sevilla Sacasa walked this fine line and stressed that any armaments "would be strictly for the purpose of internal protection."[83] Likewise, Somoza wrote that the US government's support was "a necessary measure in relation to [Nicaragua's] security against the communist threat which intensifies its gravity for the Central American countries of the type which is unfolding in Guatemala."[84]

With their new patron, Castillo Armas did what most reactionaries did and sought additional resources. At the end of July, Castillo Armas informed his CIA contact "Jacob R. Seekford" that the plot required submachine guns, pistols, bombs, mines, grenades, and more.[85] Facing pushback on his request, Castillo Armas responded with a simple offer: either the plot would continue with reduced support, such as no bombers, or the plot would continue with no support at all. His contact Seekford warned the CIA that Castillo Armas would "make the attempt even without such assistance," the central fear driving the plot's approval. Leveraging this position, the reactionary and his contact were "convinced that the best solution [was a] green light" to Somoza, who might help with the transport aircraft.[86] Right away, the CIA's contacts organized armaments for delivery.[87] Dulles and other CIA officials approved these matters.[88] By the middle of August, Colonel King reported that the light machine guns, ammunition, and grenades were ready to be shipped.[89] The soon-to-be-named Operation PBFORTUNE was moving forward.

Welcoming a New Partner into the Network

With the US government's involvement, Somoza and Castillo Armas's plot became the most concrete conspiracy yet devised. As they had for the past years, the regimes' network shared information on the plot while securing resources. Most notably, they did not see this scheme as their northern neighbor's product; rather, they interpreted the US government as one new member in their loose association. Spearheaded by Somoza, they raised the necessary funds, as the CIA ordered, which inadvertently alarmed the State Department. For the better part of a decade, the network's members had discussed reactionaries' proposals, and they did so during PBFORTUNE. Although Somoza and Castillo Armas kept the CIA informed of such matters, this intelligence sharing threatened Miller's compartmentalization and plausible deniability. In effect, the network's long-standing efforts both created and undermined PBFORTUNE.

Days after Mara's trip to Nicaragua, Somoza called on Dominican Ambassador Emilio Rodríguez Demorizi and explained that any forthcoming action would target Árbenz's government rather than Figueres in Costa Rica. To the network, Figueres remained a key target, but it was clear that the US government did not feel the same. With the "assistance" for Castillo Armas's plot on its way, members needed to maintain "absolute secrecy."[90] Upon learning of the US government's support, Somoza reached out to his allies. In mid-August, Castillo Armas traveled to Nicaragua, where the dictator promised "all the support necessary," including training grounds and bomber aircraft.[91] As expected, Somoza's son Tachito edited Castillo Armas's typically long list of requests while stressing that Nicaraguan forces could not provide transport aircraft. On top of this, Castillo Armas's forces needed to raise funds for their living expenses. The transport aircraft, though, caused a minor dispute when Tachito claimed they were not available. Castillo Armas pleaded for their use, which would be replaced if damaged or lost, according to the CIA. To remedy this conflict, the reactionary suggested that another contact or agent be deployed to Nicaragua.[92]

Despite their increased role in nurturing Guatemalan anticommunism, British officials remained out of the affair, though the network tried soliciting their support. In August 1952, the IRD's Lecours made contact with the CCN's Simmons.[93] As CIA contacts discovered, Simmons and Barrios Peña were seeking armaments for their own efforts independent of Castillo Armas and Córdova Cerna.[94] To help, Lecours introduced Simmons to Dominican Ambassador Héctor Incháustegui Cabral, who described Simmons as "the representative of the wealthy groups from Guatemala and himself a person with important property." Despite such resources, Simmons was "searching for help, weapons in a word."[95] Following protocol, Incháustegui Cabral put Simmons in touch with Bernardino, Trujillo's agent who networked with reactionaries in Mexico.[96] While Simmons met with Bernardino, on August 20 Barrios Peña met with Incháustegui Cabral and Lecours. The Guatemalan reactionary and Dominican ambassador asked the British intelligence official if it were "possible to utilize the territory of Belize to transport indispensable materials for the Guatemalan opposition, already, united, to overthrow the current Government." Restraining his zealous advocacy on the subject, Lecours diplomatically warned that issues related to Belize needed to go through another British ministry. Though he would certainly bring this request to his superiors, "it could take a while," so he mentioned that Honduras might be a more suitable location.[97]

With this suggestion, Incháustegui Cabral reached out to the interested regimes' officials in Mexico City. That same day, he contacted Venezuelan and Cuban officials, who approved of the idea and left to obtain their superiors' opinions. The next day, Incháustegui Cabral hosted the Nicaraguan, Salvadoran, and Colombian ambassadors "to learn what would be the position of their Governments regarding the possibility that there emerges a serious movement in Guatemala." "Everyone, absolutely everyone," Incháustegui Cabral confirmed, "agrees that a change of Government, in the ideology of the Government, that is, of Guatemala would be useful for the healthy coexistence of the Continent, principally in the Caribbean zone." All would "immediately communicate with their respective Governments to suggest, if possible, [putting] something like pressure on Tegucigalpa," since the Honduran ambassador was not available for the meeting.[98] As Somoza and the CIA supported Castillo Armas's forces, others were coalescing around Simmons and Barrios Peña.

Together, Somoza and Trujillo redirected this momentum back into Castillo Armas's plot. Facilitated by Lecours and Incháustegui Cabral, Simmons and Barrios Peña met with Bernardino and gained Trujillo's patronage.[99] In mid-September 1952, reactionaries seemed divided between Castillo Armas and Córdova Cerna's group on the one hand and Simmons and Barrios Peña's group on the other.[100] Fortunately for Castillo Armas, Somoza was his intermediary with Trujillo.[101] After Somoza confirmed the US government's support, Castillo Armas traveled to Honduras.[102] The next day, Bernardino arrived, and Castillo Armas requested Trujillo's support.[103] Bernardino did offer Trujillo's largesse but demanded a favor in return: the dictator wanted Castillo Armas to murder four Dominican exiles in Guatemala before the invasion.[104] Though he wanted to postpone such assassinations until after the coup, Castillo Armas told his CIA contact that he and Bernardino compromised.[105] Since his "own plans included similar action" with "special squads," he "would be glad to carry out" the executions after overthrowing Árbenz's government.[106] Days after this meeting, Trujillo ordered Simmons and Barrios Peña to cooperate with Castillo Armas.[107] It required the combined efforts of the CIA and the intelligence-sharing network, but Guatemalan reactionaries finally seemed capable of uniting after years of rivalries and disagreements.

As Castillo Armas's primary patron, Somoza tapped into the network to raise the funds the CIA expected. In early September, he met with Rodríguez Demorizi and Zuleta Ángel, the latter completing his Caribbean trip, to discuss the plot's cost. At this point, the leading patrons were Somoza and Trujillo, whom Rodríguez Demorizi claimed "carried the heaviest load." As such, it was frustrating that "el apoyo yankee (Yankee support)" was not larger. Demonstrating his government's commitment to the scheme, Zuleta Ángel interjected to proffer his assistance.[108] First, he, a former lawyer for the UFCO, would petition the corporation, who had a large investment in Colombia, to pay for more of the costs.¹⁰⁹ Then, after traveling to the Dominican Republic, he would head to Caracas to petition Pérez Jiménez before going to Cuba to meet with Batista.¹¹⁰ By September 12, Somoza informed the CIA that Trujillo and Pérez Jiménez were assisting the project.¹¹¹

Rodríguez Demorizi, though, recognized the dilemma in how the network's intelligence sharing could undo the very conspiracy it birthed. Somoza updated his allies about the plot's progress, including the arrival of an "'emissary' to 'coordinate'" with Castillo Armas and Tachito regarding the shipments. Yes, the regimes were the ones gathering the funds for the plot as the CIA wished, but the CIA did not know how many regimes collaborated. Somoza's inclusion of Zuleta Ángel had lessened the regimes' collective burden but "compromise[d] further [Somoza's] moral position regarding the number of individuals that ha[d] been made participants" in the conspiracy.¹¹² Unaware of the bureaucratic debates taking place in Washington, he recognized the dangers behind the plot's growing size.

And Trujillo, who best personified the personalist dictator unconcerned with formal bureaucratic divisions, set off this alarm. While vetting Castillo Armas and coordinating with Somoza, Trujillo ordered Ambassador Thomen to confirm the US government's participation.¹¹³ On September 11, Thomen broached the topic during a scheduled meeting with Miller. As their conversation began, Thomen stated that "the Dominican Republic was ready and anxious to do everything incumbent upon it to engage in anticommunistic activities." Compartmentalizing PBFORTUNE to ensure the State Department's plausible deniability, Miller officially documented his response that "no understandings had been arrived at as to methods of combating communism."¹¹⁴ In Thomen's view, however, Miller was plenty receptive. After describing the US government as "absolutely noninterventionist," Miller commented that "'the situation of other countries is probably very distinct' with respect to the problems of nonintervention." Admitting that the US government would welcome "a change of regime in Guatemala" and "offer recognition and support," he asked, "What would be the attitude of [Trujillo's regime]?" and "Would [Trujillo] recognize the new Government?"¹¹⁵ As Miller intended, Thomen understood the US official's position: maintain the US government's public commitment to nonintervention while allowing the scheme to progress. As a result, Thomen shared with his superiors his belief that Miller and other US officials would not "openly participate in a plan to overthrow the communist Government of Guatemala" but would "turn a blind eye" and "welcome any movement." He warned, "Knowing the duplicity of [the US government], it would not be too adventurous to assume that what [US officials] desire is that *someone else* resolves *their* problem, overthrowing the Government of Guatemala, but in such a manner that [they] could not be accused of being interventionists."[116]

Canceling Operation PBFORTUNE

As Thomen foresaw, the network dismantled Miller's plausible deniability and unraveled PBFORTUNE. Although the regimes' cooperation from July into September raised money and strengthened the scheme, it paradoxically threatened the covert nature demanded by the CIA and Miller. One reason it took months before US officials grasped such activities was their prevailing ignorance of the network. Most State Department officials in the greater Caribbean did not give significant attention to inter-American relations, focusing on their nation-state posts or the dictators' comical mannerisms. In mid-November, when interviewed about Somoza's activities after PBFORTUNE's cancelation, First Secretary Rolland Welch still did not believe that Somoza cooperated with Pérez Jiménez or other dictators.[117] US officials sympathetic to local heads of state repeated these false positions. From the mid-1940s into the mid-1950s, Ambassador Erwin insisted that Carías and Gálvez would never assist reactionaries.[118] Though PBFORTUNE made it clear that regimes supported one another, US officials were oblivious.

Another reason was that Miller wanted the plot to succeed. As with his July messages about Mara's lobbying, he never took an active role discouraging the scheme. In early September, Somoza told Whelan that the regimes were cooperating as he searched for armaments, facts the State Department and the CIA knew.[119] When Whelan reported on this development, neither Miller nor Mann responded or filed a report, passively allowing Somoza's activities. Only after meeting with Thomen did Miller act. Of course, he started by following Dulles's July suggestion: blame Somoza and Truman's military aides. On September 17, over two weeks since Somoza's conversation with Whelan but five days after meeting Thomen, Miller rebuked the dictator for "going around representing himself as an authorized agent of Uncle Sam to stamp out communism in the Caribbean," using the US government's "good name in enlisting 'allies.'" This blame also fell upon the two aides, whose "seed which Colonel Mara planted" was "growing into a greater tree than" anyone expected. Due to Mara's indiscretions, Somoza was "apt to spread this thesis even more."[120]

Adding to this conundrum was the upcoming October inauguration of Panamanian President José Antonio Remón. Those familiar with Mara's lobbying on Somoza's behalf worried what might transpire when the dictator socialized with fellow heads of state. Having "heard that Somoza considers that he got the green light from President Truman to do something in Guatemala," Ohmans confessed his fear "that, if Somoza is in Panama at the same time that Mr. Miller is, there might be talk that we are getting together to give our instructions to President Somoza."[121] The network's activities compounded this concern. Before the inauguration, Somoza asked Remón whether he would join efforts against Árbenz's government.[122] While in Caracas, Zuleta Ángel delivered a memorandum to US Ambassador Fletcher Warren, which referenced Somoza's coordination of "a mutual effort to defend against Communism in this area" as well as Trujillo's pressure to unite reactionaries.[123]

The final warning sign came from Somoza's ambassador. Up to this point, Sevilla Sacasa adeptly maneuvered to keep the plot separate from arms requests facilitated by Truman's military aides. On September 26, the ambassador met with Miller and Ohmans. Opening the conversation, Sevilla Sacasa repeated his earlier dialogue in which he recognized that the State Department and "Miller's assistance in the acquisition of arms" was only to approve Vaughan's recommendation for MDAP armaments. This did the trick, except Sevilla Sacasa then updated the two officials about the regimes' activities. He and Zuleta Ángel were sharing information about meetings with colleagues revolving around a "great understanding and concern over the growing communistic actions of the Government of Costa Rica" and a "consensus of concern over Guatemala." To address the latter issue, there was a "plan" to meet at Remón's inauguration, precisely what the State Department dreaded. Right away, Ohmans took Sevilla Sacasa to Mann. There, the ambassador summarized his previous talking points while stating "that the group was considering a 'military' plan" for "the organization of a military group to overthrow the Guatemalan Government, a kind of Caribbean Legion in reverse."[124] As with his previous discussions, Sevilla Sacasa likely thought his emphasis on the military nature of the matter was sufficient.

Instead, his conversations forced Miller and Mann to shut down any possible rumors of the US government's involvement. For the past weeks, Miller had kept the plot at a reasonable distance so as to avoid being implicated, only for these September conversations to render his efforts moot.

In Washington, Mann called Sevilla Sacasa for a tensely formal conversation in which Mann "said that he wanted to speak very frankly and very carefully to the Ambassador and emphasized that, although his remarks were in the friendliest manner possible, he was speaking officially for the State Department." He then elaborated that, despite a shared opposition to communism and Árbenz's government, the State Department did "not believe it wise to speak of military adventure against Guatemala." The US government adhered to the nonintervention principle and participated in international organizations where the slightest violation could undermine a country's reputation and influence. Furthermore, recent events made it clear that "the proposal was, as a practical matter, reckless since it would not be possible to maintain secrecy." Taking notice of Sevilla Sacasa's disappointment, Mann assured him that Miller would "speak along these same lines" to Zuleta Ángel in Panama.[125]

There, Miller's words revealed his failure to compartmentalize PBFORTUNE. Whereas Miller never filed a report on Remón's inauguration, Zuleta Ángel was glad to share details with his colleagues.[126] Supposedly, Miller soaked up the event's joyful atmosphere, and on October 1 a drunk Miller found Zuleta Ángel. When they discussed the plot, he claimed that "the State Department looked upon that concerted action with interest and sympathy and encouraged it." The next day, without the "euphoria of drinks and drinking," a sober Miller dictated the State Department's official policy, this being the one time the US official fully admitted his weeks-long efforts. He confessed that, while the US government looked favorably upon the scheme, it was essential to preserve the image of nonintervention. Miller "could allow Zuleta [Ángel] personally, as a friend, to discuss informally whatever news about the subject" he had, but he "did not even want any representative of a foreign government to inform any of [his staff] about this matter." In fact, Miller told Zuleta Ángel that the forthcoming decision to officially halt PBFORTUNE "was not at all shared by the White House, at which one detects the tendency is to liquidate the current situation in Guatemala."[127] Whether in Washington or Panama, the assistant secretary of state kept the blame upon Truman's military aides.

Placing Blame

Subsequent events shifted that blame. Still in Panama, Miller ran into Tachito, who informally remarked about the arms shipments.[128] Returning to Washington, Miller and Mann led the State Department in filing a flurry of reports. These presented the September conversations with Thomen, Sevilla Sacasa, and Zuleta Ángel as revelations into the regimes' military action against Árbenz's government, leaving out the writers' own meetings with the CIA.[129] For its part, the CIA pushed forward with PBFORTUNE. On October 4, Bedell Smith ordered his staff "to get the show on the road" and deliver the armaments.[130] Days later, he brought up the matter with Bruce, trying to reassure his State Department counterparts to stay the course.[131] Instead, an agent or contact in Managua approached Whelan about the armaments, the same day State Department officials convened "to talk over a situation in Latin America."[132]

On October 8, the State Department and the CIA shut down PBFORTUNE. All parties "agreed it would not be undertaken," but questions lingered as to what had transpired.[133] Thanks to Miller's compartmentalization, most of the State Department had been in the dark, so the various September conversations surprised many. Speaking on behalf of the CIA, Deputy Director of Plans Frank Wisner and Colonel King explained that their July records and conversations indicated that they had received the State Department's "green light." Miller retorted that his position was that "the risk of providing arms was too great but that he had no objection to monetary contributions." This claim, too, was further evidence of Miller's complicity, since Dulles repeatedly emphasized that other parties had the financial means to cover all related expenses. Similarly, Bruce maintained that his conversations with Bedell Smith did not indicate approval for the project.[134]

To remedy this dispute, participants chose to blame those outside their respective departments. Miller highlighted that Somoza was the key figure telling parties throughout the greater Caribbean that he had the US government's approval, and the CIA's representatives made it clear that they never made such assurances. Together, they followed Dulles's original idea and "agreed that [Somoza's] statements could be based only on remarks made to him by members of the White House staff," Truman's military aides.[135] For weeks, Miller looked the other way to allow those outside the State Department to overthrow a democratic government, and the CIA may have misconstrued its colleagues' position on facilitating armaments and overstepped its bounds.[136] Fortunately for those who wished to sidestep any critical examination, blaming Somoza and the aides avoided bureaucratic conflicts and rivalries.

Quickly, the blame fell heaviest upon Somoza. Once in a while, some would admit that Truman's aides played a role, but most relied on paternalistic tropes and even blatant racism to keep the focus squarely on Somoza. The CIA's King was the first to do so, arguing, "This confirmed our general belief that no Latin American can be trusted to keep his mouth shut."[137] In the State Department, Mann paternalistically suggested that "the Latinos are gradually waking up to their responsibilities" against communism.[138] Likewise, Miller repeated this stance, telling Warren that it was "good to see some of the latinos getting together on an anticommunist front." He only regretted "this business of a 'green light' from Uncle Sam" and wished that "some of the characters involved were more discreet."[139] These lukewarm sentiments flew in the face of what had just transpired and made clear their ignorance of their Latin American counterparts' beliefs and activities. For years, regimes stood against anything its members deemed communist, and they brought to the US government the foundation of what became PBFORTUNE.

Blaming Somoza became PBFORTUNE's official history. Although the State Department and CIA originally agreed that Truman's military aides were responsible for much of what transpired, most officials chose to overlook Vaughan and Mara's role. Mann claimed that "the word was being passed around" about the US government's unauthorized support of the plot due to Somoza, while Secretary Welch blamed the dictator's lack of "secrecy or caution."[140] As time passed, Somoza received all fault, and Miller would even reminisce that Somoza somehow "sold" Mara on the entire scheme, entirely forgetting how the aide had criticized the State Department's interventionist policy while lobbying on the dictator's behalf.[141]

This too was the CIA's position. Upon halting PBFORTUNE, the agency sent a message to Castillo Armas that "the indiscretions of Somoza" had "alerted" the State Department.[142] Throughout the project, Somoza and Castillo Armas regularly updated the CIA, whether in raising funds from Pérez Jiménez or soliciting Trujillo's assistance. Nevertheless, Seekford told Castillo Armas that the entire scheme ended "as a result of the indiscrete approaches to the Department by Generals Somoza and Trujillo." Unwilling to lose the potential largesse of the Western Hemisphere's most powerful government, Castillo Armas conceded, "The actions of Generals Somoza and Trujillo were ill considered. I can appreciate the reaction of the US government."[143] Castillo Armas's deference masked his and the regimes' frustrations. They had built up what had become Operation PBFORTUNE, only for the US government to back down. In fact, Zuleta Ángel made such feelings clear to Miller while in Panama and argued that "panamericanism . . . assumes as a basic idea an anticommunist America." While the State

Department treasured a fake image of nonintervention, Zuleta Ángel and others in the regimes' network believed "no measure that seeks to remove communism from America can be refuted as a violation of those principles and agreements."[144] Even with the US government's exit, Somoza tried to continue the plot by lobbying Vaughan, only for the CIA to rebuff the aide's entreaty.[145] With the US government having terminated what had been one of their most promising opportunities to finally overthrow Guatemala's democratic government, the network's members doubted the Colossus of the North.

British Worries

Inadvertently, PBFORTUNE implicated the British government, since reactionaries linked to the IRD, such as Simmons and Barrios Peña, spent August and September 1952 traveling the greater Caribbean. On September 22, Minister Gallienne warned his superiors, "The rumor is current that an anticommunist revolution will be staged at any moment and that it is not the Americans who are supporting the revolutionaries, but the British."[146] The Foreign Office, though, did not take the rumors seriously. Yes, there were meetings with reactionaries, Lecours's newspaper articles, and the IRD's patronizing anticommunist organizations behind "the unrest in certain provinces in Guatemala." Nevertheless, the Foreign Office believed these were "only a few bits of the evidence that Guatemala can produce to show we are meddling."[147] Currently, Árbenz's government was dealing with its "most pressing immediate problem," that is, "her fear of a threat to the regime, either from the opposition within . . . or from her neighbors without."[148] More importantly, British officials were finally feeling relieved thanks to the US government's increased opposition to Guatemalan communism. "Latin America is, as people in the Pentagon here put it, in a US strategic lake," one official concluded. "I am inclined to believe those here who assure me that in practice a real communist seizure of power anywhere in Latin America would be put down with US help, though the US cannot actually say so beforehand."[149]

Chapter 8

Realizing the Counterrevolution

Operation PBSUCCESS, 1953–1954

Scholars have spent the past half century examining how the US government helped overthrow Árbenz's government in 1954. What they have found is that, after taking office, the Eisenhower administration approved Operation PBSUCCESS, and the CIA under Director Dulles prepared Castillo Armas and his followers to launch a paramilitary action after some training in bases allowed by sympathetic Central American governments. However, the invasion from Honduras into Guatemala fell under a broader psychological campaign aiming to weaken the Guatemalan public and military's morale. Bribery of Guatemalan officials, radio broadcasts, the Catholic church's anticommunist warnings, and CEUA's propaganda and harassment hit their marks thanks to the CIA's support. The State Department under Secretary of State John Foster Dulles assisted with an arms embargo and an anticommunist resolution at the Tenth Inter-American Conference at Caracas in March 1954. These actions contributed to the Árbenz government's decision to purchase Eastern European armaments. Seeing the public backlash and the US government's clear antipathy, the Guatemalan military requested Árbenz's resignation, even as Castillo Armas's invasion faced defeat. After pressure from the Eisenhower administration, the military consented to a new regime under Castillo Armas, marking the 1944–1954 Guatemalan Revolution's end.

This chapter, though, does not retread the CIA's management of or the State Department's role in PBSUCCESS. Rather, this chapter recovers others' contributions: veteran Guatemalan reactionaries, Caribbean Basin dictators, the UFCO, the British government. Since the 1940s, these forces waged a transnational counterrevolution that endured into PBSUCCESS. At numerous moments, these groups acted independently or jointly to assist the US government, sometimes unknown to the CIA or the State Department. The entire operation depended on reactionaries and dictators who made clear their intent to strike against Árbenz's government with or without the US government's leadership. Glad to help at international venues, reactionaries continued their rivalries while networking with Mexican anticommunists, Caribbean Basin officials, and members of the US Congress. Throughout, the UFCO's propaganda campaign expanded to guide the anticommunist sympathies of the US media, Congress, and public. Meanwhile, the State Department's arms embargo benefited from that of its British counterpart. Ultimately, the US government played the crucial role in overthrowing Árbenz's government, but many aspects of PBSUCCESS emerged out of the preexisting counterrevolution.

The CIA Takes Charge: Salamá's Rivalries and Warnings

Following PBFORTUNE, the US government's administrative units discussed their respective roles. Calming bureaucratic tensions, the CIA stressed its "responsibilities" toward Castillo Armas in order "not to be even more embarrassed with our Central American friends."[1] Toward this end, the CIA supplied cash for the next weeks, but the lingering issue was the debacle over the halted plot. In December 1952, Bedell Smith promised that the CIA would stay "in compliance with policy guidance."[2] By March 1953, now Director Dulles offered up an outline for any future operation. It would involve installing a more aggressive ambassador, encouraging now President Dwight D. Eisenhower and Congress to openly criticize Guatemalan communism, and employing economic warfare.[3] Into early 1953, the CIA waited for the Eisenhower administration's signal to proceed.

In motion before PBFORTUNE, the counterrevolution did not wait. Reactionaries solicited their patrons for assistance, Castillo Armas warning the CIA, "I shall be obliged to develop other contacts, i.e., Venezuela, Cuba, and Mexico."[4] He did just that by maintaining his relationship with Somoza and cultivating alliances with the Dominican and Venezuelan regimes.[5] Still, this support appeared minimal in PBFORTUNE's aftermath, so he sought the US government's endorsement. His CIA contact claimed, "Neither General Trujillo or General Somoza will give us material help without being properly assured [that] the United States government approves of such help." The contact warned that, despite lacking sufficient resources, antigovernment forces were preparing "to strike" in early 1953.[6]

The resulting Salamá uprising failed due in part to reactionaries' usual rivalries. Though Castillo Armas networked with Dominican and Venezuelan officials, Trujillo and Pérez Jiménez preferred Barrios Peña and Simmons.[7] Already, they were launching a plot to seize the military garrison at Salamá in Baja Verapaz during the Good Friday holiday and spark internal uprisings with their allies inside Guatemala.[8] Invited to contribute, Somoza informed US officials that "he would not participate in any action toward Guatemala without first informing" the State Department.[9] After PBFORTUNE, Somoza would not entertain another plot without the US government's approval, but other dictators proceeded. On the eve of the uprising, Barrios Peña secured the assistance of the Dominican, Venezuelan, and Salvadoran regimes while lobbying for Batista's help.[10] Other reactionaries undermined the plot. Ydígoras Fuentes sought out Salazar, who helped his 1950 presidential campaign but now backed Castillo Armas.[11] In fact, Castillo Armas may have sabotaged the uprising. Under Somoza's protection, in mid-March 1953 he reached out to meet personally with Trujillo.[12] Abruptly, the Dominican dictator pulled out of the plot after Castillo Armas told everyone that Barrios Peña was Árbenz's spy. Despite Trujillo's withdrawal and Barrios Peña's warnings to wait, Simmons launched the uprising.[13]

Salamá's failure reverberated across the greater Caribbean. The Guatemalan military crushed the rebels as Árbenz's government detained numerous conspirators and suspects.[14] Conservative newspapers denounced the arrests of many alleged conspirators, most notably Córdova Cerna.[15] As had those under Arévalo, Árbenz's representatives fought an uphill battle to convince the people that the conspiracy was real.[16] Critics summoned the government's treatment of prisoners and inability to prove the uprising's details as evidence of unbridled persecution, while participants presented themselves as anticommunist martyrs.[17] In multiple issues of its *Boletín*, the Comité de Estudiantes Universitarios Anticomunistas Guatemaltecos en Exilio (Committee of Guatemalan Anticommunist University Students in Exile, CEUAGE) characterized these events as violations of the constitution and the UN's Declaration of Human Rights.[18] Issues described those killed in both the Salamá uprising and the 1950 Base Militar attack as "patriots" and "victims" of a "genocide" in "the claws of communism."[19] Guatemalan officials remained as vigilant as possible but faced suspicions that constitutional suspensions and mass arrests were politically calculated. In June 1953, they forwarded to Mexican officials information that Ponce and Salazar were organizing a plot with the UFCO's help, but nothing came of this.[20] If anything, Ponce spent this time failing to obtain any patron's support.[21]

The resulting arrests destroyed part of Guatemala's domestic anticommunist opposition and fractured reactionaries' relationships. Castillo Armas blamed Barrios Peña and Simmons for allowing their "personal ambitions" to waste "the economic assistance of Guatemalan and foreign capitalists" and "the military aid from other countries," while Barrios Peña spent the next two years denouncing Castillo Armas's seeming betrayal.[22] Trujillo joined Somoza in stipulating that reactionaries, roughly divided between Castillo Armas, Barrios Peña, and Ydígoras Fuentes, needed to unite.[23] Expelled, Córdova Cerna joined Castillo Armas to lobby Dominican officials regarding "their desire to obtain armaments."[24] A Dominican official then traveled to Havana to deliver Castillo Armas and Córdova Cerna's request for Batista's help.[25] In Salamá's shadow, Castillo Armas and his allies presented themselves as the most capable force, requiring fresh injections of money and armaments to replace what was just lost.[26]

The CIA saw their greatest fears realized in Salamá. Agents had warned that a premature uprising with insufficient backing would give Árbenz's government cause to eliminate the anticommunist opposition. Now, it was not clear any uprising could succeed.[27] After PBFORTUNE, the CIA waited on the margins while "it appeared possible that certain anticommunist governments of the Caribbean would lend sufficient support in arms, planes, and money." However, Salamá proved this was no longer possible, with regimes demanding "reassurance that the United States is prepared to back them effectively in maintaining a friendly attitude toward our interests and in defending themselves against aggression or self-styled retaliation on the part of Guatemala."[28] As September began, the operation against Árbenz's government was approved, now "sponsored" by the US government.[29]

New Operation, Same Reactionaries

The CIA's decision to back Castillo Armas did not end reactionaries' rivalries. Throughout the early 1950s, Ydígoras Fuentes and his son-in-law tried meeting with British officials.[30] In mid-1953, he sent Central American diplomats manifestos on behalf of the Comité Guatemalteco Anticomunista (Guatemalan Anticommunist Committee).[31] Days before Castillo Armas's invasion, the Salvadoran minister of foreign relations offered to arrange a meeting between the US ambassador in San Salvador and Ydígoras Fuentes, who "need[ed] money to buy arms and to buy the support of Guatemalan army officers."[32] Fortunately for those directing PBSUCCESS, Ydígoras Fuentes's plot failed to materialize.

Due to unsuccessful lobbying, some reactionaries joined Castillo Armas. In Guatemala, Arenas approached the US Embassy in Guatemala City, who redirected him to Julius Cahn, the counsel for the Senate Foreign Relations Committee under Senator Alexander Wiley (R-WI). In December 1953, Arenas met Wiley in Washington, DC.[33] The next month, Arenas obtained an audience with Senator Karl Mundt (R-SD), who sent the reactionary to meet with Senator Joseph McCarthy (R-WI), who embodied US anticommunist paranoia. [34] Recognizing McCarthy's status, Arenas and an associate beseeched him as "the one Government official in the United States who would be most interested in seeing that the spread of Communism ceased in Guatemala or in fact in the world." Despite their efforts, they only met the senator's aide to request five hundred thousand dollars, supplementing what the UFCO and other regimes promised, "to exert the force necessary to overthrow the Communist Government in Guatemala." Nothing immediately came of this meeting.[35] With no influential patrons, Arenas backed Castillo Armas.[36] Those refusing to endorse Castillo Armas were shut out. Ramírez and Ardón tried lobbying Nixon to no avail, and Barrios Peña was completely sidelined.[37]

Reactionaries who joined PBSUCCESS played essential roles. With their years of experience, they helped Castillo Armas propagate anticommunist views circulating since the mid-1940s. With the CIA's help, Castillo Armas published *Yo Acuso* [*I Accuse*].[38] He blamed Arévalo, "through the threads of an international network on the Continent," for spreading "International Communism" and undermining Ubico's regime.[39] In exile, CEUA repeated this theme, suggesting links between the "Argentine" Arévalo, the Legión, and the Soviet Union.[40] In a confidential memorandum shared with dictators, Castillo Armas described an anticommunist struggle against "the Red International Network" since the 1930s. Despite its being suppressed in Guatemala and El Salvador, "the Conspiracy" survived because Guatemalans abroad were "carefully indoctrinated in the Marxist disciplines and battle tactics recommended by Lenin." "Under the instructions of the central hubs in Moscow and Mexico," "communist cells" under Lombardo Toledano played a pivotal role against Ubico and Ponce. After installing Arévalo, these forces disrupted the greater Caribbean's peace with attacks against neighboring governments, complementing the "anti-US policy" against "Yankee imperialism."[41] Thanks to his alliances, Castillo Armas kept alive the anticommunist ideology of those who first plotted against Arévalo's government.

A key component of PBSUCCESS's psychological dimension, the student organizations, was derived from the counterrevolution.[42] As did British intelligence, the CIA helped CEUA and its exile organization, CEUAGE, distribute pamphlets, stickers, newsletters, and other pieces of propaganda.[43] These materials were sent to journalists, diplomats, religious leaders, and more.[44] Coronado Lira, Salazar, and Calderón Salazar helped CEUA abroad, with Coronado Lira and Salazar behind a splintering faction in El Salvador, the Frente Anticomunista de Guatemaltecos en Exilio [Anticommunist Front of Guatemalans in Exile].[45] Together, students' publications merged the mid-1940s' anticommunist claims with contemporary controversies to depict Árbenz's government as a threat to hemispheric solidarity and compare the treatment of Guatemalan prisoners to the North Korean regime's methods.[46]

Other aspects of Castillo Armas's activities relied on these reactionaries. Salazar networked between Calderón Salazar, student organizations, and the FPAM.[47] Reactionaries also bolstered Castillo Armas's reputation and influence. Calderón Salazar and Arenas stood alongside the CIA's chosen leader when warning that any who refused to endorse the Plan de Tegucigalpa, an agreement for Guatemalans to unite against Árbenz's government, would have no voice in a postcoup government.[48] As Castillo Armas's secretaries, Coronado Lira and Salazar signed bulletins and announcements.[49] Remaining almost as hidden as he was during Ubico's regime, Pinillos served as Castillo Armas's trusted agent in Tegucigalpa and the rest of the greater Caribbean, networking between reactionaries and Carías.[50] While incorporating the US government's resources, Castillo Armas's movement built on a decade of plots.

Transnational Allies at International Venues

This experience bolstered international conferences targeting Árbenz's government, specifically the Tenth Inter-American Conference at Caracas in March 1954 and the Primer Congreso Contra la Intervención Soviética en América Latina in Mexico City in May. The truth is that both events were relatively small triumphs against Guatemalan communism. In Caracas, US delegates leveraged loans and trade deals to obtain an anticommunist resolution that, after amendments, should have hindered any intervention in Guatemalan affairs.[51] In Mexico City, dozens of Mexican and Guatemalan representatives dwarfed the handful of voices from Brazil and elsewhere.[52] Nevertheless, US officials summoned the Caracas resolution and the Congreso as evidence of the Western Hemisphere's anticommunist solidarity in 1954. This delusion was not their own creation, for reactionaries' transnational alliances legitimated and magnified the two events' results.

At Caracas, the highlight was Guatemalan Foreign Minister Guillermo Toriello. After Foster Dulles denounced international communism, Toriello unleashed an anti-imperialist speech defending Guatemalan sovereignty to the delight of attendees and his country. Critics, though, reproduced a predetermined script. There, Coronado Lira and Salazar denounced Guatemalan communism, their proclamations boosted by regimes' press and radio.[53] Furthermore, they built an ideological defense against Toriello's speech. Days before Caracas, US congresspersons as well as Mexico's conservative *El Universal* derided Guatemalans' anti-imperialism as communism.[54] The UFCO's favored journalist Tomlinson mocked Guatemalan complaints of "Yankee imperialism, Yankee intervention, Yankee exploitation of helpless Latin American peasants and Indians, and of course Yankee big business."[55] Across the United States, newspapers including Ohio's *Toledo Times* denigrated Toriello and his admirers, while the American Legion portrayed the speech as proof that "communism has definitely established in Guatemala a beachhead on the American continent."[56]

This bled into widespread propaganda presenting Caracas as a victory against international communism. Assisted by the UFCO's public relations campaign, Dominican, Cuban, and Nicaraguan delegates received much coverage.[57] US outlets picked up this theme, as when Missouri's *Independence Examiner* highlighted Árbenz's government as the "lone dissenter" against the "resolution calling for a firm front against Communist infiltration in the Western Hemisphere."[58] In a feedback loop, the UFCO informed journalists and political leaders that Coronado Lira and Salazar's presence somehow "nullified in part" Toriello's positions.[59] Reactionaries then contrasted an image of hemispheric solidarity against Guatemala, which the UFCO republished.[60] These forces, inside and outside the United States, repeated the Eisenhower administration's false interpretation of the Caracas resolution.

A similar pattern emerged with the May 1954 Congreso in Mexico. Outlining in September 1953 how to restart efforts against Árbenz's government,

Dulles pondered the "creation of a real or notional society of international character for freeing Guatemala from Communism" with "agents and representatives throughout the Western Hemisphere sending out anticommunist petitions."⁶¹ Unknown to US officials, Dulles's idea was the realization of what Arenas and Prieto Laurens's FPAM envisioned in 1950. In January 1954, before backing Castillo Armas, Arenas traveled not merely to Washington, DC, but throughout the greater Caribbean Basin to meet religious leaders, workers, and student organizations.⁶² Upon joining PBSUCCESS, Arenas teamed up with Coronado Lira as they rallied their contacts in Venezuela, Nicaragua, Honduras, and El Salvador for an anticommunist conference.⁶³

The Congreso would be the product of the US government's funds, reactionaries' networking, and Mexican anticommunism. At its outset, CIA officials wanted to "smokescreen US activities in PBSUCCESS" and "create [the] maximum psychological impact on the target audience in Guatemala." Additionally, the Congreso would "build a hemisphere mechanism for combatting Soviet influence in Guatemala" and "unify the several anti-Árbenz groups in exile." In early March, one agent offered Arturo Ramírez ten thousand dollars to join, and Prieto Laurens was promised a similar amount if the FPAM would cooperate.⁶⁴ Funds might have tempted some reactionaries to coalesce around Castillo Armas, but Mexican anticommunists needed no inducement. Prieto Laurens took the money as his associate Florencio Ávila traveled the region, meeting first with Ramírez and Calderón Salazar in Mexico, Ydígoras Fuentes in El Salvador, and Castillo Armas in hopes of uniting reactionaries. Soon after, Ávila was traveling with Coronado Lira. By April, the Congreso's organizers had discussed with their allies plans for a Liga de Defensa contra el Comunismo en América (Defense League Against Communism in America) while soliciting funds from the UFCO and sympathetic regimes. This collaboration also disseminated Castillo Armas's writings and speeches among sympathetic newspapers in Cuba, the Dominican Republic, Costa Rica, Panama, Nicaragua, and Honduras, all likely to publish the conference's proceedings.⁶⁵

In effect, the resulting May 27–30 Primer Congreso Contra la Intervención Soviética en América Latina became a propagandistic coup far bigger than its immediate impact.⁶⁶ Most regimes, with the exception of Nicaragua, had no delegates, and most countries were represented by one or two figures. What stood out were the number of Mexican and Guatemalan delegates, the former including FPAM members and the latter led by Arenas, Calderón Salazar, Coronado Lira, and Salazar. After two days of lackluster proceedings, the third day centered on Guatemalan communism, and all members on the final day endorsed Arenas's and Coronado Lira's calls for hemispheric solidarity against the "Soviet yoke."[67] Despite its patronage, the CIA failed to control the event. Most panels and speeches included vague broadsides against Soviet and international communism, with Prieto Laurens's extremely conspiratorial screeds attracting a couple of walkouts and mocking press coverage. Nevertheless, attendees leveraged their networking to inform the greater Caribbean about the supposedly successful event. The CIA and anticommunist students disseminated favorable articles about the Congreso, and the UFCO advertised the reactionaries and FPAM's networking as emblematic of the region's anticommunist spirit.[68] The Congreso's real legacy was legitimating reactionaries' decade of opposition. The event's memorial opened with a brief history, stressing that exiled communists returned to Guatemala "under the plans prepared in Mexico" by Lombardo Toledano. This continued with the Legión and Arévalo's foreign policy that supported Soviet agents in overthrowing preexisting regimes and spreading "the red infiltration." Behind every regional disruption, this international communist conspiracy was at work.[69]

Uncle Sam's Best Friends: The Regimes Back PBSUCCESS

Fitting into PBSUCCESS were the regimes seeking to eliminate any antidictatorial haven. To US officials, these tensions were an exploitable asset, since strengthening nearby militaries would reshape "the balance of power" and weaken the Guatemalan military's morale.[70] While keeping such matters quiet to avoid anti-US backlash, US officials hoped Guatemalan leaders might recognize that "military aid to neighboring countries [was] an expression of US determination to eliminate Communist leadership and influence."[71] Though the funds were small, this military assistance complemented refusals to provide requested trainers and staff to US military missions, making clear the US government's position.[72]

Regimes gladly accepted these resources while uniting around Castillo Armas. As always, dictators kept their legations and embassies open to receive reactionaries' solicitations, but alliances at first seemed intact. After refuting the allegations against him, Barrios Peña returned to Trujillo's graces, and Dominican officials tried to obtain regional support.[73] However, Somoza, the UFCO, and the CIA preferred Castillo Armas.[74] No longer dictator, Carías wielded immense influence and supported Castillo Armas, but Gálvez sought proof that the US government preferred Castillo Armas, reassurances that arrived by April 1954.⁷⁵ Solidifying Gálvez's support were Honduran labor strikes blamed on Guatemalan and Mexican communism. With Trujillo soon backing him, Castillo Armas faced no significant rival, but coalescing around the CIA's candidate did not mean that regimes strictly adhered to the US government's objectives.

They still opposed Figueres. Despite his public denials, Figueres provided assistance to Auténticos-in-exile, AD-in-exile, Dominican exiles, and more.⁷⁶ For these reasons, regimes blended their opposition to Figueres into their roles in PBSUCCESS. By December 1953, Trujillo's and Pérez Jiménez's officials asked Castillo Armas to contact Calderón Guardia, who met with Castillo Armas's representative Pinillos.⁷⁷ Soon, they came to a pact against Figueres that reinforced Pérez Jiménez's participation in PBSUCCESS.⁷⁸ By April 1954, Figueres's agents reported that those training in Nicaragua at Somoza's estates to invade Guatemala were assisting Calderón Guardia's allies and preparing to "make a simultaneous attack" into Costa Rica.⁷⁹ Only because of his own frustrations with Árbenz's policies and US officials' assurances that there was no plot against him, Figueres kept quiet.⁸⁰ A failed attempt to assassinate Somoza further complicated everything. In April 1954, Nicaraguans Baéz Bone and Leal, Dominican Soler, and Honduran Ribas Montes organized a plot to kill Somoza, but the dictator bragged that he knew of the upcoming attempt on his life.⁸¹ Afterward, Somoza seized upon the exiles' relationships with Figueres to publish numerous copies of relevant diplomatic notes, survivors' forced testimonies, and captured documents that did not mention Guatemalan communism.⁸² Perturbed at the very tensions US officials sought to exploit, Foster Dulles worried these matters would "distract" from PBSUCCESS.⁸³

Foster Dulles did not foresee how this actually galvanized those behind PBSUCCESS. As some participants and many anti-Somoza activists sought asylum at the Guatemalan Embassy in Managua, Somoza summoned this as evidence that Árbenz's government was assisting "Nicaraguan citizens . . . accused of participating in communist activities" and broke diplomatic relations.⁸⁴ Upon learning of the attempt, Venezuelan officials cabled their allies throughout the region that Figueres and Betancourt ordered the assassination.⁸⁵ Following suit, Arenas described the attempt as Árbenz's scheme to disrupt the Congreso and spread "international communism."⁸⁶ Members of the US Congress endorsed this view, somehow determining that the failed assassination of Somoza and strikes in Honduras "were linked in a Communist plot, engineered in Guatemala, to seize control of all Central America."⁸⁷

Keeping Guatemala in the News: Bernays's Propaganda Campaign

Operating apart from the US government, the UFCO boosted PBSUCCESS with a simple mailing list. The company's public relations expert, Bernays, and the UFCO director of public relations, Edmund Whitman, compiled a list of contacts to receive voluminous compilations of propaganda and numerous reports critical of Árbenz's government. At a time when one had to solicit publications directly from the US government, Bernays immediately sent out copies of the Senate Special Subcommittee on Security Affairs's *Strength of the International Communist Movement*.[88] Of course, Bernays ensured that his dozens of contacts received the latest articles, including Nathaniel Weyl's "Quarantine of Red Guatemala?" in *The Freeman*, but he also shared older items such as Will Lissner's 1950 *New York Times* articles on "communist underground agents" in Guatemala.[89] In February 1954, Bernays and Whitman targeted the foreign news editors of over two dozen newspapers, from New York and Pennsylvania to California and Washington.[90]

Especially receptive to the newsletter were smaller US-based newspapers. Bernays's list of contacts included congresspersons and writers with a national audience but reached outlets unable to send journalists abroad. For example, New York's *Buffalo Evening News* asked to be put on the list.[91] Soon, the newspaper's editor prepared a "background package accessible to [his] editorial writers," with the "material . . . of help in the story now unfolding in Guatemala."[92] Bernays's reputation and influence put his writings in the hands of journalists who did travel. When the *Cleveland Plain Dealer* sent journalist Mary Hirschfield to Central America, the publicist had his newsletter waiting at her return "as background information," which she gladly received.[93] These journalists tipped off Bernays about anything related to Guatemala, allowing him to reach out to Arkansas's *Pine Bluff Commercial* when it published a favorable editorial. By the beginning of May 1954, at least seventy-five US publishers and politicians were receiving Bernays's newsletter.[94]

Bernays supplemented stand-alone articles with his "Guatemala News Notes," an edited compilation of news, articles, speeches, and anything else that cast all events in Guatemala as a product of international communism. Whereas complete articles were in English, the "Guatemala News Notes" included translations and summaries of Spanish-language materials, including articles from *El Impacto* and *La Hora*, not readily available to US readers. Bernays did defend the UFCO, but the newsletter typically stressed communism's influence and anti-US manifestations. Regarding disputes over the

Agrarian Reform, Bernays highlighted anti-imperialist protests during May Day activities. Another issue noted an "oversized photograph of the Viet-Minh Communist leader Ho Chi-Minh" and a "float [with] Uncle Sam with red claws dripping blood, reaching for a Guatemalan."[95] With the Guatemalan Congress praising Russia and Guatemalans returning from Poland or Hungary, it required little effort to denounce the Sociedades de Amigos de Guatemala (Society of Friends of Guatemala) in Mexico and elsewhere as "Communist front organizations and Communist-inspired meetings."[96] Obviously, Bernays received no pushback when spreading bombastic rumors about Soviet submarines in the Caribbean.

Such rumors were not Bernays's creation; rather, they resulted from his networking with Latin American conservatives and regimes' agents. In early 1953, the public relations expert met with Trujillo's journalist, Stanley Ross. For two hundred dollars, Ross allowed Bernays to reprint and reuse material from Ross's *Communism in Latin America* booklet, which Trujillo publicized in the mid-1940s to present all antidictatorial activities as communist.[97] Still assisting the dictator, Ross then wrote articles on Guatemala for the *New York Daily News* and offered them to Bernays for five hundred dollars.[98] The material that made up Ross's *Report on Guatemala* and *Guatemalan Communism Endangers the Americas* booklets was a boon that came out of the journalist's networking with Guatemalan editors, officials, and anticommunists.[99] His writings touched on overwhelmed but valiant anticommunists, the Legión as international communist saboteurs, and an Agrarian Reform somehow modeled on the Soviet Union's policies.[100] Much more valuable was Ross's list of contacts throughout the Western Hemisphere to help distribute reports and obtain further information. Alongside Trujillo's agents and Carías's son at the UN, the list included editors and journalists for newspapers under conservatives and regimes: Nicaragua's *Novedades*, Cuba's *Información*, Colombia's *El Colombiano*, Venezuela's *El Universal* and *La Esfera*, Mexico's *El Universal*.[101] Through these channels, Bernays's "Guatemala News Notes" disseminated stories of Soviet submarines in the Gulf of Mexico, Russian arms caches on Caribbean coasts, and other unfounded allegations from Somoza, since they were backed by a supposedly respectable Mexican newspaper.[102] Ross's array of information strengthened Bernays's narratives, as when Mexico's *El Universal* called the Sociedad de Amigos de Guatemala "a Bolshevik concentration prepared by the Mexican Communist Party and the Mexican Worker-Peasant Party."[103]

Meanwhile, the US Congress remained critical of Guatemala due in part to the UFCO's lobbying. Tomlinson sent now Senator Mansfield his articles, and Corcoran mailed various congresspersons Tomlinson's article, "Reds Have Master Plan for Middle America," with a business card asking, "China again?"[104] Targeting influential congressional leaders, Bernays inundated Hickenlooper with Russell H. Fitzgibbon's articles on Latin American communism and anything on Guatemala from *The New York Times* and the *New York Herald Tribune*.[105] As in 1952, UFCO agents paid close attention to Hickenlooper and Green's work on the Senate Subcommittee on Latin American Affairs, especially its members' late 1953 trip through the region. Despite the subcommittee's resulting report vaguely referencing Latin American opposition to "Yankee imperialism," Tomlinson praised the two congresspersons as marvelous experts, in contrast to the "politicians and so-called advisers who may control votes in Middletown and Possum Trot, U.S.A., but who [have] never been south of [the] border before and are unable [to] utter [a] word in any other language except [their] own."[106]

Working Through Wiley's Office: Bernays and Cahn

Few noticed these connections because of lobbyists' and others' efforts to keep the UFCO out of the headlines. Since the mid-1940s, the corporation stressed that the conflict was not over its bananas but over communism. The entire time, its propaganda minimized Guatemalans' complaints about economic reform and national sovereignty into a simplistic attack against the United States, a pattern repeated by US officials. Visiting Guatemala in mid-1953, Assistant Secretary of State for Inter-American Affairs John Moors Cabot wished to discuss the Agrarian Reform but could not escape Guatemalan officials' complaints about the company's anticompetitive practices and treatment of workers. He admitted that the corporation's "hands are by no means clean" but could not tolerate Guatemalan officials' and Árbenz's arguments, insisting that they "showed a fanatical hatred for American companies and their actions in Guatemala."[107] In his official October 1953 remarks, Cabot blamed US-Guatemalan tensions on communism and anti-US sentiments, making his statements a suitable resource for Corcoran to circulate. When Cabot issued an aide-memoire critical of Árbenz's government coinciding with mid-September celebrations for Guatemalan independence, Guatemalan officials posted slogans against "foreign intervention."[108] McCormack celebrated Cabot's statement as "an official confirmation" of what the UFCO's allies had described for half a dozen years.[109] The issue was not bananas but communism, epitomized in one of Hickenlooper's final statements on Guatemala: "When we say 'communism,' the Guatemalans answer, 'United Fruit Co.' When will any Guatemalan Government official answer our charges on the real and only issue, which is international communism?"[110]

Another reason few detected the corporation's involvement was that its agents covertly acted through official channels. Figures like Wiley did not appear to have any connection to the UFCO when discussing Guatemalan communism. In October 1953, Wiley spoke before the City Club of Milwaukee and blamed Moscow and Lombardo Toledano for "training [Latin America's] future Red rulers."[111] The following January, Wiley delivered an address before Congress, proclaiming, "The source of our concern is that Guatemala has become a serious beachhead for international Communism in this hemisphere." He proceeded to offer "some 22 facts," though claiming to have over two hundred, on "the stark record of the subservience by Guatemalan Communism to Moscow Communism."[112] These speeches hit their marks. From Virginia, William McNamara with the *Petersburg Progress-Index* read Wiley's speech and offered to send his own articles on Guatemalan communism.[113] Julius Cahn, Wiley's assistant as counsel for the Senate Foreign Relations Committee, assured McNamara that the senator "would indeed be interested in receiving copies . . . on this critical question of Communism in the Caribbean."[114] With Wiley as that committee chair, few wondered if his activism was related to the UFCO.

An attorney in Lima, Ohio, did. In a March 1954 letter, Elmore McClain asked "if [Wiley] obtained from or on behalf of the United Fruit Company the purported information anent Guatemala . . . included in a Senate address."[115] The senator denied the allegation. He swore, "I have not seen or been in contact with any representative of the United Fruit Company in connection with my two addresses on the Communist problem in Guatemala."[116] This was at best a half truth, evident in his insertions into the *Congressional Record*. On one hand, he submitted items clearly available to a Wisconsin senator, such as an editorial from the *Sheboygan Press* and an article from the *LaCrosse Register*.[117] On the other hand, Wiley submitted one of Tomlinson's articles along with an article from Texas's *Dallas Morning News* and two from Tennessee's *Nashville Banner*.[118] Only those on Bernays's mailing list would have recognized that the *Nashville Banner* editorials had been sent two days earlier.[119] In his letters to the newspapers about these insertions, the senator did not credit Bernays and claimed to have learned of the articles "through someone's courtesy."[120] This "someone" was likely his assistant, Cahn, who networked directly with Bernays.

The relationship between Cahn and Bernays started as early as 1953 when Bernays was preparing a report on Guatemala. Before sending it out, he approached Cahn, who arranged a subsequent meeting with Hickenlooper's staff. By April, Bernays felt the seventy-five-page report was strong enough to share with other congresspersons' staff.[121] The reason for Cahn's coordination with Bernays is unknown. It is possible they held a similar anticommunist view of Guatemalan matters or that networking with any source of information was typical of Cahn's work for Wiley and the Senate Foreign Relations Committee.

Together, Cahn and Bernays reinforced the US government's policy toward Árbenz's government. Right after Wiley's January 1954 speech, Cahn distributed copies of Wiley's statement, "Communism in Guatemala—A Menace to Hemispheric Security," to other congresspersons.[122] He then sent Bernays the statement. The next week, Bernays included Wiley's speech in his "Guatemala News Notes." This pattern continued over the next months.[123] Thanks to this circulation, Wiley's speeches reached an international audience. Near the end of January, the Guatemalan legislature denounced Wiley's speech, which emboldened the senator. He retorted that his twenty-two claims had yet to be disproven, the same response he gave to his constituents and other US citizens.[124] This was also what the State Department appreciated. As with McCormack's speeches the previous years, US officials expressed gratitude for a congressperson's scathing remarks on Guatemalan communism, Cabot cheering, "I am sure that you must be pleased and proud that your remarks directed against the Communist infiltration in Guatemala should so obviously have struck home and that no reply has been forthcoming for the simple reason that they could not be refuted."[125]

Due to Cahn's maneuvering between Bernays and the State Department, Wiley's congressional office became an outlet reassuring the public about US policy toward Guatemala. Cahn made Wiley's various speeches available for the State Department, which shared its materials with the senator's office. At one point, the State Department sent Wiley a chronology of events in Guatemala in 1953 summarizing the Agrarian Reform, Toriello's criticisms of the US press, and Fortuny's publishing an article in a Soviet-supported outlet. Wiley's staff then distributed the chronology to constituents, journalists, and anyone else interested in Guatemalan affairs. The entire time, Cahn was both receiving and sharing information from and with Bernays and the State Department.[126]

Defending US policy, Bernays and Cahn spearheaded a public relations campaign through the American Legion to rally US public support.

Beginning in March, the two were using Wiley's January 1954 speech to draft a "Guatemala reprint" for distribution throughout the United States when Bernays suggested that they work with Edward McGinnis, the American Legion's national public relations director.¹²⁷ Soon, Cahn sent McGinnis fifty sample copies.¹²⁸ With sufficient input from all involved, they titled the final draft, "Communism in Guatemala—22 Facts."¹²⁹ In April, Wiley and Cahn attended the American Legion's National Commission on Foreign Relations meeting and played a "film on Guatemala."¹³⁰ Next, Cahn provided the Pioneer Letter Company, for almost seven hundred dollars, the first of three hundred thousand flyers that would be mailed to the American Legion's posts and auxiliaries across the country.¹³¹

With such resources, congressional leaders and public servants brushed aside constituents' criticisms of US policy. From California, J. Stuart Innerst asked Wiley whether the US government should "consider the nations to the south of us sovereign states with the right to order their affairs as they see fit."¹³² Robert F. Muse of Boston asked Eisenhower's aide Maxwell Rabb why everyone doubted Guatemala's Agrarian Reform while admiring those elsewhere, as in Italy.¹³³ Born in Madison, Wisconsin, Nathalia Swanson Collver had worked in Guatemala, spurring her to write both Wiley and Hickenlooper. She wondered why the US government refused to sell weapons to the Guatemalan Army and mocked the past years' relentless "planned propaganda."¹³⁴ During the coup, she begged Wiley not to support the "rebel invasion" whose "top two leaders . . . were traitors."¹³⁵ In the socialist *Monthly Review*, Anna Louise Strong doubted Wiley's claims about links between Árbenz's government and the Soviet Union. When Frances Duncan Manning of California suggested that Wiley read Strong's article, the senator forwarded his published remarks.¹³⁶ Manning followed up, asking, "Why a mighty country, such as the US . . . , should be so disturbed at a tiny country" and "Do you really hold that if you were a Guatemalan farmer, . . . the United Fruit Company [would give] you a square deal." Wiley's office did not respond.¹³⁷

Citizens Against Guatemalan Coffee: The CIA's Failed Embargo

With the UFCO's congressional allies, the CIA rallied the US public by inspiring calls for a coffee embargo.¹³⁸ In mid-1953, agents debated alternative means to induce a coup in Guatemala that would not rely on the national opposition seemingly crippled during the Salamá uprising. Among the proposals were a handful of ideas to hurt Guatemala's economy by sabotaging coffee crops or boycotting coffee shipments.[139] As the CIA deliberated, some in Congress such as Representative William C. Lantaff (D-FL), in mid-June 1953, suggested a similar idea, lamenting that Americans "still buy and pay the highest prices in history for coffee and other products of Communist-infested Guatemala."[140] Eventually, the CIA decided to encourage a boycott of Guatemalan coffee.

To begin, the agency chose to work with right-wing radio host Fulton Lewis Jr. This was a rather odd choice due to the cold relationship between the CIA and Lewis, who spread conspiracies that the State Department and the White House shielded alleged Soviet spy Alger Hiss or schemed to smear McCarthy.[141] Despite this fraught situation, the CIA appreciated the national reach of his broadcast as well as his new fifteen-minute television program.[142] At the end of December 1953, the CIA drew up talking points for Lewis on Guatemala, probably because the topic was not a popular one. These points blended years-old unfounded allegations with recent developments to argue that Guatemalan reformers' activities paralleled those of Chinese Communists, Árbenz followed the Kremlin's orders, Lombardo Toledano controlled Fortuny and Gutiérrez, and the country was a "haven" for Latin America's "Communist agents and leaders." Regarding the boycott, talking points stressed that "the Guatemalan Communists have their weak points. . . . The country depends very heavily on its two principal export crops, coffee and bananas."[143]

Soon after, the CIA learned that Hickenlooper would appear on Lewis's program to discuss Guatemala. They had considered Hickenlooper's previous statements on anti-US sentiments in Guatemala as suitable for psychological warfare, but Dulles had an official "produce any information that might help," likely a reaction to how Hickenlooper's Senate Subcommittee on Latin American Affairs had not demonstrated a substantive knowledge of Guatemala during its recent trip.[144] Thus, the agency provided Hickenlooper a memorandum with its own analysis, resembling what was fed to Lewis. "Communism has been growing and developing in Guatemala for at least ten years and is now the most influential political creed in the country," the CIA alleged, with "at least one hundred top Guatemalan Communists, men who have been trained in the Soviet Union, who have genuine stature as Communists go, men who form an integral part of the international Communist conspiracy" overseeing "between 1,500 and 3,000 loyal Communist Party members who are available for the propaganda, agitation, and organization work that a Communist machine requires." Furthermore, "Guatemalan

Communist leaders were trained by international Communism, and they maintain[ed] close, disciplined liaison with the center of international Communism in Moscow." Under "the Kremlin conspiracy," "Guatemalan Communists have trained certainly dozens and probably hundreds of high and medium level Communists from other Central American and South American countries."[145]

With the CIA's assistance, Lewis hosted Hickenlooper, accompanied by Cahn, on his television program on January 22, 1954. Cahn denounced the Agrarian Reform, and Hickenlooper admitted that there was "no fear of a military danger from Guatemala but that the country could furnish bases for guerrilla operations in South America." He then blamed the Truman administration and the State Department for having "refused to come to grips with the problem" in Guatemala. Hopefully, the senator proclaimed, "an uprising by the Guatemalan people against the new type of servitude under the Communists, who are usurpers of the government, would some day occur." The television broadcast ended with Lewis urging his viewers "that, by refusing to accept Guatemalan coffee, the United States could cause the fall of the present Guatemalan government."[146] Not only did Lewis repeat his call for a coffee embargo on his radio broadcast but radio personality Walter Winchell did, too. Following these broadcasts, other outlets reported on the calls for an embargo.

These reports ignited a wave of public support for a boycott of Guatemalan coffee. Across the country, congresspersons received letters, cables, and petitions from constituents demanding some policy to overthrow the Communist regime in the Western Hemisphere. In Montana, the Michels family asked Mansfield to "make every effort to end all trade which might be beneficial to any communist government and as far as possible to any pro communist government."[147] Hickenlooper received letters from Iowa citizens endorsing a boycott "until Guatemala would collapse."[148] From Wisconsin, Mrs. Joe Runyan wrote Wiley, "We are very much against the importation of any coffee from Guatalamala [sic]."[149]

This domestic surge of anticommunist activism did not end at the legislative level; the State Department found itself inundated with letters from congresspersons sparked by their constituents. Representative Wingate Lucas (D-TX) forwarded a petition from Fort Worth while Representative Burr P. Harrison (D-VA) received a petition from a Veterans of Foreign Wars Auxiliary.[150] "Several" of Representative William A. Dawson's (R-UT) constituents supported a boycott.[151] "Typical of many" he received, Representative Charles E. Bennett (D-FL) described a constituent asking, "if the United States would refuse to buy coffee from Guatemala, the Red government there would soon collapse." Though confessing that he had no idea if the statements were true, Bennett stressed, "I do wish to go on record as favoring ending any trade with Communist dominated countries."[152] Similarly, due to "many statements recently appearing in the press regarding the growth of the Communist Party in Guatemala," citizens in Connecticut sent Representative Horace Seely-Brown (R-CT) letters, which forced the congressperson to ask Assistant Secretary of State for Congressional Relations Thruston B. Morton for a "proper response."[153] Senator Lester C. Hunt (D-WY) wrote Foster Dulles directly concerning the pleas of "several Wyoming constituents."[154]

This activism culminated with Senator Margaret Chase Smith (R-ME) introducing Senate Resolution 211 for Eisenhower to order an embargo on Guatemalan coffee.[155] The embargo did not happen, though, as beans became too mixed to selectively restrict one country's imports.[156] Nevertheless, Americans continued demanding an embargo against Árbenz's government. Representative James C. Davis (D-GA) recognized the myriad factors preventing a focused boycott but wanted "to urge that . . . the importation of Guatemalan coffee into this country be discouraged."[157] Many continued asking for a boycott, forcing Morton to prepare a statement assuring the US public that the State Department was working on a "solution to this problem."[158] Into March, Morton kept responding to these requests, such as one from a constituent of Representative Gerald R. Ford Jr. (R-MI).[159] Requests came even in June, very infrequently but requiring Morton's response.[160] Until the coup resolved the matter, congresspersons had to assure their constituents that their elected leaders were standing against Guatemalan communism. Hickenlooper promised petitioners across his state that the Caracas conference would address the matter while Wiley received many petitions.[161] The CIA's efforts through Congress and Lewis may not have launched the desired coffee embargo, but it channeled the nation's anticommunist fervor and provided the impetus for citizens, such as one in Minnesota, to call Árbenz "the red president of Guatemala."[162] The CIA not only collaborated with Congress during PBSUCCESS but utilized UFCO-assisted congresspersons to stoke public opposition.[163]

Not Reporting on the Conspiracy: The January 1954 Revelation Falls Flat

The UFCO's propaganda, Congress's hardline position, and the CIA's failed embargo drowned out what was meant to be the Árbenz government's great revelation in January 1954: irrefutable evidence of the counterrevolution. A Panamanian attaché in Managua, Jorge Isaac Delgado, delivered documents and messages on behalf of Castillo Armas.[164] In September 1953, Delgado began selling these items to Guatemalan officials. Over the next months, Árbenz's government collected a trove of evidence on PBSUCCESS's wide-ranging dimensions with messages between Castillo Armas and Somoza, discussions between Castillo Armas and Ydígoras Fuentes, Dominican officials' concerns about Barrios Peña, purchases of armaments and explosives, some of Castillo Armas's allies within Guatemala, and far more. In late January 1954, Árbenz's Secretaría de Propaganda y Divulgación [Secretary of Propaganda and Disclosure] released the evidence as a booklet that included an overview of the conspiracy and copies of the documents.[165] In February, it had a full write-up, "Documents Expose Invasion Plot: Newsmen Examine Proof of Threatened Attack," in their English-language publications out of their US Embassy and consulates.[166] After years of constitutional suspensions with little evidence, Guatemalan officials finally had conclusive evidence of an international scheme backed by Guatemalan reactionaries, Caribbean Basin dictators, the UFCO, and now the US government.

And it landed with a whimper. Guatemalan newspapers, including *Diario de Centro América* and *Prensa Libre*, reported the majority of the details, but almost a decade's worth of similar charges of international conspiracies, all backed with incomplete evidence, weakened the impact of the January 1954 revelation. Though supporters cheered Árbenz's government, this reaction was overlooked in the rest of the Americas.[167] News did travel in Mexico, where the Sociedad de Amigos de Guatemala shared the Guatemalan Embassy's pamphlet on the plot, but this was the sole country where the conspiracy received significant attention.[168] Most Caribbean Basin newspapers, controlled by their respective regimes, overlooked the charges or repeated their officials' denials.[169] In the United States, the revelation coincided with the CIA's campaign to embargo Guatemalan coffee. The *New York Herald Tribune* did a brief write-up, while UFCO-subsidized journalist Tomlinson defended Somoza's regime.[170] *The New York Times* had a lengthier overview, which accompanied a "special" report on Guatemalan communists' labor activities that watered down the lead story.[171] As in the rest of the greater Caribbean, most US newspapers repeated the State Department's denials with little skepticism, as when *Time* reported on the "completely fanciful" report.[172] Some Guatemalan organizations coupled the revelation with denunciations of Wiley's speeches, which took attention away from the former.[173]

Further marginalizing any notable response were the continued propaganda campaigns against Árbenz's government. In England, *The Daily Telegraph* repeated the State Department's denials.[174] Even in March, British officials mocked the revelation as symptomatic of Guatemala's "persecution complex."[175] French officials highlighted how Guatemalan agents, who had never before carried out such a successful operation, somehow obtained an astoundingly complete picture of this conspiracy.[176] For his part, Bernays buried the revelation in summaries on communists taking advantage of the Agrarian Reform and the Communist Party's commemoration of Lenin's death.[177] This turned out to be more effort than necessary, thanks to the years-long campaign that minimized Guatemalan nationalism as manifestations of communism and anti-US sentiments. *The Daily Worker* reported on the revelation and highlighted the US government's role, but congresspersons saw this as further evidence of international communism.[178] Throughout PBSUCCESS, Representative Jacob Javits (R-NY) portrayed the *Daily Worker*'s defense of Árbenz's government as proof of "the close liaison which has been established between the Communist press in the United States and the Communist press in Guatemala and the international design of communism."[179] Despite initial concerns about the revelation, the CIA determined that little had changed.[180] Even in taking away the "covert" from Operation PBSUCCESS, the issue that derailed its predecessor two years earlier, Guatemalan officials had little to show for revealing the international plot thanks to the hostile atmosphere built up by the UFCO and the CIA's propaganda. As a result, the revelation received far less fanfare than that given a few months later to a shipment of Eastern European armaments.

The "Secret" Embargo Endures: The *Alfhem* Shipment and the Monroe Doctrine

Even those behind the transnational counterrevolution were taken aback when armaments from behind the Iron Curtain arrived in Guatemala. Upon receiving the first of Delgado's materials, Árbenz in October 1953 decided to purchase weapons from Czechoslovakia, which arrived the following May on the Swedish ship the *Alfhem*. As the CIA's official history of PBSUCCESS notes, the weapons were a "propaganda bonanza," stoking fears and validating allegations of Soviet influence in Guatemala.[181] Árbenz's decision, though, did not emerge from a vacuum; it was the result of the British government's longstanding arms embargo. The US arms embargo not only "relied heavily on British cooperation" but benefited from a Foreign Office seeking to appease the US government.[182] As other governments followed suit, congresspersons and newspapers throughout the United States saw the shipment as a violation of the Monroe Doctrine comparable to other Cold War conflicts.

Throughout 1953, the Foreign Office kept in place its silent embargo due to Guatemala's anticolonialism. As with its patronage of CEUA, the Foreign Office still believed "that the American [government] must take the lead in Latin American affairs."[183] Although any slight or misunderstanding could "lead the Americans to act with less consideration of our interests in corresponding areas of British policy, e.g., the Middle East and the Commonwealth," the Foreign Office determined that the Eisenhower administration's "views are now very close to ours."[184] The outstanding matter, as it had been for a decade, was Guatemalan anticolonialism. To British officials' dismay, their US counterparts remained uninterested in the question.[185] Overlooking this disagreement, the Foreign Office denied the Árbenz government's requests.[186] In December 1952, agents with the Black Eagle and a Swiss firm were trying to purchase materiel in Switzerland and Italy.[187] After momentarily considering the purchase, the Foreign Office sounded out the State Department.[188] While waiting, the Foreign Office offered various excuses to "maintain [its] stalling policy" and suggested that the agents withdraw their application "in view of Guatemala's attitude to the British Honduras dispute."[189] Before their US counterparts admitted their preference to deny licenses, British officials had determined, "We are maintaining an arms embargo on Guatemala a) because of British Honduras, b) so as to keep in step with State Dep[t.]."[190] In early May 1953, the Foreign Office clearly articulated this policy. "While our objections to Guatemala arise primarily from the British Honduras dispute and those of the United States from their dislike of her near-communism," one official concluded, "our worldwide interests, e.g. Egyptian arms purchases, make it undesirable that we should waver in our solidarity with the United States over a situation so near to them in every sense."[191]

Into 1954, this embargo blocked Guatemalan agents' attempts, leaving Czechoslovakia as the remaining alternative. They lobbied members in the House of Commons, only for the Foreign Office to intervene.[192] In June, Guatemalan officials brought up the subject, but the Foreign Office cut the discussion based on recent complaints about Belize and an item in *Nuestro Diario* favorable toward Kenya's Mau Mau. This embargo, according to British officials, frustrated Árbenz.[193] Even after Árbenz decided to purchase Iron

Curtain armaments, the situation further deteriorated as multiple governments pursued a similar line. In February 1954, the Guatemalan Ministry of Defense obtained a contract for two hundred thousand dollars in French armaments, only for the French minister to warn that the "persistent tension between Washington and Guatemala" would not be worth the profits.[194] Before and after the *Alfhem*, US officials pressured Western European governments to halt shipments, much to the chagrin of French, Dutch, Belgian, and West German diplomats.[195] Thus, Árbenz's decision to acquire Czech armaments aimed to circumvent a plethora of embargoes placating the US government, but that would not be the reported story.

Instead, the *Alfhem* shipment became another detail in the propaganda campaigns reducing Guatemalan nationalism into a communist conspiracy, or what the French minister in Mexico City described as the Caribbean Basin's "international McCarthyism."[196] Likewise, the US Congress and newspapers were awash with denouncements of what Representative Patrick J. Hillings (R-CA) called "a clear-cut violation of the Monroe Doctrine." Representative Robert L. F. Sikes (D-FL) inserted an editorial from *The Washington Post* titled "Communist Beachhead."[197] Representative Walter Rogers (D-TX) shared an editorial from western Texas's *Memphis Democrat* summoning the Monroe Doctrine to justify intervention in Guatemala, Representative Gordon Canfield (R-NJ) submitted editorials from *The Newark Star-Ledger* invoking the doctrine to crush "the Red blight in Central America," and Senator Lyndon B. Johnson (D-TX) received praise from *The Dallas Morning News*, *The Houston Post*, and the *San Antonio Light* for offering a resolution defending intervention as the doctrine's triumph.[198]

The *Alfhem* shipment also evoked comparisons to Cold War hotspots outside the Western Hemisphere. Investigating the Katyn massacre in which the Soviet Union slaughtered Polish police and military officials, Representative Ray Madden (D-IN) insisted, "We know now that the Kremlin has succeeded in making Guatemala a Communist beachhead in the Americas."[199] Senator John Marshall Butler (R-MD) referenced the Korean War and the growing conflict in Vietnam, which Senator Barry Goldwater (R-AZ) repeated while inserting Butler's claims into the *Record*.[200] Bernays's "Guatemala News Notes" profited immensely from such coverage. The June 25, 1954, issue reproduced criticisms of the *Alfhem* shipment from the *Philadelphia Inquirer*, *Baltimore Sun*, *New York Herald Tribune*, *Washington Post*, *San Diego Union*, *Miami Herald*, *West Palm Beach Post*, *Chicago Daily News*, *Topeka State Journal*, *Phoenix Republic*, and more endorsing action against Soviet influence in Guatemala.[201] While Bernays was mailing statements from Javits and Hillings critical of the *Alfhem* shipment, a petition from the Sociedad de Amigos de Guatemala in Mexico defending Guatemalan sovereignty received no notice.[202] What had been the Árbenz government's attempt to bypass a silent, almost global embargo became more evidence of Soviet communism and another justification for intervention.

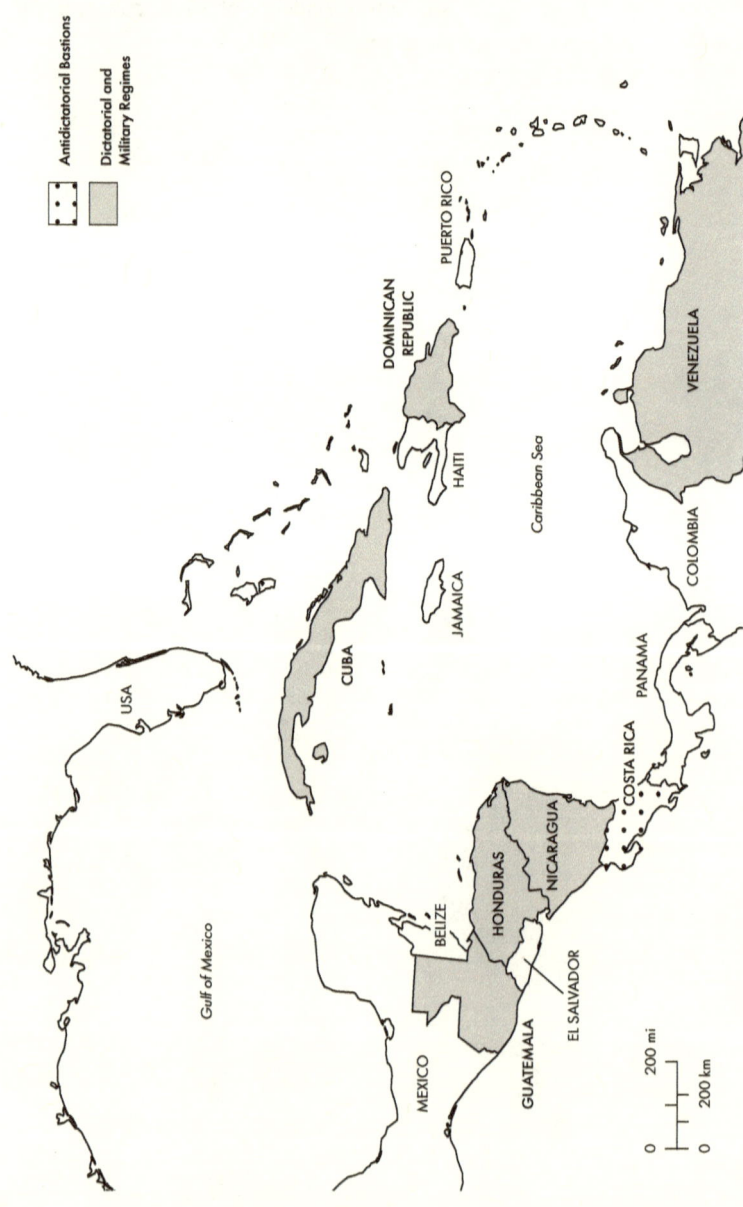

Figure 5. Map of Caribbean Basin, 1954

Conclusion

Dictators, Exiles, and the Caribbean Basin's Cold War

After a decade of failed conspiracies and political infighting, the transnational counterrevolution finally ended Guatemalan democracy thanks to the US government's decisive role. Seizing power, reactionaries unleashed their seemingly boundless vengeance upon the nation's democratic activists. Across Guatemala, Coronado Lira, Arenas, and others led multiple government agencies and elite-sponsored committees that tortured and executed thousands of union organizers, social reformers, and political leaders sympathetic to the Revolution's ideals. Throughout this systematic wave of violence, Castillo Armas and his allies blessed the bloodshed and death as an anticommunist cleansing restoring the nation's Christian status quo.[1] Successive Guatemalan regimes repeated this pattern, taking hundreds of thousands of lives. Always, self-proclaimed anticommunist foot soldiers tried silencing not just the nation's democratic legacy but evidence of these unimaginable atrocities that would only be recovered years later by the victims' allies and loved ones.[2]

The coup in Guatemala was a devastating blow to antidictatorial exiles who lost another bastion of the democratic ideals of the mid-1940s. Immediately, Castillo Armas paid his debts and targeted his patrons' foes, ordering the arrests of many Legionarios such as Ramírez and issuing warrants for the Dominican exile who bankrolled notable anti-Trujillo plots, Juancito Rodríguez, much to the regimes' delight.³ Castillo Armas's forces imprisoned Nicaraguan exile Meza, who was only released due to tragically fortunate errors resulting from the number of arrests and mixed up identities.⁴ Seeing his country once again in the throes of a dictatorship, Arévalo worried about his confidante and ally Edelberto Torres, one of Somoza's most hated targets, who miraculously escaped safely to Mexico.⁵

Costa Rica now appeared as one of the only options left for antidictatorial exiles and democratic activists. As the coup ruptured Guatemala, exiles fled, and sympathetic organizations tried to offer whatever help possible.⁶ A survivor of the attempt on Somoza, Nicaraguan exile José Félix Córdoba Boniche gained asylum through the Costa Rican Embassy.⁷ Many Dominican exiles followed, but Horacio Ornes warned their ally Figueres that Castillo Armas would hand over Ramírez and others to Trujillo.⁸ Immediately, the Costa Rican president ordered his officials to look into the matter, somehow obtaining the release of some detainees, including Ramírez.⁹ In stark contrast to the prior decade's democratic fervor, Ornes admitted that Figueres's government was "the only . . . democratic government."[10]

There was one country in the greater Caribbean led by someone sympathetic to antidictatorial exiles, which their enemies sought to remedy. Bolstered by the coup in Guatemala, the regimes' network in January 1955 launched a final, failed invasion of Costa Rica in pursuit of their long-standing agenda to eliminate democratic bastions, yet their onetime ally against Árbenz's government halted their efforts. Seeing Figueres as a liberal anticommunist ally, the US government halted the invasion, making clear its position as a pivotal force in the greater Caribbean.

As with this failed invasion, the core conflicts driving the Caribbean Basin since before the Second World War endured, but the US government no longer held the same respect it received in the mid-1940s. Yes, Somoza, Carías, Trujillo, Pérez Jiménez, and Batista finally triumphed over the Guatemalan Revolution but not the ideals it embodied. Instead, the US government's intervention on the dictators' side escalated the Cold War's stakes. On the eve of the coup, many Dominican exiles felt betrayed. They wanted to see US "democracy [reach] a high degree of perfection"; instead, the US government, in "opposing with all its might the spread of communism," undid this lofty vision and actively helped Latin America "become a fish hatchery of tyrannical governments." From Cuba, itself having fallen under Batista's dictatorship, anti-Trujillo leaders Rodríguez and Jiménes Grullón warned of a "deep resentment against those upholding their oppressors" taking hold in the region. If the US government remained a reactionary force and helped the region maintain its "semicolonial status," the resulting "benediction to the bloodiest regimes in Latin America" would bolster "the sufferings of the people [which] are the eggs out of which communism is hatched." They defended Guatemala's "national independence and sovereignty" and called out the US government for its "acquiescence" in empowering "the tyrannies of the Dominican Republic, Nicaragua, Venezuela, and El Salvador" to finally "erase from Guatemala all democratic life in order to bring to their fellow country the bloody chains [which have] been strangling" peoples across the greater Caribbean.[11]

The counterrevolution's triumph destroyed many antidictatorial figures' admiration of the United States. The "fight in Guatemala has ended," Ornes lamented. "Guatemala can be a lesson for those still seeing in the United States something good and beneficent for our peoples."[12] Arévalo agreed that the UFCO and other corporations could "count upon the backing and solid protection of North American weapons." Over the next years, his tomes on US imperialism became immensely popular, channeling the frustrations of exiles and others who expected more of the Colossus of the North.[13] Whereas Arévalo never embraced communism, others did. With an alliance of repressive regimes and the US government having suffocated democratic outlets, some Guatemalan reformers turned to radical alternatives and embraced communism and armed violence, as antidictatorial activists always warned. For the rest of the Cold War, the Central American nation was defined by right-wing repression and leftist guerrillas, with the former constantly targeting democratic activists, civilians, and Indigenous communities.[14]

This violence was not limited to Guatemala. An Argentine, Ernesto "Che" Guevara, was there during the coup and witnessed firsthand the brutality unleashed by the US government and regimes' alliance, all to stop democracy and economic reforms that Colombian democratic activist Germán Arciniegas called more moderate than those the US government accepted and encouraged in Mexico, Colombia, or Bolivia.[15] Arriving in Mexico City after PBSUCCESS, Guevara met another exile standing against a regime backed by the US government in the name of anticommunism. Fidel Castro's July 26, 1953, assault on the Moncada Barracks failed to spark an uprising and overthrow Batista's regime, but the dictator sent Castro into exile after the Cayo Confites participant's "La historia me absolverá [History will absolve me]" speech ensured that an execution would have meant martyrdom. Together, Castro and Guevara organized an antidictatorial coalition and in late 1956 unleashed a guerrilla war against Batista's forces that received moral and financial assistance from Auténticos-in-exile, AD-in-exile, Dominican exiles, Betancourt, Figueres, and more who nurtured this ideal. Upon Batista's ouster, antidictatorial exiles felt vindicated when Castro approved expeditions against the regimes in the Dominican Republic, Nicaragua, and Haiti, although the expedition into Panama seemed an odd choice.[16] These transnational allies soon felt betrayed when, following the US government and nearby regimes' Bay of Pigs fiasco, Castro as Cuba's new dictator pledged his allegiance to communism.

Even as this moment transformed the Cuban Revolution and the greater Caribbean Basin's dynamics, the region's long-standing conflicts continued. Pérez Jiménez clamped down firmer on democratic activists and political opponents, culminating in his ouster in January 1958. Welcomed back into Venezuela, Betancourt and AD restarted the democratic processes shut down ten years earlier, but the people did more than criticize the US government's support of the previous regime. When US Vice President Richard Nixon visited Caracas in May 1958, crowds threw rocks and attacked his motorcade. These riots seemed to spark new considerations among US officials, who over the next years supported AD and its democratic government against right-wing attacks and leftist guerrillas, funded respectively by Trujillo and Castro.[17]

That change in US policy seemed to register most notably in the Dominican Republic, but this shift was brief. Into the late 1950s, Trujillo refused to allow any democratic activities while enriching his estate at the people's expense. Humbled after a decade of failed expeditions, anti-Trujillo exiles never marshalled the resources or momentum seen in the mid-1940s. Instead, it was the dictator's bombastic efforts to eliminate any opposition throughout the Western Hemisphere that undid him. He deployed assassins to disappear Jesús de Galíndez from New York City in 1956 and approved the unsuccessful car bombing of Betancourt in 1960.[18] After the Caracas protests and hoping to rally opposition against Castro's communist regime, US officials cut diplomatic relations with Trujillo, who was assassinated in 1961. One of the most famous anti-Trujillo exiles, Bosch returned to the Dominican Republic and was elected president in 1962 before his expulsion by a military coup d'état. In the midst of a back-and-forth between right-wing elements and democratic factions, the US government, along with the OAS, landed military forces in 1965. After the war ended, the CIA helped Joaquín Balaguer, Trujillo's sycophant who had assisted the dictator's intelligence activities and Guatemalan reactionaries, win the 1966 elections.

In power, Balaguer built up his own regime under a smokescreen of democracy that eliminated his political opponents while relying on the US government's largesse.

The legacy of the fight against dictatorships was on full display in Nicaragua. There, Somoza held a firm grasp until his assassination in 1956. Newspapers and pamphlets throughout the greater Caribbean republished the letter of Somoza's assassin to his mother in which the young man defended this murder as the only remedy to two decades of dictatorship, and the FEU in Honduras honored the assassin by reminding the world of how Somoza embraced and then murdered the anti-imperialist hero Augusto Sandino.[19] What was supposed to be a democratic opening quickly turned to despondency, for Somoza's sons took power and unleashed a new wave of violence and repression upon the people as the US government remained beholden to the corrupt anticommunist dynasty. As a Nicaraguan exile in New York City wrote, the sons "continue[d] the same cruel, unjust, and criminal policies" of their father.[20] Again, an antidictatorial coalition emerged that borrowed directly from its predecessors as the Sandinistas took their name from the anti-imperialist icon. Antidictatorial veterans gave support to the Sandinistas, none more so than Ernesto Cardenal, who had denounced Somoza's coup in 1947 and participated in the 1954 failed assassination before becoming a priest of liberation theology and the Sandinistas' moral figurehead. Adherents to the cause even came from descendants of antidictatorial exiles who led the battles waged in the 1940s and 1950s. In 1955, Honduran exile Jorge Ribas Montes wrote his wife about his dream of a Caribbean Basin free of dictators. Years later, his daughter Sandra Ribas took up her father's ideals and joined the Sandinistas. Before his death, Ribas Montes confided that he did not wish "to impose on my children this cause of mine," only for his daughter to embrace it in her father's memory.[21] Though caught between the Cold War and the US government, these peoples and their struggle for a greater Caribbean free of dictators continued.

Epilogue

Fictitious *Historias*

After a year installed as Guatemala's president, Castillo Armas took a moment to commemorate the coup, celebrating a mythical crusade of exiles whose only crime was speaking against international communism. Abroad, in nearby countries, they received a warm welcome. "The patriots in exile came to make up important nuclei in different countries," Castillo Armas eulogized. "They were in Mexico, in El Salvador, in Honduras, in Nicaragua, and it was in those four sister countries where they found the friendly and brotherly hospitality denied them in Guatemala."[1] His flowery language left out important aspects of the decade-long counterrevolution, most notably assistance from dictators, the UFCO, and the British and US governments.

This gap in memory was not unintentional but echoed other reactionaries' tropes. Whether in the new regime's first days or in later years, they wrote memorials and testimonials, most under the Secretaría de Propaganda y Divulgación's new leadership, that presented themselves as selfless heroes fighting alone without any outside assistance. On the coup's third anniversary, the Secretaría circulated a text that set the counterrevolution's birth at the 1952 Agrarian Reform with only a few pages on "Arévalo, the Godfather of Communism."[2] Its *Así se gestó la liberación* (*How the Liberation Came to Be*) included reactionaries' publications, material from Mexico's anticommunist conference, and an entire chapter listing those imprisoned or exiled by Arévalo and Árbenz's governments. Despite including the names of Padilla, Coronado Lira, Salazar, Barrios Peña, Córdova Cerna, Arenas, and others who benefited from foreign largesse, it did not mention the conspiracies behind their arrests and expulsions.³ Whether in its one-year commemorative text or members' recollections, the CEUA never described itself as a benefactor of the US and British governments.⁴

Reactionaries began writing this fictitious *historia* immediately upon seizing power. Placed in charge of the Secretaría, Calderón Salazar released a series of radio broadcasts overlooking his and others' decade of plots.⁵ One overview ignored any antigovernment attempts before June 1954.⁶ Similarly, the Secretaría's *La intriga roja en Guatemala* (*Red Intrigue in Guatemala*) cast Castillo Armas's attack as the counterrevolution's spark and his 1954 "movement" as "the only influence" behind Árbenz's ouster.⁷ Spanish- and English-language texts mirrored each other in placing Castillo Armas as the singular force.⁸ The entire regime adhered to this dogma and rewrote the ten-year counterrevolution as the creation of a single man and his persecuted Guatemalan allies, best outlined in the Secretaría's *Liberación con sangre, sacrificios y heroísmo: se escribió la historia de nuestra segunda independencia* (*Liberation with Blood, Sacrifice, and Heroism: The History of Our Second Independence Was Written*). The UN request that the Nicaraguan and Honduran regimes not help the 1954 invasion was moot since, according to this *historia*, "the Liberation that Colonel Castillo Armas commanded was disassociated from all official support from those countries."⁹

One reason the regime kept writing this false *historia* was that, upon taking power, reactionaries faced a wide backlash. International reports stressed democratic activists' near-unanimity in denouncing the US government's blatant intervention.¹⁰ Protests spread in Mexico, and Colombian newspapers complained of the US government's methods.¹¹ In Uruguay and Brazil, pro-Árbenz letters and news articles alleged that the UFCO directed the US government's policies.¹² These sentiments escalated most notably in Chile, where solidarity organizations attracted formerly pro-US socialist Salvador Allende.¹³ This activism even reverberated in countries whose regimes backed PBSUCCESS. In Honduras, university students led pro-Árbenz protests while championing UFCO workers striking for better wages, the resulting suppression taking at least two students' lives.¹⁴ Whereas the Masacre Sampedrana ten years earlier received international attention, these demonstrations went relatively unnoticed with only a handful of photos circulating of occupied buildings and dead students as a clear message to both students and workers.[15] Aware of reprisals next door in Guatemala, Honduran unions anxiously accepted the UFCO's new contracts.[16] Elsewhere, anti-US criticisms did not receive such treatment.[17] Venezuelans demonstrated their sympathy, while Cuban anticommunists, leftist labor unions, and students denounced the coup.[18]

British Scripts

British officials were especially sensitive to this backlash, for the Foreign Office found itself in a controversy potentially weakening its government's position in the UN. Akin to that in Latin America, the European press questioned US-backed claims of an unassisted movement against Árbenz's government. Multiple Swedish newspapers condemned the intervention, with some outlets highlighting links between the UFCO and recently arrived Ambassador John Moors Cabot.[19] Sparked by reports that the US government tried halting shipments to Guatemala even before the *Alfhem*, Swiss public opinion criticized the official story.[20] West German newspapers across the political spectrum questioned the provided narrative.[21]

Further frustrating many international observers was the UN's hands-off approach. At the invasion's onset, Árbenz's government submitted a request for mediation to the Security Council, only for the US government to support a resolution from Colombia's and Brazil's delegates to take the matter to the OAS. This put the British and French representatives in a delicate position when Foster Dulles ordered the US representative at the UN to pressure his European colleagues.[22] If the two delegates did not agree to the resolution, the US government "would feel entirely free equally to be independent, if and when such matters as Egypt, Cyprus, North Africa, or the Middle East come up before the United Nations."[23] Receiving the threat, British and French representatives warned their superiors that the Eisenhower administration was keeping its eye on "areas vital to Great Britain such as Egypt or to the French such as Tunisia."[24] The Foreign Office was now in a "delicate position."[25] On one hand, British officials appreciated the UN's idealistic imagery, which granted them a "moral position" to set the schedule when it came to colonial issues.[26] On the other hand, it was important to appease the US government.[27] Fortunately, they found an amenable compromise.[28]

The European representatives abstained from the vote but endorsed the upcoming investigation of Guatemalan affairs by the OAS's Inter-American Peace Committee (IAPC), thereby passing the resolution.[29] Before the IAPC set foot in Guatemala, however, the military ousted Árbenz, rendering the procedure moot. Celebrating at a White House dinner at the week's end, Churchill assured the Eisenhower administration of his "sympathy" regarding the issue.[30] Others saw through this façade. As Britain's UN representative summarized, Foster Dulles "enunciate[d] a new kind of Monroe Doctrine," a "warning not only to international Communism but also to the United Nations itself to keep their hands off the American continent."[31] Europeans made a similar interpretation, with France's *Le Monde* wondering why the Security Council dropped the matter and West Germany's *Frankfurter Allgemeine* comparing the matter to the Korean War.[32] Latin American criticism escalated, drawing attention from Russian outlets as well as Soviet officials.[33] After years of false allegations of Guatemalan ties to international communism, it was the coup's hemispheric backlash and the UN's inaction that precipitated the Soviet Union's decision to court allies in the Western Hemisphere.[34]

British officials were not done placating their US counterparts. Following the Security Council abstentions, London too endured a fair share of criticism. Liverpool had a mass protest of around one hundred people, while the Foreign Office received questions from the Women's International League for Peace and Freedom, the National Peace Council, their own officials abroad, and members of Parliament.[35] *The Times* reported how one member in the House of Commons contrasted the UN's inaction against Nicaragua and Honduras with its intervention against "Russia and China . . . in Korea and Indo-China."[36] Other members asked if the government would investigate the bombing of a British ship or capitulate to US interests.[37] To allay these concerns, the Foreign Office in early July agreed to compile a white paper on Guatemala.[38] Their US counterparts, "still jittery about any post mortem," made clear their opposition.[39]

To maintain the US government's support, the Foreign Office walked a "tightrope."[40] Newly appointed British Minister Richard Allen selected general memoranda and reports dovetailing with the new regime's *historia*, the central document revolving around Allen's own sympathetic observations. Castillo Armas's "volunteers" triumphed over the "Communist-dominated regime in Guatemala . . . with far greater ease and speed than seemed possible." Unlike their opponents, Árbenz's government was "led by opportunists" who allowed communists to infiltrate key institutions and offices. Spurred by the *Alfhem* shipment, "some Guatemalans of considerable wealth" helped Castillo Armas obtain planes and topple the regime. Ultimately, Allen argued, "the movement of Colonel Carlos Castillo Armas was a popular one, welcome to the majority of the people here."⁴¹ This white paper came to just over 120 pages, including Allen's overview, a summary of events at the Security Council, the IAPC's pointless report, and other items offering little about Castillo Armas's patrons.⁴² This was the entire point. When the Foreign Office sent copies over, US officials were ebullient, earning "a word of appreciation" from Dulles.⁴³ As when patronizing the CEUA, the British government throughout the Cold War would continue pursuing its goals while recognizing the US government's leadership in the Western Hemisphere.⁴⁴

British officials also nurtured a harmonious relationship with Castillo Armas's regime. During PBSUCCESS, the Foreign Office kept quiet its relationships with reactionaries.⁴⁵ Afterward, it reevaluated the arms embargo. By early March 1955, Guatemalan officials requested armaments, truck parts, and other equipment denied to Árbenz's government. Initially, the Colonial Office and some in the Foreign Office hesitated, having seen "little evidence of goodwill in the Guatemalan attitude towards British Honduras."⁴⁶ A few years earlier, those reactionaries now making up Castillo Armas's cabinet had defended Guatemalan claims to Belize, with Coronado Lira alleging that Lombardo Toledano's orders prevented Arévalo from pushing back on Mexican claims.⁴⁷ This was, the new regime's architects confessed, an act. When told of his British colleagues' concerns, Castillo Armas's representative in London laughed, stating that "all Guatemalan children had been brought up for many years on the doctrine that Belize belonged to Guatemala, but his Government had, of course, no intention of doing anything about it."⁴⁸ A few weeks later, Allen told Goicolea, Castillo Armas's minister of foreign affairs, that the embargo was lifted.⁴⁹ Having worked together when the CEUA disseminated IRD propaganda, Allen was glad to help Goicolea and encourage the Foreign Office to assist the regime in harassing Guatemalan exiles.⁵⁰

Such gratitude contributed to the regime's fictitious *historia*. In early 1955, the French minister in Guatemala City found "a certain surprise" on his desk.⁵¹ Over the past weeks, he had been bombarded with the Secretaría de Propaganda's pamphlets and tomes, but this most recent item stood out: a joint Secretaría-CEUA publication with Allen's smiling portrait on the front cover.⁵² "Even more surprising" was that the pamphlet was a bilingual translation of Allen's June 1954 report to the Foreign Office. Somehow, Guatemalan officials acquired and republished Allen's "first impressions" of the coup, "the observations and the conclusions . . . obviously the most favorable to the regime." Asked about the matter, Allen admitted giving the Secretaría permission to republish the report. The French minister was thoroughly confused. "[It was] quite difficult to understand what may have pushed the Government in London first to publish, in such a short time, a white paper on events that only took place last summer in this country and that do not seem to have been of vital importance for Great Britain, then to allow foreigners to publicly use, to defend or justify their internal political action, the report of an English diplomatic agent still stationed in the country of interest." He joined his "Latin American colleagues [who] were somewhat shocked by this dissemination which they consider[ed] a kind of intervention by Britain in the internal politics of Guatemala."[53] None of them knew that providing this script for the regime's *historia* was merely the latest "intervention by Britain."

Faking It

Having ousted a democratically elected president with the help of multiple foreign entities, reactionaries returned to shape the new regime and its *historia*. Despite frequent shake-ups in Castillo Armas's cabinet, those who long undermined the Revolution played central roles propping up the façade of a righteous government eliminating communists. After myriad complaints about their supposed persecutions, they rounded up members from Arévalo's and Árbenz's governments.[54] Perhaps worried that opponents would follow in his footsteps and rally support against Castillo Armas's regime, Córdova Cerna lobbied other governments to strip Guatemalans of their diplomatic immunity and return those who sought exile.[55] These efforts went beyond state-to-state relationships. Grateful for their anticommunist allies' moral and financial support, Coronado Lira and Salazar led Guatemala's delegates and joined the FPAM's Prieto Laurens at the 1955 Segundo Congreso Contra la Intervención Soviética (Second Congress Against Soviet Intervention) in Río de Janeiro. There, they commemorated their victory against the "ignoble Bolshevik regime implanted there by the traitorous presidents, Arévalo and Árbenz," and their having cut off "from Central America the tentacles of the despicable Government of Soviet Russia."[56] This had been the plan since October 1954, when Castillo Armas sent Pinillos to express gratitude for the FPAM's support during PBSUCCESS and consider future measures for further anticommunist collaboration.[57]

Though personal rivalries complicated their returns, reactionaries populated Guatemala's subsequent regimes. One of Castillo Armas's most potent challengers, Barrios Peña, in 1956 humored the possibility of making an alliance with leftist organizations. Then, he received an invitation from his former patron Trujillo "about alleged aid [for] groups opposed to" Castillo Armas. Upon arriving in the Dominican Republic, Trujillo offered the onetime reactionary a choice: to serve as Castillo Armas's consul or remain an unofficial prisoner-in-exile under the dictator.[58] Castillo Armas's other rival, Ydígoras Fuentes, tentatively eyed the presidency after the coup. As usual, his son-in-law approached British officials to see if they would recognize an Ydígoras Fuentes government, only to be rebuffed.[59] He had to settle for an ambassadorship under Castillo Armas until the latter's assassination in 1957. With the military's backing, Ydígoras Fuentes finally became president, during which time he offered his country's resources to the CIA for the 1961 Bay of Pigs fiasco. Of course, he kept the sensational details of his conspiring against Arévalo's government out of his self-serving memoir.[60] Other reactionaries also obfuscated their activities in exile while having less dramatic roles upon returning to Guatemala. Ramírez served as Ydígoras Fuentes's ambassador to the United States, and Padilla became his nation's surgeon general, representing his country at the World Health Organization and shaking hands with one of Southeast Asia's anticommunist figureheads, Chiang Kai-shek.[61] In 1955, Archila Obregón became Castillo Armas's consul in Chiapas, Mexico, the same place where he had published anti-Arévalo bulletins and the Arévalo-Yakubovsky forgery a decade earlier.[62] Thanks to their patrons, these reactionaries survived their time in exile, undermined two democratic governments, and returned to ensure the Revolution's demise.

Just as they benefited from such largesse while abroad, they continued depending on their patrons. Across the United States, Castillo Armas's cheerleaders held up his fictitious *historia* and swore that his regime was solid. After the coup, Bernays sent his mailing list the UFCO's newest booklet, *Redemption in Guatemala: Eyewitness Accounts of the Defeat of Communism in the Western Hemisphere*. It testified that Castillo Armas and his forces "swept out the deeply entrenched Communist-ridden government and established a stable democracy," evidenced by a compilation of anonymous letters whose writers supposedly endured immense hardships under Árbenz's government.[63] Having rallied his audience to the cause, Fulton Lewis repeated claims that the US government was not involved. Upon surveying Guatemala in 1955, Lewis celebrated Castillo Armas for having conquered the Guatemalan military with "only 250 men in his army and a few planes."[64]

This *historia* masked the fragile reality in which reactionaries and their allies lobbied the US government to ensure the regime's stability.[65] One asked Father Joseph Francis Thorning, who had defended the Spanish fascist Franco and positioned himself as a Latin Americanist expert in *World Affairs*, to help Mansfield find much-needed financial assistance.[66] From the other side of the political aisle, McCarthy lambasted the State Department for "dragging its feet in Guatemala" rather than delivering the necessary assistance.[67] Newspapers soon reported that McCarthy's intervention was instrumental in compelling the Eisenhower administration to provide the regime over five million dollars.[68] Reflective of the limited attention paid to the topic after the coup, no newspaper noticed that the regime, at a cost of just under twenty thousand dollars in 1955, had retained the public relations firm of McCarthy's friend and associate John A. Clements.[69]

No matter the reason, McCarthy's intervention may have been minor, for the Eisenhower administration was investing both its money and its reputation in Castillo Armas's success. In the hopes of locating evidence of Soviet domination, the CIA approved Operation PBHISTORY, yet agents' attempts to locate proof of Guatemalan-Russian ties yielded nothing significant and failed to silence global criticism.[70] Having expounded at length about the Árbenz government's failures, it was imperative that the succeeding regime be a triumph, regardless of cost or truth. In May 1955, Assistant Secretary of State Henry Holland went so far as to blame all the regime's economic challenges on "the systematic looting carried on by the preceding government," a blatant lie.[71] In the span of a year, the US government went from reactionaries' patron to the lifeline for Castillo Armas's regime as well as its successors who utilized hundreds of millions of dollars in US aid and armaments to repress their own citizens under the cloak of hemispheric solidarity and anticommunism. Ironically, one of the reactionaries' first patrons would find itself out of any support whatsoever.

The Octopus Shrivels

In the coup's direct aftermath, the UFCO boldly proclaimed victory. It was the corporation, according to Whitman, who had "been pretty much in a lone fight for its survival in Guatemala these past several years" while standing against "the international Communist conspiracy in Guatemala and elsewhere in Latin America."[72] Corcoran chimed in, complaining that the US government long ignored the company's warnings and made the same mistakes in China that led to "the Yenan Way in Guatemala."[73] Fortunately, the UFCO fought back, defending its livelihood, Latin America, and the United States with the "one commodity utterly foreign to the international Communist conspiracy—and that is TRUTH!"[74] Inspired by this sense of vindication, the corporation boasted that its services were already resuming in Guatemala after the coup.[75] Just as the company celebrated, the Eisenhower administration approved a Justice Department antitrust suit against the UFCO. During PBSUCCESS, US officials held back on the action, concerned that it would provide fodder for nationalists who defended labor reforms as necessary against the company's machinations. Thanks to the coup, the US government proceeded.[76]

To defend itself, the company redeployed its propaganda campaign. Whitman distributed favorable editorials that questioned the antitrust action. In spite of the removal of Árbenz's government, one editorial from Fort Worth still feared any action against the UFCO that gave the "appearance of Washington confirmation of the Red charges of monopoly."[77] The corporation contacted those congresspersons with whom they networked the past years, telling Hickenlooper that "some of our shareholders and your constituents" opposed the antitrust suit.[78] By December, Whitman sent the UFCO's own "white paper" to trumpet the corporation's work improving Latin America's economy and medical capabilities.[79] They went so far as to leverage their contributions to the coup. Bernays sent his many contacts copies of the State Department's *Intervention of International Communism in Guatemala*, and Whitman distributed *How an American Company, Through Advertising and Public Relations, Has Combatted Communism in Latin America*, a bound speech in which he held the company up as the first opponent of Guatemalan communism.[80]

These attempts accomplished nothing. The UFCO's agents spent years insisting that their opposition to the Guatemalan Revolution's economic reforms was not about their bananas but about standing against communism, and it worked. Now, there was no reason to defend the company or its bananas. Representing Boston, where the corporation was headquartered, McCormack was the only congressperson to endorse the UFCO on the House Floor and in the *Congressional Record*.[81] The antitrust suit became the first in a series of events that, in less than half a century, chipped away at the corporation's once mythical status and reduced it to a smaller entity, Chiquita Brands. During this time, those officials who defended the UFCO during the 1940s and 1950s told themselves that the corporation was sacrificed by the Eisenhower administration simply to placate the coup's many anti-US protests, with Corcoran ranting that "Foster Dulles compensated a few Uruguayan rioters by bringing an antitrust suit against the Company."[82]

Well, that had been the point of the UFCO's propaganda campaign: convince the US government and the public that overthrowing Guatemala's democratically elected government had nothing to do with the company.[83] The antitrust suit sent this very message; the Eisenhower administration and the US government's Cold War foreign policies were not beholden to any corporation. The UFCO's propaganda campaign was successful.

Acknowledgments

This project only started thanks to the efforts of amazing archivists and staff at the Archivo General de la Nación in Santo Domingo. After making sense of my horrible Spanish, Óscar Feliz facilitated my requests for materials on Dominican foreign relations. Maribel, Wellington, Pulio, Viterbo, Pedro de León, and many others brought me materials for weeks, and Orquídea Correa shared an entire collection of digital items.

This help continued in Costa Rica, where Jafeth Campos Ramírez and the Archivo Nacional de Costa Rica gave me ample time to go through materials. David Díaz-Arias provided access to the Colección Carlos Meléndez with the Centro de Investigaciones Históricas de América Central at the Universidad de Costa Rica, which is where I had my first chance to share my early, formative ideas.

It was pure coincidence that I bumped into Jorge Renato Ibarra Guitart while in Santo Domingo, as he pushed me to travel to Cuba. In Havana, Servando Valdés Sánchez, Belkis Quesada, and others at the Instituto de Historia de Cuba let me type up myriad files and reports at the Archivo. After a comedy of errors, Eduardo Valido and the staff at the Archivo Central del Ministerio de Relaciones Exteriores welcomed me into their collections with pencil and paper.

Javier, César, and more at the Biblioteca Nacional de México let me take my time in Rafael Heliodoro Valle's papers, and Pilar Benito was very accommodating at the Fundación Universitaria Española in Madrid.

I do not have the words to express my gratitude to Thelma Porres and Óscar Farfán, who made available hundreds of items at the Centro de Investigaciones Regionales de Mesoamérica.

At the National Archives in College Park, Maryland, David Fort and Amanda Weimer went through far too many of my FOIA requests, as did the staff who made such materials accessible.

Randy Sowell at the Truman Presidential Library patiently helped me with my questions and requests when I had no clue what I was doing.

I still cannot believe the good archivists at the Rauner Special Collections Library fielded my requests and led me to Victor Cutter's writings.

Of course, I must thank the myriad archivists and staff who helped me at the Nettie Lee Benson Latin American Collection; the Howard Gotlieb Archival Research Center, the Baker Library, and the Massachusetts Historical Society; the Herbert Hoover Presidential Library & Museum; the Dwight D. Eisenhower Presidential Library & Museum; the Franklin D. Roosevelt Presidential Library & Museum; the Library of Congress; the Maureen and Mike Mansfield Library; Rutgers University Libraries; the Virginia Historical Society; the Wisconsin Historical Society; the University of Alabama Libraries Special Collections; Nicholls State University's Ellender Memorial Library; London's National Archives; La Courneuve's Centre des Archives Diplomatiques and Nantes's Centre des Archives Diplomatiques; the Archivo General de la Nación and Archivo Histórico Genaro Estrada; the Archivo Nacional de Cuba and Biblioteca Nacional de Cuba José Martí; and the Archivo General de Puerto Rico and Fundación Luis Muñoz Marín.

Miraculously, the descendants of notable exiles and reactionaries made available what they had. Iliana Ornes Rodríguez, Rosa Arvelo, and Luisa de Peña Díaz with the Museo Memorial de la Resistencia Dominicana welcomed me and shared their families' experiences, as did Alberto Henríquez and the family of Chito Henríquez. Porfirio, Virginia, Juan José, and Doroteo Rodríguez Iriarte offered their insights into the lives of Juan "Juancito" Rodríguez and others. Sandra Ribas, Valky Durán, and their families gave what they had on Jorge Ribas Montes, and Mauricio Ordóñez made available materials from his father, the poet Alberto Ordóñez Argüello. Likewise, Roberto, Hesed, and Jaime Padilla gave me a fascinating glimpse into Carlos Padilla y Padilla's life.

Darío Euraque and Polly Moran allowed me to go through the personal correspondence of Honduran exile Amílcar Gómez Robelo, and Kevin Coleman turned me toward Philippe Bourgois's collection. Serendipitously, Ryan Livingston shared materials on the CIA-inspired coffee boycott, and Ashley Black sent materials from Mexican intelligence collections. Richard Immerman graciously responded to too many messages about US congresspersons and the UFCO.

It is not possible to describe the invaluable mentorship I received while writing this book from those who were never my official teachers or professors. Kyle Longley gave guidance when I first set off on this project, William O. Walker III welcomed me into this scholarship, Jonathan Brown cheered for me when I was not one of his students, Alan McPherson pushed me to push my work further, Max Paul Friedman chatted about Sandino and Arévalo's legacies in Latin America, Richard Immerman offered suggestions on personal collections and congressional finds, Roberto García Ferreira gave more interest to my work than what I thought it deserved, Arturo Taracena gave his patience, and Tanya Harmer allowed me to ask about methodologies and historiographies. Any good work in this book is the result of the support given by these scholars as well as Charles Ameringer, Antonio Rafael de la Cova, and Mark Gilderhus.

Dustin Walcher, Margaret Power, Allen Wells, and Bill Booth helped with drafts, and I had a fun writing group in Michelle Chase, Emily Snyder, Molly Avery, and Luis Herrán Ávila. My colleagues Samuel Sutherland and Philip Catton read pieces, and Renata Keller and Jason Colby went through entire drafts.

I have been extremely fortunate to receive the support of multiple institutions and organizations who took a risk on my scholarship, including a William Appleman Williams Junior Faculty Research Grant and Samuel Flagg Bemis Dissertation Research Grant from the Society for Historians of American Foreign Relations; a Franklin Research Grant from the American Philosophical Society; an Andrew W. Mellon Fellowship from the Massachusetts Historical Society; a Travel Fellowship from the Frances S. Summersell Center for the Study of the South at the University of Alabama; a Bordin-Gillette Researcher Travel Fellowship from the Bentley Historical Library at the University of Michigan; a Herbert Hoover Research Travel Grant from the Hoover Presidential Foundation at the Herbert Hoover Presidential Library and Museum; a Research Travel Grant from the Eisenhower Foundation at the Dwight D. Eisenhower Presidential Library; a Grant-in-Aid from the Roosevelt Institute at the Franklin D. Roosevelt Presidential Library & Museum; a Dissertation Year Fellowship and Research Grant from the Truman Library Institute at the Harry S. Truman Presidential Library; a John Pine Memorial Scholarship from Phi Alpha Theta; a New England Regional Fellowship Consortium Travel Fellowship; and a Dirksen Congressional Center Congressional Research Grant.

It is only due to the support of Stephen F. Austin State University that I have turned years of research into some coherent stream of words. This entire time, the Department of History has supported me, as have the College of Liberal and Applied Arts and the Office of Research and Graduate Studies.

My thanks to Sarah Elizabeth Grossman and Ben Coates with Cornell University Press for taking a chance on this book.

For some reason, good people keep helping me, including Ron Gordon, Darren Swagerty, Patrick Williams, and too many friends and family members who suffered my incessant doubts, questions, and drafts that only changed by the word.

Additional thanks to Molly O'Halloran for providing remarkable maps and charts.

For my GrandPam.

For my biggest fan.

Notes

Introduction

1. Jorge Ribas Montes, 25 agosto 1955, collection of Jorge Ribas Montes (Honduran exile), access courtesy of Valky Durán. A copy of this letter is in RREE 2696, suggesting the smuggler made a photostat or the letter was intercepted and shared with regional governments, akin to the Legión Caribe's materials in box 68, OARA.

2. Ramírez, "Jorge Rivas Montes: Asesinado en las Cárceles Somocistas," *VRD: Órgano de Vanguardia Revolucionaria Dominicana* 1, no. 4 (septiembre 1957): 10, 36, folder Caribbean: Dominican Rep. 1957, box 35, DJP; Cardenal, *Mi Rebelión*; Rushdie, *Jaguar Smile*.

3. Chamorro, *Estirpe sangrienta*, 160.

4. Ribas Montes, 25 agosto 1955, JRM.

5. Ribas Montes, 25 agosto 1955, JRM.

6. A wide-ranging account is Grandin, *Blood of Guatemala*. On subalterns' attempts, see Carey, *I Ask for Justice*.

7. Handy, *Revolution in the Countryside*; Levenson-Estrada, *Trade Unionists Against Terror*; Forster, *Time of Freedom*; Rodríguez de Ita, *La participación política*; Grandin, *Last Colonial Massacre*; Taracena Arriola, *Guatemala, la República Española y el Gobierno Vasco*; Vrana, *This City Belongs to You*; Gibbings and Vrana, *Out of the Shadow*.

8. Grandin, *Last Colonial Massacre*; Weld, *Paper Cadavers*.

9. Immerman, *CIA in Guatemala*; Blasier, *Hovering Giant*; Wood, *Dismantling of the Good Neighbor Policy*; Rabe, *Eisenhower and Latin America*; Leonard, "Nationalism or Communism?"; Gleijeses, *Shattered Hope*; Lehman, "Revolutions and Attributions"; Siekmeier, *Aid, Nationalism, and Inter-American Relations*; Schlesinger and Kinzer, *Bitter Fruit*; Cullather, *Secret History*; Grow, *US Presidents and Latin American Interventions*; Rabe, *Killing Zone*.

10. Johnson, *Congress and the Cold War*; McKercher, "Steamed Up"; Barrett, *CIA and Congress*. On the UFCO and US foreign policy, see Langley and Schoonover, *Banana Men*; Langley, *Banana Wars*; Schlesinger and Kinzer, *Bitter Fruit*. On the UFCO's history, see Dosal, *Doing Business with the Dictators*; Joseph, LeGrand, and Salvatore, *Close Encounters of Empire*; Striffler and Moberg, *Banana Wars*; Bucheli, *Bananas and Business*; Bucheli, "Multinational Corporations, Totalitarian Regimes and Economic Nationalism"; Colby, *Business of Empire*; Martin, *Banana Cowboys*.

11. For a recent work on public views of Cold War conflicts, Masuda, *Cold War Crucible*.

12. Schmitz, *Thank God They're on Our Side*; Holden, *Armies Without Nations*; Grandin, *Last Colonial Massacre*; Kuzmarov, *Modernizing Repression*.

13. Whereas the Guatemalanist literature reduces Castillo Armas and others to tools of US imperialism, Piero Gleijeses, *Shattered Hope*, points out that dictators favored some reactionaries over others. Nick Cullather, *Secret History*, Richard Immerman, *CIA in Guatemala*, and Stephen Streeter, *Managing the Counterrevolution*, touch on how reactionaries competed for the US government's support in the early 1950s. Though attempting to note that reactionaries held their own worldviews and goals, Zachary Karabell relies on US-based reports and is unable to properly assess their numerous points of convergence and divergence, only claiming that reactionaries "egged on" the Eisenhower administration during PBSUCCESS without identifying how the US government took up opponents' years-long efforts (*Architects of Intervention*, 127).

14. Gould and Lauria-Santiago, *To Rise in Darkness*.

15. Hove, "The Árbenz Factor"; García Ferreira, "'El caso de Guatemala'"; Friedman, "Fracas in Caracas"; Perutka, "Arms for Árbenz,"; Getchell, "Revisiting the 1954 Coup in Guatemala"; García Ferreira, *El derrocamiento de Jacobo Árbenz*; Loaeza, "El archivo te da sorpresas"; Grandin, *Last Colonial Massacre*; Vela Castañeda, "Guatemala, 1954"; Holden, "Communism and Catholic Social Doctrine"; Harms, *Ladina Social Activism*; García Ferreira y Taracena, *Guerra fría y anticomunismo*; Weld, "Other Door." García Ferreira, "Toda Centroamérica conspiró," and Vázquez Medeles's works have begun examining links between Guatemalan anticommunists and those in the region and abroad.

16. For works on Britain and decolonization, see Darwin, *Britain and Decolonisation*; Louis and Robinson, "The Imperialism of Decolonization"; Brown and Louis, *The Oxford History of the British Empire*; Mazower, *No Enchanted Palace*; Grob-Fitzgibbon, *Imperial Endgame*; Walton, *Empire of Secrets*.

17. On the IRD, see Lucas and Morris, "A Very British Crusade"; Wilford, "Information Research Department"; Lashmar and Oliver, *Britain's Secret Propaganda War*; Shaw, "Information Research Department"; Defty, *Britain, America and Anticommunist Propaganda*; Vaughan, "'Cloak Without Dagger'"; Cormac, "Information Research Department"; McGarr, "Information Research Department." On US-British intelligence, see Aldrich, *Hidden Hand*. On Britain, Guatemala, and Guyana, see Young, "Great Britain's Latin American Dilemma"; Meers, "British Connection"; Rabe, *US Intervention in British Guiana*; Palmer, *Cheddi Jagan*; Mawby, *Ordering Independence*. On Britain and Latin America, see Miller, *Britain and Latin America*; Knight, "Britain and Latin America"; Livingstone, *Britain and the Dictatorships*; Mills and Miller, *Britain and the Growth of US Hegemony*; Cormac, "Currency of Covert Action"; McEvoy, "Before the Rubble."

18. Bethell and Roxborough, "Postwar Conjuncture in Latin America"; Rock, *Latin America in the 1940s*.

19. Bethell and Roxborough, "Postwar Conjuncture in Latin America," 2; Grandin, *Last Colonial Massacre*; Dunkerley, "Guatemala," 300.

20. Harmer, *Allende's Chile*, 2; Brands, *Latin America's Cold War*, 2, 7; McPherson, "Afterword," 308–309; Grandin, "Living in Revolutionary Time," 3–5; Joseph, "Latin America's Long Cold War," 400–411.

21. Joseph, "What We Now Know"; Kirkendall, "Cold War Latin America"; Marchesi, "Escribiendo la Guerra Fría latinoamericana"; Pettinà, *Historia mínima*; Joseph, "Border Crossings"; Casals, "Which Borders Have Not Yet Been Crossed?"; Booth, "Rethinking Latin America's Cold War."

22. Gómez Ochoa, *Constanza, Maimón y Estero Hondo*; Brown, *Cuba's Revolutionary World*; Oñate, "The Red Affair"; Kruijt, *Cuba and Revolutionary Latin America*; Salcedo Ávila, *Venezuela*; Gleijeses, *Conflicting Missions*; Gleijeses, *Visions of Freedom*.

23. Among and alongside works noted by Kirkendall, "Cold War Latin America," see Hershberg, "'High-Spirited Confusion'"; Dávila, *Hotel Trópico*; Rothwell, *Transpacific Revolutionaries*; Field, *From Development to Dictatorship*; Keller, *Mexico's Cold War*; Weld, "Spanish Civil War"; Field, Krepp, and Pettinà, *Latin America and the Global Cold War*.

24. Despite multiple governments, regimes, and popular movements, Honduras's largest role in the literature is its government's response to the Sandinista government and the Argentine- and then US-funded Contras, as in LeoGrande, *Our Own Backyard*.

25. Miller, *Precarious Paths to Freedom*.

26. Rabe, "Caribbean Triangle"; Schwartzberg, *Democracy and US Policy in Latin America*; Salcedo Ávila, "Conflictos en el Caribe"; Miller, *Precarious Paths to Freedom*; Salcedo Ávila, *Venezuela*.

27. Ameringer, *Cuban Democratic Experience*; Pettinà, "Preponderance of Politics."

28. Taking from Longley's groundbreaking *Sparrow and the Hawk*, Vanni Pettinà, (*Historia mínima*, 23) places Costa Rica alongside Mexico and Cuba in finding "opportunities" to profit from or avoid the violence of the Cold War, but Costa Ricanists such as David Díaz Arias, in *Crisis social y memorias en lucha*, stress the nation's internal political divisions and contradict these popular myths of domestic peace.

29. On the *teoría*'s history, see Crenzel, *La historia política del Nunca Más*; Franco, "La 'teoría de los dos demonios'"; Feierstein, *Los dos demonios*. For debates resulting from Cold War studies works appearing to endorse the *teoría de los demonios*, see Gaddis, *We Now Know*; Grandin, "Off the Beach"; Joseph, "What We Now Know"; Sargent et al., "Online Roundtable"; and Walcher et al., "Review of *Latin America's Cold War*."

30. Casaús Arzú y Giráldez, *Las redes intelectuales centroamericanas*; Roniger, *Transnational Politics*; Roniger, Green, and Yankelevich, *Exile & the Politics of Exclusion*; Carr, "Pioneering Transnational Solidarity in the Americas"; McPherson, *Invaded*.

31. Grandin, "Off the Beach"; Joseph, "What We Now Know"; Grandin, "Living in Revolutionary Time"; Joseph, "Latin America's Long Cold War"; Kirkendall, "Cold War Latin America"; Marchesi, "Escribiendo la Guerra Fría latinoamericana"; Pettinà, *Historia mínima*; Joseph, "Border Crossings"; Casals, "Which Borders Have Not Yet Been Crossed?"; Booth, "Rethinking Latin America's Cold War."

32. Armony, *Argentina, the United States, and the Anticommunist Crusade*; McSherry, *Predatory States*; Harmer, *Allende's Chile*; Harmer, "Brazil's Cold War"; Bell, "Matter of Western Civilisation"; Power, "Who but a Woman?"; Avery, "Promoting a 'Pinochetazo'"; exceptions being Herrán Ávila, "Las guerrillas blancas"; Casals, "Against a Communist Threat."

33. Bender, *Rethinking American History in a Global Age*; Seigel, "Beyond Compare"; Roberts, "Transnationalization of Gender History"; Briggs, McCormick, and Way, "Transnationalism"; Roniger, "Connected Histories"; Putnam, "Transnational and the Text-Searchable."

34. Pratt, *Imperial Eyes*, 6; Pratt, "Arts of the Contact Zone," 34.

35. Armony, *Argentina, the United States, and the Anticommunist Crusade*; Joseph, "Close Encounters," 5; Joseph, "What We Now Know," 7; Spenser, "Standing Conventional Cold War History," 381–382; Cohn, *Latin American Literary Boom*; Stites Mor, *Human Rights*.

1. Where the War Did Not End

1. Persio Celeste Franco et al., "Carta a un dominicano al ingresar . . .," Brooklyn (New York), 2 diciembre 1942, OF 138a, OFFDR.
2. "Dominicano Muerto en Italia," *Quisqueya Libre*, julio 1944, BNCJM.
3. Persio C. Franco, "Plan for the Liberation of the Dominican People . . .," 12 October 1947, box 708, OF 138 Miscellaneous, OFHST.
4. Andrés Requena, *Bulletin of the Dominican Republic in Exile*, 30 June 1947, box 708, OF 138 Miscellaneous, OFHST.
5. Vega, *Correspondencia entre Ángel Morales y Sumner Welles*.
6. Julius Gustman, Brooklyn, 8 March 1938, box 708, OF 138, OFHST.
7. A. J. Alfonseca and J. A. Bonilla Atiles to Harry Truman, 29 March 1947, box 708, OF 138 Miscellaneous, OFHST.
8. Leonard, *United States-Latin American Relations*; Sexton, *Monroe Doctrine*; May, *Manifest Destiny's Underworld*; Loveman, *No Higher Law*; Coates, *Legalist Empire*.
9. Pérez, *On Becoming Cuban*; Findlay, *Imposing Decency*; Gobat, *Confronting the American Dream*; Sotomayor, *The Sovereign Colony*; Verna, *Haiti and the Uses of America*; Ferrer, *Cuba*; Scarfi, *Hidden History of International Law*; Renda, *Taking Haiti*; McPherson, *Invaded*.
10. On the Good Neighbor Policy's contradictions, see Friedman, *Nazis & Good Neighbors*; Gellman, *Roosevelt and Batista*; Grow, *Good Neighbor Policy*; Roorda, *Dictator Next Door*; Wood, *Making of the Good Neighbor Policy*; Walker, "Crucial for Peace."
11. Millett, *Guardians of the Dynasty*, 125–188; Walter, *Regime of Anastasio Somoza*, 27–62; Schmitz, *Thank God They're on Our Side*, 48–57; Gould, *To Lead as Equals*; Walter, *Regime of Anastasio Somoza*; Ferrero Blanco, *La Nicaragua de los Somoza*.
12. C. H. Calhoun to Stephen Early, Canal Zone, 21 July 1939, OF 432a, OFFDR.
13. Velázquez Alemán et al., *Pavorosas Realidades*, 19.
14. "Una Oclaración de los Estudiantes Nicaragüenses," *Las Últimas Noticas*, 18 febrero 1944. On Nicaraguan students and Somoza, see Rueda, *Students of Revolution*.
15. Cordero Reyes, Wassmer y Cuadro Pasos, *Nicaragua bajo el régimen de Somoza*, 22–35.
16. "Memorándum para acuerdo presidencial: Política nicaragüense," México, 31 mayo 1944; Emilio Calderón Puig, "Informe político sobre Nicaragua," 15 agosto 1944, exp. III-255-5, AHGE; "Serán establecidas relaciones diplomáticas . . .," *Novedades*, 17 diciembre 1944.
17. Walter, *Regime of Anastasio Somoza*; Leonard, *United States and Central America*; Clark, *United States and Somoza*.
18. Exp. 9, caja 784, DGIPS; Clodomiro Urcuyo Rodríguez a Ricardo Fournier, Managua, 6 agosto 1947, RREE 2606bis.
19. Antonio Gamero, "Revelaciones con relación a su revista *Estrella de Centro América*," álbum de recortes periodísticos políticos de Alberto Ordóñez Argüello (Nicaraguan poet and exile), access courtesy of Mauricio Ordóñez
20. Álvaro Bonilla Lara, memorándum, San José, 17 noviembre 1947, RREE 2673.
21. Yanuario Landa Blanco a Rafael Heliodoro Valle, 23 junio 1948, exp. 1130, BNM. On Honduran state formation, see Euraque, *Reinterpreting the Banana Republic*.
22. Dodd, *Tiburcio Carías*; Inestroza Manzanares, *Documentos clasificados*.
23. Federal Bureau of Investigation and United States Department of Justice, *Honduras: Today* (Federal Bureau of Investigation, 1942), 16–17, folder Axis Penetration and Political Activities in Latin America, box 79, HWVP.
24. Santamaría, *La personalidad política*; Zúñiga Huete, *Cartas*; Fenner, "Puppet Dictator in the Banana Republic?"

25. Plutarco Muñoz P., Vicente Cáceres y Fernando Zepeda D., Decreto No. 44, 30 enero 1942, OF 193, OFFDR.
26. C. G. Kemball, Tegucigalpa, 12 June 1944, FO 371/37919.
27. C. G. Kemball, Ref. 966/44, Tegucigalpa, 14 July 1944; C. G. Kemball, Ref. 901/44, Tegucigalpa, 4 July 1944, FO 371/37919.
28. Zúñiga Huete, *Regalos del exilio*, 10–11.
29. Zúñiga Huete et al., *Carta abierta a Tiburcio Carías*, 8.
30. Rafael Heliodoro Valle a José R. Castro, 18 junio 1944, exp. 446, BNM.
31. José R. Castro a Silverio Laínez, Habana, 8 febrero 1944, exp. 446, BNM.
32. Derby, *Dictator's Seduction*; Peguero, *Militarization of Culture*; Turits, *Foundations of Despotism*; Manley, *Paradox of Paternalism*; Tillman, *Dollar Diplomacy by Force*.
33. Enrique A. González, Número 179, Ciudad Trujillo, 7 marzo 1946; Enrique A. González, Número 453, Ciudad Trujillo, 7 junio 1946, exp. III-824-7, AHGE.
34. "¿Y de esto que, Mr. Hull?," *Quisqueya Libre*, mayo 1944, BNCJM.
35. Mayes, *Mulatto Republic*; Paulino, *Dividing Hispaniola*; Roorda, *Dictator Next Door*; Wells, *Tropical Zion*.
36. State Department, 4 February 1938; Presidential Memorandum for the Undersecretary of State, 16 February 1939; C. K. Schmidt, 5 March 1942, OF 138, OFFDR.
37. Ellis O. Briggs, No. 70, Ciudad Trujillo, 5 July 1944, box 1, DRSCF.
38. Russell Duncan Macrae, "Political Situation in Santo Domingo," Ciudad Trujillo, September 1947, FO 371/60919.
39. John Gunther, "Trujillo: El Perfecto Dictador," *Quisqueya Libre*, junio 1944, BNCJM.
40. "Informe general que la Embajada . . .," noviembre 1944, exp. III-256-3, AHGE.
41. Sergio Alpízar, "El 'Democratismo' de Trujillo," *Quisqueya Libre*, mayo 1944, BNCJM.
42. Handwritten comment in margins, Russell Duncan Macrae, "Political Situation in Santo Domingo," Ciudad Trujillo, September 1947, FO 371/60919; Arvelo, *Nuestras luchas civiles*, 200–225; Miolán, *El Perrede desde mi ángulo*, 49–82; Bonilla, "Entre el recuerdo y el olvido"; Pou García, "Movimientos conspirativos"; Ayuso, *Lucha contra Trujillo*; Orbe, *Del Exilio Político Dominicano Antitrujillista*.
43. "Ecos del Centenario," *Quisqueya Libre*, abril 1944, BNCJM.
44. Hicks, *Blood in the Streets*.
45. Landestoy, *¡Yo también acuso!*
46. Partido Revolucionario Dominicano, *La historia del hombre*.
47. Vega, *Un interludio de tolerancia*.
48. Israel Mejías Deras a Rafael Heliodoro Valle, San Salvador, 12 octubre 1937, exp. 1309, BNM; Alemán Bolaños, *Un Lombrosiano*, 5, 74. On Sandino, see Carr, "Pioneering Transnational Solidarity in the Americas"; Katz, "Mexico, Gilberto Bosques, and the Refugees."
49. Jesús González Valencia, "Asunto: Informe sobre actividades . . .," México, 27 octubre 1945, exp. 9, caja 784, DGIPS; Ordóñez Argüello, *Arévalo visto por América*.
50. Ezequiel Padilla, Número 3109, México, 13 febrero 1945, exp. 59, caja 753, DGIPS.
51. Juan Sánchez de Tagle y Adi Stacovici, "Asunto: Informan sobre propaganda . . .," México, 22 febrero 1945, exp. 8, caja 757, DGIPS.
52. "Otro Homenaje a Sandino en Renovación," álbum de recortes de Ordóñez Argüello; Unión Democrática Centroamericana, *Centro América Libre*, marzo 1944, exp. 2, vol. 790, DGIPS.
53. Manela, *The Wilsonian Moment*; Borgwardt, *A New Deal for the World*.
54. Ángel Zúñiga Huete a Henry A. Wallace, México, 9 diciembre 1940, exp. 2219, BNM.
55. Vicente Sáenz y Francisco Lino Osegueda a Sumner Welles, 30 abril 1943, exp. 1780, BNM.

56. Vicente Sáenz a Franklin Delano Roosevelt, México, 3 julio 1944, exp. 1780, BNM.
57. Daniel Alegría, Santa Ana, 8 junio 1947, exp. 9143, leg. 589, FME.
58. Amílcar Gómez Robelo a Ángel Zúñiga Huete, Guatemala, 9 octubre 1944, AGR.
59. Ángel Zúñiga Huete a Amílcar Gómez Robelo, México, 18 octubre 1944, AGR.
60. Zúñiga Huete, *La Carta del Atlántico*.
61. Cordero Reyes, Wassmer y Cuadra Pasos, *Nicaragua bajo el régimen de Somoza*, 33–34.
62. Velázquez Alemán et al., *Pavorosas Realidades*, 22; William D. Hassett, 12 October 1944, OF 432a, OFFDR.
63. Graciela Bográn, testimonio en Apolo Musageta, "Crónica del homenaje tributado . . .," CLDHMH, 9.
64. "Trujillo ha Manchado Nuestra Historia," *Quisqueya Libre*, mayo 1944, BNCJM.
65. Ornes, *Trujillo*, 67.
66. "Trujillo ha Manchado Nuestra Historia," *Quisqueya Libre*, mayo 1944, BNCJM.
67. Esperanza Ellis to Eleanor Roosevelt, New York, 8 March 1944, folder 190, box 1352, ERP. Women were pivotal contributors to antidictatorial causes and movements throughout the Caribbean Basin, as seen in the Honduran protests or Dominican exiles' writings, but they were often forced to remain with children and family while men networked in public or abroad, resulting in the seeming "silence" of these women. See "El Callado y Heroico Sacrificio de la Mujer Dominicana," *Quisqueya Libre*, septiembre 1944, BNCJM.
68. Rivas, *Missionary Capitalist*; Friedman, *Nazis & Good Neighbors*; Rankin, *¡México, la patria!*; Humphreys, *Latin America and the Second World War*; Rout and Bratzel, *Shadow War*; Leonard and Bratzel, *Latin America During World War II*.
69. Jorrit van den Berk (*Becoming a Good Neighbor*) claims that exiles used antifascism in the late 1930s to little success.
70. Amílcar Gómez Robelo, memorándum, Guatemala, 13 diciembre 1945, AGR. As Thomas J. Dodd, *Tiburcio Carías*, and Kenneth J. Grieb, *Guatemalan Caudillo*, stress, admiration of European fascism did not translate into building mirror-image regimes; rather, regimes reflected or resembled European fascism due to preexisting factors.
71. Esteban M. Morel, "Igual que en Alemán," *Quisqueya Libre*, julio 1944, BNCJM.
72. "La paz del dictador Carías," *En Marcha*, 15 noviembre 1947, exp. 8, vol. 796, DGIPS.
73. Vicente Sáenz, "No Quedará un solo tirano en Centro América," México, 26 noviembre 1943, exp. 1780, BNM.
74. Cordero Reyes, Wassmer y Cuadra Pasos, *Nicaragua bajo el régimen de Somoza*, 21.
75. Pedro José Zepeda et al. a Ezequiel Padilla, México 21 febrero 1945, exp. III-451-1, AHGE.
76. Partido Unionista Centroamericano, *El Partido Unionista Centroamericano en la lucha*, 3, 20.
77. Frente Democrático Revolucionario Hondureño, memorándum, AGR.
78. Rafael Heliodoro Valle a José R. Castro, 8 mayo 1944, exp. 446, BNM.
79. Antonio Madrid H. a Rafael Heliodoro Valle, San Pedro Sula, 30 mayo 1946 y 5 junio 1946, exp. 1255, BNM.
80. Comité Liberal Demócrata de Honduras en México, "Mensaje para el Pueblo de Honduras," México, 1 enero 1944, exp. 8, vol. 796, DGIPS.
81. Leovigildo Cuello, "América y la Hora Internacional," *Quisqueya Libre*, enero 1945, BNCJM.
82. A Franklin Delano Roosevelt, Winston Churchill y José Stalin, México, enero 1944, exp. 826, BNM.
83. Ernestina Baez, Faustino Calcines, Ramón Ruíz Rodríguez y José Solís Miyar, Santa Clara, 1 mayo 1946, signatura 30, leg. 22, FSP. On Cuban antifascism, see Lambe, *No Barrier Can Contain It*.

84. No. 840-B, San José, 22 marzo 1945, RREE 543:7.
85. Peticiones, octubre 1945, FP 9107.
86. "Text of address . . .," 4 December 1946, exp. 1780, BNM.
87. Vicente Sáenz, "Memorándum sobre Centro América," México, 15 febrero 1944, exp. 1780, BNM; Amílcar Gómez Robelo, memorándum, Guatemala, 13 diciembre 1945, AGR.
88. Juan José Meza a Manuel Ávila Camacho, México, 5 noviembre 1945, exp. III-451-1, AHGE.
89. Andrés Requena, *Boletín of the Dominican Republic in Exile* 3 (1947), box 708, OF 138 Miscellaneous, OFHST.
90. Salvador Muñoz a Primo Villa Michel, Oficio No. 0071/45, México, 31 octubre 1945, exp. 9, caja 784, DGIPS.
91. Comité Cubano Pro Liberación de Honduras, *Yo Acuso*, 4, 6.
92. "Dominicanos y Españoles de New York Unidos en la Lucha," *Quisqueya Libre*, junio/agosto 1945, BNCJM.
93. "Dos fechas cubanas," *Quisqueya Libre*, mayo 1944, BNCJM.
94. Miolán, *El Perrede desde mi ángulo*, 37–40.
95. Juan Bosch, "El Día de un Pueblo; en Prado 615," *Quisqueya Libre*, abril 1944, BNCJM.
96. Unión Democrática Antinazista Dominicana, *América contra Trujillo*, 13–39.
97. Exp. 433/234, CMAC; Federación Estudiantil Universitaria, *Los Universitarios de Santo Domingo*; Asociación de Estudiantes Hispanoamericanos en México, *En Lucha contra Trujillo*.
98. For more on the Masacre Sampedrana, see Moulton, "Applying the Atlantic Charter."
99. John Erwin, No. A-308, Tegucigalpa, 21 December 1945; Nathan A. Brown Jr., R 128–45, 26 December 1945, box 26, USH.
100. Unión Democrática Centroamericana a Winston Churchill, México, 15 diciembre 1943, FO 371/37919.
101. Reconstruction of these marches and protests derive from Honduran exiles' collections, CLDHMH, *Homenaje a las Víctimas*, US and British reports, and regional newspapers.
102. Beatriz Galindo, "La jornada femenina del 29 de mayo," in CLDHMH, *Homenaje a las Víctimas*, 27–31, 35–36, 47–49.
103. Galindo, in CLDHMH, *Homenaje a las Víctimas*, 49–60.
104. Galindo, in CLDHMH, *Homenaje a las Víctimas*, 60–61.
105. "C . . . C . . .," "Encarcelamiento colectivo de damas . . .," in CLDHMH, *Homenaje a las Víctimas*, 66–67.
106. Memorándum, 17 junio 1945, 009, SRD; Galindo, in CLDHMH, *Homenaje a las Víctimas*, 61.
107. "Nuestra América: Honduras al borde de la revolución," *Quisqueya Libre*, junio 1944, BNCJM.
108. Rafael Heliodoro Valle a José R. Castro, 5 junio 1944, exp. 446, BNM.
109. Bográn, in CLDHMH, *Homenaje a las Víctimas*, 7; "La Masacre sampedrana," AGR.
110. Bográn, in CLDHMH, *Homenaje a las Víctimas*, 7–8; "La Masacre sampedrana," AGR.
111. Masacre Sampedrana sources are scarce. Exiles' materials offer important insights yet offer little on Carías's police and military forces' decision-making. British officials admitted that US reports were misleading and inaccurate, possibly due to the relationship between Carías's officials and US officials such as the US ambassador in Tegucigalpa John Erwin. The British vice consul at Tela provided a report (with C. G. Kemball, No. 9, Tegucigalpa, 26 July 1944, FO 371/37919) after having visited San Pedro Sula (C. G. Kemball, Ref. 966/44, Tegucigalpa, 14 July 1944, FO 371/37919). As British officials confessed, the vice consul's report confirms the atrocities documented in "La Masacre sampedrana" and Bográn, in CLDHMH, *Homenaje a las Víctimas*.

Exile documents and reports agree Gálvez was not present, though he approved the route and soldiers. Bográn, in CLDHMH, *Homenaje a las Víctimas*, 10, claims Gálvez approved and allowed the bloodshed, but there is no reason exiles or protesters would know Gálvez's orders when he was, as Bográn admits, "in a hotel, one block away" from the massacre. In an unpublished historiography, Euraque, "La Masacre del 6 de Julio en San Pedro Sula," quotes a secondhand account from Medardo Mejía published in 1972, repeated in a 2009 biography of Gálvez, that the massacre's conspirators sought to destroy Gálvez's chances at becoming Carías's successor or even kill Gálvez. This unverified claim is the only one that tries to exonerate Gálvez. The British vice consul reported, "Government officials are highly embarrassed," and "Gálvez hastily flew to the capital the following day to render a report to the President," suggesting Gálvez and Carísta officials did not order or approve the atrocities but were implicated in failing to control what took place, especially in light of Funes's actions.

112. Bográn, in CLDHMH, *Homenaje a las Víctimas*, 9.

113. Vice Consul Report with C. G. Kemball, No. 9, Tegucigalpa, 26 July 1944, FO 371/37919.

114. Bográn, in CLDHMH, *Homenaje a las Víctimas*, 9.

115. Vice Consul Report with C. G. Kemball, No. 9, Tegucigalpa, 26 July 1944, FO 371/37919.

116. C. G. Kemball, No. 9, Tegucigalpa, 26 July 1944; C. G. Kemball, Ref. 966/44, Tegucigalpa, 14 July 1944, FO 371/37919.

117. José R. Castro a Rafael Heliodoro Valle, Habana, 20 agosto 1944, exp. 446, BNM.

118. "La Masacre sampedrana," AGR.

119. Amílcar Gómez Robelo, memorándum, Guatemala, 13 diciembre 1945, AGR.

120. Zúñiga O., *Año trece de la era Tiburcia*, 40–41.

121. "No Será Presidente de Honduras," *Combate*, 1 enero 1948, exp. 8, vol. 796, DGIPS.

122. Carlos A. Perdomo a Rafael Heliodoro Valle, Guatemala, 14 julio 1945, exp. 1538, BNM.

123. Comité Cubano Pro Liberación de Honduras, *Yo Acuso*, 11.

124. Alfredo Corona Gallardo, México, 6 julio 1945, in CLDHMH, *Homenaje a las Víctimas*, 19–20.

125. Jacobo Carcamo, "Tiranía en Honduras," in CLDHMH, *Homenaje a las Víctimas*, 65; Rafael Enrique Marrero, "Oda a Carías," in CLDHMH, *Homenaje a las Víctimas*, 100–102.

126. "Nuestra América: La lección salvadoreña," *Quisqueya Libre*, mayo 1944, BNCJM.

127. "Vibrante Mitin Centroamericano," álbum de recortes de Ordóñez Argüello.

128. Serafín García a Rafael Heliodoro Valle, Guatemala, 21 diciembre 1944, exp. 869, BNM.

129. José R. Castro a Rafael Heliodoro Valle, Guatemala, 23 mayo 1945, exp. 446; José Antonio Peraza a Rafael Heliodoro Valle, Guatemala, 30 junio 1946, exp. 1536, BNM.

130. Amílcar Gómez Robelo a José Antonio Peraza, Guatemala, 28 junio 1946, AGR.

131. Amílcar Gómez Robelo a Alfredo Trejo Castillo, Guatemala, 21 mayo 1946, AGR.

2. The Transnational Postwar Conjuncture

1. Roberto Despradel, No. 275, Guatemala, 29 agosto 1945, leg. 3348, Oficios y Correspondencia, 1950, caja 2903348, SERREE.

2. Grieb, *Guatemalan Caudillo*; Dosal, *Doing Business with the Dictators*.

3. "Lo que nos dice la prensa norteamericana" (Tipografía C.D.S., 1944), item 178, folder 4, box 1, ATF.

4. Inspector P.S. 11, "Asunto: Informe de relaciones amistosas . . .," Huixtla, 2 octubre 1938, exp. 5, vol. 109, DGIPS.
5. Juan Sánchez de Tagle, "Asunto—Informa sobre las Organizaciones . . .," México, 4 abril 1944, exp. 1, caja 87, DGIPS.
6. Clemente Marroquín Rojas y Gustavo A. Trangay a Miguel Alemán, México, 22 octubre 1942, exp. 1, caja 750, DGIPS.
7. José Prado Romana, Gustavo A. Trangay, and Clemente Marroquín Rojas to Enrique Ruiz Guinazu, México, 12 January 1942, OF 439, OFFDR.
8. On students and teachers, see Galich, *Del pánico al ataque*; Vrana, *This City Belongs to You*, 27–61.
9. "Solo los nascifacistas han abierto . . ." (1944), item 390, folder 8, box 1, ATF.
10. Jorge Ubico, "Manifiesto al pueblo de Guatemala" (Tipografía Nacional, 1944), item 329, folder 7, box 1, ATF.
11. Romeo Ortega, 387, Guatemala, 15 octubre 1944, exp. III-708-1, AHGE.
12. Celestino Herrera Frimont, Número 603, San Salvador, 18 septiembre 1944, exp. III-708-1, AHGE.
13. "Ponce Pedía Aviones Para Bombardear a Guatemala," *Excelsior*, 28 octubre 1944; John D. Erwin, 313, Guatemala, 20 October 1944, box 18, USH.
14. Cardoza y Aragón, *Guatemala*, 392.
15. On the Revolution's achievements and limitations, see Villagrán Kramer, *Biografía política de Guatemala*, 25–119; Gleijeses, *Shattered Hope*, 36–49; Rodríguez de Ita, *La participación política*; Grandin, *Last Colonial Massacre*, 19–71; Levenson-Estrada, *Trade Unionists Against Terror*, 14–48; Handy, *Revolution in the Countryside*; Vrana, *This City Belongs to You*, 43–61.
16. *20 de Octubre*, abril 1945, 004, SRD.
17. Emigración hondureña a miembros del Triumvirato, Guatemala, 21 octubre 1944, AGR.
18. Declaraciones del Licenciado . . ., 238, Correspondencia de Enero a Marzo de 1945, SCJJA.
19. "Apoyo de la AEU a Nicaragüenses Democráticos," *El Imparcial*, 26 septiembre 1945.
20. Francisco Morazán, "Lo falso de las dictaduras," *Mediodía*, 8 octubre 1945.
21. "Aislamiento de las Dictaduras Centroamericanas," *El Imparcial*, 29 septiembre 1945.
22. Roberto Despradel, No. 115, Ciudad de Guatemala, leg. 3348, caja 2903348, SERREE.
23. Roberto Despradel, No. 127, Guatemala, leg. 3348, caja 2903348, SERREE.
24. Frente Unido de Partidos Políticos y Agrupaciones Cívicas, "Los que no son nada" (Tipografía América), item 133, folder 3, box 1, ATF.
25. Luis Cardoza y Aragón a Juan José Arévalo, 22 noviembre 1944, 162, Correspondencia de Noviembre, SCJJA.
26. Rafael Heliodoro Valle a Juan José Arévalo, 29 octubre 1944, 002, Correspondencia de Octubre, SCJJA.
27. Héctor Medina Planas a Juan José Arévalo, 25 octubre 1944, 014, Correspondencia de Octubre, SCJJA.
28. On Arévalo's spiritual socialism, see Friedman, "Latin American Third Way."
29. Juan José Arévalo, "Conservadores, liberales y socialistas" (Centro Editorial, 1944), item 19, folder 1, box 1, ATF; memorándum, Frente Democrático Revolucionario Hondureño, AGR.
30. Álbum de firmas, Chalchuapa, abril 1945, 006, SRD; J. Leonardo Godoy a Juan José Arévalo, San Salvador, 1 diciembre 1944, 024, Correspondencia de Diciembre, SCJJA.
31. Ernestina M. Alvarado a Juan José Arévalo, 22 noviembre 1944, 154, Correspondencia de Noviembre, SCJJA; Alvarado a Juan José Arévalo, México, 24 octubre 1944, 016, Correspondencia de Octubre, SCJJA.

32. José R. Campos a Juan José Arévalo, Chiapas, 30 octubre 1944, 017, Correspondencia de Octubre, SCJJA.
33. Manuel Peña H. y A. González Aragón, "Obreros de Honduras con el Presidente Arévalo," San Pedro Sula, 24 mayo 1946, 115, SRD.
34. José R. Castro a Rafael Heliodoro Valle, Guatemala, 23 mayo 1945, exp. 446, BNM.
35. Rafael Heliodoro Valle a Juan José Arévalo, 29 octubre 1944, exp. 121, BNM.
36. Ordóñez Argüello, *Arévalo visto por América*, 325–342.
37. Inspector P.S. 42 y P.S. 21 a Emilio Baig Serra, México, 13 abril 1946, exp. 9, caja 784, DGIPS.
38. Memorándum, Frente Democrático Revolucionario Hondureño, AGR.
39. Andrés Alvarado Puerto a José García Bauer, Guatemala, 14 agosto 1945, 016, SRD.
40. Boletín, Guatemala, 18 diciembre 1944, AGR.
41. Rafael Heliodoro Valle a Juan José Arévalo, Guatemala, 3 agosto 1945, AGR.
42. Rafael Heliodoro Valle a José Pineda, 25 julio 1945, exp. 1570, BNM.
43. Although there has not been a thorough examination of Central American unionist sentiments, whether in its entirety or the 1900s alone, see Solano Muñoz, "La república centroamericana," for more information.
44. Mendieta, *Esquema del problema unionista centroamericano*, 10–11.
45. Inspectores No. 73 y No. 361, "Asunto: Se rinde informe relacionado . . .," México, 9 octubre 1945, exp. 1, caja 750, DGIPS.
46. Unión Patriótica Centroamericana, "Si yo fuera centroamericano" (Imprenta Arimany), item 338, folder 7, box 1, ATF.
47. Unión Patriótica Centroamericana, "Ventajas que reportará . . ." (Imprenta Hispanica, 1944), item 339, folder 7, box 1, ATF.
48. Gleijeses, "Juan José Arévalo and the Caribbean Legion," 136–137, touches on Arévalo's unionist stance.
49. Joaquín García Monge a Juan José Arévalo, San José, 01 septiembre 1944, 009, Correspondencia de Septiembre, SCJJA.
50. Salvador Mendieta a Juan José Arévalo, Guatemala, 10 junio 1949, 592, SRD.
51. Carlos Castillo Ibarra a Juan José Arévalo, Panamá, 7 diciembre 1946, 164, SRD.
52. Rafael Heliodoro Valle a Amílcar Gómez Robelo, México, 15 junio 1945, AGR; "Famoso periodista de Nicaragua, se encuentra en México," AOA.
53. Ricardo Herrera, "Asunto: Se rinde informe," México, 4 febrero 1944, exp. 9, caja 784, DGIPS.
54. Partido Unionista Centroamericano, "La más unánime y grandiosa manifestación . . ." (Tipografía C.D.S., 1944), item 286, folder 6, box 1, ATF.
55. Unión Patriótica Centroamericana, "La junta directiva . . ." (Guatemala: I.E.), item 336, folder 7, box 1, ATF.
56. On Spanish Republicans and the Guatemalan Revolution, see Taracena Arriola, *Guatemala, la República Española y el Gobierno Vasco*.
57. Roberto Despradel, No. 275, Guatemala, 29 agosto 1945, leg. 3348, caja 2903348, SERREE.
58. Roberto Despradel, No. 42, Guatemala, 26 enero 1945, leg. 3348, caja 2903348, SERREE.
59. Salvador Etcheverría Brañas al Presidente de la Confederación de Trabajadores de Guatemala, Guatemala, 8 enero 1947, exp. No. 1, caja No. 115, fondo México, FUE.
60. Salvador Etcheverría Brañas, No. 89, Guatemala, 11 enero 1947, exp. No. 1, caja 115, fondo México, FUE.
61. Exp. No. 3, caja 115, fondo México, FUE.

62. Outside of Tom Long and Max Paul Friedman, "The Promise of Precommitment," there is no thorough examination of how Braden's or Larreta's ideas resonated throughout the Western Hemisphere. On how South American officials and journalists interpreted the Larreta Doctrine, see Casal Tatlock, *La Doctrina Larreta*. On Braden and Larreta's impact on the Caribbean Basin, see Ameringer, *Caribbean Legion*.

63. Carlos Félix y José Antonio Bonilla Atiles a Juan José Arévalo, 15 julio 1945, 220, SRD.

64. J. Gustavo Morales, "Igualdad de Trato Para todas las Dictaduras," *El Imparcial*, 8 octubre 1945.

65. *Quisqueya Libre*, junio 1944, BNCJM.

66. Amílcar Gómez Robelo a Rafael Heliodoro Valle, Guatemala, 27 abril 1946, AGR.

67. Gómez Robelo a Rafael Heliodoro Valle, Guatemala, 30 noviembre 1945, AGR.

68. Although most studies on European decolonization have overlooked the greater Caribbean, there are some English-language works noting links between the multifaceted and unique processes of each territory, race, sex, World War II, and the Cold War. On British territories and decolonization in the Caribbean Basin, see Parker, *Brother's Keeper*; Mawby, *Ordering Independence*; Teelucksingh, *Labour and the Decolonization Struggle*; Chamberlain, *Empire and Nation-Building in the Caribbean*. For the French, see Childers, *Seeking Imperialism's Embrace*. For the Dutch, see Oostindie and Klinkers, *Decolonising the Caribbean*; Quinn, *Black Power in the Caribbean*; Schields, "Closer Ties."

69. One of the few works attempting to examine the international factors shaping Belizean independence is Shoman, *Belize's Independence*.

70. Gleijeses, "Juan José Arévalo and the Caribbean Legion"; Shoman, *Belize's Independence*.

71. Véliz Estrada, "'El más importante asunto internacional,'" links the Belize question with Arévalo's foreign policy.

72. Virgilio Rodríguez Beteta a Juan José Arévalo, Santiago, 28 enero 1947, 175; Rodríguez Beteta a Arévalo, Santiago, 2 mayo 1946, 110; Rodríguez Beteta a Arévalo, Santiago, 20 agosto 1945, 021; Rodríguez Beteta a Arévalo, Santiago, 5 septiembre 1945, 031, SRD.

73. Roberto Despradel, No. 103, Guatemala, 3 abril 1945, leg. 3348, caja 2903348, SERREE; O. Bertholin y Gálvez a Juan José Arévalo, Grand-Saconnex, 19 enero 1946, 061; Rafael Pineda de Mont a Juan José Arévalo, París, 30 enero 1946, 062, SRD.

74. "Desfile Satírico Estudiantil . . .," exp. III-450-1, AHGE.

75. Juan Bosch, "Colonias en el continente," *Información*, 29 agosto 1944, in Céspedes Espinosa, *Juan Bosch en Cuba*.

76. Lorenzo Zelaya R. et al. a Juan José Arévalo, México, 18 marzo 1948, 344, SRD.

77. Salvador Mendieta a Juan José Arévalo, Managua, 14 abril 1948, 363, SRD.

78. Vicente Sáenz, "Puntos Esenciales Tratados . . .," Guatemala, 8 marzo 1948, 338, SRD.

79. Arévalo, "Istmania," in *Escritos políticos*; Arévalo, "Al asumir la presidencia," in *Discursos en la presidencia*; Arévalo, "El mundo en guerra," in *Despacho presidencial*.

80. Dosal, *Doing Business with the Dictators*; Bucheli, "Major Trends in the Historiography."

81. John Taylor, No. 162, Guatemala, 11 September 1944, FO 371/37933.

82. Amílcar Gómez Robelo, memorándum, Guatemala, 13 diciembre 1945, AGR.

83. Rafael Heliodoro Valle a César Ortiz, 19 junio 1944, exp. 1464, BNM.

84. C. G. Kemball, No. 12, Tegucigalpa, 4 June 1944; "Situation in Tegucigalpa," 14 June 1944, FO 371/37919.

85. J. H. Leche, No. 142, Guatemala, 28 July 1944, FO 371/37933.

86. José María Dávila, Número 127-R, Guatemala, 9 abril 1945, exp. III-450-1, AHGE.

87. Harms, *Ladina Social Activism*.

88. Rafael Heliodoro Valle a Amílcar Gómez Robelo, México, 10 diciembre 1945, AGR.
89. Jorge García Granados a Juan José Arévalo, 24 mayo 1947, 212, SRD.
90. Jorge García Granados, "Memorándum al señor Ministro de Relaciones Exteriores," 6 diciembre 1946, 163; Granados a Juan José Arévalo, New York, 11 noviembre 1947, 293, SRD.
91. Amílcar Gómez Robelo a Samuel Semurray [sic], Guatemala, 14 julio 1948, AGR.
92. José María Dávila, Número 119-R, Guatemala, 23 marzo 1945, exp. III-450-1, AHGE.
93. W. H. Gallienne, No. 84, Guatemala, 6 May 1949, FO 371/74030.
94. "No intervenimos en política extranjera," *Quisqueya Libre*, mayo 1944, BNCJM.
95. Rafael Heliodoro Valle a Carlos A. Perdomo, 25 julio 1945, exp. 1538, BNM.
96. Rafael Heliodoro Valle a Carlos A. Perdomo, México, 11 junio 1945, exp. 1538, BNM.
97. Modesto Valle, et al., a Juan José Arévalo, 19 octubre 1945, 037, SRD.
98. "Si Somoza irrespeta...," *La Hora*, 22 noviembre 1947, exp. 9, caja 784, DGIPS.
99. Juan M. Diaz, "Los Pueblos que no Luchan, son Pueblos Vencidos," *Quisqueya Libre*, agosto 1944, BNCJM.
100. Vicente Sáenz, "No Quedará un solo tirano en Centro América," México, 26 noviembre 1943, exp. 1780, BNM.
101. José R. Castro a Silverio Laínez, Habana, 8 febrero 1944, exp. 446, BNM.
102. Amílcar Gómez Robelo a Francisco J. Arana, Guatemala, 12 diciembre 1945, AGR.
103. Arvelo, *Cayo Confite y Luperón*, 34.
104. Juan José Arévalo a Jorge García Granados, Guatemala, 20 octubre 1945, 038, SRD.
105. Miguel Ángel Ramírez a Horacio Ornes, La Habana, 7 julio 1950, exp. 2, caja 5, APHO.
106. Memorándum, Frente Democrático Revolucionario Hondureño, AGR.
107. "Partido Liberal Nacional: Declaración de Principios," 001, SRD.
108. Amílcar Gómez Robelo a Ángel Zúñiga Huete, Guatemala, 9 octubre 1944, AGR.
109. Ángel Zúñiga Huete a Amílcar Gómez Robelo, México, 18 octubre 1944, AGR.
110. A la Junta de Gobierno de Guatemala, memorándum, AGR.
111. Miguel Ángel Feliú Arzeno a Horacio Ornes, Habana, 19 junio 1956, Expediente 12, Caja 5, APHO.
112. Miguel Ángel Ramírez, "Apreciación de la situación político-internacional . . .," Guatemala, 25 enero 1951, folder 350: Caribbean, box 40, USN.
113. Memorándum, Frente Democrático Revolucionario Hondureño, AGR.
114. Jorge Ribas Montes, 25 agosto 1955, collection of Ribas Montes.
115. Horacio Ornes a José Félix Córdoba Boniche, Habana, 12 mayo 1951, exp. 16, caja 6, APHO.
116. Alfredo B. Reina a Rafael Heliodoro Valle, Managua, 5 marzo 1945, exp. 1651, BNM.
117. José Antonio Peraza a Amílcar Gómez Robelo, San Marcos, 16 marzo 1946, AGR.
118. José Antonio Peraza a Juan José Arévalo, Nuevo Progreso (México), 11 julio 1947, 219, SRD.
119. "Nepotismo de Trujillo," *El Imparcial*, 9 octubre 1945; López De-Sardi, "La Libertad de Prensa en la República Dominicana," *El Tiempo*, septiembre 1945.
120. Manuel A. Peña Batlle a los Jefes de Misiones Diplomáticas, Circular No. 21, Ciudad Trujillo, 24 julio 1944, exp. Boletín, 1944, caja 2903759, SERREE.
121. Roberto Despradel, No. 367, Guatemala, 16 noviembre 1945, leg. 3348, caja 2903348, SERREE.
122. On Trujillo and Betancourt's rivalries, see Castro Ventura, *Trujillo vs. Betancourt*; Mondolfi Gudat, *El día del atentado*.
123. George Ogilvie Forbes, No. 194, Caracas, 29 October 1945; George Ogilvie Forbes, No. 198, Caracas, 31 October 1945, FO 371/45154.

124. Leake, No. 13, Guatemala City, 19 November 1945; George Ogilvie Forbes, No. 238, Caracas, 8 December 1945, FO 371/45154; Rómulo Betancourt a Juan José Arévalo, Miraflores, 22 octubre 1946, 149, SRD.
125. Roberto Despradel, No. 263, Guatemala, 5 agosto 1946, leg. 3348, caja 2903348, SERREE.
126. Virgilio Rodríguez Beteta a Juan José Arévalo, Santiago, 13 febrero 1946, 077, SRD.
127. Juan Bosch a Juan José Arévalo, Habana, 9 abril 1946, 105, SRD.
128. Rómulo Betancourt a Juan José Arévalo, Caracas, 18 febrero 1946, 105, SRD.
129. Carlos Félix y José Antonio Bonilla Atiles a Juan José Arévalo, 15 julio 1945, 220; Carlos Félix y José Antonio Bonilla Atiles a Juan José Arévalo, New York, 9 julio 1947, 244, SRD.
130. Ángel Arturo Rivera a Juan José Arévalo, Habana, 21 julio 1947, 222, SRD.
131. Juan Bosch a Juan José Arévalo, Habana, 8 julio 1947, 242, SRD.
132. J. C. Alfonseca a Juan José Arévalo, New York, 10 julio 1947, 248; Ramón de Lara a Juan José Arévalo, Caracas, 11 julio 1947, 251; F. Ellis Cambiaso a Juan José Arévalo, Caguas (Puerto Rico), 10 julio 1947, 247.
133. Augusto Charnaud MacDonald, José Manuel Fortuny y Humberto González Juárez a Juan José Arévalo, No. 9 hr, Guatemala, 10 julio 1947, 237, SRD.
134. Carlos Martínez Palma a Juan José Arévalo, No. 2.Bf., Chimaltenango, 8 julio 1947, 231; Ignacio Pashel a Juan José Arévalo, No. 1 hr/rm, Antigua, 12 julio 1947, 241, SRD.
135. J. Antonio Acevedo a Juan José Arévalo, No. 17 bf, Guatemala, 10 julio 1947, 239, SRD.
136. Jacinto Sacor Coyoy a Juan José Arévalo, No. 14.Hr., Guatemala, 9 julio 1947, 234, SRD.
137. Movimiento Socialista Revolucionario a Juan José Arévalo, Habana, 11 julio 1947, 250, SRD.
138. Ángel Arturo Rivera a Juan José Arévalo, Habana, 21 julio 1947, 222; Enrique Ovares a Juan José Arévalo, Habana, 14 julio 1947, 253; Alfredo Guevara, et al., a Juan José Arévalo, Habana, 12 julio 1947, 262, SRD.
139. Alberto Ordóñez Argüello y Carlos Castillo Ibarra a Juan José Arévalo, No. 11.Bf., Guatemala, 09 julio 1947, 232; Leonte Pallais Tiffer et al. a Arévalo, Guatemala, 10 julio 1947, 256, SRD.
140. Francisco Morazán a Juan José Arévalo, No. 18.Hr., Guatemala, 9 julio 1947, 233; Antonio Madrid H. a Juan José Arévalo, No. 22 bf/rm, Guatemala, 10 julio 1947, 238; Marco Tulio Mendieta S. a Juan José Arévalo, No. 2 bf, Guatemala, 11 julio 1947, 240, SRD.
141. "Bases y Temario para la Convención Democrática Centroamericana," julio 1947, 228, SRD.
142. Horacio Ornes a Juan José Arévalo, México, 11 agosto 1954, exp. 18, caja 6, APHO.
143. Rafael Heliodoro Valle a Amílcar Gómez Robelo, México, 10 diciembre 1945, AGR.
144. Amílcar Gómez Robelo a Francisco J. Arana, Guatemala, 12 diciembre 1946, AGR.
145. Gómez Robelo a José Antonio Peraza, Guatemala, 13 mayo 1946, AGR.
146. Amílcar Gómez Robelo a Rafael Heliodoro Valle, Guatemala, 27 abril 1946, AGR.
147. Modesto Valle, et al., a Juan José Arévalo, 19 octubre 1945, 037, SRD.
148. Vicente Sáenz a Juan José Arévalo, México, 25 noviembre 1945, 043, SRD.

3. Counterrevolutionary Signatories

1. Boaz Long, No. 2351, Guatemala City, 9 April 1945, 814.00/4-945, roll 1, DF814.
2. See intercepted cables and telephone conversations in box 12, USG.

3. "Correspondence between Guatemalan Political Exiles," 11 April 1945, box 12, USG.
4. Robert F. Woodward, No. 2437, Guatemala City, 27 April 1945, 814.00/4-2745, roll 1, DF814.
5. John Edgar Hoover, "Subject: Revolutionary Plans, Guatemala," Washington, DC, 2 June 1945, 814.00/6-245, roll 1, DF814.
6. "Re: Doctor and Colonel Carlos Padilla y Padilla," Managua, 23 August 1945, with John Edgar Hoover, "Subject: Colonel Carlos Padilla y Padilla," Washington, DC, 28 September 1945, 814.00/9-2845, roll 1, DF814.
7. Paul C. Daniels, A-191, Tegucigalpa, 21 August 1947, 814.00/8-2147; Gordon S. Reid, "Subject: Carlos Padilla," 21 August 1947, 814.00/8-2147; MOC, Carlos Padilla y Padilla and Gordon S. Reid, 26 September 1947, 814.00/9-2647, roll 1, DF814.
8. Robert F. Woodward to Hallett Johnson, Guatemala City, 11 May 1945, box 40, USC.
9. Ramsey L. Moore, "RE: Guatemalan Revolution," San Salvador, 8 June 1945, with John F. Simmons, No. 293, San Salvador, 8 June 1945, box 40, USC.
10. Fletcher Warren, A-226, Managua, 21 June 1945, 814.00/6-2145, roll 1, DF814.
11. Paul C. Daniels, A-191, Tegucigalpa, 21 August 1947, 814.00/8-2147; Gordon S. Reid, "Subject: Carlos Padilla," 21 August 1947, 814.00/8-2147; MOC, Carlos Padilla y Padilla and Gordon S. Reid, 26 September 1947, 814.00/9-2647, roll 1, DF814.
12. Fletcher Warren, A-226, Managua, 21 June 1945, 814.00/6-2145, roll 1, DF814.
13. John Erwin, A-148, 14 June 1945, 814.00/6-1445, roll 1, DF814.
14. "Re: Doctor and Colonel Carlos Padilla y Padilla," 23 August 1945, DF814.
15. John Erwin, A-148, 14 June 1945, 814.00/6-1445, roll 1, DF814.
16. Andrew E. Donovan, "Subject: Investigation of Alleged Plot," Guatemala City, 2 July 1946, 814.00/7-246; John Edgar Hoover, "Subject: Revolutionary Activities in Guatemala," 2 July 1946, 814.00/7-246, roll 1, DF814.
17. John Edgar Hoover, "Subject: Revolutionary Activities In Guatemala," 31 December 1946, 814.00/12-3146, roll 1, DF814.
18. El Salvador and its governments' activities during this era merit further investigation, whether into the impact of the 1944 uprisings, how subsequent governments attempted to maneuver between and deflect away the political pressures emanating from its neighbors, or how notable Salvadoran military and political officials cultivated important relationships with reactionaries.
19. Andrew E. Donovan, No. 3211, Guatemala City, 18 March 1947, 814.00/3-1847, roll 1, DF814.
20. Interview with Roberto Padilla (son of Carlos Padilla y Padilla, Guatemalan reactionary), 18 December 2018, arranged by Hesed Padilla and Jaime Padilla.
21. John Taylor, No. 162, Guatemala, 11 September 1944, FO 371/37933. Anzueto often appears in memoirs, such as Galich, *Del pánico al ataque*. Ramírez, Coronado Lira, and Salazar do not appear in memoirs. Pinillos appears in memoirs by Guatemalans and Venezuelans linked to Caribbean Basin dictators. Some such as Córdova Cerna only appear in the literature due to their later roles in Castillo Armas's regime. Villagrán Kramer, *Biografía política de Guatemala*, 171, 174, 187, 226; Rodríguez de Ita, *La participación política*, 176, 227.
22. Salvador Navarro Aceves, Número 141-R, Guatemala, 30 abril 1945, exp. III-450-1, AHGE.
23. Manuel Castillo R. y Guillermo Palomo A., México, 8 enero 1945, exp. 1, caja 750, DGIPS.
24. Ezequiel Padilla, Número 326, México, 9 enero 1945, exp. 1, caja 750, DGIPS. Alongside the literature on the DFS following Aguayo's foundational *La Charola*, see Margolis, "La Otra Frontera"; Aguilar, "From Comrades to Subversives."

25. See the cases of Carlos Recinos, Jorge Luis García Aceituno, General Miguel Castro Monzón, and General Mariano Méndez Rodríguez, exp. 1, caja 750, DGIPS.
26. Alejandro Ortega Romero y Francisco F. Quezada, México, 08 febrero 1946, exp. 1, caja 750, DGIPS.
27. Entrevista con Federico Ponce y Marco Antonio Archila Obregón, México, 22 abril 1946, exp. 1, caja 750, DGIPS.
28. Extracto de informes confidenciales, 15–17 junio 1945, 009, SRD.
29. *Mediodía, Radiografía del Complot* (octubre 1945), 001, Correspondencia de Octubre SPICSP.
30. Ángel Arturo Rivera a Juan José Arévalo, No. 201, San Salvador, 27 junio 1946, 118, SRD.
31. Juan José Arévalo a Roberto Arzú Cobos, Guatemala, 2 febrero 1946, 076, SRD; Ezequiel Padilla, Número 326, México, 9 enero 1945, exp. 1, caja 750, DGIPS.
32. "Memorándum para acuerdo presidencial . . .," México, 25 enero y 12 febrero 1947, exp. 1, caja 750, DGIPS.
33. Inspector I.P.S. 37 a Lamberto Ortega P., México, 19 marzo 1947, exp. 1, caja 750, DGIPS.
34. Gobat, *Confronting the American Dream*; Spenser, *Impossible Triangle*; Kiddle, *Mexico's Relations with Latin America*; Spenser, *In Combat*.
35. On the Soviet Union, the Communist International, and the Caribbean Basin, see Cruz Cerdas, *La hoz y el machete*; Ching, "El Partido Comunista de Costa Rica"; Pujals, "¿Una perla en el Caribe Soviético?"; Jéifets y Jéifets, "Los archivos rusos revelan secretos"; Zumoff, "Ojos que no ven"; Reeves, "Extracting the Eagle's Talons."
36. Gould and Lauria-Santiago, *To Rise in Darkness*; Grandin, *Last Colonial Massacre*.
37. O.S.O., *La Confabulación Nazifacista y Comunistoide Revolucionaria en América* (México: 1945), 559.1/33, CMAC.
38. Federico Ponce a Franklin Delano Roosevelt, México, 6 noviembre 1944, OF 439, OFFDR; J. H. Leche, No. 126, Guatemala, 11 July 1944; J. H. Leche, No. 171, Guatemala, 27 September 1944, FO 371/37933; Federico Ponce a Manuel Ávila Camacho, México, 26 diciembre 1944, exp. 559.1/33, CMAC; Federico Ponce to Harry Truman, Mexico City, 15 August 1945, 814.00/8-1545, roll 1, DF814.
39. *Boletín: Emigración Democrática de Guatemala*, 21 septiembre 1945, with Sidney E. O'Donoghue to John W. Carrigan, Mexico City, 4 October 1945, 814.00/10-445, roll 1, DF814.
40. Juventud Liberal de Guatemala, *Xequijel*, 15 septiembre 1945, with O'Donoghue to Carrigan, 4 October 1945, 814.00/10-445, roll 1, DF814.
41. C.R. 3,550, San José, 11 April 1945, with No. 273, San José, 11 April 1945, box 12, USG.
42. Coronado Lira, *Totalitarismo espiritualista*, 16.
43. Luis Coronado Lira, "Violación constitucional y fracaso rotundo de un régimen," in Comité de Defensa Patria, *La Tribuna de la libertad*, 16.
44. Marco Archila C., "Un liberal y militar guatemalteco"; Luis Coronado Lira, "Del Licenciado Coronado Lira al Embajador de los EE.UU. Mexicanos," in Comité de Defensa Patria, *La Tribuna de la libertad*, 24, 21.
45. Memorándum, México, 26 noviembre 1946, with S. Walter Washington, No. 1,961, Mexico City, 29 November 1946, 814.00/11-2946, roll 1, DF814.
46. Juan Pinillos a Edward R. Stettinius, 23 mayo 1945, box 26, USH; Pinillos a James Byrnes, Tegucigalpa, 23 mayo 1946, with Department of State Central Translating Division, 23 May 1946, 814.00/5-2346, roll 1, DF814.
47. George S. Messersmith, A-1140, Mexico City, 10 April 1945, 814.00/4-1045, roll 1, DF814.
48. PS-12, "Asunto: Rinde informe de la investigación . . .," México, 05 abril 1941, exp. 22, caja 322, DGIPS.

49. Comité de Defensa Patria, *La Tribuna de la libertad*.
50. Calderón Salazar, *Guatemala bajo el signo rojo*.
51. Comité de Ayuda a los Exiliados Guatemaltecos, "Señores delegados de la UNESCO" (1947), No. 732, folder 719–759, box 2, ATF.
52. Jorge Matamoros a Julio Acosta García, Santa Tecla, 16 septiembre 1944, RREE 1961.
53. Serafín García a Rafael Heliodoro Valle, 1 diciembre 1944, exp. 869, BNM; Héctor García Godoy, No. 98, Managua, 26 noviembre 1945, exp. Nicaragua, caja 2903348, SERREE; Servicio Internacional de Prensa, Tegucigalpa, 22/23 mayo 1945, SP 1813.
54. Harold D. Finley, No. 2823, Managua, 16 January 1945, box 12, USG; Víctor A. Fernández J., No. 308, Tegucigalpa, 5 agosto 1947, caja 2903349, SERREE.
55. Fletcher Warren, No. 55, Managua, 6 June 1945, box 26, USH.
56. Memorandum of Conversation (MOC), Julián R. Cáceres, Robert Newbegin, and Gordon S. Reid, 2 October 1947, box 34, USH.
57. Office of the Legal Attaché of US Embassy in Guatemala City, "RE: Communism In Guatemala," Guatemala City, 18 July 1946, box 14, USG.
58. Edward L. Reed, No. 17,049, Buenos Aires, 13 January 1945, 814.00/1-1345, roll 1, DF814.
59. MOC, Jorge Toriello and Edwin J. Kyle, 26 and 28 September 1945, with Edwin J. Kyle, No. 681, Guatemala City, 1 October 1945, 814.00/10-145, roll 1, DF814.
60. Harold E. Montemat, memorandum, Tegucigalpa, 2 December 1947, box 34, USH.
61. Federico Ponce a Sidney E. O'Donoghue, México, 4 octubre 1945, with O'Donoghue to Carrigan, 4 October 1945, 814.00/10-445, roll 1, DF814.
62. Juventud Liberal de Guatemala, *Xequijel*, 15 septiembre 1945, with O'Donoghue to Carrigan, 4 October 1945, DF814.
63. Carlos Padilla, Tegucigalpa, 21 noviembre 1947, with Harold E. Montemat, memorandum, Tegucigalpa, 2 December 1947, box 34, USH.
64. Juan Pinillos a John B. Faust, Tegucigalpa, 19 agosto 1946, box 32, USH.
65. Comité de Ayuda a los Exiliados Guatemaltecos, "Señores delegados de la UNESCO" (noviembre 1947), No. 732, folder 719–759, box 2, ATF.
66. Gustavo Santiso Gálvez a Eugenio Silva Peña, Guatemala, 16 abril 1947, 196, SRD.
67. Víctor Ant. Fernández J., No. 375, Tegucigalpa, 22 septiembre 1947, caja 2903349, SERREE; Legal Attaché at the US Embassy in Guatemala City, "Juan Pinillos," 29 August 1944, box 11, USG.
68. Maurice M. Bernbaum, 268, Managua, 1 July 1947, box 58, USC.
69. Joaquín Balaguer, No. 837, México, 8 septiembre 1949, exp. 1948–1950, caja 2903961, SERREE.
70. Robert A. Lovett to "Certain American Diplomatic Officials," 18 August 1947, 814.00/8-1847; Paul C. Daniels, A-191, Tegucigalpa, 21 August 1947, 814.00/8-2147; Gordon S. Reid, "Subject: Carlos Padilla," 21 August 1947, 814.00/8-2147, roll 1, DF814.
71. Willard L. Thorp, No. 114, 19 March 1948, 814.00/3-1948, roll 2, DF814.
72. Andrew E. Donovan, "Subject: Interview with Guatemalan Minister," Guatemala City, 14 August 1946, box 14, USG; MOC, Luis Coronado Lira and Robert E. Wilson, 16 October 1947, 814.00/10-1647; Albert F. Nufer, No. 1818, San Salvador, 30 October 1947, 814.00/10-3047, roll 1, DF814.
73. Jorge García Granados a Juan José Arévalo, 02 octubre 1946, 153, SRD.
74. Roberto Despradel a Manuel A. Peña Batlle, No. 336, Ciudad de Guatemala, 16 octubre 1945, Legajo 3348, Caja 2903348, SERREE.
75. Gustavo Santiso Gálvez a Eugenio Silva Peña, Guatemala, 16 abril 1947, 196, SRD.

76. Adolfo (sin apellido) a Juan José Arévalo, México, 30 marzo 1947, 185, SRD.
77. Embaguate a Relaciones Guatemala, Washington, DC, 18 julio 1947, 230, SRD.
78. John Erwin, No. 1558, 28 December 1944, box 10, USG; Nathan A. Brown, No. 24–45, 5 April 1945, box 26, USH.
79. Wallace F. Estill, "Re: Carlos Padilla y Padilla," 21 June 1945, folder 800: 1945, box 9, USN.
80. Arturo Despradel a Rafael Trujillo, "Memorándum al Excelentísimo Señor Presidente . . .," Ciudad de Trujillo, 16 julio 1947, caja 2903349, SERREE.
81. Dominican Republic Foreign Office, "Official Announcement," 18 July 1947, with Julio Ortega Frier, No. 2238, 23 julio 1947, caja 2903349, SERREE.
82. Víctor Antonio Fernández, No. 285, Tegucigalpa, 25 julio 1947, caja 2903349, SERREE.
83. Gustavo Julio Henríquez, cable 407, México, 9 julio 1947, caja 2903349, SERREE.
84. Comité Patriótico Guatemalteco, "El Comunista Presidente de Guatemala sabotea la conferencia de Río de Janeiro," with José A. Paniagua, No. 432, México, 17 julio 1947, caja 2903349, SERREE.
85. Víctor Ant. Fernández Jiménez, "Refutaciones . . .," Tegucigalpa, 31 julio 1947, with Víctor Ant. Fernández J., No. 308, Tegucigalpa, 5 agosto 1947, caja 2903349, SERREE.
86. Arturo Ramírez a Nathan A. Brown, Tegucigalpa, 17 julio 1947, box 34, USH.
87. Arturo Ramírez a Rafael Trujillo, Tegucigalpa, 8 julio 1947, with Emilio García Godoy, Núm. 19809, Ciudad Trujillo, 18 julio 1947, caja 2903349, SERREE.
88. Emilio García Godoy, Núm. 19809, Ciudad Trujillo, 18 julio 1947, caja 2903349, SERREE.
89. Arturo Ramírez, "Exposición Sobre Los Asuntos Relacionados con Guatemala," Tegucigalpa, 27 julio 1947, with Víctor Ant. Fernández J., No. 290, Tegucigalpa, 28 julio 1947, caja 2903349, SERREE.
90. Ramírez, "Exposición Sobre Los Asuntos," 27 July 1947; versión descifrada del párrafo de Arturo Ramírez, "EXPOSICIÓN," con Arturo Despradel, No. 20463, Ciudad Trujillo, 5 agosto 1947, caja 2903349, SERREE.
91. Ramírez, "Exposición Sobre Los Asuntos," 27 julio 1947, caja 2903349, SERREE.
92. Emilio García Godoy, No. 22297, Ciudad Trujillo, 22 agosto 1947, exp. 070-057, CBV.
93. Víctor Ant. Fernández J., No. 347, Tegucigalpa, 6 septiembre 1947, caja 2903349, SERREE.
94. Juan Pinillos a Víctor Ant. Fernández J., Tegucigalpa, 18 octubre 1947, exp. 070-089, CBV.
95. Víctor Ant. Fernández J., No. 415, Tegucigalpa, 18 octubre 1947; Virgilio Díaz Ordóñez, No. 28956, Ciudad Trujillo, 31 octubre 1947, exp. 070-090, CBV.
96. Gleijeses, *Shattered Hope*, 75.
97. Andrés Pastoriza a Rafael Trujillo, memorándum, Londres, 21 agosto 1947, exp. 070-106, CBV.
98. Miguel Ydígoras Fuentes, "Memorándum De La Situación Política, etc., de Guatemala," 9 agosto 1947, exp. 070-106, CBV.
99. H. Aguilar Kestler a Miguel Ydígoras Fuentes, Nueva York, 1 agosto, 1947, exp. 070-106, CBV.
100. Telésforo R. Calderón, Núm. 24002, Ciudad Trujillo, 1 septiembre 1947, caja 2903349, SERREE.
101. Andrew B. Wardlaw to Rudolph Schoenfeld, William Krieg, John C. Hill, office memorandum, "Subject: Conversation about Discussions with President TRUJILLO . . .," 18 September 1953, folder 350: Guatemala, Aug.-Dec. 1953, box 3, USGC.
102. José María Dávila, Número 127-R, Guatemala, 9 abril 1945; Dávila a Relaciones, cable 126, Guatemala, 8 abril 1945, exp. III-450-1, AHGE.

103. "La Disertación del Sr. Manuel Galich," *Diario de Centro América*, 12 abril 1945, exp. III-450-1, AHGE.

104. "Fueron conducidas ante el jefe," *El Demócrata*, 6 abril 1945, exp. III-450-1, AHGE.

105. "Distinguidos elementos políticos guardan prisión," "Acompañaron al exilio al coronel Ovidio Pivaral," and "A última hora: Otros expatriados," *El Demócrata*, 7 abril 1945, exp. III-450-1, AHGE.

106. José María Dávila, Número 131-R, Guatemala, 16 abril 1945, exp. III-450-1, AHGE.

107. "Purga Política en Guatemala de Elementos Adversos al Régimen," *La Prensa*, 22 mayo 1945; "Los liberales no complotan," *Novedades*, 22 mayo 1945.

108. "En Guatemala no ha Habido 'Purga,'" *El Nacional*, 23 mayo 1945.

109. "Complicado en el Reciente Complot Antirrevolucionario," *El Imparcial*, 15 octubre 1945, exp. III-450-1, AHGE.

110. "El Complot a Luz," *El Imparcial*, 8 octubre 1945, exp. III-450-1, AHGE.

111. Salvador Navarro Aceves, Número 248-R, Guatemala, 6 octubre 1945; "Complicados en el reciente," *El Imparcial*, 15 octubre 1945, exp. III-450-1, AHGE.

112. Relaciones Exteriores a Juan José Arévalo, Número 218, 27 octubre 1947, 285, SRD.

113. MOC, Jorge Toriello, Carlos Salazar Jr., Luis Coronado Lira, Norman Stines, Robert E. Wilson, 6 October 1947, 814.00/10-647, roll 1, DF814.

114. MOC, Toriello, Salazar, Coronado Lira, Stines, Wilson, 6 October 1947, 814.00/10-647, roll 1, DF814.

115. Moulton, "El frustrado bombardeo."

116. S. Walter Washington, No. 4023, Mexico City, 24 June 1947, 814.00/6-2447, roll 1, DF814.

117. José Paniagua, cable 433, México, 17 julio 1947; Arturo Despradel, No. 18908, Ciudad Trujillo, 22 julio 1947, caja 2903349, SERREE.

118. Walter C. Thurston, No. 916, Mexico City, 21 August 1947, 814.00/8-2147, roll 1, DF814.

119. Thurston, No. 916, DF814.

120. Robert A. Lovett, No. 248, Washington, DC, 22 August 1947, 814.00/8-2147; Lovett, No. 796, Washington, DC, 22 August 1947, 814.00/8-2147, roll 1, DF814.

121. Entrevista con Federico Ponce, México, 25 agosto 1947, exp. 1, caja 750, DGIPS.

122. Gustavo Julio Henríquez, cable 558, México, 27 agosto 1947, caja 2903349, SERREE.

123. Rafael Trujillo a Gustavo Julio Henríquez, 28 agosto 1947, caja 2903349, SERREE.

124. Edwin Kyle, No. 361, Guatemala City, 9 October 1947, 814.00/10-947, roll 1, DF814.

125. Gustavo Julio Henríquez, 20 septiembre 1947, caja 2903349, SERREE.

126. Rafael Trujillo a Gustavo Julio Henríquez, 23 septiembre 1947, caja 2903349, SERREE.

127. Juan Pinillos, Tegucigalpa, 4 octubre 1947, with Víctor Ant. Fernández J., No. 401, Tegucigalpa, 6 octubre 1947, caja 2903349, SERREE.

128. "Alcance al número 43," *Diario de Centro América*, 16 septiembre 1947, No. 740, folder 719–759, box 2, ATF.

129. Andrew E. Donovan II, No. 2657, Guatemala City, 6 October 1947, 814.00/10-647, roll 1, DF814; Víctor Ant. Fernández J., No. 391, Tegucigalpa, 1 octubre 1947, caja 2903349, SERREE.

130. Pinillos, 4 October 1947, caja 2903349, SERREE.

131. *El Imparcial*, 4 octubre 1947.

132. Edwin Kyle, No. 367, Guatemala City, 15 October 1947, 814.00/10-1547; Milton K. Wells, No. 2672, Guatemala City, 16 October 1947, 814.00/10-1647, roll 1, DF814.

133. Edwin Kyle, No. 361, Guatemala City, 9 October 1947, 814.00/10-947, roll 1, DF814.

134. Federico Ponce, memorandum, with S. Walter Washington, No. 4976, Mexico City, 7 November 1947, 814.00/11-747, roll 1, DF814.

135. "El Partido Renovación Nacional . . ." (Imp. Minerva, 23 septiembre 1947), No. 783, folder 760–803, box 2, ATF.

136. Partido Acción Revolucionaria, "Manifiesto del Partido Acción Revolucionaria . . ." (Imp. Minerva, enero 1948), No. 866, folder 841–880, box 3, ATF.

137. Wells, No. 2722, Guatemala City, 18 November 1947, 814.00/11-1847, roll 1, DF814.

138. Andrew E. Donovan II, No. 2639, Guatemala City, 19 September 1947, roll 1, DF814. See L. C. Hughes-Hallett's reports, FO 371/60828.

139. J. Luis García A., "Ciudadanos de América" (14 enero 1947), No. 724, folder 719–759, box 2, ATF.

140. "Carta abierta de acusación . . ." (octubre 1947), No. 722, folder 719–759, box 2, ATF.

141. Comité de Ayuda a los Exiliados Guatemaltecos, "Señores delegados de la UNESCO" (noviembre 1947), No. 732, folder 719–759, box 2, ATF.

142. Harold E. Montemat, memorandum, Tegucigalpa, 23 September 1947, box 34, USH.

143. Vicente L. Beneitez, Número 1330, 1 diciembre 1947, Guatemala; Beneitez, Número 0268, 24 febrero 1948, Guatemala; Manuel Tello, 53705, 12 marzo 1948, exp. III-708-1, AHGE.

144. G. Wallace LaRue, No. 20, 12 July 1951, 714.00/7-1251, roll 1, DF714.

145. "Guatemalan Internal Political Situation, January-February 1949"; W. H. Gallienne, No. 230, Guatemala, 28 December 1948, FO 371/74030.

146. Alongside US and British reports, see caja 2903961 and caja 2903825, SERREE, for letters from counterrevolutionaries who spread rumors surrounding Arana's assassination. On Arana's death, see Gleijeses, "Death of Francisco Arana"; Gleijeses, *Shattered Hope*, 50–71.

147. W. H. Gallienne to R. Cecil, 1011/96/51, Guatemala, 12 December 1951, FO 371/90727.

148. Whitman, *How an American Company*, 5–7, HBS; Victor C. Folsom, "Agrarian Reform—The Myth?" folder Banana Study: UNIFRUITCO Co. Information pamphlets, 1916–1968, box 7, HBA.

149. Cutter, *Trade Relations with Latin America*, 5–6.

150. T. W. Willard to C. W. Diebold, 24 March 1948, UFCO. Alongside various scholarly theses on the UFCO's approach to tropical environments and diseases, one can consult collections of UFCO scientists whose works circulated throughout the 1900s, such as the Papers of Joseph Charles Bequaert, Pusey Library, Harvard University Archives, and Richard P. Strong Papers, Center for the History of Medicine, Francis A. Countway Library of Medicine, Harvard University.

151. E. F. Spence to C. W. Diebold, 17 March 1947, UFCO; Memorandum, "Subject: Discussion with Dr. Sarasgeta . . .," folder Banana Study: United Fruit Notes, Interviews, 1963–1967, box 8, HBA.

152. Thomas E. Sunderland, "A Century of Private Investment Abroad—And a Look to the Future," 21 June 1967, folder Banana Study: United Fruit Notes, Interviews, 1963–1967, box 8, HBA.

153. John S. Kelley, untitled and undated memorandum; R. H. Hamer to A. A. Pollan, San José, 1 February 1943, UFCO.

154. Hamer to Pollan, San José, 1 February 1943, UFCO.

155. Federico Picado Sáenz a Eduardo F. Spence, Limón, 16 marzo 1947; To Sam G. Baggett, Panamá, 12 February 1952, UFCO.

156. Pedro J. Urbina to G. A. Myrick, Boston, 28 September 1949, UFCO.

157. G. A. Myrick to A. A. Pollan, Almirante, 18 October 1945, UFCO.

158. "Present Conditions in Spain: January 1938," Baltimore, 23 February 1938, 05, 14, 378–379, 382, 389–390, 415, WCF.

159. Folsom, "Agrarian Reform—The Myth?," box 7, HBA.

160. Victor Cutter to Ernest Martin Hopkins, 5 January 1934, folder 9, box 6940, DCOP.

161. Galileo Solís a V. T. Mais, Panamá, 17 abril 1950, UFCO.

162. Among the works that discuss the positives and negatives in the 1947 Labor Code's construction and implementation and the Arévalo government's approach to labor, see Gleijeses, *Shattered Hope*, 30–49; Dosal, "Political Economy of Industrialization"; Levenson-Estrada, *Trade Unionists Against Terror*, 14–48; Handy, *Revolution in the Countryside*, 22–86; Forster, *Time of Freedom*, 74–106.

163. Memorandum, untitled and undated, folder Typescripts re: Guatemala, box C644, LFP.

164. John Taylor, No. 161, Guatemala, 2 September 1944, FO 371/37933.

165. W. H. Gallienne, No. 48 E, Guatemala, 22 February 1949, FO 371/74048. DF814 and DF714 are replete with Taillon's lobbying of US officials.

166. Whitman, *Why Interdependence Is a "Must*," 1–2, folder W, Miscellany, WH, box 88, TGC

167. "Communism in Guatemala," undated, folder "Typescripts re: Guatemala," box C644, LFP.

168. Whitman, *Why Interdependence Is a "Must*," 1–2.

169. Cutter, *Trade Relations with Latin America*, 6.

170. "Communism in Guatemala," undated, folder Typescripts re: Guatemala, box C644, LFP.

171. Gleijeses, *Shattered Hope*, 103–107.

172. W. H. Gallienne, No. 231E, Guatemala, 29 December 1948; W. H. Gallienne, No. 2E, Guatemala, 3 January 1949, FO 371/74048.

173. W. H. Gallienne, No. 54E, Guatemala, 11 March 1949, FO 371/74048.

174. W. H. Gallienne, No. E28, Guatemala, 25 January 1949, FO 371/74048.

175. Moulton, "'We Are Meddling.'"

176. J.H. Leche, No. 1, Guatemala, 01 January 1944, FO 371/37932.

177. L.C. Hughes-Hallett, No. 45, Guatemala, 26 March 1947, FO 371/60828.

178. FO 371/44861; FO 371/44862.

179. R. H. Hadow, Ref. 243/72/47, Washington, DC, 9 August 1947, FO 371/61318.

180. G. Jackson, minutes, "Information on the questions," 29 August 1952, FO 371/97350.

181. A. Young, minutes, "Information on the questions," 29 August 1952, FO 371/97350.

182. H. F. A. Gates, Guatemala, 15 May 1947, FO 371/60828.

183. C. E. Rudlaw, minutes, "Manifestations in Guatemala on Labour Day, 1st May," 30 May 1947, FO 371/60828.

184. L. C. Hughes-Hallett to I. A. D. Wilson-Young, Guatemala City, 8 August 1947, FO 371/60828.

185. J. McQuillen, minutes, "Relations between USSR and Guatemala," 23 April 1945, FO 371/44897.

186. FO 371/37933; FO 371/44859; FO 371/44860.

187. FO 371/61316.

188. Minutes, "Guatemalan Ambassador in San Salvador," 13 December 1948, FO 371/67960A.

189. George Ogilvie-Forbes, No. 34, Caracas, 10 March 1948; George Ogilvie-Forbes, No. 48, 9 March 1948, FO 371/68302.

190. R. Cecil, minutes, "Details of the make up of the Caribbean Legion," 18 November 1948, FO 371/67952.

191. Minutes, "Suspension of Guatemalan Constitutional guarantees," 17 October 1945, FO 371/44861.

192. J. McQuillen, minutes, "Suspension of Guatemalan Constitutional Guarantees," 16 October 1945, FO 371/44861.
193. Office of the Legal Attaché of US Embassy in Guatemala City, "RE: Communism In Guatemala," Guatemala City, 18 July 1946, box 14, USG.
194. Robert Newbegin, office memorandum, 6 August 1946, 814.00/8-646, roll 1, DF814.
195. "Memorándum para acuerdo presidencial," México, 17 julio 1946, exp. 1, caja 750, DGIPS.
196. Luis Cardoza y Aragón a Juan José Arévalo, México, 12 noviembre 1945, 042; Cardoza y Aragón a Arévalo, 27 diciembre 1945, 056; Cardoza y Aragón a Arévalo, 18 enero 1946, 066, SRD.
197. S. Walter Washington, No. 392, Mexico City, 11 July 1946; Secretary of State, No. 589, Washington, DC, 29 November 1946, box 14, USG; Robert E. Wilson, No. 1680, San Salvador, 1 August 1947, 8140.00/8-147, roll 1, DF814.
198. S. Walter Washington, No. 392, Mexico City, 11 July 1946, box 14, USG.
199. "Memorándum para acuerdo presidencial," México, 17 julio 1946, exp. 1, caja 750, DGIPS.
200. Francisco Castillo Nájera, Número 57929, México, 23 julio 1946, exp. 1, caja 750, DGIPS.
201. M. Antonio Archila Obregón, "Pueblo Guatemalteco," México, 10 julio 1946, with Francisco Castillo Nájera, Número 57929, México, 23 julio 1946, exp. 1, caja 750, DGIPS.
202. Marco Antonio Archila Obregón, "Juan José Arévalo," México, 10 julio 1946, exp. 1, caja 750, DGIPS.
203. Comité de Defensa Patria, *La Tribuna de la libertad*; Calderón Salazar, *Guatemala bajo el signo rojo*.
204. William Dawson to Ellis O. Briggs, New York, 5 December 1946, 814.00B/12-546, roll 1, DF814.
205. Ángel Arturo Rivera a Juan José Arévalo, No. 208, San Salvador, 8 julio 1946, 127, SRD.
206. MOC, Toriello, Salazar Coronado Lira, Stines, Wilson, 6 October 1947, 814.00/10-647, roll 1, DF814.
207. W. H. Gallienne to A. S. Fordham, 52/91/49, Guatemala, 26 December 1949, FO 371/81402.
208. Gabriel Arroyo, "Juan José Arévalo organizó la fracasada invasión contra la República Dominicana," *Novedades*, 2 septiembre 1949, with César Pina Barinas a Virgilio Díaz Ordóñez, Managua, 2 septiembre 1949, exp. Nicaragua, caja 2903350, SERREE.

4. Drawing Up Pacts

1. Juan Bosch, "Informe confidencial sobre la situación . . .," Habana, 17 junio 1948, 416, SRD.
2. Humberto Vázquez García, *La expedición de Cayo Confites*, remains the most thorough discussion of the expedition. Studies by Charles Ameringer, Jorge Renato Ibarra Guitart, and Eliades Acosta Matos offer details on US and Caribbean responses to the expedition. Descriptions of the expedition and its supporters are derived from these works, exiles' correspondence, and participants' memoirs.
3. Manuel Galich, "Informe sobre la Misión Confidencial . . .," [1947], 304, SRD.
4. Cablegrama de Port au Prince, 24 agosto 1947, 271; Mensajes cablegráficos, 31 agosto y 4 septiembre 1947, 288, SRD.

5. The "Haitian connection" deserves further investigation. Works on the Cayo Confites affair note that Dominican exiles and their allies lobbied Estimé's government for support and that Trujillo's officials later charged Haitian officials for even allowing such conversations, yet no study has delved into the decision-making and political calculus regarding Haiti and Cayo Confites. Works on Dominican-Haitian relations stress Trujillo's notorious interventions in Haitian matters, which could have either encouraged Estimé (with his own record of issues related to Trujillo's regime) and his government to support the affair or discouraged Haitian officials who feared incurring further hostilities with Trujillo. Likewise, such factors could have led Estimé to strategically limit his support for the expedition so as to provide assistance without any public knowledge in the hope of avoiding further Dominican-Haitian tensions.

6. Juan José Meza a Juan José Arévalo, 22 noviembre 1945, 041, SRD.
7. Rosendo Argüello, Guatemala, 18 julio 1947, box 68, OARA.
8. Meza a Arévalo, 29 julio 1946, 132, SRD.
9. Rosendo Argüello, Guatemala, 18 julio 1947, box 68, OARA.
10. Rosendo Argüello, Guatemala, 18 julio 1947, box 68, OARA. Cuadra, *Hombre del Caribe*, 226, confirms this support.
11. Cuadra, *Hombre del Caribe*, 230.
12. Enrique C. Henríquez a Juan José Arévalo, Habana, 20 julio 1947, 261, SRD.
13. Juan Bosch a Juan José Arévalo, Habana, 12 julio 1947, 258, SRD.
14. Manuel Galich, "Informe sobre la Misión Confidencial . . .," [1947], 304, SRD; Rafael Paíno Pichardo a Rafael Trujillo, memorándum, exp. 073–034, CBV.
15. José R. Castro a Rafael Heliodoro Valle, Habana, 22 octubre 1947, exp. 446, BNM.
16. Rogelio Caparros a Alejo Cossio del Pino, Habana, 17 octubre 1947, sig. 8, box 49, FSP.
17. Registro, 17 octubre 1947, sig. 8, caja 49, FSP.
18. Jorge Ribas Montes a Juan Rodríguez, Habana, 1 enero 1948, box 68, OARA; Ángel Arturo Rivera a Rafael González Muñoz, Habana, 8 enero 1948, 315, SRD; Juan Rodríguez a José Horacio Rodríguez, Guatemala, 17 enero 1948; Miguel Ángel Ramírez a Jorge Ribas Montes, 2 febrero 1948, box 68, OARA.
19. José R. Castro a Rafael Heliodoro Valle, Habana, 22 octubre 1947, exp. 446, BNM.
20. Cuadra, *Hombre del Caribe*, 227–228, 246–247.
21. Ángel Morales Nadler, "Memorándum al Señor Ministro," México, 12 diciembre 1947, 307, SRD.
22. "Convenio," Habana, 14 noviembre 1947, box 68, OARA.
23. Although newly available materials might prove otherwise, Kenneth J. Grieb, "Myth of a Central American Dictators' League," claims there was no "dictators' league" in the 1930s.
24. On these discussions, see Moulton, "Building Their Own Cold War."
25. Luis F. Thomen a Rafael Trujillo, 4502, 19 diciembre 1947, leg. 14, caja 707576, FSERREE.
26. César Pina Barinas a Virgilio Díaz Ordóñez, No. 884-A, Managua, 3 diciembre 1949, exp. Nicaragua, caja 2903350, SERREE.
27. Castro Ventura, *Trujillo vs. Betancourt*; Mondolfi Gudat, *El día del atentado*.
28. Moulton, "The Counterrevolution's Patron."
29. For more, see Moulton, "El cuasi-bombardeo de Caracas."
30. "Informe Referente A La Situación Política-Militar En La República De Nicaragua," Guatemala, 21 diciembre 1948, 231, JAG.
31. Alfredo Chocano, Maurice M. Bernbaum, MOC, "Tension between Guatemalan and Nicaraguan Governments," 2 February 1948, folder 800a: Guatemala, 1948, box 23, USN.

32. Alfredo Chocano, Maurice M. Bernbaum, MOC, "Reported Landing of Foreign Aircraft at Puerto Cabezas," 2 February 1948, folder 800a: Guatemala, 1948, box 23, USN.

33. See boxes 24–28, USN, and boxes 62–65, USV.

34. Walter J. Donnelly to US Embassy in Managua, cable, 1 February 1948, folder 800: Venezuela, Revolutionary Activities, box 65, USV; Rómulo Betancourt a Víctor M. Román y Reyes, "Mensajes cruzados," Caracas, 1 febrero 1948, exp. 077–097, CBV.

35. Víctor M. Román y Reyes a Rómulo Betancourt, Managua, 3 febrero 1948, exp. 077–097, CBV.

36. Virgilio Díaz Ordóñez, Núm. 3472, Ciudad Trujillo, 3 febrero 1948, exp. 077–097, CBV.

37. Gordon S. Reid to Maurice M. Bernbaum, 16 March 1948, folder 800: Nicaragua, General conf file, 1948, box 26, USN; Rafael Paíno Pichardo a Rafael Trujillo, Memorándum No. 3, febrero 1948, exp. 077–097, CBV.

38. Alberto Posse Rivas a Álvaro Bonilla Lara, No. 72, San José, 2 febrero 1948, RREE 4306.

39. Paíno Pichardo a Trujillo, Memorándum No. 3, febrero 1948, exp. 077–097, CBV.

40. On this era of social reform and turmoil, see Molina Jiménez, *Anticomunismo reformista*; Díaz Arias, *Crisis social y memorias en lucha*.

41. On Costa Ricans in Mexico in the 1940s, see Mejía Flores y Moreno Rodríguez, "El exilio costarricense."

42. Benito Herrera Porra, "Memorándum," Habana, 22 agosto 1947, exp. 6517, leg. 413, FME.

43. Rosendo Argüello, Guatemala, 18 julio 1947, box 68, OARA; Cuadra, *Hombre del Caribe*, 226.

44. Juan José Meza a Juan José Arévalo, 22 noviembre 1945, 041; Salvador Mendieta a Juan José Arévalo, Managua, 3 noviembre 1947, 292, SRD.

45. Mauricio Ordóñez (son of Alberto Ordóñez Argüello), correspondence with Aaron Coy Moulton, 19 August 2017.

46. Historians continue to argue over Ulate's seeming ten-thousand-vote lead and uncounted votes. Molina Jiménez, "El resultado de las elecciones."

47. Costa Rica's Seguridad Pública [Public Security] caught individuals funneling armaments to Figueres's finca. Mario Araya C. a Rogelio Granados Ch., 0234, San José, 29 diciembre 1945, SP 1886.

48. Cuadra, *Hombre del Caribe*, 252.

49. "Tercer partido político en la Rep. de Nicaragua," álbum de recortes de Ordóñez Argüello; Juan Bosch, "Informe confidencial sobre la situación . . .," Habana, 17 junio 1948, 416, SRD.

50. Jorge García Granados a Juan José Arévalo, 1 febrero 1946, 069, SRD.

51. "Informe Confidencial . . .," 2 abril 1945, 002, SRD.

52. "NOTA," Guatemala, 16 diciembre 1947, in "Convenio," Habana, 14 noviembre 1947, box 68, OARA.

53. José Figueres a Juan Rodríguez, San José, 22 diciembre 1947, box 68, OARA.

54. José Figueres a Juan José Arévalo, San José, 3 diciembre 1947, 002, Correspondencia, Diciembre 1947, SPICSP; Edelberto Torres, "Memorándum para el señor Presidente," Guatemala, 24 febrero 1948, 324, SRD.

55. Juan Rodríguez a José Figueres, Guatemala, 12 marzo 1948, box 68, OARA.

56. Juan José Arévalo a Rómulo Betancourt, Guatemala, 26 diciembre 1947, 302, SRD.

57. Figueres a Rodríguez, Cuartel La Lucha, 13 marzo 1948, box 68, OARA.

58. Ordóñez, correspondence with Moulton, 19 August 2017. No English-language work has examined the entire Costa Rican Civil War, but the most thorough Spanish-language source remains López, *Los cuarenta días de 1948*.

59. Anexo No. 2, "Libro de la Legión Caribe," caja 10, APHO.
60. "Libro de la Legión Caribe," caja 10, APHO.
61. Rodríguez a Figueres, Guatemala, 12 marzo 1948; Figueres a Arévalo, Santa María de Dota, 17 marzo 1948, 334, SRD.
62. Juan Rodríguez a Horacio Ornes, Guatemala, 18 marzo 1948, box 68, OARA.
63. Nathaniel P. Davis, "Extract from my Diary," 5 March 1948, box 1, NPD.
64. Figueres a Arévalo, Santa María de Dota, 17 marzo 1948, 334; "Memorándum: Resúmen de la conversación . . .," 20 marzo 1948, 335, SRD.
65. Nathaniel P. Davis, "Extract from my Diary," 20 March 1948, box 1, NPD.
66. "Memorándum: Resúmen de la conversación . . .," 20 marzo 1948, 335, SRD.
67. Carlos Darío Ojeda, Número 311, San José, 23 marzo 1948, exp. III-1024-2, AHGE.
68. Kyle Longley (*Sparrow and the Hawk*, 63–85) stresses how US officials feared the combination of Costa Rican communists and dictatorial support for Calderón Guardia as possibly exacerbating the civil war.
69. Francisco Morazán a Juan Rodríguez, San Isidro, 2 abril 1948, box 68, OARA; Central Intelligence Agency, "The Caribbean Legion," ORE 11–49, 17 March 1949, Box 216, CIRF.
70. Teodoro Picado y Mario Fernández Piza, with Maurice Bernbaum, No. 205, Managua, 20 April 1948, folder 800: CR, Vol. III, April 1948, Confidential, box 65, USC. On dictators and Costa Rica, see Moulton, "The Dominican Dictator's Funds and Guns."
71. Francisco Calderón Guardia y Vicente Urcuyo R. a Víctor M. Román y Reyes, Managua, 16 abril 1948, with Maurice Bernbaum, No. 205, Managua, 20 April 1948, folder 800: CR, Vol. III, April 1948, Confidential, box 65, USC.
72. A. Somoza a Rafael Trujillo, Managua, 17 abril 1948, exp. 1948, caja 2904052, SERREE.
73. Nathaniel P. Davis, "Extract from my Diary," 18 March–16 April 1948, box 1, NPD.
74. Nathaniel P. Davis, "Extract from my Diary," 16 April 1948 and 17 April 1948, box 1, NPD; Legaguate a Relaciones, No. 48, San José, 19 abril 1948, 351, SRD.
75. Davis, "Extract from my Diary," 19 April 1948, box 1, NPD; Ojeda a Relaciones, cable 392, San José, 16 abril 1948; Ojeda a Relaciones, cable 400, San José, 18 abril 1948, exp. III-1024-2, AHGE.
76. Díaz Arias, *Crisis social y memorias en lucha*.
77. Maurice Bernbaum, No. 205, Managua, 20 April 1948, folder 800: CR, Vol. III, April 1948, Confidential, box 65, USC; Davis, 21 April 1948, box 1, NPD.
78. Virgilio Díaz Ordóñez a Rafael Trujillo, 12434, Ciudad Trujillo, 23 abril 1948, exp. 1948–1951, caja 2903825, SERREE.
79. Enrique Muñoz Meany, Número 132, 20 abril 1948, 352, SRD.
80. Virgilio Díaz Ordóñez, 15092, Ciudad Trujillo, 17 mayo 1948, exp. 1945–1953, caja 2903920, SERREE.
81. Virgilio Díaz Ordóñez a Óscar Sevilla Sacasa, proyecto de cablegrama, con Telésforo R. Calderón a Virgilio Díaz Ordóñez, Núm. 12191, Ciudad Trujillo, 24 abril 1948, exp. 1948–1951, caja 2903825, SERREE.
82. "Libro de la Legión Caribe," caja 10, APHO.
83. Olander, "Costa Rica in 1948," 250; Alemán, "Nicas belicosos," 130.
84. Miguel Ángel Ramírez a Juan José Arévalo, San José, 19 julio 1948, 427, SRD.
85. Figueres's supposed "break" with the Legión merits further consideration. Much of the literature has focused on published accounts by Figueres and Rosendo Argüello, which have delved into their personal rivalry following Figueres's decision to not support Argüello, who then considered Figueres's action a "betrayal," against Figueres's claims that Argüello had little support from Nicaraguan exiles and behaved erratically in Costa Rica (Argüello, *Quiénes y*

cómo nos traicionaron; Argüello, *Sobre el caso de Figueres;* Ameringer, *Don Pepe*). However, exiles' correspondence and dictators' reports highlight closer relations between Figueres and those organizing against dictators. Asked by Guillermo Villegas Hoffmeister about this, Ornes admitted Rodríguez was always upset about the decision, but other Legionarios understood the decision and maintained amicable relations with Figueres. For the narrow view that only highlights Rodríguez's frustrations and some exiles' original concerns that Figueres's financial payments did not live up to what the exiles gave him during the conflict, based on Ornes's Legión accounting book or correspondence, without examining other relevant resources or issues, see Ferrero and Eiroa, "La oposición antitrujillista."

86. Miguel Ángel Ramírez a Juan José Arévalo, Cartago, 22 abril 1948, 349, SRD.

87. Miguel Ángel Ramírez y Francisco Morazán a Juan José Arévalo, San José, 20 mayo 1948, 381, SRD.

88. "Pacto Complementario del pacto de 16 de diciembre de 1947," San José, 31 mayo 1948, 301, SRD.

89. "Estado Mayor del Ejército de Liberación del Caribe," San José, 25 mayo 1948, 409, SRD.

90. Felipe Argüello Bolaños a Juan José Arévalo, San José, 24 mayo 1948, 387, SRD.

91. Carlos Pasos et al., San José, 20 mayo 1948, 407, SRD.

92. Yanuario Landa Blanco a Rafael Heliodoro Valle, 23 junio 1948, exp. 1130, BNM.

93. Alemán, "Nicas belicosos"; Argüello, *Quiénes;* Argüello, *Sobre el caso;* Ameringer, *Don Pepe;* Anexo No. 3, "Libro de la Legión Caribe," caja 10, APHO.

94. Juan José Meza a Juan José Arévalo, San José, 7 mayo 1948, 380, SRD.

95. Francisco Valdés Calderón a Juan José Arévalo, San José, 11 mayo 1948, 391; Adolfo Báez Bone a Juan José Arévalo, Guatemala, 18 junio 1948, 422, SRD.

96. Rosendo Argüello, hijo, a Miguel Ángel Ramírez, "Asunto: Transmisión de órdenes," San José, 9 diciembre 1948, box 68, OARA.

97. "Acta de Fundación del Frente de Unidad Revolucionaria Hondureña," San José, 18 agosto 1948, 449, SRD.

98. Jorge Ribas Montes, Francisco Sánchez y Marcial Aguiluz, San José, 8 diciembre 1948; Eduardo J. Carrasco, Antonio Miralda Santos y Enrique Aguiluz Rosa, Esquipulas, 23 octubre 1948, box 68, OARA.

99. Rafael Heliodoro Valle a José R. Castro, 20 mayo 1946, exp. 446, BNM.

100. Heliodoro Valle a Castro, 29 enero 1948, exp. 446, BNM; Unión Democrática Centroamericana, "Rafael H. Valle . . .," México, 30 diciembre 1947, AGR.

101. H. N. Steptoe to P. Broad, Ref. B/4/1, San Salvador, 11 August 1948, FO 371/67951.

102. Julián López Pineda a Rafael Heliodoro Valle, Tegucigalpa, 22 abril 1948, exp. 1225, BNM.

103. Nathaniel P. Davis, MOC, San José, 18 April 1948, box 1, NPD.

104. Paul C. Daniels and Rafael Ángel Calderón Guardia, MOC, 24 May 1948, folder CPA, General: 1948, Costa Rica, box 1, BIAA.

105. Robert Newbegin and Norman Armour, "Memorandum Presented by Rafael Calderón Guardia," 4 June 1948, folder CPA, General: 1948, Costa Rica, box 1, BIAA.

106. Gellman, *Secret Affairs.* Another possible complication was Welles's opposition to Trujillo and sympathy for Dominican exiles such as Ángel Morales (Vega, *Correspondencia entre Ángel Morales y Sumner Welles*), though there is no evidence Welles or others were aware of the Calderón Guardia–Somoza–Trujillo alliance.

107. Handwritten note, 22 May 1948, folder 3, box 131, SWP.

108. Sumner Welles to R. A. Calderón Guardia, Bar Harbor, 30 June 1948, folder 3, box 131, SWP.

109. Sumner Welles to Guillermo Sevilla Sacasa, Bar Harbor, 30 June 1948, folder 3, box 131, SWP.

110. Costa Rican Embassy in Washington, DC, press release, [June 1948,] folder 3, box 131, SWP.

111. José Vicente Pepper, "Un Cargamento Marxista para Estados Unidos"; "La Segunda República Comunista," *Novedades*, 11 julio 1948, folder 3, box 131, SWP.

112. R. A. Calderón Guardia a Sumner Wells [sic], Diriamba, 18 julio 1948, folder 3, box 131, SWP.

113. Sumner Welles to Rafael A. Calderón Guardia, Bar Harbor, 22 July 1948, folder 3, box 131, SWP.

114. Welles to Calderón Guardia, Bar Harbor, 29 July 1948, folder 3, box 131, SWP.

115. Calderón Guardia a Wells [sic], Diriamba, 19 agosto 1948, folder 3, box 131, SWP.

116. Calderón Guardia a Wells [sic], Diriamba, 6 agosto 1948, folder 3, box 131, SWP.

117. Joaquín Balaguer a Rafael Trujillo, cable 562, México, 21 julio 1948, exp. 1948–1950, caja 2903961, SERREE.

118. Luis E. Bonetti a Virgilio Díaz Ordóñez, No. 196, 7 agosto 1948, exp. 1948–1949, caja 2904052, SERREE.

119. Luis E. Bonetti a Rafael Trujillo, Núm. 207, 26 agosto 1948, exp. 1948–1949, caja 2904052, SERREE. Emphasis in original.

120. Arturo Calventi a Telésforo R. Calderón, cable 210, Managua, 30 mayo 1948, exp. 1948–1951, caja 2903825, SERREE.

121. Luis Manuel Debayle a Arturo Calventi, No. 21, Managua, 6 julio 1948, exp. 1945–1953, caja 2903920; Anastasio Somoza a Rafael Trujillo, Managua, 4 septiembre 1948, exp. Sec. Calderón, 1948, caja 2904052, SERREE.

122. Arturo Calventi a Virgilio Díaz Ordóñez, No. 366, Managua, 7 septiembre 1948, exp. Nicaragua, caja 2903958, SERREE. Further research could shed light on the alliances and divisions between Mexican officials, dictators, and antidictatorial forces. Whereas former Mexican President Lázaro Cárdenas provided sympathy and support to refugees from the 1940s into the 1950s, his successors were far more conservative when it came to their nation's image as a bastion of liberal reform, as noted in the recent literature on the Partido Revolucionario Institucional.

123. Calventi a Díaz Ordóñez, No. 366, 7 septiembre 1948, exp. Nicaragua, caja 2903958, SERREE.

124. Virgilio Díaz Ordóñez a Telésforo R. Calderón, 27434, Ciudad Trujillo, 11 septiembre 1948; Calderón a Díaz Ordóñez, Núm. 28370, Ciudad Trujillo, 11 septiembre 1948, exp. Nicaragua, caja 2903958, SERREE.

125. Somoza a Embajada Nicaragua, sin fecha, exp. 1948–1950, caja 2903961, SERREE.

126. Telésforo R. Calderón a Rafael Damirón Diaz, Ciudad Trujillo, 25 septiembre 1948; SPC a Embajadom Mexico; Damirón Diaz a Calderón, exp. 1948–1950, caja 2903961, SERREE.

127. Damirón Diaz a Calderón, No. 712, México, 27 septiembre 1948, exp. 1948–1950, caja 2903961, SERREE.

128. [Francisco Calderón Guardia], memorándum, 27 septiembre 1948, exp. 1948–1950, caja 2903961, SERREE.

129. Telésforo R. Calderón a Rafael Damirón Diaz, Ciudad Trujillo, 2 octubre 1948, exp. 1948–1950, caja 2903961, SERREE.

130. Rafael Damirón Diaz a Telésforo R. Calderón, No. 737, Ciudad de México, 8 octubre 1948, exp. 1948–1950, caja 2903961, SERREE.

131. Rafael Damirón Diaz a Telésforo R. Calderón, No. 747, Ciudad de México, 9 octubre 1948, exp. 1948–1950, caja 2903961, SERREE.

132. Rafael Damirón Diaz a Telésforo R. Calderón, No. 756, Ciudad de México, 15 octubre 1948, exp. 1948–1950, caja 2903961, SERREE.
133. Calderón a Damirón Diaz, No. 32755, Ciudad Trujillo, 18 octubre 1948, exp. 1948–1950, caja 2903961, SERREE.
134. "Asesoria Especial: Informe Sobre Costa Rica," exp. 3884, leg. 280, FME; René de Lamar y Capó a Carlos Hevia, No. 99, Tegucigalpa, 14 diciembre 1948, caja A. Latina/Costa Rica, ACMINREX.
135. "Informe Referente A La Situación Política-Militar En La República De Nicaragua," Guatemala, 21 diciembre 1948, in "Confidencial . . . (Primera parte)," GT-CIRMA-AH-099-001-002-231" and "Confidencial . . . (Segunda parte)," GT-CIRMA-AH-099-001-002-233," JAG.
136. "Memorandum of Telephone Conversation . . .," [Washington, DC,] 12 December 1948, doc. 397, *FRUS48*.
137. "The Ambassador in Nicaragua (Shaw) to the Secretary of State," Managua, 12 December 1948, doc. 398, *FRUS48*.
138. Doc. 399–402, *FRUS48*.
139. Maurice Bernbaum, No. 172, 2 April 1948, folder 800: Nicaragua, General Confidential, 1948, box 26, USN.
140. George Marshall, "Unsettled Conditions in Central American-Caribbean Area," 25 June 1948, box 64, USC.
141. B. P. Sullivan, No. 57, San José, 2 November 1948, FO 371/67952.
142. W. H. Gallienne, No. 19, Guatemala, 17 January 1948, FO 371/67951.
143. W. H. Gallienne, No. 114, Guatemala, 6 June 1948, FO 371/67951.
144. Luis Cardoza y Aragón a Enrique Muñoz Meany, París, 19 diciembre 1948, in Taracena Arriola, Mendoza, and Soria, *El placer de corresponder*.
145. Juan Isidro Jiménes Grullón a Luis Muñoz Marín, Morovis, 4 enero 1949, exp. 258, ALMM.
146. Ornes, *Desembarco en Luperón*, 29.
147. Enrique C. Henríquez a Juan José Arévalo, Habana, 21 diciembre 1947, 310, SRD. Emphasis in original.
148. Luis Nicolau d'Olwer, No. 76, México, 13 octubre 1948, exp. No. 4, caja No. 115, fondo México, FUE.

5. Building a Transnational Counterrevolution

1. Rómulo Betancourt a Luis Muñoz Marín, Habana, 7 noviembre 1950, exp. 54, ALMM.
2. Moulton, "Counterrevolution's Patron."
3. Secretaría de Estado de Relaciones Exteriores, *Boletín Hebdomadario de Información*, No. 256, Ciudad Trujillo, 7 abril 1949, exp. República Dominicana, 1949–50, caja 1629, AGPR.
4. Miguel Ángel Ramírez a Horacio Ornes, Guatemala, 17 octubre 1950, exp. 2, caja 5, APHO.
5. José Félix Córdoba Boniche a Horacio Ornes, San José, 23 agosto 1950, exp. 16, caja 6, APHO.
6. On dictators' intelligence sharing, see Moulton, "Dictators' Domino Theory."
7. Ramón Brea Messina a Rafael Trujillo, Caracas, 4 junio 1951, exp. Informaciones Confidenciales, caja 2903956, SERREE.
8. Héctor Incháustegui Cabral a José Benjamín Uribe Macías, No. 90, México, 26 enero 1951, exp. México, caja 2903961, SERREE.

9. Pellerano a Trujillo, cable 102, México, 14 agosto 1949, exp. Informaciones Confidenciales, caja 2903959, SERREE.

10. Raymond G. Leddy, 833, Caracas, 17 May 1950, folder 350 Dom Rep, box 80, USV, FOIA.

11. Virgilio Díaz Ordóñez, 20005, Ciudad Trujillo, 30 junio 1950, exp. Nicaragua, caja 2903958, SERREE.

12. Moulton, "Counterrevolutionary Friends."

13. MOC Francisco Aguirre and Gordon S. Reid, 19 March 1948, folder 800: Nicaragua, General conf file, 1948, box 26, USN.

14. Carlos Salazar, hijo, "Memorándum sobre última situación política en Guatemala," con Virgilio Díaz Ordóñez, 14960, Ciudad Trujillo, 17 mayo 1948, caja 2903349, SERREE.

15. Luis Bonetti a Rafael Trujillo, No. 208, Tegucigalpa, 30 agosto 1948, exp. 1948–1949, caja 2904052, SERREE. Despite ceding official power, Carías maintained immense influence over Honduran affairs.

16. Manuel Melgar de la Cerda, memorándum, México, 29 septiembre 1948; Manuel Melgar de la Cerda, "Personas Que Responden Del Memorandum Anexo," con Rafael Damirón Díaz a Telésforo R. Calderón, No. 232, México, 01 octubre 1948, exp. 1948–1949, caja 2904052, SERREE. This appears to be related to the Black Christ of Esquipulas, which was caught in the nation's political divisions during the Guatemalan Revolution. Sullivan-González, *Black Christ of Esquipulas*. On religion and the Guatemalan Revolution, see Harms, *Ladina Social Activism*; Holden, "Communism and Catholic Social Doctrine."

17. Anastasio Somoza a Embanic Cdtrujillord, Managua, 25 octubre 1948, exp. 1948–1949, caja 2904052, SERREE.

18. Moulton, "Becoming the Dictator's Agents."

19. Joaquín Balaguer a Rafael Trujillo, No. 802, México, 05 septiembre 1949, exp. 1948–1950, caja 2903961, SERREE.

20. Joaquín Balaguer a Rafael Trujillo, No. 837, México, 8 septiembre 1949, exp. 1948–1950, caja 2903961, SERREE.

21. Arturo Calventi, hijo, "Memorándum de Conversación . . .," Ciudad Trujillo, 29 noviembre 1949, exp. Salvador, 1949–1952, caja 2903956, SERREE.

22. "Guatemala (w/ Attachment)," 19 January 1950, doc. 0000915053, CREST; Gleijeses, *Shattered Hope*, 67–68.

23. "Guatemala (w/ Attachment)," 19 January 1950, doc. 0000915053, CREST.

24. Legadom a Telésforo R. Calderón, Cable 7, San Salvador, 24 enero 1950, exp. Salvador, 1949–1952, caja 2903956, SERREE.

25. "Plans of Colonel Carlos Castillo Armas . . .," 24 August 1950, doc. 0000915075, CREST.

26. Gleijeses, *Shattered Hope*, 72–84.

27. "La oposición por diputados dignos para Chimaltenango" (noviembre 1950), No. 1269, folder 1269–1280; "Coronel Árbenz," No. 1053, folder 1024–1072, box 3, ATF.

28. "Conciudadanos," No. 1023, folder 1022–1023, box 3, ATF.

29. Miguel Ydígoras Fuentes a Rafael Trujillo, Londres, 27 julio 1949, caja 2903349, SERREE.

30. Due to the challenges in acquiring relevant archival materials and party members' concealing their international activities, the 1950 opposition parties have yet to receive a thorough scholarly examination. Gleijeses, *Shattered Hope*, 72–84; Villagrán Kramer, *Biografía política de Guatemala*, 81–86.

31. "Organización del Partido Reconciliación Democrática Nacional (Redención)," No. 1124, folder 1108–1158; "¡Guatemaltecos!," Guatemala, mayo 1950, No. 1074, folder 1073–1107; "El General Ydígoras Fuentes expresa su satisfacción . . .," Guatemala, 5 diciembre 1950, No. 1154, folder 1108–1158, box 3, ATF.

32. Rafael Damirón Díaz a Telésforo R. Calderón, No. 94, Tegucigalpa, 03 abril 1950, exp. 1949–1953, caja 2903825, SERREE.
33. Rafael Damirón Díaz a Telésforo R. Calderón, No. 104, Tegucigalpa, 15 abril 1950, exp. 1949–1953, caja 2903825, SERREE
34. Damirón Díaz a Calderón, No. 94, Tegucigalpa, 3 abril 1950, exp. 1949–1953, caja 2903825, SERREE.
35. "Proclama de 'Juventud Nacionalista' a la ciudadanía guatemalteca," Guatemala, mayo 1950, No. 1081, folder 1073–1107, box 3, ATF.
36. "Guatemaltecos: ¡Cumplamos con nuestro deber!," Guatemala, 19 julio 1950, No. 1075, folder 1073–1107, box 3, ATF.
37. Wardlaw to Schoenfeld, Krieg, Hill, 18 September 1953.
38. "Decreto Número 24," El Guatemalteco, 23 julio 1950, No. 1073, folder 1073–1107, box 3, ATF.
39. Carlos Salazar, hijo, y Jesús Unda Murillo, "Publicaciones [del Partido] 'Reconciliación Democrática Nacional' (Redención)," Guatemala, 12 mayo 1950, No. 1122, folder 1108–1158, box 3, ATF.
40. Jesús Unda Murillo y Carlos Salazar, hijo, "Publicaciones del Partido Reconciliación Democrática Nacional-Redención," Guatemala, 1 junio 1950, No. 1125, folder 1108–1158, box 3, ATF.
41. "Manifiesto a los Guatemaltecos," San Salvador, 15 agosto 1950, No. 1084, folder 1073–1107, box 3, ATF.
42. TRC, Ciudad Trujillo, 29 agosto 1950, caja 2903349, SERREE.
43. Emblem, No. 1280, folder 1269–1280, 1950; Nos. 1192 and 1197, folder 1159–1197, box 3, ATF.
44. Héctor Incháustegui Cabral a Telésforo R. Calderón, No. 1355, México, 26 septiembre 1950, caja 2903349, SERREE.
45. José Luis Arenas, "Puntos Principales que hay . . .," México, leg. 3348, caja 2903348, SERREE.
46. Arenas, "Puntos Principales que hay . . ."; "Cuestión de fechas," leg. 3348, caja 2903348, SERREE.
47. Legadom, cable 304, 9 [noviembre 1950], con Secretario Presidencia a Legadom, cable, Ciudad Trujillo, 10 noviembre 1950, exp. 1949–1953, caja 2903825, SERREE.
48. Gleijeses, Shattered Hope, 82–83.
49. Dávila Córdova's political activities remain unclear. He appears to have supported anti-Carías activities in 1944 ("¿Ya leyó TIME?," Time, 21 August 1944). During PBSUCCESS, the CIA reported Dávila Córdova as a representative for Ydígoras Fuentes. "General-PBSUCCESS," 27 January 1954, doc. 0000913999; "General-PBSUCCESS," 3 February 1954, doc. 0000923901, CREST.
50. Consejo Supremo del Movimiento Revolucionario Anticomunista, "Manifiesto al pueblo de Guatemala," noviembre 1950, leg. 3348, caja 2903348, SERREE. Emphasis in original.
51. Legadom, cable 46, Tegucigalpa, 10 febrero 1951, exp. 1949–1953, caja 2903825, SERREE.
52. Virgilio Díaz Ordóñez, Núm. 6933, Ciudad Trujillo, 7 marzo 1949, exp. 1948–1949, caja 2904052, SERREE.
53. Rafael Damirón Díaz, No. 105, Tegucigalpa, 15 abril 1950, exp. 1949–1953, caja 2903825, SERREE.
54. "Informe reglamentario correspondiente al mes de marzo 1950," exp. III-1212-II, AHGE.
55. Thomas G. Corcoran to James W. Gerard, 4 December 1950, folder Gerard, James W., 1945–51, box 60, TGC.
56. Edward L. Bernays to Thomas G. Corcoran, 6 October 1947, folder B: Miscellany, Ber-Bez, box 50, TGC.

57. Bruce Barton to Russell G. Partridge, 11 July 1949; R. G. Partridge to Bruce Barton, 13 July 1949, folder United Fruit, 1948–1957, box 80, BBP; folders SD.2 and United Fruit Co., Bananas, 1931–1949, box 34, JWR.

58. *Bananas: A Food Children Need* (United Fruit Company Educational Department, n.d.); *A Study of the Banana: Its Every Day Use and Food Value (Teacher's Manual)* (United Fruit Company Home Economics Department, n.d.), folder 2, box 26, JWR.

59. Thomas D. Cabot to Bruce Barton, 8 April 1949; E. S. Whitman to Bruce Barton, 25 April 1949, folder United Fruit, 1948–1957, box 80, BBP.

60. Wallace A. Walker to Hope Martinez, 22 June 1949; W. C. Swartley to Art J. Barry, 17 June 1949; Karl R. Nelson to Pete Soutter, 17 June 1949; Frank Hatch to Bruce Barton, 30 August 1955, folder United Fruit, 1948–1957, box 80, BBP.

61. Bruce Barton to Samuel Zemurray, 23 May 1949, folder United Fruit, 1948–1957, box 80, BBP.

62. Barton to Zemurray, 26 September 1949, folder United Fruit, 1948–1957, box 80, BBP.

63. Bruce Barton to George Sokolsky, 16 August 1949, folder United Fruit, 1948–1957, box 80, BBP.

64. Immerman, *CIA in Guatemala*, 111–118; Gleijeses, *Shattered Hope*, 129–133; Cullather, *Secret History*, 15–19.

65. McKean, *Peddling Influence*.

66. "Presidente de la United Fruit . . .," *La Nación*, 25 enero 1947, with Walter E. Turnbull to Robert La Follette, 8 February 1947, folder 1947, Travel, Central America, box C622, LFP.

67. Thomas G. Corcoran to H. Harold Whitman, 22 July 1948, folder Stout, F. Sturgis, 1948, box 83; Thomas G. Corcoran to Thomas D. Cabot, 11 August 1948, folder Cabot, Thomas D., 1948–81, box 52, TGC.

68. Thomas G. Corcoran to Mr. and Mrs. Roger T. Stone, 30 June 1950, folder Stone, Roger T., 1947–74, box 83; Thomas G. Corcoran to John C. McClintock, 16 November 1949, folder McClintock, John C., 1947–74, box 71, TGC.

69. Robert M. La Follette Jr. to Bourke B. Hickenlooper, 6 August 1947, folder La Follette, Robert M., Jr., 1947, box 25, personal files, BHP; John Willard Carrigan to Bourke Blakemore Hickenlooper, San José, 31 October 1947, folder Foreign Central America, 1947; handwritten note, folder Foreign Central America, 1947; Joseph W. Montgomery to Bourke R. [sic] Hickenlooper, 2 December 1947; B. B. Hickenlooper to Joseph Montgomery, 5 December 1947; Joseph W. Montgomery to B. B. Hickenlooper, 10 December 1947, folder Foreign Central America, 1947, box 30, speeches and trips files, BHP.

70. Juan José Arévalo, Guatemala, 29 October 1946; Rafael Samayoa to Edwin Jackson Kyle, Guatemala, 20 March 1947; and José Gallegos del Rio to Edwin J. Kyle, Guatemala, 23 September 1947, folder Guatemala, General 1942–52, box 195, files of Senate committees, BHP.

71. Claude Pepper to Thomas G. Corcoran, 16 February 1949; Pepper to Corcoran, 2 March 1949, folder Pepper, Claude, 1941–62, box 77, TGC.

72. Lister Hill to T. Jefferson Coolidge, 04 March 1949, LHP.

73. On Corcoran and McCormack, see Moulton, "Anticommunist Bananas."

74. Thomas G. Corcoran to John W. McCormack, 10 May 1949, folder McCormack, John W., 1941–59, box 71; Harold J. Sullivan to Thomas Corcoran, 20 November 1950, folder McCormack, John W., 1941–59, box 71; Thomas G. Corcoran to Joseph Montgomery, 27 September 1951, folder Zemurray, Samuel, 1949–61, box 188, TGC. According to undated handwritten notes, McCormack discussed Guatemala with Spellman. John W. McCormack to Martin, n.d., folder B33F3, box 33, HGBU. Spellman's role could not be further investigated as access to Spellman's

papers was restricted during legal investigations of the New York Archdiocese related to the Catholic church's institutional protection of child abuse.

75. Thomas G. Corcoran to John W. McCormack, 23 July 1949, folder McCormack, John W., 1941–59, box 71, TGC.

76. Donald L. Jackson and Mike Mansfield to Charles A. Eaton, 29 June 1948, folder 2–4, box 2, Series IV, MMP.

77. Mike Mansfield, travel notebook, folder 2–4, box 2, Series IV, MMP.

78. Jackson and Mansfield to Eaton, 29 June 1948, MMP.

79. Thomas D. Cabot to Donald L. Jackson and Mike Mansfield, 20 August 1948, folder 1–7, box 1, Series IV, MMP; Cabot to Mansfield, 5 November 1948, folder 1–1, box 1, Series IV, MMP.

80. Edward Tomlinson, "Copy of Letter . . .," Panama Canal Zone, 19 April 1948, folder 2, box 1, ETP.

81. E. S. Whitman to Edward Tomlinson, 1 July 1949, folder 2; Edward Tomlinson to Scripps Howard Newspaper Alliance, cable, 21 September 1954, folder 3, box 1, ETP.

82. Edward Tomlinson, "Uncle Sam Chief Whipping Boy"; Edward Tomlinson to Ann Watkins Inc., "Suggestion for Article . . .," n.d., folder 3, box 3, ETP.

83. Tomlinson to Mansfield, 14 February 1949, folder 23–27, box 23, Series IV, MMP.

84. Memorandum, "Subject: The Application of Point 4 to Latin America," 4 February 1949, folder 1–1, box 1, Series IV, MMP.

85. T. S. Corcoran to Mike Mansfield, 14 February 1949, folder 1–1, box 1, Series IV, MMP.

86. Henry Cabot Lodge, "Point 4 of the President's Inaugural Address," 95 Cong. Rec. 1 (daily ed. 14 February 1949), 1172.

87. Claude Pepper, "Enlargement and Extension of the Marshall Plan," 95 Cong. Rec. 1 (daily ed. 17 February 1949), 1353.

88. Lister Hill, "Enlargement and Extension of the Marshall Plan," 95 Cong. Rec. 1 (daily ed. 17 February 1949), 1353.

89. John McCormack, "Reckless Minorities in Latin America," 95 Cong. Rec. 1, (daily ed. 21 February 1949), 1464. Author's emphasis.

90. Christian A. Herter, "Guatemala and the United Fruit Co.," 95 Cong. Rec. 2 (daily ed. 24 February 1949), 1496.

91. Mike Mansfield, "Point 4 of the President's Inaugural Speech," 95 Cong. Rec. 2 (daily ed. 24 February 1949), 1498.

92. Thomas G. Corcoran to Everett Dirksen, 26 April 1949, folder Dirksen, Everett M., 1948–69, box 56, TGC.

93. T. Jefferson Coolidge to Mike Mansfield, 1 March 1949; Mansfield to Coolidge, 7 March 1949, folder 1–1, box 1, Series IV, MMP.

94. Tom Corcoran to Mike Mansfield, 3 March 1949, folder 1–1, box 1, Series IV, MMP.

95. John W. McCormack, speech draft, undated, folder McCormack, John W., 1941–59, box 71; John W. McCormack, speech draft, undated, folder Zemurray, Samuel, 1949–61, box 188, TGC; John McCormack, "Political Trends in Guatemala," 96 Cong. Rec. 14 (daily ed. 3 April 1950), A2538-A2541.

96. W. H. Gallienne, No. 115, Guatemala, 6 June 1948, FO 371/67954A.

97. R. Cecil, minutes, "Information concerning the assassination . . .," 7 September 1949, FO 371/74031.

98. W. H. Gallienne to A. S. Fordham, 52/91/49, 26 December 1949, FO 371/81402.

99. W. H. Gallienne, No. 166, Guatemala, 20 October 1949, FO 371/74031.

100. Gallienne to Fordham, 1011/19/50, Guatemala, 11 March 1950, FO 371/81402.
101. Gallienne, No. 166, 20 October 1949.
102. R. Cecil to Geoffrey Scoones, AN 3692/1193/8, 14 December 1949, FO 371/74047.
103. G. Meade to Philip Broad, Ref. 151/20/48, 31 July 1948, FO 371/67951.
104. P. S. Stephens to A. M. MacKintosh, AN 2479/436/8, 7 July 1948, FO 371/67951. See FO 371/81116; and Pach, *Arming the Free World*.
105. R. Cecil, minutes, "Measures being taken by the Americans . . .," 15 June 1951; M. B. Anstee, minutes, "Further conversation with members of State Department . . .," 31 July 1951, FO 371/90727.
106. Overview of OIE Program in Guatemala, 1946–1947, folder Foreign Central America, 1947, box 30, speeches and trips files, BHP.
107. Lucas and Morris, "A Very British Crusade"; Wilford, "Information Research Department"; Shaw, "Information Research Department"; Vaughan, "'Cloak Without Dagger'"; Jenks, *British Propaganda and News Media*; Defty, *Britain, America and Anticommunist Propaganda*; Cormac, "Information Research Department"; McGarr, "Information Research Department."
108. "Lista del cuerpo diplomático acreditado en Venezuela," *Gaceta Oficial de los Estados Unidos de Venezuela*, 22 diciembre 1950.
109. "Table Showing Countries Receiving Translations from Caracas (Venezuela)," FO 1110/400.
110. Information Department, 52/47/49, Guatemala, 4 August 1949, FO 953/491.
111. Emile P. Lecours, Ref. No. 134/C.3, 5 May 1951, FO 1110/400.
112. M. B. Anstee, 1 March 1950, AG1015/3, FO 371/81402.
113. H. Bienvenido Gómez, "Reportaje para su Excelencia," febrero 1950, con Telésforo R. Calderón a Virgilio Díaz Ordóñez, Ciudad Trujillo, 25 febrero 1950, exp. 1949–1950, caja 2904052, SERREE.
114. J. Magowan, No. 16, 27 February 1950, FO 371/81402.
115. Stanley Gudgeon, No. 16, 3 March 1950, FO 371/81402.
116. M. B. Anstee, 9 March 1950, FO 371/81402.
117. R. Cecil, 3 March 1950, AG1015/3, FO 371/81402.
118. MOC Thomas Corcoran, Thomas C. Mann, 15 May 1950, doc. 457, in *FRUS50*.
119. Cullather, *Secret History*, 17.
120. MOC Thomas Corcoran, Thomas C. Mann, 15 May 1950, doc. 457, in *FRUS50*.
121. Immerman, *CIA in Guatemala*; Blasier, *Hovering Giant*; Wood, *Dismantling of the Good Neighbor Policy*; Rabe, *Eisenhower and Latin America*; Leonard, "Nationalism or Communism?"; Gleijeses, *Shattered Hope*; Lehman, "Revolutions and Attributions"; Cullather, *Secret History*; Siekmeier, *Aid, Nationalism, and Inter-American Relations*; Schlesinger and Kinzer, *Bitter Fruit*; Grow, *US Presidents and Latin American Interventions*; Rabe, *Killing Zone*.
122. The best work on the "McCarthy-like inferences rather than facts [used by US officials] to find evidence of Guatemalan Communism" remains Immerman, *CIA in Guatemala*, 93.
123. Quoted in Longley, *In the Eagle's Shadow*, 208–210; Rabe, *Killing Zone*, 31–53.

6. Waiting for the Colossus

1. Foto de Jacobo Árbenz y Jorge Ribas Montes, JRM.
2. J. G. Boyd to Robin Cecil, 2191/27/51G, Washington, DC, 16 July 1951, FO 371/90727.
3. Gleijeses, *Shattered Hope*, 120–121.

4. Beisner, *Dean Acheson*; Allcock, *Thomas C. Mann*.
5. MOC Ismael González Arévalo et al., "Subject: Guatemalan Ambassador Calls On the Under Secretary," 16 September 1949, 814.00/9-1649, roll 1, DF814.
6. "The Chargé in Guatemala (Wells) to the Department of State," Guatemala [City], 7 July 1950, doc. 462, *FRUS50*; "Memorandum by the Director . . .," [Washington, DC,] 14 July 1950, doc. 463, *FRUS50*. On US Ambassador Richard Patterson, see Marshall, "The United Fruit Lobby."
7. See docs. 459, 464, 471, and 472, *FRUS50*.
8. Gleijeses, *Shattered Hope*, 127–133.
9. "Policy Statement Prepared in the Department of State," Washington, DC, 2 May 1951, doc. 800, *FRUS51*. On Árbenz's ties to Guatemalan communists, see Gleijeses, *Shattered Hope*, 134–148.
10. "Paper Prepared for the Under Secretary's Meeting," [Washington, DC,] 12 June 1951, doc. 801, *FRUS51*.
11. Charles H. Deerwester, untitled report on Miguel Ángel Ramírez, no date, folder 350: Caribbean, box 40, USN.
12. "Notes of the Under Secretary's Meeting, Department of State, 9:30 a.m., October 3, 1951," doc. 804, *FRUS51*.
13. "Notes of the Undersecretary's Meeting, Department of State, 10:15 a.m., June 15, 1951," doc. 802, *FRUS51*.
14. "The Secretary of State to the Deputy Director of the Office of International Trade, Department of Commerce (Macy)," Washington, DC, 30 July 1951, doc. 803, *FRUS51*.
15. Edward G. Miller Jr. to W. Tapley Bennett Jr., "Subject: Review of Recent Developments in Communist Penetration of Guatemala," Washington, DC, 7 June 1951, FW714.001/6-751, box 3249, DF1950.
16. "Notes of the Undersecretary's Meeting, Department of State, 10:15 a.m., June 15, 1951," doc. 802, *FRUS51*.
17. Handwritten notes and "Guatemala Railroad and Highway," 26 June 1952, folder 8, box 1445, AJEP.
18. Joseph Montgomery to Allen J. Ellender, Boston, 19 March 1952; Allen J. Ellender to Mrs. A. G. Matthews, 13 March 1952, folder 8, box 1445, AJEP.
19. Robert M. La Follette Jr. to John W. McCormack, 29 June 1951; John W. McCormack to Robert M. La Follette Jr., 30 June 1951, folder B33F3, box 33, HGBU.
20. John McCormack, "Military and Naval Construction," 97 Cong. Rec. 7 (daily ed. 10 August 1951), 9808–9809.
21. Andrew B. Wardlaw, No. 202, 22 August 1951, folder B33F3, box 33, HGBU; Peter Sedgwick, No. 38, 13 August 1951, FO 371/90727; Rudolf Schoenfeld to Edward W. Clark, Guatemala City, 28 August 1951, folder B33F3, box 33, HGBU.
22. Andrew B. Wardlaw, No. 239, 31 August 1951, folder B33F3, box 33, HGBU.
23. Thomas G. Corcoran to Samuel Zemurray, 13 August 1951, folder Zemurray, Samuel, 1949–61, box 188, TGC.
24. Thomas C. Mann to John W. McCormack, 17 September 1951, folder B33F3, box 33, HGBU.
25. J. G. Boyd to Robin Cecil, 2191/27/51G, Washington, DC, 16 July 1951, FO 371/90727.
26. W. H. Gallienne, No. 4, Guatemala, 3 January 1951; W. H. Gallienne, "Record of conversation . . .," 17 March 1951, FO 371/90734; Gerald Meade to Robin Cecil, Washington, DC, 2191/12/51G, 8 June 1951, FO 371/90727.
27. R. Cecil, minutes, "Measures being taken . . .," 15 June 1951, FO 371/90727.

28. "Minutes of a Meeting Held on 10th July . . .," FO 1110/452.
29. Peter Sedgwick to J. G. Boyd, 2192/47/51, Guatemala, 8 August 1951, FO 371/90727.
30. "Minutes of a Meeting Held on 10th July . . .," FO 1110/452.
31. J. H. A. Watson to R. Cecil, S2193/40/52G, Washington, DC, 22 May 1952, FO371/97350.
32. G. H. S. Jackson, minutes, "Communism in Latin America," 22 January 1952, FO 371/103115.
33. R. Cecil to B. Salt, AG1018/11G, 26 August 1951, FO 371/90727.
34. G. H. S. Jackson, minutes, "Communism in Latin America," 21 March 1951, FO 371/97350.
35. Barbara Salt to R. Cecil, 2191/59/51, 23 October 1951; Gerald Meade to R. Cecil, 10236/45/51, Washington, DC, 25 October 1951, FO 371/90727.
36. J. H. Peck to J. W. Taylor, PR 111/11/51/G, 23 July 1951, FO 1110/452. This reinforces Andrew Defty's analysis in *Britain, America and Anticommunist Propaganda* that, despite some conflicts, British intelligence cooperated with US intelligence on certain targets and regions.
37. "Minutes of a Meeting Held on 10th July . . .," FO 1110/452.
38. Peter Sedgwick to Herbert Morrison, No. 122, Guatemala, 27 August 1951, FO 371/90727.
39. Emile P. Lecours, "Memorandum," 25 August 1951, with Peter Sedgwick to Herbert Morrison, No. 122, Guatemala, 27 August 1951, FO 371/90727.
40. Sedgwick to Morrison, No. 122, 27 August 1951.
41. Lecours, "Memorandum," 25 August 1951. .
42. Gerald Meade to R. Cecil, 10236/45/51, Washington, DC, 25 October 1951, FO 371/90727.
43. Harms, *Ladina Social Activism*.
44. "Manifiesto del Partido Unificación Anticomunista," *El Imparcial*, 3 octubre 1951.
45. Comité de Estudiantes Universitarios Anticomunistas, "Tretas del Comunismo," No. 1514, folder 1456–1537, box 4, ATF; Comité Central, "El Comité de Estudiantes Universitarios Anticomunistas Al Pueblo de Guatemala, Hace Saber," Guatemala, septiembre 1951, No. 1322; Comité de Estudiantes Universitarios Anticomunistas, "Una es nuestra bandera . . .," No. 1334, folder 1285–1354, 1952, box 4, ATF.
46. Comité Estudiantes Universitarios Anticomunistas, Guatemala, No. 1325; Comité de Estudiantes Universitarios Anticomunistas, "No permitamos más . . .," No. 1331, folder 1285–1354, 1952, box 4, ATF.
47. Comité Cívico Nacional y el Comité de Estudiantes Universitarios Anticomunistas, Guatemala, noviembre 1951, No. 1424, folder 1407–1432, box 4, ATF.
48. Roberto Barrios Peña y Guillermo Sosa, "El Comité de Estudiantes . . .," Guatemala, 16 noviembre 1951, No. 1422, folder 1407–1432, box 4, ATF.
49. Comité de Estudiantes Universitarios Anticomunistas, "Comité Cívico Nacional: Convención Nacional Anticomunista," Guatemala, 25 noviembre 1951, No. 1354, folder 1285–1354, 1952, box 4, ATF.
50. "Conclusiones de la magna . . .," Guatemala, noviembre 1951, No. 1423, folder 1407–1432, box 4, ATF.
51. W. H. Gallienne, No. 162, Guatemala City, 27 November 1951, FO 371/90727.
52. Some IRD materials have been retained, so questions remain about how Lecours contacted CEUA and who his contacts were. Lecours's CEUA report includes the third and first person, suggesting he and his staff were transcribing materials provided by CEUA leaders. As a result, multiple reports offer an estimation of the IRD-CEUA's networking.
53. "Activities of the Anticommunist University Students in Guatemala," with T. S. Tull to J. H. A. Watson, PR 111/60/G, 24 March 1952, FO 1110/452.

54. Photographs with Package C with Tull to Watson, PR 111/60/G, 24 March 1952, FO 1110/452.
55. Posters with Package C with Tull to Watson, 24 March 1952, FO 1110/452.
56. Stencil with Package C with Tull to Watson, 24 March 1952, FO 1110/452.
57. "Activities of the Anticommunist University Students in Guatemala."
58. "Activities of the Anticommunist University Students in Guatemala."
59. E. P. Lecours, "Memorandum on Anticommunist Activities in Guatemala," 6 December 1951, FO 1110/452.
60. Emile Lecours to J. H. Peck, Havana, 13 December 1951, FO 1110/452.
61. Richard Allen, No. 120, 7 August 1954, FO 371/108973. Allen identifies the contact as "the new Secretary General of the Ministry of Foreign Affairs (the first man appointed has just resigned)" in Castillo Armas's regime after the 1954 coup. There were many changes among these positions, but Carlos Salazar, hijo, was named secretario de relaciones exteriores (secretary of foreign relations) at the beginning of Castillo Armas's regime while Goicolea (CEUA officer, 1951–1954) was the sub-secretario de relaciones exteriores. Upon Salazar's resignation, Goicolea would have assumed the position.
62. W. H. Gallienne to R. Cecil, 1051/8/52G, Guatemala City, 13 February 1952, FO 371/97495.
63. Comité Cívico Nacional, "La gran manifestación . . .," Guatemala, 20 marzo 1952, No. 1486, folder 1456–1537, box 4, ATF.
64. W. H. Gallienne, No. 49, Guatemala, 8 April 1952, FO 371/97495.
65. "Impresionante Repudio Ciudadano al Comunismo," El Imparcial, 24 marzo 1952; Comité Cívico Nacional, "Gran Manifestación Anticomunista," 23 marzo 1952, No. 1485, folder 1456–1537, box 4, ATF.
66. "El Comité Cívico . . .," Guatemala, marzo 1952, No. 1488, folder 1456–1537, box 4, ATF.
67. Comité de Estudiantes Universitarios Anticomunistas, "Guatemaltecos," No. 1498, folder 1456–1537, box 4, ATF.
68. Comité de Estudiantes Universitarios Anticomunistas, "Manifiesto al Pueblo de Guatemala," Guatemala, 20 marzo 1952, No. 1503, folder 1456–1537, box 4, ATF.
69. Peter Sedgwick to G. H. S. Jackson, 1015/21/52, Guatemala, 12 March 1952, FO 371/97495.
70. Comité de Estudiantes Universitarios Anticomunistas, "Cárceles 'Revolucionarias' Tipo," Guatemala, 19 junio 1952, No. 1494; Comité de Estudiantes Universitarios Anticomunistas, "Sistema de Tortura Usado . . .," Guatemala, 19 junio 1952, No. 1512, folder 1456–1537, box 4, ATF.
71. Comité de Estudiantes Universitarios Anticomunistas, "En el país de la nueva vida," Guatemala, 19 junio 1952, No. 1497; Comité de Estudiantes Universitarios Anticomunistas, "¿Habrá Justicia en Guatemala?," No. 1502, folder 1456–1537, box 4, ATF.
72. Comité de Estudiantes Universitarios Anticomunistas, "Pueblo de Guatemala," Guatemala, 2 mayo 1952, No. 1509, folder 1456–1537, box 4, ATF.
73. Comité de Estudiantes Universitarios Anticomunistas, "Boletín del Anticomunismo," No. 1493, folder 1456–1537, box 4, ATF. Capitalization in original.
74. Throughout the literature and the sources, Carlos Simmons's name has been spelled as "Carlos Simmons" and "Carlos Simons."
75. W. H. Gallienne, No. 49, Guatemala, 8 April 1952, FO 371/97495.
76. "(Est. Pub Date) Honduras . . .," 1 December 1953 (estimated), doc. 0000923964, CREST.

77. "General Situation of the country as of December 4th, 1951," with Tull to Watson, PR 24 March 1952, FO 1110/452. The language resembles that which Castillo Armas used elsewhere, and Castillo Armas's brother-in-law Federico Paiz Herrera was a prominent CEUA leader.

78. T. S. Tull to J. H. A. Watson, PR 111/60/G, 24 March 1952, FO 1110/452.

79. Gallienne, No. 9, 25 March 1952, FO 371/97495.

80. W. H. Gallienne, No. 49, Guatemala, 8 April 1952, FO 371/97495.

81. R. E. Barclay, minutes, "The views on the . . .," 25 April 1952, FO 371/97495.

82. Barclay, "The views on the . . .," 25 April 1952; Gallienne, No. 49, 8 April 1952.

83. Duncan Aikman, "Red Front Tightens Grip on Guatemala," *Washington Post*, 17 February 1952, with Everett McKinley Dirksen to Bourke B. Hickenlooper, 25 February 1952, folder Guatemala, General 1942–52, box 195, files of Senate committees, BHP.

84. "Guatemala: The Price of Caviar," *Time*, 11 February 1952.

85. Ludwell Denny, "Marriage of Convenience: Communist Clique Runs Guatemala," *Washington Daily News*, 13 February 1952; Ludwell Denny, "Economic Suicide in Guatemala: Reds Out to Wreck United Fruit Co.," *Washington Daily News*, 14 February 1952, with La Follette to Hickenlooper, 15 February 1952; Ludwell Denny, "Central America Rich Field for Reds," *Washington Daily News*, 15 February 1952, with Dirksen to Hickenlooper, 25 February 1952, folder Guatemala, General 1942–52, box 195, files of Senate committees, BHP.

86. Folder 1, box 3, LDP.

87. Denny, "Marriage of Convenience."

88. G. S., handwritten comments, "Communism in Latin America," 21 March 1952, FO 371/97350.

89. Robert La Follette Jr. to John W. McCormack, 15 February 1952, folder B33F3, box 33, HGBU.

90. John W. McCormack, "Aliens Entering or Remaining in the United States Illegally," 98 Cong. Rec. 1 (daily ed. 25 February 1952), 1335.

91. Martin, "Aliens Entering or Remaining," 1338.

92. John W. McCormack to Robert M. La Follette Jr., 28 February 1952; Kenneth H. Redmond to John W. McCormack, 26 February 1952, folder B33F3, box 33, HGBU.

93. James Rowe Jr. to Mike Mansfield, 1 March 1952, folder 23-2, box 23, Series IV, MMP.

94. Mike Mansfield, "The Crisis in Guatemala," 98 Cong. Rec. 8, Appendix (daily ed. 3 March 1952), A1316–1317.

95. James Rowe Jr. to Mike Mansfield, 4 March 1952, folder 23-2, box 23, Series IV, MMP.

96. Denny, "Latin American Reds."

97. Rowe to Mansfield, 4 March 1952, MMP.

98. B. A. B. Burrows, 1684/13/52, Washington, DC, 12 March 1952, FO 371/97350; Henri Bonnet, No. 1056/AM, Washington, DC, 28 Février 1952, dossier Plan d'action contre communisme, 1948–55, numéro 49, série Santo Domingo, CADN.

99. Thomas G. Corcoran to Samuel Zemurray, 26 February 1952, folder Zemurray, Samuel, 1949–61, box 188, TGC.

100. « Communisme au Guatemala et à Cuba », 8 mars 1952, dossier 1952, numéro 4, série La Havane, CADN.

101. Edward L. Bernays to Edmund S. Whitman, 18 April 1952, folder 10, box III/37, ELB.

102. Robert M. La Follette Jr. to Bourke B. Hickenlooper, 15 February 1952; Dirksen to Hickenlooper, 25 February 1952, folder Guatemala, General 1942–52, box 195, files of Senate committees, BHP.

103. Dirksen to Hickenlooper, 25 February 1952, BHP.

104. B. B. Hickenlooper to Robert M. La Follette Jr., 26 February 1952; B. B. Hickenlooper to Everett M. Dirksen, 26 February 1952, folder Guatemala, General 1942–52, box 195, files of Senate committees, BHP.
105. Thomas G. Corcoran to Samuel Zemurray, 26 February 1952, folder Zemurray, Samuel, 1949–61, box 188, TGC.
106. Virgilio Díaz Ordóñez a Gustavo Sotolongo, 35520, Ciudad Trujillo, 23 noviembre 1950, exp. sin título [República Dominicana], ACMINREX; Robert Urquhart, No. 136, Caracas, 20 November 1951, FO 371/90774.
107. Braulio A. Mendez L. a José Benjamín Uribe Macías, No. 844, Habana, 22 junio 1951, exp. V, 1948–1953, caja 2904034, SERREE.
108. On Auténticos' opposition to Batista, see Ameringer, "Auténtico Party and the Political Opposition in Cuba."
109. César Pina Barinas, No. 399-A, Managua, 15 marzo 1952, carp. 1951–1953, Nicaragua, caja 2903352, SERREE.
110. Cristián de Tattenbach a Lara Bustamante, N. 781-E, Guatemala, 29 mayo 1952, RREE 1927.
111. Luis F. Thomen a Rafael Trujillo, Ciudad Trujillo, 20 agosto 1952, exp. D, 1948–1952, caja 2902307, SERREE.
112. Al Coronel Manuel Larrubis y Paneque, SOP 102, Estado Mayor General, Ciudad Militar, 20 abril 1952, exp. Confidencias de conspiraciones . . ., AIHC.
113. Reporte de Inteligencia No. 1, 6 agosto 1952, Estado Mayor General, Ciudad Militar, RIE.
114. José Arroyo Maldonado a Virgilio Díaz Ordóñez, Habana, 24 marzo 1952, exp. Relaciones con Cuba, caja 2904035, SERREE.
115. Héctor Incháustegui Cabral a Telésforo R. Calderón, No. 706, México, 3 mayo 1952, exp. México, caja 2903957, SERREE.
116. Salvador A. Monclús a Virgilio Díaz Ordóñez, Núm. 1799, Habana, 8 abril 1952, exp. Informaciones Confidenciales, caja 2903956, SERREE.
117. Cabral a Calderón, No. 957, México, 1 julio 1952, exp. México, Caja 2903957, SERREE.
118. Petronio S. Caamaño a Virgilio Díaz Ordóñez, No. 160, 8 agosto 1952, exp. Guatemala, caja 2903351, SERREE.
119. César Pina Barinas, No. 149-A, Managua, 04 febrero 1952, carp. 1951–1953, Nicaragua, caja 2903352, SERREE.
120. Rubén Suro, No. 104, Panamá, 16 junio 1952, exp. Panamá, caja 2903958, SERREE.
121. Emilio Rodríguez Demorizi, No. 816-B, Managua, 1 julio 1952, exp. 084–030, CBV.
122. Emilio Rodríguez Demorizi a César A. Piantini, Managua, 2 octubre 1952; Emilio Rodríguez Demorizi, No. 1032-A, Managua, 8 octubre 1952, carp. 1951–1953, Nicaragua, caja 2903352, SERREE.
123. Ramón Brea Messina, Caracas, 28 mayo 1952, exp. Informaciones Confidenciales, caja 2903956, SERREE.
124. Ramón Brea Messina, Caracas, 5 agosto 1952, exp. Informaciones Confidenciales, caja 2903956, SERREE.
125. Emilio Rodríguez Demorizi, Managua, 10 septiembre 1952, exp. Nicaragua, Sec. Calderón, caja 2903958; Ramón Brea Messina, "Situación política venezolana," septiembre 1952, exp. Informaciones Confidenciales, caja 2903956, SERREE.
126. Richard F. Lankenau, Despatch 182, 29 August 1952, folder 350: Nic. Pol. Jan. to Dec. 1953, box 39, USN.
127. Alejandro Ortega Romero, 00289, México, 28 julio 1952, exp. 1, caja 750, DGIPS.

128. Due to limited sources, Bernardino lacks a complete examination, though he regularly appears in works on Trujillo's intelligence apparatus such as Cruz Infante, *Hombres de Trujillo*; Vega, *Almoina, Galíndez y otros crímenes*.
129. "Denuncian la presencia en México . . .," *El Popular*, 7 octubre 1952, exp. 1, caja 750, DGIPS.
130. Alejandro Ortega Romero, 00289, México, 28 julio 1952, exp. 1, caja 750, DGIPS.
131. "Sigue tronando el cuete . . .," *La Prensa*, 24 septiembre 1952, exp. 1, caja 750, DGIPS.
132. Jorge Prieto Laurens, "Conspiración Roja Contra América," *El Universal*, 9 octubre 1952, exp. 1, caja 750, DGIPS.
133. Frente Popular Anticomunista de México, "¡Alerta, Mexicanos!," exp. III-1255-3, AHGE.
134. Jorge Prieto Laurens a Demetrio Flores Fagoaga, memorándum, México, exp. 1, caja 750, DGIPS.
135. Prieto Laurens a Flores Fagoaga, memorándum, DGIPS; Marcelo C. Fernández Baeza a Demetrio Flores Fagoaga, México, 13 octubre 1952, exp. 1, caja 750, DGIPS.
136. Prieto Laurens to Flores Fagoaga, memorándum, DGIPS.
137. Rubén Suro, No. 333, Panamá, 8 diciembre 1951, exp. Panamá, caja 2903958, SERREE.
138. Virgilio Díaz Ordóñez, 15016, Ciudad Trujillo, 3 mayo 1952, exp. Guatemala, caja 2903351, SERREE.
139. Álvaro Logroño Batlle, No. 49, Managua, 26 abril 1952, exp. Guatemala, caja 2903351, SERREE.
140. Byron E. Blankinship to Charles H. Deerwester, Tegucigalpa, 15 April 1952, folder 350: Guatemala, box 47, USH, FOIA.

7. Uncle Sam Signs On

1. Spruille Braden to Ellis Briggs, 21 November 1951, folder 3-3, box 3, EBP. Emphasis in original.
2. Cullather, *Secret History*, 15; "Special Estimate 13," 24 September 1951, doc. 71, in Warner, *CIA Under Harry Truman*.
3. "Memo to Deputy Director . . .," 5 November 1951, doc. 0000915073, CREST.
4. "Report," Washington, DC, 8 October 1952, *FRUSG*.
5. On Córdova Cerna and Corcoran, see Schlesinger and Kinzer, *Bitter Fruit*, 121–122.
6. "Memorandum from the Chief . . .," Washington, DC, 11 January 1952, doc. 2, *FRUSG*. The CIA claimed "a Peruvian group" backed Castillo Armas, and Peruvian officials did share regimes' concerns, but to date, there has not been any evidence.
7. "Cable to OPC/OSO . . .," 23 January 1952, doc. 0000915068; "Cable to State . . .," 24 January 1952, doc. 0000915067, CREST; "Memorandum from the . . .," Washington, DC, 17 March 1952, doc. 7, *FRUSG*.
8. "Memorandum from the . . .," 17 March 1952, *FRUSG*.
9. M. Ydígoras F. y Carlos Castillo A., "Pacto de caballeros . . .," San Salvador, 31 marzo 1952, in Villagrán Kramer, *Biografía política de Guatemala*, 105–108.
10. "(Estimated Pub Date) . . .," 5 May 1952, doc. 0000135837, CREST.
11. Immerman, *CIA in Guatemala*, 61–67; Gleijeses, *Shattered Hope*, 149–170; Handy, *Revolution in the Countryside*; Cullather, *Secret History*, 20–27.
12. Rollin S. Atwood to Fletcher Warren, 3 July 1952, 714.001/7-352; Roy R. Rubottom Jr. to William O'Dwyer, 3 July 1952, 714.001/7-352, box 3249, DF1950.

13. Dean Acheson, A-167, Guatemala City, 2 April 1952, 714.001/4-252, box 3249, DF1950, FOIA.
14. "Monthly Report on Articles Published in Guatemala," May 1952, FO 1110/483.
15. "General Review of the Press . . .," FO 1110/707; "List of Articles Produced . . . June, 1952," FO 1110/472.
16. Rudolf E. Schoenfeld to Edward W. Clark, Guatemala City, 23 June 1952, 714.001/6-2352, box 3249, DF1950.
17. Thomas E. Whelan to Edward G. Miller Jr., Managua, 20 February 1952, folder Nicaragua, box 8, EGM.
18. Edward G. Miller, Jr., to Thomas E. Whelan, 25 February 1952, folder Nicaragua, box 8, EGM. On White House renovations, see Klara, *The Hidden White House*.
19. Edward G. Miller Jr. to Dean Acheson, memorandum, 9 April 1952, folder Nicaragua, box 8, EGM.
20. Harold B. Hinton, "Vaughan Admits Deep-Freeze Gifts and Defends Them," *New York Times*, 14 August 1949; "The Administration: The Deep Freeze Set," *Time*, 22 August 1949.
21. Hess, Oral History Interview.
22. C. J. Mara to Joseph H. Lewis, 26 August 1949, folder Pearson, Drew, 1949–54, box 6, JMP.
23. Jeansonne, *Gerald L. K. Smith*.
24. Gerald L. K. Smith, *Drew Pearson: Enemy of the Catholic Church* (Christian Nationalist Crusade, 1949): 1, folder 1949, Pearson, Drew (Smith brochures about), box 28, GLKS.
25. Gerald L. K. Smith, *Drew Pearson: Blackmailer* (Christian Nationalist Crusade, 1949): 1–2, folder 1949, Pearson, Drew (Smith brochures about), box 28; Gerald L. K. Smith to Harry Vaughan, 23 October 1949, folder 1949, V, miscellaneous, box 29, GLKS.
26. Vaughan to Smith, 26 October 1949, folder 1949, V, miscellaneous, box 29, GLKS.
27. Smith to Vaughan, Tulsa, 9 January 1951, folder 1951, V, miscellaneous, box 36; Gerald L. K. Smith to C. J. Mara, Tulsa, 11 January 1951, folder 1951, M, miscellaneous, box 35, GLKS.
28. MOC Harry H. Vaughan, Paul C. Daniels, James H. Webb, "Subject: Visit of Army . . .," 20 August 1948, folder 800, Guatemala, 1948, box 13, USN.
29. Ernest V. Siracusa to Thomas C. Mann, 3 January 1951, folder Chronological Memoranda, 1951, box 3, BIAA.
30. James E. Webb to Harry S. Truman, memorandum, "Subject: Designation of . . .," 1 March 1951, folder Guatemala, OF 439, box 1435, OFHST.
31. MOC Harry Vaughan et al., "Subject: Trip to Honduras . . .," 8 January 1952, folder Chronological Memoranda, 1951, box 3, BIAA.
32. MOC Ernest V. Siracusa, Cornelius J. Mara, "Subject: Trip to Honduras . . .," 5 January 1951, folder Trips, Vaughan and Graham . . ., box 4, BIAA.
33. Ernest V. Siracusa, "Visit of Generals Vaughan . . .," 30 January 1951, folder Trips, Vaughan and Graham . . ., box 4, BIAA.
34. *Dominican Republic: A Bulletin of the Dominican Embassy* 136 (September 1951): 3, exp. 030.1, caja 1625, AGPR.
35. Harry H. Vaughan to Harry S. Truman, 7 April 1952, folder N, box 161, FAF.
36. Truman to Vaughan, 9 April 1952, folder N, box 161, FAF.
37. Ernest V. Siracusa to Harry S. Truman, "Subject: Unofficial Visit . . .," 9 April 1952, folder Nicaragua, box 8, EGM.
38. Edward G. Miller Jr. to Thomas C. Mann et al., "General Somoza's Proposed Visit to the US," 10 April 1952, folder Nicaragua, box 8, EGM.
39. Luis F. Thomen a Rafael L. Trujillo, 05 mayo 1952, exp. 1945–1953, caja 2903920, SERREE.

40. Matthews, *A World in Revolution*, 262–263.
41. Luis F. Thomen a Rafael L. Trujillo, 05 mayo 1952, Expediente "1945–1953," Caja 2903920, SERREE.
42. "(Est. Pub Date) Memo . . .," est. date 1954, doc. 0000914985, CREST. On Truman's informal/unofficial reception of foreign leaders/representatives, see Savage, "Truman in Historical, Popular, and Political Memory."
43. William Kirten Jr., 181–52, 28 November 1952, with Rolland Welch to John L. Ohmans, Managua, 22 December 1952, folder Nicaragua: General Somoza, box 2, ROMAA.
44. Rolland Welch, Anastasio Somoza Jr., office memorandum, "Subject: The previously proposed plan . . .," 9 March 1953, folder Nicaragua: General Somoza, box 2, ROMAA.
45. Kirten, 181–52, 28 November 1952, ROMAA.
46. Charles B. Layton, CARMA S-2-52, Managua, 1 December 1952, with Garrison B. Coverdale, G-2-CDR, Washington, DC, 24 December 1952, folder Nicaragua: General Somoza, box 2, ROMAA.
47. Emilio Rodríguez Demorizi a Rafael Trujillo, Managua, 21 julio 1952, exp. Nicaragua, Sec. Calderón, caja 2903958, SERREE.
48. Rodríguez Demorizi to Trujillo, Managua, 21 July 1952; "Memorándum: Conversaciones con el Dr. Eduardo Zuleta Ángel, en Panamá, del 2 al 5 de octubre 1952," exp. Panamá, caja 2903958, SERREE.
49. Anastasio Somoza to Harry H. Vaughan, telegram, New York, 21 June 1952; Robert B. Landry to Harry S. Truman, "Memorandum for the President," 24 June 1952, folder Nicaragua, OF 432, box 1434, OFHST; John L. Ohmans to Thomas E. Whelan, 23 June 1952, folder Nicaragua: General Somoza, box 2, ROMAA.
50. Anastasio Somoza to Harry H. Vaughan, telegram, New York, 23 June 1952, folder Nicaragua, OF 432, box 1434, OFHST; Rolland Welch, Despatch No. 11, Managua, 11 July 1952, 717.00(W)/7-1152, box 3263, DF1950; Cornelius J. Mara to Óscar Sevilla Sacasa, 17 July 1952; Cornelius J. Mara to Anastasio "Tachito" Somoza, 18 July 1952, folder Nicaragua, OF 432, box 1434, OFHST.
51. "Memorandum of Interview," Washington, DC, 13 November 1952, doc. 31, *FRUSG*.
52. John L. Ohmans to Thomas C. Mann, "Subject: Conversations with Colonel . . .," 21 July 1952, 717.00/7-2152, box 3262, DF1950. In note 2, doc. 14, *FRUSG*, the editors wrote, "No record was found of Mara's trip to Nicaragua with Somoza." Fortunately, William Kamman ("A Friendly Problem," 88) consulted these items, which confirm Somoza's and Mara's activities.
53. Cornelius J. Mara to Harry S. Truman, "Memorandum for the President," 11 July 1952, folder G, box 156, FAF.
54. Cornelius J. Mara, handwritten note, folder G, box 156, FAF.
55. Ohmans to Mann, "Subject: Conversations with Colonel . . .," 21 July 1952, DF1950.
56. Rodríguez Demorizi a Trujillo, 21 julio 1952, SERREE; "Memorándum: Conversaciones con el Dr. Eduardo Zuleta Ángel, en Panamá, del 2 al 5 de octubre 1952," SERREE.
57. MOC Roberto Barrios Peña, Ernest Siracusa, Edward W. Clark, "Subject: Conversation with Colonel Peña," 27 May 1952, box 3243, DF1950, FOIA.
58. "Memo re Guatemala 1954 Coup," 23 May 1952, doc. 0000915046, CREST. On these debates, see Moulton, "Guatemalan Exiles."
59. "Cable to (Deleted) . . .," 23 June 1952, doc. 0000915042; "Cable re: Funds Transfer," 23 June 1952, doc. 0000136382, CREST. Nick Cullather (*Secret History*, 28) references declassified sources indicating, "At Vaughan's urging, Truman instructed DCI Smith to follow up" on Somoza's lobbying that led to an agent arriving in Guatemala City by 16 June.
60. "Misc re: Guatemala 1954 Coup," 7 July 1952, doc. 0000915039, CREST.

61. "Cable to Operations . . .," 9 July 1952, doc. 0000915032; "General-DYCLUCK-Specific-TP-REDUCE (w/Attachments)," 25 June 1952, doc. 0000915040, CREST; "Telegram from the CIA . . .," [place not declassified,] 25 June 1952, doc. 10, *FRUSG*; "Cable to Operations . . .," 9 July 1952, doc. 0000915031, CREST.

62. "Memorandum from [name not declassified] . . .," Washington, DC, 9 July 1952, doc. 12, *FRUSG*; "Cable to Operations . . .," 9 July 1952, doc. 0000915032, CREST.

63. "Memorandum from [name not declassified] . . .," Washington, DC, 8 October 1952, doc. 21, *FRUSG*; "Guatemala (handwritten)," 10 July 1952, doc. 0000915033, CREST. Miller and Mann never documented this meeting, but Dulles and another official recorded the results in two reports, one typed and one handwritten.

64. "Guatemala (handwritten)," 10 July 1952, doc. 0000915033, CREST.

65. "Memorandum from [name not declassified] . . .," Washington, DC, 8 October 1952, doc. 21; "Chronology Prepared in . . .," Washington, DC, 8 October 1952, doc. 22, *FRUSG*.

66. "Memorandum from [name not declassified] . . .," Washington, DC, 8 October 1952, doc. 21, *FRUSG*. As with Miller and Mann, Bruce never documented these conversations in VHS.

67. "Memorandum from [name not declassified] . . .," Washington, DC, 9 July 1952, doc. 12, *FRUSG*.

68. "Report," Washington, DC, 8 October 1952, doc. 20; "Memorandum for the Record," Washington, DC, 15 July 1952, doc. 13, *FRUSG*.

69. "Memorandum for the Record," Washington, DC, 15 July 1952, doc. 13, *FRUSG*.

70. Thomas Corcoran to Floyd Odlum, undated, folder United Fruit Company, 1951–52, box 12, FBO.

71. "MOC," Washington, DC, 21 July 1952, doc. 14, *FRUSG*.

72. "MOC," 21 July 1952, doc. 14, *FRUSG*. The cable appears to be "Cable Providing Headquarters . . .," 21 July 1952, doc. 0000136383, CREST.

73. "MOC," 21 July 1952, doc. 14, *FRUSG*.

74. "MOC," 21 July 1952, doc. 14, *FRUSG*.

75. "Memorandum from [name not declassified] . . .," Washington, DC, 9 July 1952, doc. 12, *FRUSG*, footnote 2; "Packaging and Transportation . . .," 28 July 1952, doc. 0000915029, CREST.

76. On plausible deniability, see Cormac and Aldrich, "Grey Is the New Black."

77. John L. Ohmans to Thomas C. Mann, "Subject: Conversations with Colonel . . .," 21 July 1952, 717.00/7-2152, box 3262, DF1950.

78. Edward G. Miller Jr. to H. Freeman Matthews, 23 July 1952, 717.00/7-2152, box 3262, DF1950.

79. H. Freeman Matthews to Dean Acheson, 26 July 1952, 717.00/7-2152, box 3262, DF1950.

80. "Memorandum of Interview," Washington, DC, 13 November 1952, doc. 31, *FRUSG*.

81. MOC Guillermo Sevilla Sacasa, John L. Ohmans, "Subject: Call of . . .," 8 August 1952, folder Nicaragua: Military Assistance Program, box 1, ROMAA.

82. On the MDAP, see Pach, *Arming the Free World*.

83. Sevilla Sacasa, Ohmans, "Subject: Call of . . ," 8 August 1952, ROMAA.

84. "Letter to General . . .," 8 October 1952, doc. 0000915011, CREST.

85. "Supplement 'B,'" 31 July 1952, doc. 0000915027, CREST.

86. "Conference with Seekford . . .," 4 August 1952, doc. 0000915026, CREST.

87. "Shipment of Foreign . . .," 6 August 1952, doc. 0000915025; "Shipment of Foreign . . .," 8 August 1952, doc. 0000915024, CREST.

88. "Report," Washington, DC, 8 October 1952, doc. 20; "Chronology Prepared in . . .," Washington, DC, 8 October 1952, doc. 22, *FRUSG*.

89. "Memo to Director . . .," 19 August 1952, doc. 0000915003, CREST; "Chronology Prepared in . . .," Washington, DC, 8 October 1952, doc. 22, *FRUSG*.

90. Rodríguez Demorizi a Trujillo, Managua, 21 julio 1952, SERREE.

91. "Intermediate Report on . . .," Washington, DC, 1 September 1952, doc. 16, *FRUSG*. In note 2, the editors of *FRUSG* state that this document, with other documents also dated "01 September 1952," is incorrect in placing the Castillo Armas–Somoza meeting on "30 September 1952." Although they place the date at "30 July 1952," this too would be incorrect. The meeting appears to have taken place after Somoza received the "green light" discussed in early August. It is more likely that Somoza and Castillo Armas met in person in mid-August after the "green light" was approved, and Castillo Armas returned on "30 August 1952."

92. "Intermediate Report on . . .," Washington, DC, 1 September 1952, doc. 16, *FRUSG*.

93. Details of the August 1952 meeting comes from Héctor Incháustegui Cabral a Rafael Trujillo, México, 21 agosto 1952, exp. México, 1951–1952, caja 2903957, SERREE; and E. P. Lecours, "Political Report on the Caribbean Area," 25 September 1952, FO 371/97353. Incháustegui Cabral does not note Lecours's first contact in Mexico City but notes Lecours's second contact, Barrios Peña, while Lecours does not note Barrios Peña but admits his information "comes from Carlos Simons, who recently visited Mexico," and notes "the Carlos Simons group," suggesting he saw Barrios Peña as Simmons's representative/ally.

94. "Cable to Director . . .," 9 September 1952, doc. 0000915021, CREST. CIA reports include Barrios Peña's name but do not reference Simmons but rather, someone under the code name "KMEGGCUP." Considering Barrios Peña and Simmons's work with the CCN and Lecours's meeting with Barrios Peña and Simmons at this time, it is likely "KMEGGCUP" refers to Simmons while the two were seeking assistance independent of Castillo Armas's and Córdova Cerna's activities. This also suggests—based on "MOC," Washington, DC, 21 July 1952, doc. 14, *FRUSG*—that the CIA with the State Department's permission had begun working with Simmons's allies to produce anticommunist propaganda.

95. Incháustegui Cabral a Trujillo, 21 agosto 1952, SERREE.

96. Incháustegui Cabral a Trujillo, 21 agosto 1952, SERREE; Lecours, 25 September 1952, FO 371/97353.

97. Incháustegui Cabral a Trujillo, 21 agosto 1952, SERREE.

98. Incháustegui Cabral a Trujillo, 21 agosto 1952, SERREE.

99. E. P. Lecours, "Political Report on the Caribbean Area," 25 September 1952, FO 371/97353.

100. "Cable to Director . . .," 9 September 1952, Doc. 0000915021, CREST.

101. "Intermediate Report on . . .," Washington, DC, 1 September 1952, doc. 16, *FRUSG*.

102. José A. Paniagua, Núm. 570, Tegucigalpa, 10 septiembre 1952, exp. Guatemala, caja 2903351, SERREE.

103. José A. Paniagua, Núm. 572, Tegucigalpa, 12 septiembre 1952, exp. 1949–1953, caja 2903825, SERREE.

104. "Memorandum from Jacob . . .," Washington, DC, 18 September 1952, doc. 18, *FRUSG*.

105. José A. Paniagua, Núm. 572, Tegucigalpa, 12 septiembre 1952, exp. 1949–1953, caja 2903825, SERREE.

106. "Memorandum from Jacob . . .," Washington, DC, 18 September 1952, doc. 18, *FRUSG*.

107. Lecours, 25 September 1952, FO 371/97353. Zuleta Ángel confirmed these details as described in a letter. Fletcher Warren to Edward G. Miller Jr., Caracas, 25 September 1952, folder Nicaragua: Political Relations with Neighbors, box 2, ROMAA.

108. Emilio Rodríguez Demorizi a Rafael Trujillo, Managua, 10 septiembre 1952, exp. Nicaragua, Sec. Calderón, caja 2903958, SERREE.
109. Edward G. Miller Jr. to James Clement Dunn, 27 April 1952, folder Colombia, 1950–1951, box 4, EGM; Rodríguez Demorizi a Trujillo, 10 septiembre 1952, SERREE.
110. Rodríguez Demorizi a Trujillo, 10 septiembre 1952; Arturo Calventi, No. 2602, Habana, 18 septiembre 1952, exp. V, 1948–1953, caja 2904034, SERREE.
111. "Telegram from the . . .," [place not declassified,] 12 September 1952, doc. 17, *FRUSG*.
112. Rodríguez Demorizi a Trujillo, 10 septiembre 1952, SERREE.
113. Telésforo R. Calderón a Luis F. Thomen, Núm. 33307, Ciudad Trujillo, 5 septiembre 1952, exp. Nicaragua, Sec. Calderón, caja 2903958, SERREE.
114. MOC Luis Francisco Thomen, Edward G. Miller Jr., "Subject: Conversation Between . . .," 11 September 1952, folder Dominican Republic, 1949–1952, box 6, EGM.
115. Luis F. Thomen a Telésforo R. Calderón, 3248, 12 septiembre 1952, exp. Nicaragua, Sec. Calderón, caja 2903958, SERREE.
116. Thomen a Calderón, 12 septiembre 1952, SERREE. Emphasis in original.
117. "Memorandum of Interview," Washington, DC, 13 November 1952, doc. 31, *FRUSG*.
118. John D. Erwin, Desp. No. 688, 15 May 1952, box 48, USH, FOIA.
119. Thomas E. Whelan to Rolland Welch, "Subject: Memo of Conversation . . .," 2 September 1952, with Rolland Welch to Thomas C. Mann, Managua, 3 September 1952, 717.00/9-352, box 3262, DF1950; "Telegram from the . . .," [place not declassified,] 12 September 1952, Doc. 17, *FRUSG*.
120. Edward G. Miller Jr. to Thomas E. Whelan, 17 September 1952, folder Nicaragua, box 8, EGM.
121. John L. Ohmans to Rolland Welch, 12 September 1952, folder Nicaragua: Political Relations with Neighbors, box 2, ROMAA.
122. Rolland Welch to Edward G. Miller Jr., Managua, 23 September 1952, box 8, EGM, FOIA.
123. Fletcher Warren to Edward G. Miller Jr., Caracas, 25 September 1952, folder Nicaragua; Political Relations with Neighbors, box 2, ROMAA.
124. MOC Guillermo Sevilla Sacasa, Thomas C. Mann, John L. Ohmans, "Subject: Action Against Guatemala," folder Nicaragua, box 8, EGM.
125. Guillermo Sevilla Sacasa, Thomas C. Mann, John L. Ohmans, "MOC . . .," [Washington, DC,] 29 September 1952, doc. 59, *FRUS52*.
126. Edward G. Miller Jr., 109, 26 September 1952, folder Colombia, 1952, box 4, EGM. On Miller and Zuleta Ángel's relationship, see folder Colombia, 1950–1951, box 4, EGM.
127. "Memorándum: Conversaciones con el Dr. Eduardo Zuleta Ángel, en Panamá, del 2 al 5 de octubre 1952," SERREE.
128. Matthews, *A World in Revolution*, 263.
129. "Memorandum by the . . .," [Washington, DC,] 3 October 1952, 714.00/10-352, doc. 413, *FRUS52*.
130. "Cable to (Deleted) . . .," 4 October 1952, doc. 0000915014; "Cable re: Shipments . . .," 6 October 1952, doc. 0000136384, CREST; "Report," Washington, DC, 8 October 1952, doc. 20, *FRUSG*.
131. 7 October 1952, VHS.
132. Thomas E. Whelan to Thomas C. Mann, Managua, 12 October 1952, DAS; 7 October 1952, VHS.
133. 8 October 1952, VHS.
134. "Memorandum for the Record," Washington, DC, 8 October 1952, doc. 23, *FRUSG*.

135. "Memorandum for the Record," 8 October 1952, *FRUSG*.
136. On Dulles's possibly overstepping the State Department's parameters, see Lockhart, "The Dulles Supremacy."
137. J. C. King, "Memorandum for the Record," Washington, DC, 8 October 1952, doc. 24, *FRUSG*; Thomas Corcoran, Thomas C. Mann, "MOC," 15 May 1950, doc. 457, *FRUS50*.
138. Thomas C. Mann to Thomas E. Whelan, 22 October 1952, folder Nicaragua: 1952, Arms . . ., box 1, ROMAA.
139. Edward G. Miller Jr. to Fletcher Warren, 8 October 1952, folder Venezuela, 1949–1952, box 14, EGM.
140. Mann to Whelan, 13 October 1952, folder Nicaragua: Political Relations with Neighbors; Rolland Welch to John L. Ohmans, Managua, 22 December 1952, folder Nicaragua: General Somoza, box 2, ROMAA.
141. Matthews, *A World in Revolution*, 263.
142. J. C. King, "Memorandum for the Record," Washington, DC, 10 October 1952, doc. 26, *FRUSG*.
143. "Memorandum from Jacob . . .," Washington, DC, 28 October 1952, doc. 29, *FRUSG*.
144. "Memorándum: Conversaciones con el Dr. Eduardo Zuleta Ángel, en Panamá, del 2 al 5 de octubre 1952," SERREE.
145. "Memo to Major General . . .," 16 October 1952, doc. 0000937555, CREST.
146. W. H. Gallienne to R. Cecil, 1041/281/52, Guatemala, 22 September 1952, FO 371/97358.
147. Young, minutes, "Guatemalan attitude towards British Honduras . . .," 7 October 1952, FO 371/97358.
148. G. H. S. Jackson, minutes, "Guatemalan attitude towards British Honduras . . .," 7 October 1952, FO 371/97358.
149. J. H. A. Watson to J. P. E. C. Henniker-Major, Washington, DC, 17 September 1952, FO 371/97351.

8. Realizing the Counterrevolution

1. "Memorandum for the Record," Washington, DC, 9 October 1952, doc. 25, *FRUSG*.
2. 17 December 1952, VHS.
3. "Memorandum for the Record," Washington, DC, 8 March 1953, doc. 36, *FRUSG*.
4. "Memorandum from Jacob . . .," Washington, DC, 28 October 1952, doc. 29, *FRUSG*.
5. Le Ministre de France au Honduras, No. 247/AM, Tegucigalpa, 6 Juillet 1954, dossier Politique Intérieure, numéro 19, sous série Guatemala, CADC.
6. "Report Prepared in the Central Intelligence Agency," Washington, DC, 1 December 1952, doc. 32, *FRUSG*.
7. "Cable to Director . . .," doc. 0000914950, CREST; MOC Zuleta Ángel, Thomas C. Mann, 4 February 1953, 714.00/2-453, roll 2, DF714.
8. "Report re: Guatemalan 1954 Coup," doc. 0000924021, CREST.
9. John Moors Cabot, Thomas C. Mann, John L. Ohmans, "Visit of Ambassador Sevilla-Sacasa," 10 March 1953, folder Nicaragua: 1952, Personnel, box 1, ROMAA.
10. "Background Information . . .," doc. 0000928378; "The Affair at Salamá . . .," doc. 0000914863, CREST.
11. "Background Information . . .," doc. 0000928378, CREST.

12. José A. Paniagua, cable 120, Ciudad Trujillo, 16 marzo 1953, exp. 1949–1953, caja 2903825, SERREE.
13. "Report re: Guatemalan 1954 Coup," doc. 0000924021, CREST; "MOC," Washington, DC, 8 October 1953, doc. 57, *FRUSG*.
14. "Detalles del Complot de Salamá se dan a Conocer," *Prensa Libre*, 24 abril 1953, con Número 00313, 24 abril 1953, exp. III-1488-2, AHGE.
15. "Informe mensual reglamentario correspondiente a abril 1953," exp. III-1488-1, AHGE.
16. "Árbenz y el proceso de Salamá," *Prensa Libre*, 4 marzo 1954, con "Memorándum para información presidencial," México, marzo 1954, exp. III-1572-3, AHGE.
17. Secretaría de Propaganda y Divulgación de la Presidencia de la República, *Así se gestó la Liberación*, 39.
18. "Bajo la egida de la democracia: el imperio del crimen," *Boletín del CEUAGE*, no. 4, 10 agosto 1953, BDC.
19. "La Masacre de la Base Militar," *Boletín del CEUAGE*, no. 6, 15 septiembre 1953, BDC; "Daniel Villagrán, sobreviviente de la Base," *Boletín del CEUAGE*, no. 18, 2 enero 1954, BDC.
20. Nota "Estrictamente Confidencial," 27 junio 1953, Guatemala, folder 1-4, '53, box 70, GDC; "Memorándum: Supuesto Movimiento para derrocar al Gobierno guatemalteco," México, 20 julio 1953, exp. III-1488-2, AHGE.
21. Rolland Welch, Desp. No. 272, Managua, 12 January 1954, 714.00/1-1254, roll 2, DF714.
22. Carlos Castillo Armas, "El Comunismo en Guatemala," 13 mayo 1953, con José A. Paniagua a Rafael Trujillo, Tegucigalpa, 14 mayo 1953, carpetilla 2, caja 2903352, SERREE; "MOC," Washington, DC, 8 October 1953, doc. 57, *FRUSG*.
23. John Calvin Hill Jr., "Subject: Trujillo Drops Interest . . .," 3 November 1953; MOC Aurelio Montenegro, John E. Peurifoy, William L. Krieg, "Subject: Efforts to Overthrow the Guatemalan Government," 6 November 1953, roll 2, DF714.
24. José A. Paniagua a Rafael Trujillo, Tegucigalpa, 14 mayo 1953, carpetilla 2, caja 2903352, SERREE.
25. Víctor A. Fernández Jiménez, "Memorándum Confidencial," Ciudad Trujillo, 18 mayo 1953, carpetilla 2, caja 2903352, SERREE.
26. "Memo re: Guatemala 1954 Coup," doc. 0000914902, CREST.
27. "Report Summary Prepared in the Central Intelligence Agency," Washington, DC, 18 June 1953, doc. 38, *FRUSG*.
28. "Memorandum from the Chief . . .," Washington, DC, 17 August 1953, doc. 41, *FRUSG*.
29. "Memorandum for the Record," Washington, DC, 3 September 1953, doc. 46, *FRUSG*.
30. FO 371/108929.
31. Lara a Miguel Ydígoras Fuentes, San José, 15 julio 1953, RREE 1010.
32. MOC Robert E. Canessa and Michael J. McDermott, 3 June 1954, box 1, ESGU, FOIA.
33. Joaquín Ocaña to Alexander Wiley, New Orleans, 26 May 1954, folder 7-33-18, box 15, Series 7, AWP.
34. "Cable to Director . . .," doc. 0000914100, CREST.
35. James Juliana to Francis P. Carr, memorandum, "Subject: Communist Activities in Guatemala," 11 January 1954, folder Guatemala, 1954, box 4, JMP.
36. "Cable to Director . . .," doc. 0000914048, CREST; "Contact Report," [place not declassified], 27 February 1954, doc. 106, *FRUSG*.
37. "Letter to Mr. Vice President . . .," doc. 0000923230, CREST; "Contact Report," [place not declassified], 27 February 1954, doc. 106, *FRUSG*.
38. "Memorandum for the Record," Washington, DC, 29 October 1953, doc. 61, *FRUSG*.
39. "Coronel Carlos Castillo Armas," doc. 0000914970, CREST.

40. "El 'Argentino' Arévalo en Guatemala," *Boletín del CEUAGE*, no. 14, 5 diciembre 1953, BDC.
41. Carlos Castillo Armas, "El Comunismo en Guatemala," 13 mayo 1953, con José A. Paniagua a Rafael Trujillo, Tegucigalpa, 14 mayo 1953, carpetilla 2, caja 2903352, SERREE.
42. "Memorandum for the Chief . . .," Washington, DC, 6 January 1954, doc. 80, *FRUSG*.
43. "Memorandum for the Record," Washington, DC, 29 October 1953, doc. 61, *FRUSG*.
44. "(Est Pub Date) Honduras—Comité . . .," doc. 0000923964, CREST.
45. Luis Coronado Lira, "Acta de organización . . .," San Salvador, noviembre 1953, No. 1675, folder 1655–1706, box 4, ATF.
46. "Nacionalismo: Base Sólida del Anticomunismo," *Boletín del CEUAGE*, Núm. 10, 7 noviembre 1953, BDC; "En esta forma democrática permite . . .," *El Rebelde* 29 marzo 1954, ERG; "El Gobierno de Guatemala, una amenaza a la Solidaridad Continental," *Boletín del CEUAGE*, Núm. 32, 10 abril 1954, BDC; "Las Atrocidades de los Comunistas: ¿dónde está la diferencia?," *Boletín del CEUAGE*, Núm. 21, 23 enero 1954, BDC; "Los Derechos Humanos en la 'Nueva Guatemala,'" *Boletín del CEUAGE*, Núm. 20, 16 enero 1954, BDC.
47. "General—KUGOWN/PBSUCCESS . . .," doc. 0000917348, CREST.
48. "Cable to Director . . .," doc. 0000916049, CREST.
49. "General Operational—Specific . . .," doc. 0000920770, CREST.
50. Flores Avendaño, *Memorias*, 448.
51. Friedman, "Fracas in Caracas"; García Ferreira, "'El caso de Guatemala.'"
52. On Brazilian anticomunism, see Cowan, *Moral Majorities Across the Americas*. On Guatemalan delegates at anticommunist conferences, see works of Juan Carlos Vázquez Medeles.
53. Summary, Radio from Ciudad Trujillo, FO 371/108738. The best discussion of Toriello's experience remains Gleijeses, *Shattered Hope*.
54. "Guatemala News Notes," 2 March 1954, folder 11, box III/37, ELB.
55. Edward Tomlinson to Scripps Howard News Service, cable, 5 March 1954; Tomlinson to Scripps, cable, 4 March 1954, folder 3, box 1, ETP.
56. Frazier Reams, "Advice to a Diplomat," 100 Cong. Rec. 17, Appendix (daily ed. 10 March 1954), A1869; Alexander Wiley, "Report of the Foreign Relations Commission of the American Legion," 100 Cong. Rec. 19 (daily ed. 13 May 1954), A3529–3531.
57. "Guatemala News Notes," 18 March 1954, folder 11, box III/37, ELB.
58. Jeffrey P. Hillelson, "Editorial Comment," 100 Cong. Rec. 17, Appendix (daily ed. 29 March 1954), A2349.
59. "Guatemala News Notes," 25 March 1954, folder 11, box III/37, ELB.
60. "Moción Anticomunista aprobada," *El Rebelde*, 29 marzo 1954, ERG; "Guatemala News Notes," 18 March 1954, folder 11, box III/37, ELB.
61. "MOC," Washington, DC, 15 September 1953, doc. 52, *FRUSG*.
62. "Cable to Director . . .," doc. 0000914142, CREST.
63. This is referenced in the nota de la Sexta Sesión, 30 mayo 1954, "Preside el Sr. Jorge Prieto Laurens," doc. 0000922999, CREST.
64. "General—KUGOWN—PBSUCCESS . . .," doc. 0000928364; "Instructions for (Deleted) . . .," doc. 0000923858, CREST.
65. "General—Operational—Specific . . .," doc. 0000916802; "Preside el Sr. Jorge Prieto Laurens," doc. 0000922999; "KUGOWN—Operational—Congreso . . .," doc. 0000916380; "KUGOWN/SUMMIT—Travel Report . . .," doc. 0000923393, CREST.
66. Names ranged from the "Congreso Anticomunista" (Anticommunist Conference) to "Congreso de los Combatientes Progresivos Contra el Comunismo" (Congress for the Progressive Combatants Against Communism), and the name slightly differed in correspondence and publications.

67. "Preside el Sr. Jorge Prieto Laurens," doc. 0000922999, CREST.
68. "KUGOWN Operations—Report . . .," doc. 0000922842, CREST; "Guatemala News Notes," 15 April 1954 and 21 April 1954, folder 12, box III/37, ELB.
69. Comisión Permanente del Primer Congreso Contra la Intervención Soviética en América Latina, *El Libro Negro del Comunismo en Guatemala*, 14, 49–52.
70. "Memorandum for the Record," Washington, DC, 4 September 1953, doc. 47, *FRUSG*.
71. "Special Paper Prepared in the Division . . .," Washington, DC, 26 May 1953, doc. 37, *FRUSG*.
72. "Contact Report," Washington, DC, 22 December 1953, doc. 77, *FRUSG*.
73. "Sr. Bernadino's [sic] Visit with Caligeris . . .," doc. 0000914861, CREST.
74. "Memorandum from Jacob R. Seekford . . .," Washington, DC, 15 December 1953, doc. 76, *FRUSG*; "Sr. Bernadino's [sic] Visit with Caligeris . . .," doc. 0000914861, CREST.
75. "Sr. Bernadino's [sic] Visit with Caligeris . . .," doc. 0000914861, CREST; "Contact Report," [place not declassified], 27 February 1954, doc. 106, *FRUSG*; "Dispatch from Operation PBSUCCESS Headquarters . . .," [place not declassified], 9 March 1954, doc. 112, *FRUSG*; "Telegram from Operation PBSUCCESS . . .," [place not declassified], 11 April 1954, doc. 126, *FRUSG*.
76. Arvelo, *Memorias*.
77. "Proposed Visit by (Deleted) . . .," doc. 0000914654, CREST; Warren, No. 132, 23 December 1953, 714.00/12-2353, roll 2, DF714.
78. "List re: Guatemala 1954 Coup," doc. 0000917472, CREST.
79. A Mario Esquivel, 21 abril 1954, RREE 2637; "Cable to Director . . .," doc. 0000916052, CREST.
80. "Cable to Director . . .," doc. 0000916052, CREST.
81. "Talk with American Ambassador," with Michel Leroy-Beaulieu, No. 155/AM, San José, 7 juin 1953, dossier Politique Intérieure, numéro 13, sous série Costa Rica, CADC.
82. Ministerio de Relaciones Exteriores, *Nota de la Cancillería de Nicaragua*.
83. "The Secretary of State to the Embassy in Nicaragua," Washington, DC, 18 May 1954, 617.18/5-1754, doc. 607, *FRUS52*.
84. Rubén Darío a Anthony Eden, 47 54, Londres, 20 mayo 1954, FO 371/108946.
85. Laureano Vallenilla Lanz, cable, Caracas, 8 abril 1954, exp. 088–027, CBV.
86. "Operational—José Luis Arenas . . .," doc. 0000915460, CREST.
87. Charles J. Kersten, "Communist Ties of Guatemala's Former President Árbenz," 100 Cong. Rec. 22, Appendix (daily ed. 16 August 1954), A6073-A6075.
88. Handwritten note, 14 January 1954, folder 11; handwritten note, 27 May 1954, folder 12, box III/37, ELB.
89. Handwritten note, 25 February 1954, folder 11; handwritten note, 21 June 1954, folder 12, box III/37, ELB.
90. "Suggested ELB letter to 25 Foreign Editors of US papers," folder 6, box III/38, ELB.
91. Dick Burke, 23 June 1954, folder 1, box III/38, ELB.
92. Dick Burke to Edward L. Bernays, 30 June 1954, folder 1, box III/38, ELB.
93. Edward L. Bernays to Mary Hirschfeld, 15 April 1954; Mary Hirschfeld to Edward L. Bernays, 13 April 1954, folder 12, box III/37, ELB.
94. Edward L. Bernays to Gordon N. Freedman, 1 July 1954, folder 1, box III/38; handwritten note, 5 May 1954, folder 12, box III/37, ELB.
95. "Guatemala News Notes," 25 March 1954, folder 11; "Guatemala News Notes," 5 May 1954 and 12 May 1954, folder 12, box III/37, ELB.
96. "Guatemala News Notes," 10 March 1954 and 10 February 1954, folder 11; "Guatemala News Notes," 1 April 1954, folder 12, box III/37, ELB.

97. Stanley Ross to Edward L. Bernays, Brooklyn, 12 March 1953, folder Ross, Stanley, 1953, box 28, ELB.
98. Stanley Ross to Edward L. Bernays, 12 March 1953, folder Ross, Stanley, 1953, box 28, ELB.
99. Stanley Ross, *Report on Guatemala*, folder 7-9-15, box 7, Series 7, AWP.
100. Ross, *Guatemalan Communism Endangers the Americas*, 10.
101. Stanley Ross to Edward L. Bernays, 18 March 1953, folder Ross, Stanley, 1953, box 28, ELB.
102. "Guatemala News Notes," 25 February 1954, folder 11; "Guatemala News Notes," 18 May 1954, folder 12, box III/37, ELB.
103. "Guatemala News Notes," 2 March 1954, folder 11, box III/37, ELB.
104. Edward Tomlinson to Mike Mansfield, Jesup, Georgia, 5 January [1953], General Drawer Edw. Tomlinson, box 19, Series XII, MMP; Edward Tomlinson, "Reds Have Master Plan for Middle America," *Washington Daily News*, 25 May 1953, folder American Republics Affairs Subcommittee, General, 1953, box 174, files of Senate committees, BHP.
105. Edward L. Bernays to Bourke B. Hickenlooper, 29 July 1953; Bernays to Hickenlooper, 20 October 1953, folder Guatemala, Bernays, Edward L., 1953–59, box 195, files of Senate committees, BHP.
106. US Senate Committee on Foreign Relations, *South America*, 3; Edward Tomlinson to Scripps Howard News Service, cable, 2 March [1954], folder 3, box 1, ETP.
107. John Moors Cabot to Elisabeth Cabot, 25 April 1953; John Moors Cabot to Elisabeth Cabot, 29 April 1952, JMC.
108. W. H. Gallienne, No. 114, Guatemala, 22 September 1953, FO 371/103357.
109. John W. McCormack to Thomas G. Corcoran, 26 October 1953, folder McCormack, John W., 1941–59, box 71, TGC.
110. Bourke B. Hickenlooper, "The Guatemalan Threat," 100 Cong. Rec. 6 (daily ed. 17 June 1954), 8443.
111. Alexander Wiley, "The United States and Latin America: A Challenge to Understanding, Excerpts from an Address Delivered at the City Club of Milwaukee," 16 October 1953, 9–10, folder American Republics Affairs Subcommittee, General, 1953, box 174, files of Senate committees, BHP.
112. Alexander Wiley, "Communism in Guatemala—A Menace to Hemispheric Security," 100 Cong. Rec. 1 (daily ed. 14 January 1954), 248–250.
113. William M. McNamara to Alexander M. Wiley, Petersburg, Virginia, 7 January 1954, folder 7-33-18, box 15, Series 7, AWP.
114. Julius N. Cahn to William M. McNamara, 25 January 1954, folder 7-33-18, box 15, Series 7, AWP.
115. Elmer McClain to Alexander Wiley, 8 March 1954, folder 7-33-18, box 15, Series 7, AWP.
116. Alexander Wiley to Elmer McClain, 10 March 1954, folder 7-33-18, box 15, Series 7, AWP.
117. Alexander Wiley to A. Matt Werner, 27 May 1954; Alexander Wiley to Anthony Wagener, 20 July 1954, folder 7-33-18, box 15, Series 7, AWP.
118. Alexander Wiley, "The Crisis in Guatemala," 16 June 1954, 100 Cong. Rec. 20, Appendix (daily ed. 16 June 1954), A4443-A4445.
119. Handwritten note, 14 June 1954, folder 12, box III/37, ELB.
120. Alexander Wiley to Wayne Gard, 17 June 1954; Alexander Wiley to Editor, *Nashville Banner*, 17 June 1954, folder 7-33-18, box 15, Series 7, AWP.
121. Edward L. Bernays to Dan O'Brien, 29 April 1953, folder Guatemala, Bernays, Edward L., 1953–59, box 195, files of Senate committees, BHP.

122. Alexander Wiley, "Communism in Guatemala—A Menace to Hemispheric Security," 14 January 1954, with Wiley to Hickenlooper, 13 January 1954, folder Guatemala, General, 1953–54, box 195, files of Senate committees, BHP.

123. Julius N. Cahn to Edward L. Bernays, 15 January 1954, folder 7-33-18, box 15, Series 7, AWP; "Guatemala News Notes," 20 January 1954, folder 11, box III/37, ELB; Cahn to Bernays, 5 February 1954, folder 7-33-18, box 15, Series 7, AWP.

124. Alexander Wiley, "Criticism by Legislature of Guatemala of Remarks by Senator Wiley," 100 Cong. Rec. 1 (daily ed. 4 February 1954), 1321–1323; Alexander Wiley to Elmer McClain, 10 March 1954, folder 7-33-18, box 15, Series 7, AWP.

125. John M. Cabot to Alexander Wiley, 9 February 1954, folder 7-33-18, box 15, Series 7, AWP.

126. Julius N. Cahn to Charles Burrows, 27 March 1954, folder 7-33-18, box 15; American Embassy, "Chronology of 1953 Events," Guatemala City, folder 7-9-15, box 7; Julius N. Cahn to Patrick McMahon, 5 April 1954, folder 7-33-18, box 15, Series 7, AWP; Walter J. Stoessel Jr. to Julius Cahn, 2 June 1954, folder 3-74-4, box 74, Series 3, AWP.

127. Julius N. Cahn to Edward L. Bernays, 30 April 1954; Julius N. Cahn to Edward McGinnis, 13 March 1954; Julius N. Cahn to William Manzullo, 11 May 1954, folder 7-33-18, box 15, Series 7, AWP.

128. Julius N. Cahn to Edward McGinnis, 27 March 1954, folder 7-33-18, box 15, Series 7, AWP.

129. Julius N. Cahn to Edward L. Bernays, 27 March 1954; Julius N. Cahn to William Manzullo, 11 May 1954, folder 7-33-18, box 15, Series 7, AWP.

130. Alexander Wiley, "Meeting of Foreign Relations Commission of the American Legion," 100 Cong. Rec. 19, Appendix (daily ed. 13 May 1954), A3542.

131. Cahn to Bernays, 30 April 1954; Cahn to Manzullo, 11 May 1954, AWP.

132. J. Stuart Innerst to Alexander Wiley, Santa Ana, California, 25 June 1954, folder 7-33-18, box 15, Series 7, AWP.

133. Robert F. Muse to Maxwell Rabb, 24 March 1953, folder Mu, box 34, MMR.

134. Nathalia Collver to Bourke Hickenlooper, 18 May 1954; Hickenlooper to Collver, 19 May 1954; Collver to Hickenlooper, 24 May 1954, folder Guatemala, General, 1953–54, box 195, files of Senate committees, BHP.

135. Nathalia Swanson Collver to Alexander Wiley, cable, New York, 22 June 1954, folder 7-33-18, box 15, Series 7, AWP.

136. Frances D. Manning to Alex Wiley, Burbank, California, 2 June 1954; Alexander Wiley to Francis [sic] D. Manning, 9 June 1954, folder 7-33-18, box 15, Series 7, AWP.

137. Manning to Wiley, Burbank, California, 15 June 1954, folder 7-33-18, box 15, Series 7, AWP.

138. On PBSUCCESS and coffee, see Livingston, "Operation FIBER."

139. "Guatemala Coffee project," doc. 0000914953, CREST.

140. Robert L. F. Sikes, "Aviation and Miami International Airport," 99 Cong. Rec. 11, Appendix (daily ed. 30 June 1953), A3975-A3976.

141. "Memorandum for the Director," doc. CIA-RDP74-00297R000900090116-9; "Fulton Lewis, Jr., Comments on CIA," doc. CIA-RDP74-000900070014-4; "Fulton Lewis, Jr., Comments on C.I.A.," doc. CIA-RDP74-00297R000900090117-8; "Fulton Lewis, Jr., Conference . . .," doc. CIA-RDP75-00001R000200350033-2, CREST.

142. "Memorandum for the Director," doc. CIA-RDP74-00297R000900090108-8, CREST.

143. "Material for Fulton Lewis, Jr.," doc. CIA-RDP74-00297R000900090112-3, CREST.

144. "Subject: Sen. Hickenlooper's Statement on Guatemala," 24 November 1953, doc. 0000914709; "Deputies Meeting," doc. CIA-RDP80B01676R002300140017-6, CREST.

145. "Memorandum for: Senator Bourke B. Hickenlooper," doc. 0000914680, CREST.
146. "Fulton Lewis's TV Program . . .," doc. CIA-RDP74-00297R000900090107-9, CREST.
147. R. W. Michels and Mrs. R. W. Michels to Mike Mansfield, Hungry Horse, Montana, 8 February 1954, folder 17–14, box 17, Series XIII, MMP.
148. A. M. Johnston to Bourke Hickenlooper, Keokuk, Iowa, 11 February 1954, folder Colombia, 1948–66, box 185, files of Senate committees, BHP.
149. Mrs. Joe Runyan to Alexander Wiley, West Bend, Wisconsin, 8 February 1954, folder 7-33-18, box 15, Series 7, AWP.
150. Wingate Lucas, 10 February 1954, 814.2333/2-1054; Burr P. Harrison to Thruston B. Morton, 12 March 1954, 814.2333/3-1254, folder 1, box 4507, DF1950. Thanks to Ryan Livingston for sharing these items.
151. William A. Dawson to Thruston B. Morton, 15 February 1954, 814.2333/2-1554, folder 1, box 4507, DF1950.
152. Charles E. Bennett, 15 February 1954, 814.2333/2-1654, folder 1, box 4507, DF1950.
153. Mabel L. Sisisky to Horace Seely-Brown Jr., Thompsonville, Connecticut, 10 February 1954, with Horace Seely-Brown Jr. to Thruston B. Morton, 16 February 1954, 814.2333/2-1654, folder 1, box 4507, DF1950.
154. Lester C. Hunt to John Foster Dulles, 17 February 1954, 814.2333/2-1754, folder 1, box 4507, DF1950.
155. Margaret Chase Smith, "Investigation of Communist Movement in Guatemala and Its Effect on Price of Imported Coffee," 100 Cong. Rec. 2 (daily ed. 8 February 1954), 1475.
156. Cullather, *Secret History*, 52.
157. James C. Davis to John Foster Dulles, 20 February 1954, 814.2333/2-2054, folder 1, box 4507, DF1950.
158. Thruston B. Morton to Charles E. Bennett, 24 February 1954, 814.2333/2-1654, folder 1, box 4507, DF1950.
159. Thruston B. Morton to Gerald R. Ford Jr., 2 March 1954, 814.2333/2-2654, folder 1, box 4507, DF1950.
160. Thruston B. Morton to Price Daniel, 16 June 1954, 814.2333/6-254, folder 1, box 4507, DF1950.
161. B. B. Hickenlooper to C. H. Brown, 8 March 1954; B. B. Hickenlooper to Dale Emmert, 8 March 1954; B. B. Hickenlooper to Frances Templin, 8 March 1954; B. B. Hickenlooper to Winifred English, 8 March 1954, folder Colombia, 1948–66, box 185, Files of Senate Committees, BHP; Alexander Wiley to Mrs. Joe Runyan, 1 March 1954; Alexander Wiley to Floyd W. Millett, 9 February 1954, folder 7-33-18, box 15, Series 7, AWP.
162. J. G. Eddy, St. Paul, Minnesota, 22 July 1954, folder 21-7-14, box 7, ULB.
163. Barrett, *CIA and Congress*; Trenta, Fahey, and Atkinson, "Secrecy and the Politics."
164. On Delgado, see Gleijeses, *Shattered Hope*, 258–260; Cullather, *Secret History*, 53–56.
165. Secretaría de Propaganda y Divulgación de la Presidencia de la República, *La democracia amenazada*.
166. "Documents Expose Invasion Plot," *Guatemala*, 1 February 1954, folder 7, box 505, MLP.
167. "Castillo Armas da cuenta Somoza de sus proyectos," *Prensa Libre*, 30 enero 1954, con Nicolás Graham Gurría, Número 00075, 29 enero 1954, exp. III-1572-3, AHGE.
168. Secretaría de Propaganda y Divulgación de la Presidencia de la República, *Comunicado de la Secretaría de Propaganda y Divulgación*.
169. W. H. Gallienne, No. 22, Guatemala, 3 February 1954, FO 371/108946; Roger Robert du Gardier, No. 7/11, Guatemala, 30 Janvier 1954, dossier Politique Intérieure, numéro 19, sous série Guatemala, CADC.

170. "Guatemala Sees Invasion Threat," *New York Herald Tribune*, 30 January 1954; Edward Tomlinson to Scripps Howard News Service, cable, [01 March 1954,] folder 3, box 1, ETP.
171. "Guatemala Sees Neighbors and US Plot an Invasion," *New York Times*, 30 January 1954; "Red Labor Chiefs Meet," *New York Times*, 30 January 1954.
172. "Guatemala: Plot Within a Plot," *Time*, 8 February 1954.
173. Henri Bonnet, No. 373/AM, Washington, DC, 04 février 1954, dossier Politique Intérieure, numéro 19, sous série Guatemala, CADC.
174. "Plot Denial: Reply to Guatemala," *Daily Telegraph*, 1 February 1954.
175. M. G. G. Man, minutes, "Transmits a report . . .," 23 March 1954; R. McC. Andrew, in "Transmits a report . . .," FO 371/108927.
176. Roger Robert du Gardier, No. 70/AM, Guatemala, 16 Février 1954, dossier Politique Intérieure, numéro 19, sous série Guatemala, CADC.
177. "Guatemala News Notes," 29 January 1954, folder 11, box III/37, ELB.
178. "US Plots Our Overthrow—Says Guatemala Govt.," *Daily Worker*, 1 February 1954.
179. Jacob K. Javits, "Communist Infiltration in Guatemala," 100 Cong. Rec. 20 (daily ed. 11 June 1954), A4328.
180. Documents 91–94, *FRUSG*.
181. Cullather, *Secret History*, 79. The best discussion of Árbenz's decision-making is Gleijeses, *Shattered Hope*, 279–283. On Czechoslovakia and Latin America, see Perutka, "Arms for Árbenz."
182. Meers, "British Connection," 413.
183. A. G. Maitland to W. D. Allen, 10414/1/53, Washington, DC, 7 December 1953, FO 371/103131.
184. Minutes, "Anglo-United States Relations over Latin America," FO 371/103131; J. H. A. Watson to T. W. Garvey, S1088/4/54G, Washington, DC, 14 January 1954; J. H. Lewen, minutes, "Guatemalan Communism and its intentions: US opinion," 4 March 1954, FO 371/108936.
185. Watson to Garvey, 14 January 1954; T. W. Garvey to J. H. A. Watson, AG1016/1G, 15 March 1954, FO 371/108936.
186. T. W. Garvey to H. Gummer, AG1016/1G, 11 February 1954, FO 371/108936.
187. Taft to Carnahan, 4 December 1952, box 1, ESGU, FOIA; W. P. Grant, GWPG/3142/52, 31 December 1952, FO 371/103353.
188. G. W. P. Grant, GWPG/3142/52, 31 December 1952; W. H. Gallienne to G. H. S. Jackson, 1201/9/53G, Guatemala, 4 March 1953; R. H. B. Swann, minutes, "Sale of arms to Guatemala," 25 March 1953, FO 371/103353.
189. R. H. B. Swann, minutes, "Equipment to Guatemala," 20 February 1953; G. H. S. Jackson, minutes, "Arms to Guatemala," 16 January 1953, FO 371/103353.
190. G. H. S. Jackson to P. A. Wilkinson, G 1192/5G, 2 May 1953; G. H. S. Jackson, minutes, "Sale of Arms to Guatemala," 27 March 1953, FO 371/103353.
191. G. H. S. Jackson to W. H. Gallienne, AG 1192/7G, 01 May 1953, FO 371/103353.
192. Selwyn Lloyd to H. R. Mackeson, AG 1192/10G, 11 May 1953, FO 371/103353.
193. T. W. Garvey to W. H. Gallienne, No. 37, 6 June 1953; W. H. Gallienne to G. H. S. Jackson, 1201/33/53G, Guatemala, 29 June 1953, FO 371/103353.
194. Roger Robert du Gardier, No. 65/AM, Guatemala, 12 Février 1954, dossier Fournitures d'armes au Guatemala, numéro 18, sous série Guatemala, CADC.
195. D. P. Reilly, No. 216, 31 May 1954, FO 371/108962; M. C. G. Man, "Arms for Guatemala," 8 June 1954; R. L. Speaight, "Arms for Guatemala," 9 June 1954, FO 371/108963.
196. Le Ministre de France au Mexique, No. 274/AM, Mexico, 10 juin 1954, dossier Coup d'État au Guatemala, numéro 21, sous série Guatemala, CADC.

197. Patrick J. Hillings, "Communist Aggression in Guatemala," 100 Cong. Rec. 5 (daily ed. 18 May 1954), 6768; Robert L. F. Sikes, "Communist Beachhead," 100 Cong. Rec. 19, Appendix (daily ed. 25 May 1954), A3845.

198. Walter Rogers, "Red Arms for Guatemala," 100 Cong. Rec. 20, Appendix (daily ed. 15 June 1954), A4406; Gordon Canfield, "Our Monroe Doctrine Still Makes Sense," 100 Cong. Rec. 19, Appendix (daily ed. 26 May 1954), A3909; Lyndon B. Johnson, "Monroe Doctrine Is Still Sound," 100 Cong. Rec. 20, (daily ed. 28 June 1954), A4673; Lyndon B. Johnson, "Johnson Resolution Reaffirms United States Ban on Foreign Interference," 100 Cong. Rec. 20, Appendix (daily ed. 28 June 1954), A4674-A4675; Lyndon B. Johnson, "Modernizing the Monroe Doctrine," 100 Cong. Rec. 20 (daily ed. 30 June 1954), A4755.

199. Ray Madden, "Katyn and Baltic Committees Expose Communist Blueprint," 100 Cong. Rec. 6 (daily ed. 8 June 1954), 7880.

200. John Marshall Butler, "The Situation in Guatemala," 100 Cong. Rec. 20, Appendix (daily ed. 15 June 1954), A4380-A4381; Barry M. Goldwater, "Address by Hon. John Marshall Butler . . .," 100 Cong. Rec. 20 (daily ed. 22 June 1954), A4525-A4526.

201. "Guatemala News Notes," 25 June 1954, folder 12, box III/37, ELB.

202. Handwritten note, 10 June 1954; handwritten note, 11 June 1954, folder 12, box III/37, ELB; Petition 1012, 100 Cong. Rec. 6 (daily ed. 14 June 1954), 8196.

Conclusion

1. Grandin, *Last Colonial Massacre*, 65–71.
2. Weld, *Paper Cadavers*.
3. Gilberto Morillo de Soto, cable 45, Guatemala, 24 agosto 1954, exp. 1954, Caja 3114954, SERREE.
4. Juan José Arévalo a Horacio Ornes, Santiago, 16 abril 1955, exp. 18, caja 6, APHO.
5. Arévalo a Ornes, Santiago, 7 octubre 1954; Ornes a Arévalo, México, 15 diciembre 1954, exp. 18, caja 6, APHO.
6. Horacio Ornes a José Figueres, México, 14 agosto 1954, exp. 9, caja 5, APHO.
7. Ornes a Figueres, México, 23 agosto 1954, exp. 9, caja 5, APHO.
8. Horacio Ornes a Ángel Morales, México, 3 agosto 1954, exp. 7, caja 5; Ornes a Figueres, México, 29 julio 1954, exp. 9, caja 5, APHO.
9. Figueres a Ornes, San José, 24 agosto 1954; Ornes a Figueres, México, 14 agosto 1954, exp. 9, caja 5, APHO; Fernando Fournier a Jorge Matamoros Loria, No. DVM-733-C, San José, 17 noviembre 1954, RREE 965.
10. Ornes a Figueres, México, 19 enero 1955, exp. 9, caja 5, APHO.
11. "The Foreign Policy of the United States"; "Exiliados Dominicanos Condenan Intervención . . .," *Pluma y Espada*, enero-abril 1954, exp. República Dominicana, caja 1625, AGPR.
12. Ornes a Morales, México, 14 julio 1954, exp. 7, caja 5, APHO.
13. Arévalo a Ornes, Santiago, 7 octubre 1954, exp. 18, caja 6, APHO; Arévalo, *Guatemala*; Arévalo, *Shark and the Sardines*; Arévalo, *Anti-Kommunism in Latin America*.
14. Grandin, *Last Colonial Massacre*.
15. Germán Arciniegas, "La lección de Guatemala," *Mirador*, 9 julio 1954.
16. Brown, *Cuba's Revolutionary World*.
17. Salcedo, *Venezuela*; Miller, *Precarious Paths to Freedom*.
18. Vega, *Almoina, Galíndez y otros crímenes*; Castro Ventura, *Trujillo vs. Betancourt*.

19. Federación de Estudiantes Universitarias de Honduras, *A Rigoberto López Pérez* (1956), exp. Nicaragua, caja 1630, AGPR.

20. Graciela a Luis Muñoz Marín, New York, 26 noviembre 1956, exp. Nicaragua, caja 1630, AGPR.

21. Jorge Ribas Montes, 25 agosto 1955, collection of Ribas Montes.

Epilogue

1. Castillo Armas, Guatemala, 3 julio 1955, con Francisco A. de Icaza, Número 00720, Guatemala, 4 julio 1955, exp. III-1717-7, AHGE.

2. Gandarias, *Democracia*, 31–53. Imprints came out under the "Secretaría de Propaganda y Divulgación," "Secretaría de Propaganda, Cultura y Turismo de la Presidencia de la República," and "Secretaría de Divulgación, Cultura y Turismo de la Presidencia de la República."

3. Secretaría de Propaganda y Divulgación de la Presidencia de la República, *Así se gestó la Liberación*, 33–40.

4. Comité de Estudiantes Universitarios Anticomunistas, *El Calvario de Guatemala*.

5. Calderón Salazar, *Letras de Liberación*, 1, 14.

6. Secretaría de Divulgación, Cultura y Turismo, *Efemérides del movimiento de liberación nacional*.

7. Secretaría de Divulgación y Propaganda de la Presidencia de la República, *La intriga roja en Guatemala*.

8. Moya Posas, *La jornada épica de Castillo Armas*; *Story of the President and Mrs. Castillo Armas of Guatemala*.

9. Secretaría de Propaganda y Divulgación de la Presidencia de la República, *Liberación con sangre, sacrificios y heroísmo*.

10. Note pour le Secrétaire General « as. Répercussions en Amérique latine de l'affaire guatémaltèque », paris, 3 juillet 1954, dossier Coup d'État au Guatemala, numéro 21, sous série Guatemala, CADC.

11. W. Sullivan, No. 85, Mexico City, 16 June 1954; W. Sullivan, No. 97, Mexico City, 1 July 1954; R. Keith Jopson, No. 65, Bogotá, 23 June 1954, FO 371/108530. On Mexico, see Loaeza, "La fractura mexicana."

12. Espinosa, cable 24, 10 junio 1954, leg. 208, FME; G. Thompson, No. 32, 25 June 1954, FO 371/108928. On Uruguay, see García Ferreira, "'El caso de Guatemala.'"

13. H. A. Hankey, No. 121S, Santiago, 23 June 1954, FO 371/108928. On Chile, see Hove, "The Árbenz Factor."

14. John Coghill, No. 18, Tegucigalpa, 23 June 1954, FO 371/108927; John Coghill, No. 71, Tegucigalpa, 29 June 1954, FO 371/108930.

15. Le Ministre de France au Honduras, No. 247/AM, Tegucigalpa, 6 Juillet 1954, dossier Politique Intérieure, numéro 19, sous série Guatemala, CADC.

16. Vicente Machado Valle a Rafael Heliodoro Valle, Tegucigalpa, 6 julio 1954, exp. 1253, BNM.

17. Smith, No. 8, 25 June 1954, FO 371/108929.

18. Sigalas, No. 244, Caracas, 24 juin 1954, dossier Coup d'État au Guatemala, numéro 21, sous série Guatemala, CADC; W.H. Gallienne, 1024/54, Havana, 06 July 1954, FO 371/108931.

19. Chancery to Northern Department, 10218/12/54, Stockholm, 21 June 1954, FO 371/108927; Chancery of Stockholm, 10218/20/54, Stockholm, 1 July 1954, FO 371/108929.

20. G. H. S. Jackson to M. C. G. Man, 1196/5/54, Berne, 30 June 1954, FO 371/108930.
21. Chancery at Bonn, 102/51/1/54, Bonn, 25 June 1954, FO 371/108928.
22. On Britain at the UN during PBSUCCESS, see Meers, "British Connection."
23. "Memorandum of Telephone Conversation Between the Secretary and Ambassador Lodge," 24 June 1954, reel 4, HCL.
24. P. Dixon, No. 552, 24 June 1954, FO 371/108742; "Guatemala: Record of Meeting . . .," FO 371/108743.
25. United Kingdom Delegation, No. 765, 22 June 1954, FO 371/108742.
26. K. Pridham, minutes, "Guatemalan Situation," 21 June 1954, FO 371/108742. On the British government's use of international bodies regarding decolonization, see Mazower, *No Enchanted Palace*; Grob-Fitzgibbon, *Imperial Endgame*.
27. Foreign Office, No. 785, 24 June 1954, FO 371/108742.
28. Pierson Dixon, "Guatemala," 25 June 1954, FO 371/108743.
29. P. Dixon, No. 557, 24 June 1954, FO 371/108742; "Guatemala: Record of Meeting . . .," FO 371/108743; Pierson Dixon, "Guatemala," 25 June 1954, FO 371/108743.
30. Henry Cable Lodge Jr. and Winston Churchill, "Memorandum of Conversation," 26 June 1954, reel 3, HCL.
31. P. Dixon, No. 561, 25 June 1954; P. Dixon, No. 560, 25 June 1954, FO 371/108742.
32. D. P. Reilly, No. 243, 26 June 1954, FO 371/108929; R. M. B. Chevallier, "Guatemala," 21 June 1954, FO 371/108927.
33. "Joint Press Reading Service," 22 June 1954, FO 371/108928.
34. Getchell, "Revisiting the 1954 Coup in Guatemala."
35. D. Ellward, "For the perusal of the US Consul General . . .," in "Encloses a statement submitted . . .," FO 371/108929. For more on the British backlash, see FO 371/108932; Young, "Great Britain's Latin American Dilemma."
36. Philip Noel-Baker, "U.N. and Guatemala," *Times* (London), 25 June 1954, with Foreign Office, No. 793, 25 June 1954, FO 371/108743.
37. See FO 371/108744; Young, "Great Britain's Latin American Dilemma."
38. No. 3184, 5 July 1954, FO 371/108744. On the white paper, see Meers, "British Connection."
39. B. Salt to S. Williams, 10227/1/81/54, Washington, DC, 8 July 1954, FO 371/108744.
40. M. C. G. Man to P. M. Crosthwaite, A1076/108, 17 July 1954; C. L. S. Cope, minutes, "Report of the Inter American . . .," 16 July 1954; J. S. Ward, minutes, "Guatemala: State Dept. views . . .," 21 July 1954; Foreign Office, No. 942, 24 July 1954, FO 371/108745.
41. Richard Allen, No. 76, Guatemala, 26 July 1954, FO 371/108933. With pencil markings.
42. Secretary of State for Foreign Affairs, *Report on Events Leading up to and Arising out of the Change of Regime in Guatemala*.
43. R. H. Scott to R. L. Speaight, 10227/1/130/54, Washington, DC, 29 October 1954, FO 371/108935.
44. Livingstone, *Britain and the Dictatorships*; Mills and Miller, *Britain and the Growth of US Hegemony*; Cormac, "Currency of Covert Action"; McEvoy, "Before the Rubble."
45. M. C. G. Man to R. H. Stuart, AG 1591/1, 12 May 1954, FO 371/108973.
46. Foreign Office, No. 11, 1 April 1955, FO 371/114204.
47. Luis Coronado Lira, "Carta abierta del licenciado . . ." (Editorial Nosotros, 1948), item 854, folder 841–880, box 3, ATF.
48. Reading, "Record of Conversation with the Guatemalan Minister," 04 July 1955, FO 371/114204.
49. Richard Allen to Domingo Goicolea, No. 48, Guatemala, 28 September 1955, FO 371/114204.

50. Allen, No. 120, 7 August 1954, FO 371/108973.
51. Roger Robert du Gardier, No. 57, Guatemala, 1 Février 1955, dossier Relations avec l'Europe Occidentale, numéro 18, sous série Guatemala, CADC.
52. Secretaría de Publicidad y Propaganda de la Presidencia, *El Ministro de su Majestad en Guatemala*, avec Gardier, 1 Février 1955, CADC.
53. Gardier, 1 Février 1955, CADC.
54. On persecution of Guatemalan exiles, see Black, "Politics of Asylum."
55. Frank G. Wisner to Henry Holland, "Subject: Proposal for Combined Department of State and CIA . . .," 6 August 1954, box 1, ESGU, FOIA.
56. Confederación Interamericana de Defensa del Continente, *Memoria del Segundo Congreso*, 9.
57. Leandro Castillo Venegas, "Se informe en relación . . .," México, 25 octubre 1954, DFS. Thanks to Ashley Black for this item.
58. Information Report, "Subject: Roberto Barrios Peña," early May 1956, Doc. 0000671746, CREST.
59. Holt, No. 17, 06 July 1954, FO 371/108929.
60. Ydígoras Fuentes, *My War with Communism*.
61. Photograph of Carlos Padilla y Padilla and Chiang Kai-shek, late 1950s, personal collection of family of Roberto Padilla, possession of Jaime Padilla and Hesed Padilla.
62. Secretaría de Relaciones Exteriores, *Diario Oficial*, 19 febrero 1955.
63. *Redemption in Guatemala*.
64. "Memorandum for the Director," Doc. CIA-RDP74-00297R000900090101-5; "Memorandum for the Director," Doc. CIA-RDP74-00297R000900090095-3, CREST.
65. The best work on the US government's assistance and Guatemala's Cold War-era regimes remains Streeter, *Managing the Counterrevolution*.
66. Joseph F. Thorning to Mike Mansfield, no date, folder 2–9, box 2, Series XIII, MMP.
67. Joe McCarthy to Harold Stassen, cable, 22 October 1954, folder Guatemala, box 4, JMP.
68. "$6,425,000 Offered Guatemala in Aid," *New York Times*, 31 October 1954.
69. US Attorney General, "Report of the Attorney General to the Congress of the United States on the Administration of the Foreign Agents Registration Act of 1938, as Amended, for the Calendar Year 1955," 88.
70. Holland, "Operation PBHISTORY."
71. Carl Marcy to Hickenlooper, 27 May 1955, folder Guatemala, General, 1953–54, box 195, Files of Senate Committees, BHP.
72. Whitman, *How an American Company*, 1.
73. Thomas G. Corcoran to Robert B. Dresser, 17 June 1954, folder Dresser, Robert B., box 56, TGC.
74. Whitman, *How an American Company*, 19–20. Capitalization in original.
75. E. S. Whitman to Bourke B. Hickenlooper, 27 July 1954, folder Guatemala, General, 1953–54, box 195, Files of Senate Committees, BHP.
76. Sam G. Baggett, "Factual account," with Emery N. Leonard to Bourke B. Hickenlooper, 18 August 1954, folder Guatemala, General, 1953–54, box 195, Files of Senate Committees, BHP.
77. "Spreading the Risks," *Fort Worth Star-Telegram*, 21 October 1954, with E. S. Whitman, 12 January 1955, folder U, General 1953–58, box 73, Files of Senate Committees, BHP.
78. Leonard to Hickenlooper, 18 August 1954, Folder Guatemala, General, 1953–54, Box 195, BHSC.
79. E. S. Whitman, New York, 16 December 1954, folder Guatemala, General, 1953–54, box 195, Files of Senate Committees, BHP.

252   Notes to Pages 190–191

80. Edward L. Bernays, 20 October 1954, folder Guatemala, General, 1953–54, box 195; Edmund S. Whitman, folder United Fruit Company, 1955, box 160, Files of Senate Committees, BHP.

81. John W. McCormack, "United States Government Showed Unfortunate Timing in Filing Monopoly Suit Against United Fruit Co.," 100 Cong. Rec. 22, Appendix (daily ed. 17 August 1954), A6092.

82. Thomas G. Corcoran to Thomas D. Cabot, 16 April 1975, folder Cabot, Thomas D., 1948–81, box 52, TGC.

83. Floyd B. Odlum to George E. Allen, 14 June 1954, folder Argentine Project, 1953–54, box 14, FBO.

Note on Sources

The best sources on Caribbean Basin regimes come from their nation-states' respective depositories. The Secretaría de Estado de Relaciones Exteriores collection (SERREE) from Santo Domingo's Archivo General de la Nación (AGN) and Havana's Archivo del Instituto de Historia de Cuba and Archivo Central del Ministerio de Relaciones Exteriores contain reports on regimes' opposition to and networking against democratic movements and governments. Collections at the Archivo Nacional de Costa Rica provide a contrasting perspective. On British officials' views and patronizing of Guatemalan anticommunists, the National Archives in London (TNA) has declassified relevant materials. SERREE and the National Archives and Records Administration II (NARAII) in College Park, Maryland, have reactionaries' letters. Supplemented by items from the TNA and the Centres des Archives Diplomatiques at La Courneueve and Nantes, relevant materials on the US government's policies toward the Caribbean Basin come from NARAII, multiple presidential libraries and congressional collections, the CIA's Freedom of Information Act Electronic Reading Room and CIA Records Search Tool (CREST) Library, the Massachusetts Historical Society (MHS), and the Virginia Historical Society.

Recapturing antidictatorial figures' and groups' views can be quite challenging. As scholars of exile movements emphasize, restoring the experiences of those whose activities defied nation-states and the archives designed to collect nation-state histories is a daunting task. The 1940s and 1950s were turbulent years in the Caribbean Basin, and many who contributed to this era's developments participated in later events such as the Cuban Revolution and the Sandinista movement. As a result, critical materials in the personal collections of Juan "Juancito" Rodríguez and Jorge Ribas Montes were destroyed or lost. Nevertheless, their descendants graciously shared all possible. Led by Dominican exiles' descendants, the Museo Memorial de la Resistencia Dominicana in Santo Domingo granted access to militant Dominican exile Horacio Ornes's personal collection. Mauricio Ordóñez shared an album and personal recollections related to his father, Nicaraguan poet Alberto Ordóñez Argüello. Darío Euraque and Polly Moran made available the personal collection of Honduran Amílcar Gómez Robelo, and Roberto Padilla recounted the history of his father, reactionary Carlos Padilla y Padilla.

The personal archive of Honduran Rafael Heliodoro Valle at the Biblioteca Nacional de México, copies of Dominican exile newspaper *Quiqueya Libre* at the Biblioteca Nacional de Cuba José Martí, and photostatic copies of exiles' writings at NARAII restored many exiles' voices. Materials from Antigua's Centro de Investigaciones Regionales de Mesoamérica (CIRMA) and Madrid's Archivo del Gobierno de la II República Española en el Exilio revealed hundreds of writings from Caribbean Basin democrats to Arévalo. My efforts to reconstruct the region's ambience benefited from reports at NARAII; CIRMA; Mexico City's Archivo General de la Nación, Acervo Histórico Diplomático, and Archivo Histórico Genaro Estrada; San Juan's Archivo General de Puerto Rico and Fundación Luis Muñoz Marín; and the Arturo Taracena Flores Collection with the Nettie Lee Benson Latin American Collection at the University of Texas at Austin.

Despite or perhaps because of its size, there is no accessible central depository offering a complete window into the UFCO's global operations. The corporation's worldview can be rebuilt from items at the MHS, Harvard Business School, the Library of Congress, the Wisconsin Historical Society (WHS), and Philippe Bourgois's Bocas del Toro collection, which Kevin Coleman shared. Until recently the UFCO's congressional lobbying campaign remained hidden. Fortuitously, relevant congressional collections across the United States are now available. The John McCormack Collection at Boston University; the Allen J. Ellender Papers at the Ellender Memorial

Library at Nicholls State University; the Lister Hill Papers at the University of Alabama; the Bourke B. Hickenlooper Papers at the Hoover Presidential Library; the Alexander Wiley Papers at the WHS; and the Mike Mansfield Papers at the University of Montana revealed the connections between congresspersons and the corporation's agents.

Bibliography

In citing works in the notes, short titles have generally been used. Works from manuscript collections and archives have been identified by the following abbreviations:

ACMINREX—Archivo Central del Ministerio de Relaciones Exteriores, Havana
AGPR—Oficina del Gobernador, Tarea 96–20, Archivo General de Puerto Rico, San Juan
AGR—Documentos Privados del Ingeniero Don Amílcar Gómez Robelo, San Pedro Sula (Honduran exile). Access courtesy of Darío A. Euraque and Polly Moran.
AHGE—Acervo Histórico Diplomático, Archivo Histórico Genaro Estrada, Ciudad de México
AIHC—Colección Jefe de Estado, Fondo Ejército 1952–1958, Archivo del Instituto de Historia de Cuba, Havana
AJEP—Allen J. Ellender Papers, Ellender Memorial Library, Nicholls State University, Thibodaux, Louisiana
ALMM—Sección V, Serie 2, Archivo Luis Muñoz Marín, Fundación Luis Muñoz Marín, San Juan

Bibliography

APHO—Archivo Personal de Horacio Ornes, Museo Memorial de la Resistencia Dominicana, Santo Domingo
ATF—Arturo Taracena Flores Collection, 1814–1968, Nettie Lee Benson Latin American Collection, University of Texas at Austin
AWP—Alexander Wiley Papers, Wisconsin Historical Society, Madison, Wisconsin
BBP—Bruce Barton Papers, Wisconsin Historical Society, Madison, Wisconsin
BDC—Comité de Estudiantes Universitarios Anticomunistas, *Boletín del CEUAGE* (Tegucigalpa), microfilm, Nettie Lee Benson Latin American Collection, University of Texas at Austin
BHP—Bourke B. Hickenlooper Papers, Herbert Hoover Presidential Library & Museum, West Branch, Iowa
BIAA—Bureau of Inter-American Affairs/Office of Middle American Affairs, Subject Files, 1947–1956, Record Group 59, National Archives and Records Administration II, College Park, Maryland
BNCJM—Colección Quisqueya Libre (Habana), Biblioteca Nacional de Cuba José Martí, Havana
BNM—Fondo Reservado, Archivo Personal de Rafael Heliodoro Valle, Biblioteca Nacional de México, Ciudad de México
CADC—Série B, Amérique, 1952–1963, Centre des Archives Diplomatiques, La Courneuve
CADN—Collection Archives Rapatriées des Postes, Centre des Archives Diplomatiques, Nantes
CBV—Colección Bernardo Vega, Fondo Presidencia, Archivo General de la Nación, Santo Domingo
CIRF—Central Intelligence Reports File, Intelligence File, Subject File 1940–1953, Harry S. Truman Presidential Library, Independence, Missouri
CMAC—Colección Manuel Ávila Camacho, Fondo Presidencial, Archivo General de la Nación, Ciudad de México
CREST—Freedom of Information Act Electronic Reading Room and CIA Records Search Tool (CREST) Library, Central Intelligence Agency
DAS—folder Nicaragua, 1947–1952, box 4, subject file: 1945–1956, Bureau of Inter-American Affairs, Records of Deputy Assistant Secretaries of State for Inter-American Affairs, 1945–1956, Record Group 59, National Archives and Records Administration II, College Park, Maryland
DCOP—Dartmouth College Office of the President Records, DP-12, Rauner Special Collections Library, Dartmouth College, Hanover, New Hampshire

DF714—decimal file 714, Records of the Department of State Relating to Internal Affairs of Guatemala, 1950–1954, Record Group 59, National Archives and Records Administration II, College Park, Maryland, National Archives Microfilm Publication M1527

DF814—decimal file 814, Records of the Department of State Relating to Internal Affairs of Guatemala, 1945–1949, Record Group 59, National Archives and Records Administration II, College Park, Maryland, National Archives Microfilm Publication M1527

DGIPS—Dirección General de Investigaciones Políticas y Sociales, Archivo General de la Nación, Ciudad de México

DJP—Series 2, Daniel James Papers, Holt-Atherton Department of Special Collections, University of the Pacific, Stockton, California

DRSCF—Box 1, Dominican Republic, Strictly Confidential Files, 1929–1945, Record Group 84, National Archives and Records Administration II, College Park, Maryland

EBP—Ellis Briggs Papers, ML-93, Dartmouth College, Hanover, New Hampshire

EGM—Bureau of Inter-American Affairs, Office of the Assistant Secretary of State for Inter American Affairs, Edward G. Miller, subject file 1949–1953, Record Group 59, National Archives and Records Administration II, College Park, Maryland

ELB—The Papers of Edward L. Bernays, Manuscript Division, Library of Congress, Washington, DC

ERG—Comité de Estudiantes Universitarios Anticomunistas, *El Rebelde* (Guatemala), microfilm, Nettie Lee Benson Latin American Collection, University of Texas at Austin

ERP—Anna Eleanor Roosevelt Papers, Franklin D. Roosevelt Presidential Library & Museum, Hyde Park, New York

ESGU—Bureau of Inter-American Affairs, Office of Middle American Affairs, Records Relating to El Salvador and Guatemala, 1942–1954, Record Group 59, National Archives and Records Administration II, College Park, Maryland

ETP—Edward Tomlinson Papers, Wisconsin Historical Society, Madison, Wisconsin

FAF—Foreign Affairs File, Harry S. Truman Papers: President's Secretary's Files, Harry S. Truman Presidential Library, Independence, Missouri

FBO—Floyd B. Odlum Papers, 1892–1976, Dwight D. Eisenhower Presidential Library & Museum, Abilene, Kansas

FME—Fondo Ministerio de Estado, Archivo Nacional de Cuba, Havana

FO—Foreign Office, The National Archives, London
FP—Fondo Presidencia, Archivo Nacional de Costa Rica, San José
FSERREE—Fondo Secretaría de Estado de Relaciones Exteriores, Archivo General de la Nación, Santo Domingo
FSP—Fondo Secretaría de la Presidencia, Archivo Nacional de Cuba, Havana
FUE—Archivo del Gobierno de la II República Española en el Exilio, Fundación Universitaria Española, Madrid
GDC—Guatemalan Documents Collection, 1944–1954, Manuscript Division, Library of Congress, Washington, DC
GLKS—Gerald L. K. Smith Papers, 1922–1976, call number 85818 Aa 2, Bentley Historical Library, University of Michigan, Ann Arbor
HBA—Henry B. Arthur Papers, 1915–1988, Baker Library Special Collections, Bloomberg Center, Harvard Business School, Boston
HBS—Baker Library Special Collections, Baker Library, Bloomberg Center, Harvard Business School, Boston
HCL—Papers of Henry Cabot Lodge II, microfilm #P-373, Manuscript Collection #N-166, Massachusetts Historical Society, Boston
Hess, Jerry N. Oral History Interview with Brigadier General Cornelius J. Mara. 7 June, 9 June 1971. Harry S. Truman Presidential Library, Independence, Missouri
HGBU—John McCormack Collection, Howard Gotlieb Archival Research Center, Boston University
HWVP—Henry A. Wallace Papers as Vice President, 1941–1945, Franklin D. Roosevelt Presidential Library & Museum, Hyde Park, New York
JAG— Subfondo Correspondencia, Fondo Archivo particular y presidencial de Coronel Árbenz, Archivo Personal de Jacobo Árbenz Guzmán, Archivo Histórico, Centro de Investigaciones Regionales de Mesoamérica, Antigua Guatemala
JMC—The Diplomatic Papers of John Moors Cabot, microfilm, Edward Ginn Library, Fletcher School of Law and Diplomacy, Tufts University, Medford, Massachusetts
JMP—Joseph R. McCarthy Papers, Raynor Memorial Libraries, Marquette University, Milwaukee
JWR—Papers of Jean Wade Rindlaub, MC 693, Schlesinger Library on the History of Women in America, Harvard Radcliffe Institute, Harvard University, Boston

LDP—Ludwell Denny Papers, Wisconsin Historical Society, Madison, Wisconsin
LFP—La Follette Family Papers, 1781–1988, Manuscript Division, Library of Congress, Washington, DC
LHP—Lister Hill Papers, MSS-0670, W. S. Hoole Special Collections Library, The University of Alabama, Tuscaloosa
MMP—Mike Mansfield Papers, Maureen and Mike Mansfield Library, University of Montana, Missoula
MMR—Maxwell M. Rabb Papers, 1938–1958, 1989, Dwight D. Eisenhower Presidential Library & Museum, Abilene, Kansas
NPD—Nathaniel P. Davis Papers, Harry S. Truman Presidential Library, Independence, Missouri
OARA—Office of American Republic Affairs, Its Predecessors, and Its Successors, Records Relating to the Caribbean Legion, 1947–51, Record Group 59, National Archives and Records Administration II, College Park, Maryland
OFFDR—Franklin D. Roosevelt, Papers as President: The President's Official File, 1933–1945, Franklin D. Roosevelt Presidential Library & Museum, Hyde Park, New York
OFHST—Official File, Harry S. Truman Papers: President's Secretary's Files, Harry S. Truman Presidential Library, Independence, Missouri
RIE—Expediente Reportes de inteligencia del Ejército sobre todos los opositores, 1952–1955, Colección Jefe de Estado, Fondo Ejército 1952–1958, Archivo del Instituto de Historia de Cuba, Havana
ROMAA—Records of the Office of Middle American Affairs, Records Relating to Costa Rica and Nicaragua, 1951–1955, Record Group 59, National Archives and Records Administration II, College Park, Maryland
RREE—Fondo Relaciones Exteriores, Archivo Nacional de Costa Rica, San José
SCJJA – Subserie Correspondencia, Serie Campaña presidencial de 1944, Subfondo Actividad política, Fondo Archivo Personal de Juan José Arévalo Bermejo, Archivo Histórico, Centro de Investigaciones Regionales de Mesoamérica, Antigua Guatemala
SERREE—Colección Secretaría de Estado de Relaciones Exteriores, Fondo Presidencia, Archivo General de la Nación, Santo Domingo
SP—Fondo Seguridad Pública, Archivo Nacional de Costa Rica, San José

SPICSP—Subserie Presupuesto interno confidencial, Serie Presidencia de la República, 1945–1951, Subfondo Actividad política, Fondo Archivo Personal de Juan José Arévalo Bermejo, Archivo Histórico, Centro de Investigaciones Regionales de Mesoamérica, Antigua Guatemala

SRD—Subserie Relaciones diplomáticas, Series Presidencia de la República 1945–1951, Subfondo Actividad política, Fondo Archivo Personal de Juan José Arévalo Bermejo, Archivo Histórico, Centro de Investigaciones Regionales de Mesoamérica, Antigua Guatemala

SWP—Sumner Welles Papers, Franklin D. Roosevelt Presidential Library & Museum, Hyde Park, New York

TGC—The Papers of Thomas G. Corcoran, Manuscript Division, Library of Congress, Washington, DC

UFCO—United Fruit Company Historical Archive of Letters from 1912–1982, Bocas del Toro Division, Philippe Bourgois. Courtesy of Kevin Coleman.

ULB – Usher L. Burdick Papers, Chester Fritz Library, University of North Dakota, Grand Forks

USC—Costa Rica, US Embassy, San José, Classified General Records, 1938–1961, Record Group 84, National Archives and Records Administration II, College Park, Maryland

USG—Guatemala, US Embassy, Guatemala City, Classified General Records, 1937–1961, Record Group 84, National Archives and Records Administration II, College Park, Maryland

USGC—Guatemala, US Embassy, Guatemala City, Classified & Unclassified General Records, 1953–1956, Record Group 84, National Archives and Records Administration II, College Park, Maryland

USH—Honduras, Tegucigalpa Legation and Embassy, Classified General Records, 1940–1958, Record Group 84, National Archives and Records Administration II, College Park, Maryland

USN—Nicaragua, US Legation and Embassy, Managua, Classified General Records, 1938–1961, Record Group 84, National Archives and Records Administration II, College Park, Maryland

USV—Venezuela, US Legation and Embassy, Caracas, Classified General Records, 1935–1961, Record Group 84, National Archives and Records Administration II, College Park, Maryland

VHS—Diary 15, David K. E. Bruce Papers, 1918–1971, Mss 1 B8303 a Manuscripts, Virginia Historical Society, Richmond

WCF—W. Cameron Forbes Journals, typescript, Second Series, V: 1935–1946, Massachusetts Historical Society, Boston

Published Sources

Alemán Bolaños, Gustavo. *Un Lombrosiano: Somoza. Los pobres diablos.* Editorial Hispania, 1947.
Alemán Bolaños, Gustavo. *¡Sandino! Estudio completo del héroe de las Segovias.* Imprenta La República, 1932.
Arévalo, Juan José. *Anti-Kommunism in Latin America: An X-Ray of the Process Leading to a New Colonialism.* Translated by Carleton Beals. Lyle Stuart, 1963.
Arévalo, Juan José. *Despacho presidencial: obra póstuma.* Editorial Oscar de León Palacios, 1998.
Arévalo, Juan José. *Discursos en la presidencia (1945–1948).* Tipografía Nacional, 1948.
Arévalo, Juan José. *Escritos políticos.* Tipografía Nacional, 1945.
Arévalo, Juan José. *Guatemala: la democracia y el imperio.* Editorial América Nueva, 1954.
Arévalo, Juan José. *The Shark and the Sardines.* Lyle Stuart, 1961.
Argüello, Rosendo, hijo. *Quiénes y cómo nos traicionaron.* Mexico City, 1952.
Argüello, Rosendo, hijo. *Sobre el caso de Figueres: el impostor que siendo un pigmeo quiere pasar a la historia como un gigante (Carta Abierta a don Otilio Ulate).* N.p., 1962.
Arvelo, Tulio H. *Cayo Confite y Luperón: Memorias de un Expedicionario.* Editora de la Universidad Autónoma de Santo Domingo, 1981.
Arvelo, Tulio H. *Memorias.* Museo Memorial de la Resistencia Dominicana, 2013.
Arvelo, Tulio H. *Nuestras luchas civiles, 1844–1965.* Editora Universitaria-Universidad Autónoma de Santo Domingo, 2005.
Asociación de Estudiantes Hispanoamericanos en México. *En Lucha contra Trujillo.* Mexico City, 1945.
Calderón Salazar, José. *Guatemala bajo el signo rojo.* Comité Patriótico Guatemalteco, 1947.
Calderón Salazar, José. *Letras de Liberación.* Tomos 1 y 2. Tipografía Nacional de Guatemala, 1955.
Cardenal A., Luis G. *Mi Rebelión: la dictadura de los Somoza.* Ediciones Patria y Libertad, 1961.
Cardoza y Aragón, Luis. *Guatemala: las líneas de su mano.* Editorial Universitaria, 2002.
Céspedes Espinosa, Luis F., ed. *Juan Bosch en Cuba.* Fundación Global Democracia y Desarrollo (FUNGLODE) y la Cátedra Juan Bosch de la Universidad de La Habana, 2009.
Chamorro, Pedro Joaquín. *Estirpe sangrienta: Los Somoza.* Patria y Libertad, 1957.
CLDHMH (Comité Liberal Demócrata de Honduras en México), eds. *Homenaje a las Víctimas de San Pedro Sula.* Mexico, 1945.
Comisión Permanente del Primer Congreso Contra la Intervención Soviética en América Latina. *El Libro Negro del Comunismo en Guatemala.* S. Turanzas del Valle, 1954.
Comité Cubano Pro Liberación de Honduras. *Yo Acuso . . . (al tirano Carías Andino).* Imprenta Cooperación, 1946.
Comité de Defensa Patria. *La Tribuna de la libertad: Voz de los Guatemaltecos en el destierro.* Plutarco, 1946.

Comité de Estudiantes Universitarios Anticomunistas. *El Calvario de Guatemala*. Tipografía Nacional de Guatemala, 1955.

Comité de Estudiantes Universitarios Anticomunistas. *Plan de Tegucigalpa*. N.p., 1953.

Confederación Interamericana de Defensa del Continente. *Memoria del Segundo Congreso Contra la Intervención Soviética en América Latina*. Mexico City, 1956.

Cordero Reyes, Manuel, Carlos A. Castro Wassmer, and Carlos Cuadra Pasos. *Nicaragua bajo el régimen de Somoza: a los gobiernos y pueblos de América*. Imprenta Funes, 1944.

Coronado Lira, Luis. *Totalitarismo espiritualista: Tres panoramas y un caso de nacionalidad*. Alajuela, 1946.

Cuadra, Abelardo. *Hombre del Caribe: Memorias presentadas y pasadas en limpio por Sergio Ramírez*. Editorial Universitaria Centroamericana, 1977.

Cutter, Victor M. *Trade Relations with Latin America*. Boston: United Fruit Company, 1929.

Federación Estudiantil Universitaria. *Los Universitarios de Santo Domingo Frente a la Dictadura Trujillista*. Mexico City, 1945.

Flores Avendaño, Guillermo. *Memorias (1900–1970)*. Tomo 2. Editorial del Ejército, 1974.

FRUS48 *(Foreign Relations of the United States, 1948, The Western Hemisphere, Volume IX)*. Edited by Almon R. Wright, Velma Hastings Cassidy, and David H. Stauffer. US Government Printing Office, 1972.

FRUS50 *(Foreign Relations of the United States, 1950, The United Nations; The Western Hemisphere, Volume II)*. Edited by Ralph R. Goodwin, David W. Mabon, and David H. Stauffer. US Government Printing Office, 1976.

FRUS51 *(Foreign Relations of the United States, 1951, The United Nations; The Western Hemisphere, Volume II)*. Edited by Ralph R. Goodwin, N. Stephen Kane, and Harriet D. Schwar. US Government Printing Office, 1979.

FRUS52 *(Foreign Relations of the United States, 1952–1954: The American Republics, Volume IV)*. Edited by N. Stephen Kane and William F. Sandford Jr. US Government Printing Office, 1983.

FRUSG. *(Foreign Relations of the United States, 1952–1954: Guatemala)*. Edited by Susan K. Holly and David S. Patterson. US Government Printing Office, 2003.

Galich, Manuel. *Del pánico al ataque*. 2nd ed. Universidad de San Carlos de Guatemala, 1949.

Gandarias, León, ed. *Democracia: la mejor arma contra el Comunismo*. Ediciones Liberación, 1957.

Gómez Ochoa, Delio. *Constanza, Maimón y Estero Hondo: la victoria de los caídos*. Academia Dominicana de la Historia, 2010.

Grullón, José Diego. *Cayo Confites: La revolución traicionada*. Editora Alfa & Omega, 1989.

Hicks, Albert C. *Blood in the Streets*. Creative Age Press, 1946.

Inestroza Manzanares, Jesús Evelio. *Documentos clasificados de la policía secreta de Carías (1937–1944)*. Instituto Hondureño de Antropología e Historia, 2009.

Landestoy, Carmita. *¡Yo también acuso!* 2nd ed. Editorial LEX, 1946.

Matthews, Herbert L. *A World in Revolution: A Newspaperman's Memoir*. Charles Scribner's Sons, 1971.
Mendieta, Salvador. *Esquema del problema unionista centroamericano*. Guatemala, 1949.
Ministerio de Relaciones Exteriores. *Nota de la Cancillería de Nicaragua a la de Costa Rica, con motivo del atentado contra el señor Presidente de Nicaragua, General Anastasio Somoza*. Tipografía Heuberger, 1954.
Miolán, Ángel. *El Perrede desde mi ángulo*. Editorial Letras de Quisqueya, 1984.
Moya Posas, Emma. *La jornada épica de Castillo Armas vista desde Honduras*. La República, 1955.
Orbe, Justino José. *Del Exilio Político Dominicano Antitrujillista, en Cuba*. Editora Taller, 1983.
Ordóñez Argüello, Alberto. *Arévalo visto por América: La opinión continental en torno a la personalidad del primer presidente de la nueva Guatemala*. Editorial del Ministerio de Educación Pública, 1951.
Ornes, Germán E. *Trujillo: Little Caesar of the Caribbean*. Thomas Nelson, 1958.
Ornes, Horacio. *Desembarco en Luperón*. Ediciones Humanismo, 1956.
Partido Revolucionario Dominicano. *La historia del hombre que se proclamó igual a Dios*. Partido Revolucionario Dominicano, 1943.
Partido Unionista Centroamericano. *El Partido Unionista Centroamericano en la lucha contra la Dictadura de Somoza, y en la Campaña Electoral de 1946 a 1947*. Imprenta Democrática, 1947.
Redemption in Guatemala: Eyewitness Accounts of the Defeat of Communism in the Western Hemisphere. United Fruit Company, 1954.
Ross, Stanley. *Guatemalan Communism Endangers the Americas*. New York, 1953.
Rushdie, Salman. *The Jaguar Smile: A Nicaraguan Journey*. Random House, 2008.
Santamaría, Ramón. *La personalidad política del licenciado Ángel Zúñiga Huete*. New Orleans, 1936.
Secretaría de Divulgación, Cultura y Turismo de la Presidencia de la República. *Efemérides del movimiento de liberación nacional: junio y julio de 1954*. Guatemala, [1955].
Secretaría de Divulgación y Propaganda de la Presidencia de la República. *La intriga roja en Guatemala*. Talleres Gutenberg, n.d.
Secretaría de Propaganda, Cultura y Turismo de la Presidencia de la República. *Así se gestó la Liberación*. Tipografía Nacional de Guatemala, 1956.
Secretaría de Propaganda y Divulgación de la Presidencia de la República. *Comunicado de la Secretaría de Propaganda y Divulgación de la Presidencia de la República de Guatemala respecto al complot descubierto*. N.p., 1954.
Secretaría de Propaganda y Divulgación de la Presidencia de la República. *La democracia amenazada: el caso de Guatemala*. Tipografía Nacional de Guatemala, 1954.
Secretaría de Propaganda y Divulgación de la Presidencia de la República. *Liberación con sangre, sacrificios y heroísmo: se escribió la historia de nuestra segunda independencia*. Guatemala, n.d.
Secretaría de Publicidad y Propaganda de la Presidencia. *El Ministro de su Majestad en Guatemala al Secretario de Estado en el Despacho de R. R. E. E. de la Gran Bretaña*. Talleres Gráficos Liberación C.E.U.A., [1955].

Secretary of State for Foreign Affairs. *Report on Events Leading up to and Arising out of the Change of Régime in Guatemala, 1954*. London: Her Majesty's Stationery Office, 1954.

The Story of the President and Mrs. Castillo Armas of Guatemala. N.p., n.d.

Taracena Arriola, Arturo, Arely Mendoza, and Julio Pinto Soria, eds. *El placer de corresponder: Correspondencia entre Cardoza y Aragón, Muñoz Meany y Arriola*. Editorial Universitaria, [2004].

Unión Democrática Antinazista Dominicana. *América contra Trujillo*. Habana: Unión Democrática Antinazista Dominicana, 1944.

US Attorney General. "Report of the Attorney General to the Congress of the United States on the Administration of the Foreign Agents Registration Act of 1938, as Amended, for the Calendar Year 1955." US Government Printing Office, 1956.

US Senate Committee on Foreign Relations. *South America: Report of Senator Theodore Francis Green on a Study Mission*. US Government Printing Office, 1954.

Vega, Bernardo, ed. *Almoina, Galíndez y otros crímenes de Trujillo en el extranjero*. Fundación Cultural Dominicana, 2001.

Vega, Bernardo, ed. *Correspondencia entre Ángel Morales y Sumner Welles*. Archivo General de la Nación, 2013.

Velázquez Alemán, Arturo, et al. *Pavorosas Realidades de la Política Dictatorial de Somoza: Nicaragua vive una falsa democracia*. Imprenta Española, 1951.

Villagrán Kramer, Francisco. *Biografía política de Guatemala: Los pactos políticos de 1944 a 1970*. 2nd ed. FLACSO, 1993.

Warner, Michael, ed. *The CIA Under Harry Truman*. Center for the Study of Intelligence, Central Intelligence Agency, 1994.

Whitman, Edmund S. *How an American Company, Through Advertising and Public Relations, Has Combatted Communism in Latin America*. N.p., 1955.

Ydígoras Fuentes, Miguel. *My War with Communism*. Translated by Mario Rosenthal. Prentice Hall, 1963.

Zúñiga O., Manuel Francisco. *Año trece de la era Tiburcia*. Tegucigalpa, 1946.

Zúñiga Huete, Ángel. *La Carta del Atlántico*. Mexico City, 1943.

Zúñiga Huete, Ángel. *Cartas: Una actitud y una senda, Veleidades de una veleta*. Mexico City, 1949.

Zúñiga Huete, Ángel. *Regalos del exilio*. Mexico City, 1943.

Zúñiga Huete, Ángel, et al. *Carta abierta a Tiburcio Carías Andino*. Mexico City: 1943.

Secondary Works

Acosta Matos, Eliades. *La telaraña cubana de Trujillo*. 2 tomos. Archivo General de la Nación, 2012.

Aguayo, Sergio. *La Charola: Una historia de los servicios de inteligencia en México*. Grijalbo, 2001.

Aguilar, Kevan Antonio. "From Comrades to Subversives: Mexican Secret Police and 'Undesirable' Spanish Exiles, 1939–60." *Journal of Latin American Studies* 53, no. 1 (2021): 1–24.

Aldrich, Richard J. *The Hidden Hand: Britain, America, and Cold War Secret Intelligence.* Overlook Press, 2002.

Alemán, Carlos Enrique. "Nicas belicosos: nicaragüenses en la Guerra Civil de Costa Rica, 1948." *Anuario de Estudios Centroamericanos* 39 (2013): 111–141.

Allcock, Thomas Tunstall. *Thomas C. Mann: President Johnson, the Cold War, and the Restructuring of Latin American Foreign Policy.* University Press of Kentucky, 2018.

Ameringer, Charles D. "The Auténtico Party and the Political Opposition in Cuba, 1952–57," *Hispanic American Historical Review* 65, no. 2 (May 1985): 327–351.

Ameringer, Charles D. *The Caribbean Legion: Patriots, Politicians, Soldiers of Fortune, 1946–1950.* Pennsylvania State University Press, 1996.

Ameringer, Charles D. *The Cuban Democratic Experience: The Auténtico Years, 1944–1952.* University Press of Florida, 2000.

Ameringer, Charles D. *The Democratic Left in Exile: The Antidictatorial Struggle in the Caribbean, 1945–1959.* University of Miami Press, 1974.

Ameringer, Charles D. *Don Pepe: A Political Biography of José Figueres of Costa Rica.* University of New Mexico Press, 1978.

Armony, Ariel C. *Argentina, the United States, and the Anticommunist Crusade in Central America, 1977–1984.* Ohio University Center for International Studies, 1997.

Avery, Molly. "Promoting a 'Pinochetazo': The Chilean Dictatorship's Foreign Policy in El Salvador During the Carter Years, 1977–81." *Journal of Latin American Studies* 52, no. 4 (2020): 759–784.

Ayuso, Juan José. *Lucha contra Trujillo, 1930–1961.* Editorial Letra Gráfica, 2010.

Barrett, David M. *The CIA and Congress: The Untold Story from Truman to Kennedy.* University Press of Kansas, 2017.

Beisner, Robert L. *Dean Acheson: A Life in the Cold War.* Oxford University Press, 2006.

Bell, Aaron T. "A Matter of Western Civilisation: Transnational Support for the Salvadoran Counterrevolution, 1979–1982." *Cold War History* 15, no. 4 (October 2014): 511–531.

Bender, Thomas, ed. *Rethinking American History in a Global Age.* University of California Press, 2002.

Bethell, Leslie, and Ian Roxborough. "The Postwar Conjuncture in Latin America: Democracy, Labor, and the Left." In *Latin America Between the Second World War and the Cold War, 1944–1948*, edited by Leslie Bethell and Ian Roxborough. Cambridge University Press, 1992.

Black, Ashley. "The Politics of Asylum: Cold War Revolutionaries, Human Rights, and Mexican Foreign Policy, 1944–1961." PhD diss. Stony Brook University, 2018.

Blasier, Cole. *The Hovering Giant: US Responses to Revolutionary Change in Latin America, 1910–1985.* 2nd ed. University of Pittsburgh Press, 1985.

Bonilla, Walter R. "Entre el recuerdo y el olvido: las memorias de los exiliados antitrujillistas." *Revista Mexicana del Caribe* 8, no. 15 (2003): 79–105.

Booth, William A. "Rethinking Latin America's Cold War." *The Historical Journal* (2020): 1–23.

Borgwardt, Elizabeth. *A New Deal for the World: America's Vision for Human Rights.* Harvard University Press, 2005.

Brands, Hal. *Latin America's Cold War*. Harvard University Press, 2010.
Briggs, Laura, Gladys McCormick, and J. T. Way. "Transnationalism: A Category of Analysis." *American Quarterly* 60, no. 3 (2008): 625–648.
Brown, Jonathan. *Cuba's Revolutionary World*. Harvard University Press, 2017.
Brown, Judith M., and Wm. Roger Louis, eds. *The Oxford History of the British Empire*. Vol. IV, *The Twentieth Century*. Oxford University Press, 1999.
Bucheli, Marcelo. *Bananas and Business: The United Fruit Company in Colombia, 1899–2000*. New York University Press, 2005.
Bucheli, Marcelo. "Major Trends in the Historiography of the Latin American Oil Industry." *Business History Review* 84, no. 2 (2010): 339–362.
Bucheli, Marcelo. "Multinational Corporations, Totalitarian Regimes and Economic Nationalism: United Fruit Company in Central America, 1899–1975." *Business History* 50, no. 4 (2008): 433–454.
Carey, David, Jr. *I Ask for Justice: Maya Women, Dictators, and Crime in Guatemala, 1898–1944*. University of Texas Press, 2013.
Carr, Barry. "Pioneering Transnational Solidarity in the Americas: The Movement in Support of Augusto C. Sandino, 1927–1934." *Journal of Iberian and Latin American Research* 20, no. 2 (2014): 141–152.
Casal Tatlock, Alvaro. *La Doctrina Larreta*. Montevideo: Ediciones de la Plaza, 1997.
Casals, Marcelo. "Against a Communist Threat: Transnational Anticommunist Networks of the Chilean Right Wing in the 1950s." *Journal of Latin American Studies* 51, no. 3 (August 2019): 523–548.
Casals, Marcelo. "Which Borders Have Not Yet Been Crossed? A Supplement to Gilbert Joseph's Historiographical Balance of the Latin American Cold War." *Cold War History* 20, no. 3 (2020): 141–170.
Casaús Arzú, Marta Elena, and Teresa García Giráldez. *Las redes intelectuales centroamericanas: Un siglo de imaginarios nacionales (1820–1920)*. F&G Editores, 2005.
Castro Ventura, Santiago. *Trujillo vs. Betancourt: ¡rivalidad perpetua!* Editora Manatí, 2008.
Chamberlain, Mary. *Empire and Nation-Building in the Caribbean: Barbados, 1937–66*. Manchester University Press, 2013.
Childers, Kristen Stromberg. *Seeking Imperialism's Embrace: National Identity, Decolonization, and Assimilation in the French Caribbean*. Oxford University Press, 2016.
Ching, Erik. "El Partido Comunista de Costa Rica, 1931–1935: los documentos del Archivo Ruso del Comintern." *Revista de Historia* 37 (enero-junio 1998): 7–226.
Clark, Paul Coe, Jr. *The United States and Somoza, 1933–1956: A Revisionist Look*. Praeger, 1992.
Coates, Benjamin Allen. *Legalist Empire: International Law and American Foreign Relations in the Early Twentieth Century*. Oxford University Press, 2016.
Cohn, Deborah. *The Latin American Literary Boom and US Nationalism During the Cold War*. Vanderbilt University Press, 2012.
Colby, Jason. *The Business of Empire: United Fruit, Race, and US Expansion in Central America*. Cornell University Press, 2011.

Cormac, Rory. "The Currency of Covert Action: British Special Political Action in Latin America, 1961–64." *Journal of Strategic Studies* 45, no. 6–7 (2022): 893–917.

Cormac, Rory. "The Information Research Department, Unattributable Propaganda, and Northern Ireland, 1971–1973: Promising Salvation but Ending in Failure?" *English Historical Review* 131, no. 552 (October 2016): 1074–1104.

Cormac, Rory, and Richard J. Aldrich. "Grey Is the New Black: Covert Action and Implausible Deniability." *International Affairs* 94, no. 3 (2018): 477–494.

Cowan, Benjamin A. *Moral Majorities Across the Americas: Brazil, the United States, and the Creation of the Religious Right*. University of North Carolina Press, 2021.

Crenzel, Emilio. *La historia política del Nunca Más: La memoria de las desapariciones de la Argentina*. Siglo XXI, 2008.

Cruz Cerdas, Rodolfo. *La hoz y el machete: La Internacional Comunista, América Central y la revolución en Centro América*. Universidad Estatal a Distancia, 1986.

Cruz Infante, José Abigaíl. *Hombres de Trujillo*. Letra Gráfica, 2006.

Cullather, Nick. *Secret History: The CIA's Classified Account of Its Operations in Guatemala, 1952–1954*. 2nd ed. Stanford University Press, 2006.

Darwin, John. *Britain and Decolonisation: The Retreat from Empire in the Post-War World*. Macmillan Press, 1988.

Dávila, Jerry. *Hotel Trópico: Brazil and the Challenge of African Decolonization, 1950–1980*. Duke University Press, 2010.

Defty, Andrew. *Britain, America and Anticommunist Propaganda, 1945–53: The Information Research Department*. Routledge, 2004.

Derby, Lauren. *The Dictator's Seduction: Politics and the Popular Imagination in the Era of Trujillo*. Duke University Press, 2009.

Díaz Arias, David. *Crisis social y memorias en lucha: guerra civil en Costa Rica, 1940–1948*. EUCR, 2015.

Dodd, Thomas J. *Tiburcio Carías: Portrait of a Honduran Political Leader*. Louisiana State University Press, 2005.

Dosal, Paul J. *Doing Business with the Dictators: A Political History of United Fruit in Guatemala, 1899–1944*. Scholarly Resources, 1993.

Dosal, Paul J. "The Political Economy of Industrialization in Revolutionary Guatemala, 1944–1954." *Canadian Journal of Latin American and Caribbean Studies* 15, no. 29 (1990): 17–36.

Dunkerley, James. "Guatemala." In *Latin America Between the Second World War and the Cold War, 1944–1948*, edited by Leslie Bethell and Ian Roxborough. Cambridge University Press, 1992.

Euraque, Darío A. "La Masacre del 6 de Julio en San Pedro Sula ante la historiografía de Honduras." Unpublished, 2016.

Euraque, Darío A. *Reinterpreting the Banana Republic: Region & State in Honduras, 1870–1972*. University of North Carolina Press, 1996.

Feierstein, Daniel. *Los dos demonios (recargados)*. Marea Editorial, 2018.

Fenner, Adam. "Puppet Dictator in the Banana Republic?: Re-examining Honduran-American Relations in the Era of Tiburcio Carías Andino, 1933–1938." *Diplomacy & Statecraft* 25, no. 4 (2014): 613–629.

Ferrer, Ada. *Cuba: An American History.* Charles Scribner's Sons, 2022.

Ferrero Blanco, María Dolores. *La Nicaragua de los Somoza: 1936–1979.* 2nd ed. Instituto de Historia de Nicaragua y Centro América, 2013.

Ferrero, María Dolores, and Matilde Eiroa. "La oposición antitrujillista, La Legión del Caribe y José Figueres de Costa Rica (1944–1949)." *Revista Complutense de Historia de América* 42 (2016): 175–201.

Field, Thomas C. *From Development to Dictatorship: Bolivia and the Alliance for Progress in the Kennedy Era.* Cornell University Press, 2014.

Field, Thomas C., Stella Krepp, and Vanni Pettinà, eds. *Latin America and the Global Cold War.* University of North Carolina Press, 2020.

Findlay, Eileen J. Suárez. *Imposing Decency: The Politics of Sexuality and Race in Puerto Rico, 1870–1920.* Duke University Press, 1999.

Forster, Cindy. *The Time of Freedom: Campesino Workers in Guatemala's October Revolution.* University of Pittsburgh Press, 2001.

Franco, Marina. "La 'teoría de los dos demonios': un símbolo de la posdictadura en la Argentina." *Contracorriente* 11, no. 2 (2014): 22–52.

Friedman, Max Paul. "Fracas in Caracas: Latin American Diplomatic Resistance to United States Intervention in Guatemala in 1954." *Diplomacy & Statecraft* 21, no. 4 (2010): 669–689.

Friedman, Max Paul. "A Latin American Third Way: Juan José Arévalo's Spiritual Socialism, 1916–1963." *The Americas* 81, no. 1 (January 2024): 67–91.

Friedman, Max Paul. *Nazis & Good Neighbors: The United States Campaign Against the Germans of Latin America in World War II.* Cambridge University Press, 2003.

Gaddis, John Lewis. *We Now Know: Rethinking Cold War History.* Oxford University Press, 1997.

García Ferreira, Roberto. "'El caso de Guatemala': Arévalo, Árbenz y la izquierda uruguaya, 1950–1971." *Mesoamérica* 49 (diciembre 2007): 25–58.

García Ferreira, Roberto, ed. *El derrocamiento de Jacobo Árbenz y la guerra fría en América Latina: Nuevas fuentes.* In *Revista de Historia de América* 149 (July-December 2015).

García Ferreira, Roberto. "Toda Centroamérica conspiró con la CIA contra Árbenz." *El Faro,* 15 febrero 2016.

García Ferreira, Roberto, and Arturo Taracena, eds. *Guerra fría y anticomunismo en Centroamérica.* Serviprensa, 2017.

Gellman, Irwin F. *Roosevelt and Batista: Good Neighbor Diplomacy in Cuba, 1933–1945.* University of New Mexico Press, 1973.

Gellman, Irwin F. *Secret Affairs: Franklin Roosevelt, Cordell Hull, and Sumner Welles.* Enigma Books, 1995.

Getchell, Michelle Denise. "Revisiting the 1954 Coup in Guatemala: The Soviet Union, the United Nations, and 'Hemispheric Solidarity.'" *Journal of Cold War Studies* 172 (Spring 2015): 73–102.

Gibbings, Julie, and Heather Vrana, eds. *Out of the Shadow: Revisiting the Revolution from Post-Peace Guatemala.* University of Texas Press, 2020.

Gleijeses, Piero. *Conflicting Missions: Havana, Washington, and Africa, 1959–1976.* University of North Carolina Press, 2002.

Gleijeses, Piero. "The Death of Francisco Arana: A Turning Point in the Guatemalan Revolution." *Journal of Latin American Studies* 22, no. 3 (October 1990): 527–552.

Gleijeses, Piero. "Juan José Arévalo and the Caribbean Legion." *Journal of Latin American Studies* 21, no. 2 (February 1989): 133–145.

Gleijeses, Piero. *Shattered Hope: The Guatemalan Revolution and the United States, 1944–1954*. Princeton University Press, 1991.

Gleijeses, Piero. *Visions of Freedom: Havana, Washington, Pretoria, and the Struggle for Southern Africa, 1976–1991*. University of North Carolina Press, 2013.

Gobat, Michel. *Confronting the American Dream: Nicaragua under US Imperial Rule*. Duke University Press, 2005.

Gould, Jeffrey L. *To Lead as Equals: Rural Protest and Political Consciousness in Chinandega, Nicaragua, 1912–1979*. University of North Carolina Press, 1990.

Gould, Jeffrey L., and Aldo A. Lauria-Santiago. *To Rise in Darkness: Revolution, Repression, and Memory in El Salvador, 1920–1932*. Duke University Press, 2008.

Grandin, Greg. *The Blood of Guatemala: A History of Race and Nation*. Duke University Press, 2000.

Grandin, Greg. *The Last Colonial Massacre: Latin America in the Cold War*. University of Chicago Press, 2004.

Grandin, Greg. "Living in Revolutionary Time: Coming to Terms with the Violence of Latin America's Long Cold War." In *A Century of Revolution: Insurgent and Counterinsurgent Violence During Latin America's Long Cold War*, edited by Greg Grandin and Gilbert M. Joseph. Duke University Press, 2010.

Grandin, Greg. "Off the Beach: The United States, Latin America, and the Cold War." In *A Companion to Post-1945 America*, edited by Jean-Christophe Agnew and Roy Rosenzweig. Blackwell, 2002.

Grieb, Kenneth J. *Guatemalan Caudillo: The Regime of Jorge Ubico, Guatemala, 1931–1944*. Ohio University Press, 1979.

Grieb, Kenneth J. "The Myth of a Central American Dictators' League." *Journal of Latin American Studies* 10, no. 2 (November 1978): 329–345.

Grob-Fitzgibbon, Benjamin. *Imperial Endgame: Britain's Dirty Wars and the End of Empire*. Palgrave Macmillan, 2011.

Grow, Michael. *The Good Neighbor Policy and Authoritarianism in Paraguay: United States Economic Expansion and Great-Power Rivalry in Latin America During World War II*. Regents Press of Kansas, 1981.

Grow, Michael. *US Presidents and Latin American Interventions: Pursuing Regime Change in the Cold War*. University of Kansas Press, 2008.

Handy, Jim. *Revolution in the Countryside: Rural Conflict and Agrarian Reform in Guatemala, 1944–1954*. University of North Carolina Press, 1994.

Harmer, Tanya. *Allende's Chile & the Inter-American Cold War*. University of North Carolina Press, 2011.

Harmer, Tanya. "Brazil's Cold War in the Southern Cone, 1970–1975." *Cold War History* 12, no. 4 (2012): 659–681.

Harms, Patricia. *Ladina Social Activism in Guatemala City, 1871–1954*. University of New Mexico Press, 2020.

Herrán Ávila, Luis Alberto. "Las guerrillas blancas: anticomunismo transnacional e imaginarios de derechas en Argentina y México, 1954–1972." *Quinto Sol* 19, no. 1 (junio 2015): 1–26.

Hershberg, James G. "'High-Spirited Confusion': Brazil, the 1961 Belgrade Non-Aligned Conference, and the Limits of an 'Independent' Foreign Policy During the High Cold War." *Cold War History* 7, no. 3 (2007): 373–388.

Holden, Robert H. *Armies Without Nations: Public Violence and State Formation in Central America, 1821–1960*. Oxford University Press, 2004.

Holden, Robert H. "Communism and Catholic Social Doctrine in the Guatemalan Revolution of 1944." *Journal of Church and State* 50, no. 3 (January 2008): 495–517.

Holland, Max. "Operation PBHISTORY: The Aftermath of SUCCESS." *International Journal of Intelligence and Counterintelligence* 17, no. 2 (2004): 300–332.

Hove, Mark T. "The Árbenz Factor: Salvador Allende, US-Chilean Relations, and the 1954 US Intervention in Guatemala." *Diplomatic History* 31, no. 4 (September 2007): 623–663.

Humphreys, R. A. *Latin America and the Second World War, 1939–1942*. Athlone Press, 1981.

Ibarra Guitart, Jorge Renato. *Las relaciones cubano-dominicanas: su escenario hemisférico, 1944–1948*. Archivo General de la Nación, 2011.

Immerman, Richard H. *The CIA in Guatemala: The Foreign Policy of Intervention*. University of Texas Press, 1982.

Jeansonne, Glen. *Gerald L. K. Smith: Minister of Hate*. Louisiana State University Press, 1997.

Jéifets, Víctor, and Lázar Jéifets. "Los archivos rusos revelan secretos: El movimiento de la izquierda latinoamericana a la luz de los documentos de la Internacional Comunista." *Anuario Americanista Europeo* 8 (2010): 35–64.

Jenks, John. *British Propaganda and News Media in the Cold War*. Edinburgh University Press, 2006.

Johnson, Robert David. *Congress and the Cold War*. Cambridge University Press, 2012.

Joseph, Gilbert M. "Border Crossings and the Remaking of Latin American Cold War Studies." *Cold War History* 19, no. 1 (2019): 141–170.

Joseph, Gilbert M. "Close Encounters: Toward a New Cultural History of US-Latin American Relations." In Joseph, LeGrand, and Salvatore, *Close Encounters of Empire*.

Joseph, Gilbert M. "Latin America's Long Cold War: A Century of Revolutionary Process and US Power." In *A Century of Revolution: Insurgent and Counterinsurgent Violence During Latin America's Long Cold War*, edited by Greg Grandin and Gilbert M. Joseph. Duke University Press, 2010.

Joseph, Gilbert M. "What We Now Know and Should Know: Bringing Latin America More Meaningfully into Cold War Studies." In *In from the Cold: Latin America's New Encounter with the Cold War*, edited by Gilbert M. Joseph and Daniela Spenser. Duke University Press, 2008.

Joseph, Gilbert M., Catherine C. LeGrand, and Ricardo D. Salvatore, eds. *Close Encounters of Empire: Writing the Cultural History of US-Latin American Relations*. Duke University Press, 1998.

Kamman, William. "A Friendly Problem: Washington's Assessment of Anastasio Somoza García." In *Presidents, Diplomats, and Other Mortals: Essays Honoring Robert H. Ferrell*, edited by J. Garry Clifford and Theodore A. Wilson. University of Missouri Press, 2007.

Karabell, Zachary. *Architects of Intervention: The United States, the Third World, and the Cold War, 1946–1962*. Louisiana State University Press, 1999.

Katz, Friedrich. "Mexico, Gilberto Bosques, and the Refugees." *The Americas* 57, no. 1 (July 2000): 1–12.

Keller, Renata. *Mexico's Cold War: Cuba, the United States, and the Legacy of the Mexican Revolution*. Cambridge University Press, 2015.

Kiddle, Amelia M. *Mexico's Relations with Latin America During the Cárdenas Era*. University of New Mexico Press, 2016.

Kirkendall, Andrew J. "Cold War Latin America: The State of the Field." *H-Diplo Essay*, no. 119 (November 2014).

Klara, Robert. *The Hidden White House: Harry Truman and the Reconstruction of America's Most Famous Residence*. Thomas Dunne, 2013.

Knight, Alan. "Britain and Latin America." In *The Oxford History of the British Empire*. Vol. III, *The Nineteenth Century*, edited by Andrew Porter. Oxford University Press, 1999.

Kruijt, Dirk. *Cuba and Revolutionary Latin America: An Oral History*. Zed Books, 2017.

Kuzmarov, Jeremy. *Modernizing Repression: Police Training and Nation-Building in the American Century*. University of Massachusetts Press, 2012.

Lambe, Ariel Mae. *No Barrier Can Contain It: Cuban Antifascism and the Spanish Civil War*. University of North Carolina Press, 2019.

Langley, Lester D. *The Banana Wars: United States Intervention in the Caribbean, 1898–1934*. Rev. ed. SR Books, 2002.

Langley, Lester D., and Thomas Schoonover. *The Banana Men: American Mercenaries & Entrepreneurs in Central America, 1880–1930*. University Press of Kentucky, 1995.

Lashmar, Paul, and James Oliver. *Britain's Secret Propaganda War: The Foreign Office and the Cold War, 1948–77*. Sutton, 1998.

Leonard, Thomas M., ed. *United States-Latin American Relations, 1850–1903: Establishing a Relationship*. University of Alabama Press, 1999.

Leonard, Thomas M., and John F. Bratzel, eds. *Latin America During World War II*. Rowman & Littlefield, 2007.

Lehman, Kenneth. "Revolutions and Attributions: Making Sense of Eisenhower Administration Policies in Bolivia and Guatemala." *Diplomatic History* 21, no. 2 (Spring 1997): 185–213.

LeoGrande, William M. *Our Own Backyard: The United States in Central America, 1977–1992*. University of North Carolina Press, 1998.

Leonard, Thomas M. "Nationalism or Communism?: The Truman Administration and Guatemala, 1945–1952." *Journal of Third World Studies* 7, no. 1 (Spring 1990): 169–191.

Leonard, Thomas M. *The United States and Central America, 1944–1949: The Perceptions of Political Dynamics*. University of Alabama Press, 1984.

Levenson-Estrada, Deborah. *Trade Unionists Against Terror: Guatemala City, 1954–1985*. University of North Carolina Press, 1994.

Livingston, Ryan. "Operation FIBER: 'Communist Coffee' and Covert Economic Warfare in Guatemala." *Diplomatic History* 48, no. 5 (November 2024): 744-771.

Livingstone, Grace. *Britain and the Dictatorships of Argentina and Chile, 1973–82: Foreign Policy, Corporations and Social Movements*. Palgrave Macmillan, 2018.

Loaeza, Soledad. "El archivo te da sorpresas, sorpresas te da el archivo." *Nexos*, 1 diciembre 2016.

Loaeza, Soledad. "La fractura mexicana y el golpe de 1954 en Guatemala." *Historia Mexicana* 66, no. 2 (octubre-diciembre 2016), https://historiamexicana.colmex.mx/index.php/RHM/article/view/3346/3147.

Lockhart, James. "The Dulles Supremacy: Allen Dulles, the Clandestine Service, and PBFortune." In *Spy Chiefs*. Vol. 1, *Intelligence Leaders in the United States and United Kingdom*, edited by Christopher Moran, Mark Stout, Ioanna Iordanou, and Paul Maddrell. Georgetown University Press, 2018.

Long, Tom, and Max Paul Friedman. "The Promise of Precommitment in Democracy and Human Rights: The Hopeful, Forgotten Failure of the Larreta Doctrine." *Perspectives on Politics* 18, no. 4 (2020): 1088–1103.

Longley, Kyle. *In the Eagle's Shadow: The United States and Latin America*. Harland Davidson, 2002.

Longley, Kyle. *The Sparrow and the Hawk: Costa Rica and the United States During the Rise of José Figueres*. University of Alabama Press, 1997.

López, Juan Diego. *Los cuarenta días de 1948: La guerra civil en Costa Rica*. Editorial Costa Rica, 1998.

Louis, Wm. Roger, and Ronald Robinson. "The Imperialism of Decolonization." *Journal of Imperial and Commonwealth History* 22, no. 3 (1994): 462–511.

Loveman, Brian. *No Higher Law: American Foreign Policy and the Western Hemisphere Since 1776*. University of North Carolina Press, 2010.

Lucas, Scott, and C. J. Morris. "A Very British Crusade: The Information Research Department and the Origins of the Cold War." In *British Intelligence, Strategy and the Cold War*, edited by Catherine Utting. Routledge, 1992.

Manley, Elizabeth S. *The Paradox of Paternalism: Women and the Politics of Authoritarianism in the Dominican Republic*. University Press of Florida, 2017.

Manela, Erez. *The Wilsonian Moment: Self-Determination and the International Origins of Anticolonial Nationalism*. Oxford University Press, 2007.

Marchesi, Aldo. "Escribiendo la Guerra Fría latinoamericana: entre el Sur 'local' y el Norte 'Global.'" *Estudos Históricos* 30, no. 60 (janeiro-abril 2017): 187–202.

Margolis, Aaron. "La Otra Frontera: Exiles, Engineering, and State Power in the Chiapan Borderlands." PhD diss. University of Texas–El Paso, 2015.

Marshall, Jonathan. "The United Fruit Lobby: Revisiting Truman's Guatemala Policy." *Diplomatic History* 48, no. 1 (January 2024): 102–126.

Martin, James W. *Banana Cowboys: The United Fruit Company and the Culture of Corporate Colonialism*. University of New Mexico Press, 2018.

Masuda, Hajimu. *Cold War Crucible: The Korean Conflict and the Postwar World*. Harvard University Press, 2015.

Mawby, Spencer. *Ordering Independence: The End of Empire in the Anglophone Caribbean, 1947–69*. Palgrave Macmillan, 2012.

May, Robert E. *Manifest Destiny's Underworld: Filibustering in Antebellum America*. University of North Carolina Press, 2003.

Mayes, April J. *The Mulatto Republic: Class, Race, and Dominican National Identity*. University Press of Florida, 2014.

Mazower, Mark M. *No Enchanted Palace: The End of Empire and the Ideological Origins of the United Nations*. Princeton University Press, 2009.

McEvoy, Kevin John. "Before the Rubble: Britain's Secret Propaganda Offensive in Chile (1960–1973)." *Contemporary British History* 35, no. 4 (2021): 597–619.

McGarr, Paul M. "The Information Research Department, British Covert Propaganda, and the Sino-Indian War of 1962: Combating Communism and Courting Failure?" *International History Review* 41, no. 1 (2019): 130–156.

McKean, David. *Peddling Influence: Thomas "Tommy the Cork" Corcoran and the Birth of Modern Lobbying*. Steerforth, 2004.

McKercher, Asa. "Steamed Up: Domestic Politics, Congress, and Cuba, 1959–1963." *Diplomatic History* 38, no. 3 (2014): 599–627.

McPherson, Alan. "Afterword: The Paradox of Latin American Cold War Studies." In *Beyond the Eagle's Shadow: New Histories of Latin America's Cold War*, edited by Virginia Garrard-Burnett, Mark Atwood Lawrence, and Julio E. Moreno. University of New Mexico Press, 2013.

McPherson, Alan. *The Invaded: How Latin Americans and Their Allies Fought and Ended US Occupations*. Oxford University Press, 2014.

McSherry, J. Patrice. *Predatory States: Operation Condor and Covert War in Latin America*. Rowman & Littlefield, 2005.

Meers, Sharon I. "The British Connection: How the United States Covered Its Tracks in the 1954 Coup in Guatemala." *Diplomatic History* 16, no. 3 (1992): 409–428.

Mejía Flores, José Francisco, and Laura Beatriz Moreno Rodríguez. "El exilio costarricense en México en la década de 1940." *Cuadernos Americanos* 2, no. 152 (2015): 51–73.

Miller, Aragorn Storm. *Precarious Paths to Freedom: The United States, Venezuela, and the Latin American Cold War*. University of New Mexico Press, 2016.

Miller, Rory. *Britain and Latin America in the 19th and 20th Centuries*. Routledge, 1993.

Millett, Richard. *Guardians of the Dynasty: A History of the US Created Guardia Nacional de Nicaragua and the Somoza Family*. Orbis Books, 1977.

Mills, Thomas C., and Rory M. Miller, eds. *Britain and the Growth of US Hegemony in Twentieth-Century Latin America: Competition, Cooperation and Coexistence*. Palgrave Macmillan, 2020.

Molina Jiménez, Iván. *Anticomunismo reformista: Competencia electoral y cuestión social en Costa Rica (1931–1948)*. Editorial Costa Rica, 2007.

Molina Jiménez, Iván. "El resultado de las elecciones de 1948 en Costa Rica. Una revisión a la luz de nuevos datos." *Revista de Historia de América* 130 (2002): 57–96.

Mondolfi Gudat, Edgardo. *El día del atentado: El frustrado magnicidio contra Rómulo Betancourt*. Editorial Alfa, 2013.

Moulton, Aaron Coy. "Anticommunist Bananas: The United Fruit Company versus the Guatemalan Revolution." *Diplomatic History* 47, no. 3 (June 2023): 472–500.

Moulton, Aaron Coy. "Applying the Atlantic Charter to the Caribbean Basin: Antifascism and the 1944 Honduran Masacre Sampedrana." In *New Approaches to the History of Antifascism in Latin America*, edited by Sandra McGee Deutsch and Jorge Nallim. Cambridge University Press, forthcoming.

Moulton, Aaron Coy. "Becoming the Dictator's Agents: Dominican Counterintelligence in Mexico City and the Spanish Exiles' Sabotage of the 1949 Luperón Expedition," *Journal of Iberian and Latin American Research* 26, no. 2 (2020): 207–225.

Moulton, Aaron Coy. "Building Their Own Cold War in Their Own Backyard: The Transnational, International Conflicts in the Greater Caribbean Basin, 1944–1954." *Cold War History* 15, no. 2 (2015): 135–154.

Moulton, Aaron Coy. "The Counterrevolution's Patron: Rafael Trujillo versus Venezuela's Acción Democrática Governments." *Journal of Latin American Studies* 54, no. 1 (February 2022): 29–53.

Moulton, Aaron Coy. "Counterrevolutionary Friends: Caribbean Basin Dictators and Guatemalan Exiles Against the Guatemalan Revolution, 1945–50." *The Americas* 76, no. 1 (January 2019): 107–135.

Moulton, Aaron Coy. "El cuasi-bombardeo de Caracas en 1948: Dictadores, exiliados y proyectos contrarrevolucionarios propios." *Boletín de la Academia Nacional de la Historia* 53, no. 412 (octubre-diciembre 2020): 10–44.

Moulton, Aaron Coy. "The Dictators' Domino Theory: A Caribbean Basin Anticommunist Network, 1947–1952." *Intelligence and National Security* 34, no. 7 (2019): 945–961.

Moulton, Aaron Coy. "The Dominican Dictator's Funds and Guns in Costa Rica's Wars of 1948." *Journal of Military History* 85, no. 3 (July 2021): 713–733.

Moulton, Aaron Coy. "El frustrado bombardeo a la Ciudad de Guatemala: El General Federico Ponce y Rafael Trujillo en 1947." *Anales de la Academia de Geografía e Historia de Guatemala* 93 (2018): 151–176.

Moulton, Aaron Coy. "Guatemalan Exiles, Caribbean Basin Dictators, Operation PBFORTUNE, and the Transnational Counterrevolution Against the Guatemalan Revolution, 1944–1952." PhD diss. University of Arkansas, 2016.

Moulton, Aaron Coy. "'We Are Meddling': Anticolonialism and the British Cold War Against the Guatemalan Revolution, 1944–1954." *International History Review* 44, no. 5 (October 2021): 1108–1126.

Olander, Marcia. "Costa Rica in 1948: Cold War or Local War?" *The Americas* 52, no. 4 (April 1996): 465–493.

Oñate, Andrea. "The Red Affair: FMLN-Cuban Relations During the Salvadoran Civil War, 1981–92." *Cold War History* 11, no. 2 (May 2011): 133–154.

Oostindie, Gert, and Inge Klinkers. *Decolonising the Caribbean: Dutch Policies in a Comparative Perspective*. Amsterdam University Press, 2003.

Pach, Chester J., Jr. *Arming the Free World: The Origins of the United States Military Assistance Program, 1945–1950*. University of North Carolina Press, 1991.

Palmer, Colin A. *Cheddi Jagan and the Politics of Power: British Guiana's Struggle for Independence*. University of North Carolina Press, 2010.

Parker, Jason C. *Brother's Keeper: The United States, Race, and Empire in the British Caribbean, 1937–1962*. Oxford University Press, 2008.

Paulino, Edward. *Dividing Hispaniola: The Dominican Republic's Border Campaign Against Haiti, 1930–1961*. University of Pittsburgh Press, 2016.

Peguero, Valentina. *The Militarization of Culture in the Dominican Republic, from the Captains General to General Trujillo*. University of Nebraska Press, 2004.

Pérez, Louis A., Jr. *On Becoming Cuban: Identity, Nationality, and Culture*. University of North Carolina Press, 1999.

Perutka, Lukáš. "Arms for Árbenz: Czechoslovakia's Involvement in the Cold War in Latin America." *Central European Journal of International & Security Studies* 7, no. 3 (September 2013): 59–76.

Pettinà, Vanni. *Historia mínima de la Guerra Fría en América Latina*. El Colegio de México, 2018.

Pettinà, Vanni. "A Preponderance of Politics: The Auténtico Governments and US-Cuban Economic Relations, 1945–1951." *Journal of Latin American Studies* 46, no. 4 (November 2014): 723–753.

Pou García, Francis. "Movimientos conspirativos y el papel del exilio en la lucha antitrujillista." *Clío* 78, no. 177 (enero-junio 2009): 13–72.

Power, Margaret. "Who but a Woman? The Transnational Diffusion of Anticommunism Among Conservative Women in Brazil, Chile and the United States During the Cold War." *Journal of Latin American Studies* 47, no. 1 (February 2015): 93–119.

Pratt, Mary Louise. "Arts of the Contact Zone." *Profession* (1991): 33–40.

Pratt, Mary Louise. *Imperial Eyes: Travel Writing and Transculturation*. Routledge, 1992.

Pujals, Sandra. "¿Una perla en el Caribe Soviético?: Puerto Rico en los archivos de la Comintern en Moscú, 1921–1943." *Op. Cit.* 17 (2006–2007): 117–157.

Putnam, Lara. "The Transnational and the Text-Searchable: Digitized Sources and the Shadows They Cast." *American Historical Review* 121, no. 2 (April 2016): 377–402.

Quinn, Kate. *Black Power in the Caribbean*. University Press of Florida, 2014.

Rabe, Stephen G. "The Caribbean Triangle: Betancourt, Castro, and Trujillo and US Foreign Policy, 1958–1963." *Diplomatic History* 20, no. 1 (1996): 55–78.

Rabe, Stephen G. *Eisenhower and Latin America: The Foreign Policy of Anticommunism*. University of North Carolina Press, 1988.

Rabe, Stephen G. *The Killing Zone: The United States Wages Cold War in Latin America*. Oxford University Press, 2012.

Rabe, Stephen G. *US Intervention in British Guiana: A Cold War Story*. University of North Carolina Press, 2005.

Rankin, Monica A. *¡México, la patria!: Propaganda and Production During World War II*. University of Nebraska Press, 2009.

Reeves, Michelle Denise. "Extracting the Eagle's Talons: The Soviet Union in Cold War Latin America." PhD diss. University of Texas, 2014.

Renda, Mary A. *Taking Haiti: Military Occupation and the Culture of US Imperialism, 1915–1940*. University of North Carolina Press, 2001.

Rivas, Darlene. *Missionary Capitalist: Nelson Rockefeller in Venezuela*. University of North Carolina Press, 2002.

Roberts, Mary Louise. "The Transnationalization of Gender History." *History and Theory* 44, no. 3 (2005): 456–468.

Rock, David, ed. *Latin America in the 1940s: War and Postwar Transitions*. University of California Press, 1994.

Rodríguez de Ita, Guadalupe. *La participación política en la primavera guatemalteca: una aproximación a la historia de los partidos durante el periodo 1944–1954*. Universidad Autónoma de México, 2003.

Roniger, Luis. "Connected Histories, Power and Meaning: Transnational Forces in the Construction of Collective Identities." *Journal of Classical Sociology* 11, no. 3 (2011): 251–268.

Roniger, Luis. *Transnational Politics in Central America*. University Press of Florida, 2011.

Roniger, Luis, James N. Green, and Pablo Yankelevich. *Exile & the Politics of Exclusion in the Americas*. Sussex Academic Press, 2012.

Roorda, Eric Paul. *The Dictator Next Door: The Good Neighbor Policy and the Trujillo Regime in the Dominican Republic, 1930–1945*. Duke University Press, 1998.

Rothwell, Matthew D. *Transpacific Revolutionaries: The Chinese Revolution in Latin America*. Routledge, 2013.

Rout, Leslie B., Jr., and John F. Bratzel. *The Shadow War: German Espionage and United States Counterespionage in Latin America During World War II*. University Publications of America, 1986.

Rueda, Claudia. *Students of Revolution: Youth, Protest, and Coalition Building in Somoza-Era Nicaragua*. University of Texas Press, 2019.

Salcedo Ávila, Gustavo Enrique. "Conflictos en el Caribe: Eisenhower y Pérez Jiménez, historia de cooperación y enfrentamiento." *Revista Politeia* 48, no. 35 (2012): 33–62.

Salcedo Ávila, Gustavo Enrique. *Venezuela, campo de batalla de la Guerra Fría. Los Estados Unidos y la era de Rómulo Betancourt (1958–1964)*. Ediciones Nuevas, 2017.

Sargent, Daniel, Jonathan Haslam, Max Paul Friedman, and Hal Brands. "Online Roundtable: Hal Brands' *Latin America's Cold War*." *Journal of American Studies* 46, no. 1 (February 2012), https://www.cambridge.org/core/journals/journal-of-american-studies/article/abs/online-roundtable-hal-brands-latin-americas-cold-war-hal-brands-latin-americas-cold-war-cambridge-ma-harvard-university-press-2010-2180-pp-385-isbn978-0-674-05528-5/38F2B63ED92A1EE107DF74B1102A3296.

Savage, Sean J. "Truman in Historical, Popular, and Political Memory." In *A Companion to Harry S. Truman*, edited by Daniel S. Margolies. Blackwell, 2012.

Scarfi, Juan Pablo. *The Hidden History of International Law in the Americas*. Oxford University Press, 2017.

Schields, Chelsea. "Closer Ties: The Dutch Caribbean and the Aftermath of Empire, 1942–2012." PhD diss. City University of New York, 2017.

Schlesinger, Stephen, and Stephen Kinzer. *Bitter Fruit: The Story of the American Coup in Guatemala*. Rev. ed. Harvard University Press, David Rockefeller Center for Latin American Studies, 2005.

Schmitz, David F. *Thank God They're on Our Side: The United States & Right-Wing Dictatorships, 1921–1965*. University of North Carolina Press, 1999.

Schwartzberg, Steven. *Democracy and US Policy in Latin America During the Truman Years*. University Press of Florida, 2003.

Seigel, Micol. "Beyond Compare: Comparative Method After the Transnational Turn." *Radical History Review* 91 (2005): 62–90.

Sexton, Jay. *The Monroe Doctrine: Empire and Nation in Nineteenth-Century America*. Hill and Wang, 2011.

Shaw, Tony. "The Information Research Department of the British Foreign Office and the Korean War, 1950–53." *Journal of Contemporary History* 34, no. 2 (1999): 263–281.

Shoman, Assad. *Belize's Independence and Decolonization in Latin America: Guatemala, Britain, and the UN*. Palgrave Macmillan, 2010.

Siekmeier, James. *Aid, Nationalism, and Inter-American Relations: Guatemala, Bolivia, and the United States, 1945–1961*. Edwin Mellen, 1999.

Solano Muñoz, Edgar. "La república centroamericana en la visión de Salvador Mendieta y el Partido Unionista." *Revista de Historia de América* 141 (julio-diciembre 2009): 39–52.

Sotomayor, Antonio. *The Sovereign Colony: Olympic Sport, National Identity, and International Politics in Puerto Rico*. University of Nebraska Press, 2016.

Spenser, Daniela. *In Combat: The Life of Lombardo Toledano*. Haymarket Books, 2020.

Spenser, Daniela. *The Impossible Triangle: Mexico, Soviet Russia, and the United States in the 1920s*. Duke University Press, 1999.

Spenser, Daniela. "Standing Conventional Cold War History on Its Head." In Joseph, LeGrand, and Salvatore, *Close Encounters of Empire*.

Stites Mor, Jessica. *Human Rights and Transnational Solidarity in Cold War Latin America*. University of Wisconsin Press, 2013.

Streeter, Stephen M. *Managing the Counterrevolution: The United States and Guatemala, 1954–1961*. Ohio University Center for International Studies, 2000.

Striffler, Steve, and Mark Moberg. *Banana Wars: Power, Production, and History in the Americas*. Duke University Press, 2003.

Sullivan-González, Douglass. *The Black Christ of Esquipulas: Religion and Identity in Guatemala*. University of Nebraska Press, 2016.

Taracena Arriola, Arturo. *Guatemala, la República Española y el Gobierno Vasco en el exilio (1944–1954)*. Universidad Nacional Autónoma de México y el Colegio de Michoacán, 2017.

Teelucksingh, Jerome. *Labour and the Decolonization Struggle in Trinidad and Tobago*. Palgrave Macmillan, 2015.

Tillman, Ellen D. *Dollar Diplomacy by Force: Nation-Building and Resistance in the Dominican Republic*. University of North Carolina Press, 2016.

Trenta, Luca, Kevin T. Fahey, and Douglas B. Atkinson. "Secrecy and the Politics of Selective Disclosures: The US Government's Intervention in Guatemala." *Intelligence and National Security* 39, no. 4 (2023): 1–20.

Turits, Richard Lee. *Foundations of Despotism: Peasants, the Trujillo Regime, and Modernity in Dominican History.* Stanford University Press, 2003.

van den Berk, Jorrit. *Becoming a Good Neighbor Among Dictators: The US Foreign Service in Guatemala, El Salvador, and Honduras.* Palgrave Macmillan, 2018.

Vaughan, James. "'Cloak Without Dagger': How the Information Research Department Fought Britain's Cold War in the Middle East, 1948–56." *Cold War History* 4, no. 3 (2004): 56–84.

Vázquez García, Humberto. *La expedición de Cayo Confites.* 2nd ed. Archivo General de la Nación y Editorial Oriente, 2014.

Vázquez Medeles, Juan Carlos. "'El caso de Guatemala': doctrina y praxis de la delegación guatemalteca en el I Congreso Anticomunista Latinoamericano." *Latinoamérica. Revista de Estudios Latinoamericanos* 73, no. 2 (julio-diciembre 2021): 11–39.

Vázquez Medeles, Juan Carlos. "La presencia guatemalteca en los Congresos anticomunistas latinoamericanos (1954–1980)." *Cuadernos Intercambio sobre Centroamérica y el Caribe* 17, no. 2 (2020): 20–48.

Vega, Bernardo. *Un interludio de tolerancia: el acuerdo de Trujillo con los comunistas en 1946.* Fundación Cultural Dominicana, 1987.

Vela Castañeda, Manolo E. "Guatemala, 1954: las ideas de la contrarrevolución." *Foro Internacional* 45, no. 1 (marzo 2005): 89–114.

Véliz Estrada, Rodrigo. "'El más importante asunto internacional': Belice, el Imperio británico y la política exterior guatemalteca en la posguerra (1945–1948)." *Anuario de Estudios Centroamericanos* 46 (2020): 1–38.

Verna, Chantalle F. *Haiti and the Uses of America: Post-US Occupation Promises.* Rutgers University Press, 2017.

Vrana, Heather. *This City Belongs to You: A History of Student Activism in Guatemala, 1944–1996.* University of California Press, 2017.

Walcher, Dustin, Mark T. Gilderhus, Tanya Harmer, et al. "Review of *Latin America's Cold War* by Hal Brands." *H-Diplo* 12, no. 27 (2011), https://issforum.org/roundtables/PDF/Roundtable-XII-27.pdf.

Walker, William O., III. "Crucial for Peace: Herbert Hoover, Modernization, and Economic Growth in Latin America." *Diplomatic History* 30, no. 1 (January 2006): 83–117.

Walter, Knut. *The Regime of Anastasio Somoza.* University of North Carolina Press, 1993.

Walton, Calder. *Empire of Secrets: British Intelligence, the Cold War, and the Twilight of Empire.* Abrams Press, 2013.

Weld, Kirsten. *Paper Cadavers: The Archives of Dictatorship in Guatemala.* Duke University Press, 2014.

Weld, Kirsten. "The Other Door: Spain and the Guatemalan Counterrevolution, 1944–54." *Journal of Latin American Studies* 51, no. 2 (2019): 307–331.

Weld, Kirsten. "The Spanish Civil War and the Construction of a Reactionary Historical Consciousness in Augusto Pinochet's Chile." *Hispanic American Historical Review* 98, no. 1 (2018): 77–115.

Wells, Allen. *Tropical Zion: General Trujillo, FDR, and the Jews of Sosua.* Duke University Press, 2009.

Wilford, Hugh. "The Information Research Department: Britain's Secret Cold War Weapon Revealed." *Review of International Studies* 24, no. 3 (1998): 353–369.

Wood, Bryce. *The Dismantling of the Good Neighbor Policy*. University of Texas Press, 1985.

Wood, Bryce. *The Making of the Good Neighbor Policy*. Columbia University Press, 1961.

Young, John W. "Great Britain's Latin American Dilemma: The Foreign Office and the Overthrow of 'Communist' Guatemala, June 1954." *International History Review* 8, no. 4 (1986): 573–592.

Zumoff, J. A. "Ojos que no ven: The Communist Party, Caribbean Migrants, and the Communist International in Costa Rica in the 1920s and 1930s." *Journal of Caribbean History* 45, no. 2 (2011): 212–247.

Index

abaca, 105, 108
El abrazo de la muerte, 15
Acción Democrática, 43, 97–8; in exile, 97, 127–8, 161, 180
Acheson, Dean, 115, 136–7, 141
Africa, 184
Aguiluz, Marcial, 87–8
Aikman, Duncan, 124–5
air-bomb plots, 49, 62–4, 79–80
Alabama, 106
Alaska, 54
Alfhem, 172–5, 184–5
Alianza Femenina Guatemalteca, 38
Alianza Popular Revolucionaria Americana, 32
Allen, Richard, 185–7
Allende, Salvador, 183
Almirante, 66
Alonso, Cruz, 76–7
Amaya de García, Graciela, 21
América contra Trujillo, 20
American Legion, 158, 166–7
Amigos de la URSS, 129
Antigua, 45
Anzueto, Roderico, 30, 47, 49, 52–3, 55, 99
Arana, Francisco Javier, 30, 47, 61, 65, 72, 80, 100

Archila Obregón, Marco Antonio, 50–2, 71, 128, 188
Arciniegas, Germán, 179
Ardón Fernández, José Enrique, 98, 103, 130, 156
Arenas, José Luis, 103–4, 119, 129–30, 156–61, 177, 183
Arévalo visto por América, 32
Arévalo-Yakubovsky forgery, 70–2, 110, 130, 188
Argentina, 32, 35, 51, 75, 107, 156, 179
Argüello, Leonardo, 12, 18, 39, 43, 78
Argüello, Rosendo, 76, 78, 81, 83, 87
Arkansas, 162
arms embargoes, 110, 117–8, 172–5, 186
Armstrong, J. P., 67
Arroyo Maldonado, José, 127
Artículo 32, 120–3
Arvelo, Tulio, 40, 76
Así se gestó la liberación, 182–3
Asia, 110, 188
Asociación de Estudiantes Hispanoamericanos, 20
Asociación de Estudiantes Universitarios, 30–1, 34
Asociación Mexicana Pro Francia, 25

Index

Asociación Reivindicadora Dominicana del Exilio, 10, 19, 35, 44
Atlantic Charter, 13, 17–9, 21–4, 28, 36–8, 42
Ávila, Florencio, 159

Báez, Mauricio, 76, 129
Báez Bone, Adolfo, 1, 12, 83, 87, 161
Balaguer, Joaquín, 99, 180–1
Baltimore Sun, 174
banana, 68, 104–5, 107–8, 164, 168, 190
banana republic, 16, 37
Barrios Peña, Roberto, 120, 138–9, 143–4, 151, 154–6, 160, 171, 183, 188
Barton, Bruce, 105, 108
Batista, Fulgencio, 127–8, 145, 154–5, 178–80
Batten, Barton, Durstine & Osborn, 104–5
Bay of Pigs, 180, 188
Beals, Carleton, 15, 20
Belgium, 174
Belize / British Honduras, 36, 38, 68–70, 83, 110, 173, 186; as location for plots, 54, 118, 143
Bennett, Charles E., 169–70
Bernardino, Félix W., 129, 143–4
Bernays, Edward, 104, 126, 162–7, 172, 174, 188, 190
Biblioteca Nacional (Mexico), 15
Blanco, Andrés Eloy, 20
Blood in the Streets, 14
Bolívar, Simón, 19, 41–2, 44
Bordas, Diego, 76
Bográn, Graciela, 17, 23, 36
Boletín (CEUAGE), 154
Boletín: Emigración Democrática de Guatemala, 51
Bonilla, Emma, 21
Bosch, Juan, 14, 36, 44, 73–5, 77, 82, 97, 180
Boston, 89, 106, 134, 167, 190
Braden, Spruille, 35, 38, 132
Brazil, 158, 183–4
Bruce, David, 139–40, 149
Buffalo Evening News, 162
Butler, John Marshall, 174

Cabot, John Moors, 164, 166, 184
Cabot, Thomas, 107
Cahn, Julius, 156, 164–7, 169
Calderón Guardia, Francisco, 84, 91
Calderón Guardia, Rafael Ángel, 81–92, 161
Calderón Salazar, José, 53, 57, 98, 157, 159, 183
California, 162, 167
Cámara de Diputados (Mexico), 15
Canfield, Gordon, 174
Caracas, 44, 79–80, 110–1, 145, 147, 170, 180
Cardenal, Ernesto, 46, 181

Cardenal, Luis G., 1
Cárdenas, Lázaro, 51
Cardoza y Aragón, Luis, 29–32, 70–1, 93
Castillo Ibarra, Carlos, 34, 45, 87
Castro, Fidel, 6, 75, 77, 179–80
Castro, José R., 13, 25, 32, 39, 77
Catholicism, 51–2, 57, 81, 98, 106, 119–21
Cayo Confites, 74–8, 80–1, 84, 179
Ceballos, Carlos Humberto, 98
Chamorro, Emiliano, 78, 87
Chamorro, Pedro Joaquín, 1
Charnaud MacDonald, Augusto, 44
Chiang Kai-Shek, 188
Chiapas, 50, 188
Chibás, Eduardo, 75
Chicago Daily News, 174
Chile, 183
Chimaltenango, 45
China, 105–6, 108, 164, 185, 188–9
Chiquita, 104, 190
Churchill, Winston, 17, 19–21, 185
El Ciudadano, 111
Clements, John A., 189
Cleveland Plain Dealer, 162
Club Femenino ProUnión, 34
Club Terraza, 136
coconut, 105
coffee, 50, 117, 167–71
Collver, Nathalia Swanson, 167
Colombia, 106–8, 128, 143–5, 163, 179, 183–4
El Colombiano, 163
Colonial Office, 186
Comayagüela, 22, 25
Comité Anticomunista de Estudiantes de Ciencias Comerciales, 122
Comité Central Anticomunista Femenino, 122
Comité Cívico Nacional, 120–3, 133, 138–9, 143
Comité Cubano Pro Liberación de Honduras, 20
Comité de Ayuda a los Exiliados Guatemaltecos, 53, 65
Comité de Ayuda al Pueblo Español, 19
Comité de Defensa Patria, 52, 71
Comité de Estudiantes Universitarios Anticomunistas, 120–3, 133, 156–7, 173, 183, 186
Comité de Estudiantes Universitarios Anticomunistas Guatemaltecos en Exilio, 154, 157
Comité de Unidad de la Emigración Guatemalteca, 50, 98
Comité Femenino ProUnión Centroamericana, 34

Comité Liberal Demócrata de Honduras, 18, 25, 31, 41
Comité Patriótico Guatemalteco, 53, 57, 71
Comité Patriótico Nicaragüense, 45
Comité Pro Liberación de Guatemala, 129–30
Comité Proliberación de Presos Políticos, 21
Comité Revolucionario Nicaragüense, 39, 46
Communism in Latin America, 163
La Confabulación Nazifascista y Comunistoide Revolucionaria en América, 51
Confederación de Trabajadores de América Latina, 20, 31, 45, 129
Confederación de Trabajadores de Cuba, 19
Confederación de Trabajadores de Guatemala, 34
Conferencia Interamericana sobre Problemas de la Guerra y de la Paz, 15, 42
Congressional Record, 125, 165, 190
Connecticut, 170
Consejo Supremo del Movimiento Revolucionario Anticomunista, 103, 130
Convención Nacional Anticomunista, 120–2
Corcoran, Thomas, 105–9, 111–2, 117, 125–6, 133, 140, 164, 189–90
Cordero Reyes, Manuel, 12, 16
Córdoba Boniche, José Félix, 178
Córdova Cerna, Juan, 50, 133, 139, 143–4, 154–5, 183, 187
Coronado Lira, Luis, 49–55, 61–2, 71–2, 98, 102, 157–60, 177, 183, 186–7
Costa Rican Civil War, 81–90, 92–3, 106–7
Costa Rican 1948 Invasion, 88–92
Costa Rican 1955 Invasion, 178
Cuadra, Abelardo, 76
Cuadra Pasos, Carlos, 12, 15–6, 18, 46, 77, 87
Cuban Revolution, 6, 180
Curaçao, 36
Cutter, Victor, 66–7
Cyprus, 184
Czechoslovakia, 129, 172–4

d'Olwer, Luis Nicolau, 93–4
The Daily Telegraph, 172
The Daily Worker, 172
Dallas Morning News, 165, 174
Dávila Córdova, Guillermo, 103
Davis, James C., 170
Davis, Nathaniel, 89
Dawson, William A., 169
Defense Department, 136
Delgado, Jorge Isaac, 171–2
Delgado, Ramón, 61
El Demócrata, 60
Denny, Ludwell, 124–6

Diario de Centro América, 116, 171
Diario Latino (El Salvador), 71
Díaz, José Gregorio, 60
Díaz, Juan, 39
Díaz Lozano, Argentina, 21
Díaz Medrano, Teodoro, 60
Dirección Federal de Seguridad, 50
Dirección General de Investigaciones Políticas y Sociales, 12, 15, 50–1, 129–30
Dirksen, Everett, 109, 126
Droguería Nacional (Honduras), 23–4
Dulles, Allen, 112, 139–42, 146, 149, 153, 158–9, 168, 186
Dulles, John Foster, 158, 161, 170, 184–5, 190

Eastern Europe, 55, 96, 172
economic reform, 18, 30–3, 38, 42, 51–2
Egypt, 173, 184
Eisenhower, Dwight D., 153, 158, 167, 170, 173, 184–5, 189–91
Ellender, Allen, 116
Ellis, Esperanza, 17
Ellis Cambiaso, Gerardo, 17
Ellis Guerra, Gerardo, 17
La Época, 18, 21, 48, 72
Erwin, John, 48, 146
Escuintla, 121
La Esfera, 163
Esquipulas, 98
Estimé, Dumarsais, 75, 218n5
Europe, 9–11, 59, 66, 174, 184–5; Cold War in, 89, 105; colonial influence, 15, 36–7, 83; fascism, 18–9, 29

Falange, 19, 38, 45
Federación Estudiantil Universitaria, 20, 45, 75, 181
Federal Bureau of Investigation, 13, 47–8, 79
Fernández, Eufemio, 75–6
Figueres, José, 76, 81–93, 106–7, 127–8, 142, 161, 178, 180
Fitzgibbon, Russell H., 164
Florida, 64, 106
Folsom, Victor, 67
Forbes, W. Cameron, 67
Ford, Gerald R., Jr, 170
Foreign Office, 68–70, 110–1, 114, 117–23, 151, 173, 184–7
Fortuny, José Manuel, 45, 100, 166, 168
Four Freedoms, 17–8, 22, 28, 43, 45
France, 25, 36, 172, 174, 184–7
Franco, Francisco, 19–20, 29, 32–5, 38–9, 67, 69, 189
Franco, Persio Celeste, 9
Frankfurter Allgemeine, 185

Index

The Freeman, 162
French Guiana, 36, 83
Frente Anticomunista de Guatemaltecos en Exilio, 157
Frente de Unidad Revolucionario Hondureña, 87
Frente Democrático Dominicano, 44
Frente Democrático Revolucionario Hondureño, 18, 31–3, 36, 40–2, 45
Frente Nacional Democrático de Guatemala, 52, 60–1
Frente Popular Anticomunista de México, 103, 129–30, 157, 159–60, 187
Frente Unido de Liberación Dominicana, 44
Funes, Ángel, 23, 203–4n111

Galich, Manuel, 30
Galíndez, Jesús, 180
Gallienne, William H., 109–10, 123–4, 151
Gálvez, Juan Manuel, 23–4, 88, 93, 138–9, 146, 160–1, 203–4n111
García Bauer, José, 32
Germany, 16, 18–9, 185
Goicolea Villacorta, Domingo, 122, 186, 231n61
Goldwater, Barry, 174
Gómez, Máximo, 20, 42, 76
Gómez Robelo, Amílcar, 16, 19, 24–6, 35, 37–8, 40–1, 46
Good Neighbor Policy, 11, 16–7, 35, 37–8, 115
Gran Manifestación, 122–4
Grau San Martín, Ramón, 74–5, 77, 87
Great Depression, 11–2, 18, 29
Green, Theodore, Francis, 126, 164
Guanacaste, 90, 92
Guardia Nacional (Nicaragua), 11–2, 48, 84
Guatemala, 1950 elections, 99–104, 110–2, 115; Agrarian Reform, 134, 163–4, 166–7, 169, 172, 182; Base Militar attack, 103–4, 130, 154; constitutional suspensions, 60–5, 70, 102, 120, 122, 155; Labor Code, 31, 38, 49, 67–8, 105–9; local elections, 65
Guatemala bajo el signo rojo, 53, 71
Guatemala City, 30–1, 48–9, 62–5, 78, 124
"Guatemala News Notes," 162–3, 166, 174
Guatemalan Army and military, 32; role in coup plots, 47–9, 61; versus antigovernment plots, 49, 154; Guardia Civil, 64, 102; importance in coup plots, 58–9, 62, 80, 98–9, 100, 103–4, 160; Junta Nacional Electoral, 102
Guatemalan Communism Endangers the Americas, 163

Guevara, Ernesto, 179
Guillén, Nicolás, 20
Guiteras, Antonio, 45
gunrunners, 50, 63–4
Gutiérrez, Víctor Manuel, 100, 124, 168
Guyana/British Guiana, 36, 83

Haiti, 11, 14, 17, 75, 180, 218n5
Harrison, Burr P., 169
Hearst Press, 106
Heliodoro Valle, Rafael, 13, 18, 22, 29, 31–3, 38–9, 46, 88; as Honduran ambassador, 136
hemp, 105, 108
Henríquez, Enrique Cotubanamá, 20, 42
Henríquez, Federico, 76
Herrera, Manuel María, 60
Herter, Christian A., 108
Hickenlooper, Bourke B., 106, 126, 164, 166–70, 190
Hicks, Albert, 14
Hidalgo, Miguel, 19
Hill, Lister, 106, 108
Hillings, Patrick J., 174
Hirschfield, Mary, 162
Hiss, Alger, 168
La historia del hombre que se proclamó igual a Dios, 14–5
Hitler, Adolf, 13, 17–20, 22, 25, 29, 35–6
Ho Chi Minh, 163
Holland, Henry, 189
Homenaje a las Víctimas de San Pedro Sula, 25
Hoover, Herbert, 11
La Hora, 64, 116, 118, 134, 162
La Hora Dominical, 116
Hotel Majestic, 136
Hotel San Luis, 76
House of Commons, 173, 185
House Committee on Foreign Affairs, 107
The Houston Post, 174
How an American Company, Through Advertising and Public Relations, Has Combatted Communism in Latin America, 190
Huixtla, 50
human rights, 24, 35, 45, 96
Hungary, 163
Hunt, Lester C., 170

El Impacto, 118, 134, 162
El Imparcial, 31, 35, 61, 64
Incháustegui Cabral, Héctor, 143–4
Independence Day (July 4), 13, 21–3
Información, 163
Information Research Department, 110–1, 114, 118–21, 123, 134, 151, 186

intellectuals, 15, 24–5, 29–30, 32, 34
intelligence sharing, 78–81, 90, 97–9, 127–8, 142, 144–5
Inter-American Treaty of Reciprocal Assistance, 57, 64, 115
Intercambio Cultural Mexicano-Ruso, 129
International Railways of Central America, 37–8, 50, 67, 106, 121, 125
Intervention of International Communism in Guatemala, 190
La intriga roja en Guatemala, 183
Iowa, 169
Irías, Alejandro, 23–4
Iron Curtain, 96, 172–4
Italy, 16, 18–9, 167, 173

Jackson, Donald L., 106–7
Japan, 16, 18–9, 28
Javits, Jacob, 172
Jiménes Grullón, Juan Isidro, 44, 74, 93, 178
Johnson, Lyndon B., 174
Juárez, Benito, 19
Julian, Hubert, 118, 173
Justice Department, 190–1
Juventud Liberal de Guatemala, 51, 54
Juventud Liberal Hondureña, 25
Juventud Nacionalista, 101–2

Kenya, 173
King, J. C., 133, 142, 149–50
Korean War, 112, 115, 174, 185
Krause, Karl Christian Friedrich, 31
Kremlin, 67, 116, 120, 168–9, 174

La Follette, Robert, Jr, 106, 109, 116, 125–6
labor, workers, and unions, 19–21, 29–30, 34, 38, 51, 66–7, 76, 81; fears of communist infiltration in, 51–2, 68, 70, 107
Lacayo, Chester, 46
LaCrosse Register, 165
Landestoy, Carmita, 14
Lantaff, William C., 168
Larreta, Eduardo Rodríguez, 35
Larreta Doctrine, 35
Lawrence, David, 105
Leal, Pablo, 1, 161
Lecours, Emile, 110–1, 118–23, 143–4, 151
Legión Caribe, 86–8, 90, 92–3, 97–8, 163; British concerns of, 110–1; Castillo Armas regime targeting of, 177–8; reactionaries' concerns of, 156, 160; regimes as reverse of, 147; US concerns of, 115
Legion of Merit, 136

Lenin, Vladimir, 156, 172
Lewis, Fulton, Jr, 168–70, 188
Liberación con sangre, sacrificios y heroísmo, 183
Liga Anticomunista Escuintleca, 121
Lima (Ohio), 165
Lissner, Will, 162
Liverpool, 185
Lodge, Henry Cabot, Jr, 108
Lombardo Toledano, Vicente, 12, 20, 29, 45; British opposition to, 70; Costa Rican reactionaries' opposition to, 90; dictators' opposition to, 51, 58, 88; Guatemalan reactionaries' opposition to, 51–2, 54, 57, 103, 120, 156, 160, 186; UFCO opposition to, 67; US opposition to, 124, 165, 168
London, 59, 185–7
Lucas, Wingate, 169

Madden, Ray, 174
Mainardi Reyna, Virgilio, 76, 83
Managua, 48, 84, 91–2, 136–7, 141, 149, 161, 171
Mann, Thomas, 111–2, 115–9, 132, 134, 137, 139–40, 146–50
Manning, Frances Duncan, 67
Manrique Ríos, Adán, 50
Mansfield, Mike, 106–9, 125, 163, 169, 189
Mara, Cornelius, 135, 137–42, 146–7, 150
En Marcha, 18
Marroquín Rojas, Clemente, 29–30, 116, 118, 134
Marshall, George, 106
Martí, José, 19–20, 41–2
Martin, Joseph W., Jr, 125–6
Martínez, Maximiliano Hernández, 25, 31, 37
Masacre Sampedrana, 21, 23–5, 32, 76, 88, 183
Masferrer, Rolando, 75–6
Massachusetts, 124–5
Matthews, H. Freeman, 116, 141
Mau Mau, 173
May Day, 32, 38, 69, 163
McCarthy, Joseph, 112, 156, 168, 174, 189
McClain, Elmore, 165
McCormack, John, 106, 108–9, 116–7, 125–6, 164, 166, 190
McGinnis, Edward, 167
McNamara, William, 165
Mediodía, 24, 31, 50
Melgar de la Cerda, Manuel, 50, 98–9, 103
Memphis Democrat, 174
Mendieta, Salvador, 33, 37, 81

288   Index

El Mercurio, 60
Mexican Revolution, 38, 51
Meza, Juan José, 19, 29, 46, 76, 81, 87, 178
Miami, 79
Miami Herald, 174
Middle East, 110, 173, 184
Miller, Edward G., Jr, 112, 114–7, 126, 132, 134–42, 145–50
Milwaukee, 165
Minnesota, 170
Molina, Marco Antonio, 99–100
Moncada Barracks, 179
Le Monde, 185
Monroe Doctrine, 11, 38, 112, 174, 185
Montana, 169
Monthly Review, 167
Monumento a la Independencia (Mexico), 15
Morales, Ángel, 10, 14
Morales, Baltazar, 118
Morazán, Francisco (exile), 31, 45, 83, 87
Morazán, Francisco (Central American figure), 22, 33, 41–2
Morones, Luis, 103
Morton, Thruston B., 170
Moscow, 71, 100, 118, 124–5, 129, 156, 165, 169
Movimiento Socialista Revolucionario, 45, 75
Mundt, Karl, 156
Muñoz Marín, Luis, 96
Mussolini, Benito, 13, 18, 22, 25, 29, 35, 67
Mutual Defense Assistance Program, 141, 147

La Nación, 14
El Nacional, 60
Nashville Banner, 165
National Fund for the Prevention of Infantile Paralysis, 14
Nazism and Nazis, 13–4, 17–20, 24, 30, 35, 43, 47; with communism, 51–2, 54, 67
Netherlands, 36, 174
New York, 20, 44, 74, 106, 129, 162
New York City, 129, 141, 180–1
New York Daily News, 163
New York Herald Tribune, 90, 164, 171, 174
The New York Times, 126, 162, 164, 171
The Newark Star-Ledger, 174
Newsweek, 125–6
Ninth International Conference of American States, 106
Nixon, Richard, 156, 180
El Norte, 32
North Korea, 157

Novedades, 48, 60, 72, 127, 163
Nuestro Diario, 173

O'Higgins, Bernardo, 19
Office of the Coordinator of Inter-American Affairs, 17
Ohio, 158, 165
Ohmans, John, 137–8, 147
Operation PBHISTORY, 189
Orden al Mérito Juan Pablo Duarte, 136
Orden del Quetzal, 44
Ordóñez Argüello, Alberto, 12, 25, 32, 34, 45, 81–2
Organization of American States, 92, 137, 180, 184; Inter-American Peace Committee, 184–5
Ornes, Horacio, 42, 45–6, 77, 83, 86, 93, 178–9
Ornes, Pericles Franco, 44

Pacto del Caribe, 78, 81–2, 86–7
Padilla, Visitación, 21
Padilla y Padilla, Carlos, 47–50, 52–5, 60–1, 130, 135–6, 183, 188
Paiz Herrera, Federico, 122
Panama, 66, 130, 147–8, 150, 159, 171, 180
Panama Canal, 54, 67–8
Parliament, 185
Parque La Libertad, 22
Partido Acción Nacional, 60
Partido Acción Revolucionaria, 45, 100, 102
Partido Comunista Mexicano, 129
Partido Conservador (Nicaragua), 78, 87
Partido Constitucional Democrático, 60
Partido de Unión Democrática, 101
Partido del Pueblo Cubano, 75
Partido Dominicano, 14
Partido Liberal Independiente, 78
Partido Liberal Nacional (Nicaragua), 40, 87
Partido Nacional de Trabajadores, 60
Partido Renovación Nacional, 45, 64, 100
Partido Revolucionario Cubano-Auténtico, 20, 74–8, 87, 93, 127; in exile, 127–8, 161, 180
Partido Revolucionario Dominicano, 14, 18, 20, 74
Partido Socialista Revolucionario, 34
Partido Unificación Anticomunista, 101–2, 119, 121–2
Partido Unionista Centroamericano, 16, 18, 33–4
Paz y Paz, Alberto, 31
Pearson, Drew, 135–6
Pennsylvania, 162
Pepper, Claude, 106, 108

Peraza, José Antonio, 23, 43
Pérez Jiménez, Marcos, 97, 145–6, 150, 154, 161, 178, 180
Perón, Juan, 35, 51, 75
Peru, 32, 234n6
Petersburg Progress-Index, 165
Philadelphia Inquirer, 174
Phoenix Republic, 174
Picado, Teodoro, 81–5
Pine Bluff Commercial, 162
Pinillos, Juan, 50, 52, 55–6, 58, 101, 157, 161, 187
Pioneer Letter Company, 167
Pivaral, Ovidio, 50–1
Plan de Tegucigalpa, 157
Plaza Morazán, 22
Point IV, 105, 107–9
Poland, 55, 129, 163, 174
Ponce, Federico, 30, 34, 50–4, 62–5, 71, 79–81, 128, 155, 157
Por la unidad americana, 15
La Prensa (Mexico), 60, 129
Prensa Libre (Guatemala), 171
Prieto Laurens, Jorge, 103, 129–30, 159–60, 187
Primer Congreso Contra la Intervención Soviética en América Latina, 158–61
Prío Socarrás, Carlos, 73, 87, 91, 93, 127
Puebla, 99
Puerto Barrios, 65, 68
Puerto Cabezas, 79, 90, 92, 141
Puerto Limón, 84
Puerto Rico, 11, 44, 74, 83, 96

Quetzal, 52
Quetzaltenango, 34
quinine, 105
Quisqueya Libre, 9, 14, 18–20, 25, 35

racism, 66–7, 124, 149–50
radio, 19, 25, 52, 60–1, 64–5, 121–3, 158, 168–9, 183
Radiografía del Complot, 50
Ramírez, Arturo, 47, 49, 52–3, 55–60, 71, 99–100, 103–4, 133, 156, 159, 188
Ramírez, Miguel Ángel, 40–2, 74, 76–7, 83, 86–7, 127, 177–8
Reader's Digest, 106–7
Reconciliación Democrática Nacional, 101–3
Redemption in Guatemala, 188
Remón, José Antonio, 147–8
Report on Guatemala, 163
Requena, Andrés, 10, 19, 129
Ribas, Sandra, 181

Ribas Montes, Jorge, 1–2, 21–2, 42, 76–7, 83, 87, 114, 161, 181
Rindlaub, Jean Wade, 104
Río de Janeiro Conference (1942), 29
Río de Janeiro Conference (1947), 57, 64
Rodríguez, Juan, 74–8, 82–3, 86, 178
Rodríguez Demorizi, Emilio, 142, 144–5
Rogers, Walter, 174
Romania, 55
Roosevelt, Eleanor, 17
Roosevelt, Franklin Delano, 11–4, 16–22, 30, 38, 105
Ross, Stanley, 163
Rowe, James, 125
rubber, 105, 108
Rushdie, Salman, 1

Sáenz, Vicente, 16, 18–9, 29, 33–4, 37, 39, 46
Salamá, 154–5, 167
Salazar, Carlos, hijo, 50, 72, 98, 102, 128, 130, 154–5, 157–9, 183, 187
San Antonio Light, 174
San Diego Union, 174
San Isidro, 83
San José, 87, 92
San Martín, José, 19
San Pedro Sula, 18, 23–5, 32, 88
Sánchez, Francisco, 83, 87
Sánchez Arango, Aureliano, 127
Sandinista movement, 181
Sandino, Augusto, 11, 15, 41–2, 51, 76, 181
Santo Domingo/Ciudad Trujillo, 15, 59, 85, 91, 111
Scripps-Howard Newspaper Alliance, 124
Secretaría de Propaganda y Divulgación, 171, 182, 186, 249n2
Seekford, Jacob R., 142, 150
Seely-Brown, Horace, 170
Segundo Congreso Contra la Intervención Soviética, 187
Seguridad Pública, 12, 219n47
Senate Foreign Relations Committee, 126, 156, 165–6
Senate Resolution 211, 170
Senate Special Subcommittee on Security Affairs, 162
Senate Subcommittee on Latin American Affairs, 126
Sevilla Sacasa, Guillermo, 78–80, 85, 89, 141, 147–9
Sheboygan Press, 165
Sikes, Robert L. F., 174
Simmons, Carlos, 123, 139, 143–4, 151, 154–5, 231n74

Smith, Gerald L. K., 135
Smith, Margaret Chase, 170
Smith, Walter Bedell, 139, 149, 153
social security, 31, 81
Sociedad de Amigos de Guatemala, 163, 171, 175
Sociedad de Obreros "La Fraternidad," 32
Soler, Amado, 76, 84, 161
Sokolsky, George, 105, 108
Somoza, Anastasio "Tachito," 1, 143, 145, 148
Sosa, Guillermo, 120
Southeast Asia, 110, 188
Soviet submarines, 129, 163
Spain, 19, 35, 45, 124
Spanish Civil War, 75–6
Spanish exiles, 19–20, 34, 69, 76, 93–4
Spanish-American-Cuban-Filipino War, 11
Spellman, Francis, 106, 226–7n74
spiritual socialism, 31, 40
Stalin, Joseph, 19–20, 107, 120, 125
Standard Oil, 38
Strength of the International Communist Movement, 162
Strong, Anna Louise, 167
Suriname / Surinam, 36
Sweden, 71, 172, 184
Switzerland, 173

Taillon, William L., 67–8, 106
Tapachula, 50–1
Tegucigalpa, 21–3, 25, 48, 50, 55, 58, 92, 101, 104, 144, 157
Tennessee, 165
Tenth Inter-American Conference, 152, 157–9, 170
teoría de los dos demonios, 6
Tercero, José María, 77, 83, 87
Texas, 64, 165, 169, 174, 190
Thomen, Luis, 78, 145–6, 149
Thorning, Joseph Francis, 189
Thurston, Walter, 63–4
Tijerino, Toribio, 77–8, 87
Time, 125, 171
The Times, 185
Tiquisate, 37
Tomlinson, Edward, 107, 116, 158, 163–5, 171
Topeka State Journal, 174
Toriello, Guillermo, 158, 166
Toriello, Jorge, 30
Torres, Edelberto, 30, 87, 178
La tragedia dominicana, 44
"Tres Heroés," 42
La Tribuna de la libertad, 52, 71
Tribunal Nacional Electoral, 82
Trinidad, 36
Truman Doctrine, 69
Tunisia, 184

Ulate, Otilio, 82–3
Umansky, Konstantin, 51
Unión Democrática Centroamericana, 15–6, 18, 21, 29, 31, 33, 46, 76, 88
Unión Democrática Hondureña, 18
Unión Democrática Nacional de Guatemala, 52
Unión Democrática Nicaragüense, 18
Unión Femenina ProDefensa de la Libertad de Guatemala, 32
Unión Popular Revolucionaria Guatemalteca, 52
Unión Revolucionaria Nicaragüense, 20
unionism of Central America, 15–6, 33–4, 37–9, 81, 109
United Nations, 17–9, 21, 24, 30, 72, 137, 163; and colonialism, 69, 184; and Francisco Franco, 19, 34; and Guatemalan reactionaries, 53, 55, 64; and 1954 coup, 183–6; and Universal Declaration of Human Rights, 122, 154
El Universal (Mexico), 57, 129, 158, 163
El Universal (Venezuela), 163
Universidad de San Carlos, 30, 34, 36
Universidad Nacional Autónoma de México, 20
Universitarios Anticomunistas, 121
Uruguay, 35, 183, 190
U.S. News & World Report, 105

Vaughan, Harry, 135–8, 141, 147, 150–1
Vela, David, 30–2, 116, 134
Velázquez, Angela Ochoa, 21
Veterans of Foreign Wars, 169
Vietnam, 174
Virginia, 165

Wallace, Henry, 16
War Office, 69
Warren, Fletcher, 48, 147, 150
Washington, 162
Washington, George, 13, 22
The Washington Daily News, 124
The Washington Post, 89–90, 124–5, 174
The Washington Star, 107
Washington Times-Herald, 17
Welch, Rolland, 146, 150
Welles, Sumner, 10, 16, 89–91
West Germany, 174, 184–5
West Palm Beach Post, 174
Western Arms Corporation, 110
Weyl, Nathaniel, 162

Whelan, Thomas, 134, 137–8, 141, 146, 149
White House, 97, 134, 136, 148–9, 168, 185
white papers, 126, 185–7, 190
Whitman, Edmund S., 162, 189–90
Wiley, Alexander, 109, 156, 164–7, 169–71
Winchell, Walter, 169
Wisconsin, 165, 167, 169
Wisner, Frank, 149
women and women's organizations, 17, 32, 34, 38, 120–2, 185
World Health Organization, 188
Wyoming, 170

Xequijel, 51

Ydígoras Fuentes, Miguel, 59, 101–4, 110, 133, 154–6, 159, 171, 188
Yugoslavia, 124

Zemurray, Samuel, 106, 126
Zepeda, Pedro José, 15
Zepeda Durón, Fernando, 21, 48
Zuleta Ángel, Eduardo, 128, 144–5, 147–51
Zúñiga Huete, Ángel, 13, 16, 30, 41

www.ingramcontent.com/pod-product-compliance
Lightning Source LLC
Chambersburg PA
CBHW030118240426
43673CB00041B/1324